CQ GUIDE TO

CURRENT AMERICAN GOVERNMENT

Fall 2002

CQ PRESS

A Division of Congressional Quarterly Inc.

Washington, D.C.

Congressional Quarterly Inc.

Congressional Quarterly Inc., an editorial research service and publishing company, serves clients in the fields of news, education, business and government. It combines the specific coverage of Congress, government and politics contained in the *CQ Weekly* with the more general subject range of an affiliated service, the *CQ Researcher*.

Under the CQ Press imprint, Congressional Quarterly also publishes college political science textbooks and public affairs paperbacks on developing issues and events, information directories and reference books on the federal government, national elections and politics. Titles include the *Guide to the Presidency*, the *Guide to Congress*, the *Guide to the U.S. Supreme Court*, the *Guide to U.S. Elections* and *Politics in America*. CQ's A-Z collection is a reference series that provides essential information about American government and the electoral process. The *CQ Almanac*, a compendium of legislation for one session of Congress, is published each year. *Congress and the Nation*, a record of government for a presidential term, is published every four years.

CQ publishes the *Daily Monitor*, a report on the current and future activities of congressional committees. An online information system, CQ.com on Congress, provides immediate access to CQ's databases of legislative action, votes, schedules, profiles and analyses. Visit www.cq.com for more information.

CQ Press
A Division of Congressional Quarterly Inc.
1255 22nd St. N.W., Suite 400
Washington, DC 20037
202-729-1900; toll free, 1-866-4-CQ-PRESS (1-866-427-7737)

www.cqpress.com

Copyright © 2002 by CQ Press, a division of Congressional Quarterly Inc.

Cover photos: Scott J. Ferrell

All rights reserved. No part of this publication may be reproduced or transmitted in any form or by any means, electronic or mechanical, including photocopy, recording or any information storage and retrieval system, without permission in writing from the publisher.

Printed and bound in the United States of America
06 05 04 03 02   5 4 3 2 1

∞ The paper used in this publication meets the minimum requirements of the American National Standard for Information Sciences—Permanence of Paper for Printed Library Materials, ANSI Z39.48-1992.

ISBN 1-56802-729-X
ISSN 0196-612-X

Contents

Introduction • v

Foundations of American Government • 1

Bush's Swift, Sweeping Plan
Is Work Order for Congress
White House proposal for security department goes beyond lawmakers' request • 2
By Adriel Bettelheim and Jill Barshay

Proposal Presages Turf Wars
Committee chairmen bristle at notion of losing some jurisdiction • 9
By David Nather and Karen Foerstel

How to Resurrect Congress
After a Debilitating Attack
Talk grows about ways to speed the filling of House vacancies if disaster strikes • 13
By David Nather

Risk Enough for All In *Walker v. Cheney*
GAO's document quest is a high-stakes game for Congress and White House alike • 16
By Jill Barshay

Political Participation • 23

Safe House: Incumbents
Face Worry-Free Election
Is glut of secure seats dangerous to nation's political health? • 24
By Bob Benenson, Gregory L. Giroux and Jonathan Allen

House Democratic Leadership
To Undergo Complete Overhaul
Contentious races expected regardless of party control • 37
By Karen Foerstel

Campaign Finance Passage
Ends a Political Odyssey
Supporters and critics alike say legislation's effect will be unpredictable • 41
By Karen Foerstel

Government Institutions • 47

Congress

Politics Muddies the Water Around Sept. 11 Investigation
Democrats nearly paralyzed by pressure on both sides of intelligence probe • 48
By David Nather with Jill Barshay and Chuck McCutcheon

Members Return From Afghanistan
Urging Greater Postwar U.S. Role
Some in delegation see need for greater involvement in reconstruction, peacekeeping • 52
By Miles A. Pomper

The Duel of Bush and Daschle:
Men of Genteel Steel
Both men walk a fine line in power struggle over domestic policy • 56
By Jill Barshay

Presidency

Indecision, Disagreements
Hamper Bush's Foreign Policy
Conservatives lean toward taking more aggressive measures with Arafat • 60
By Miles A. Pomper

Will a New Era of Deficits
Be Bush's Budget Legacy?
Conservatives troubled by red ink's return may fight spending plans • 63
By Daniel J. Parks

Bureaucracy

Powell's Congressional Army Guards His Flank
Moderate in Bush administration courts allies on the Hill • 68
By Miles A. Pomper with Jonathan Broder

Army's Three-Part Plan Causes Budget, Hill Disharmony
Military seeks faster, lighter, smarter weapons of tomorrow • 74
By Pat Towell

Contents

Politics and Public Policy • 79

New Pot of Federal Dollars Has Admirers From All Over
Homeland Security spending could threaten other programs • 80
By Daniel J. Parks and Mary Dalrymple

FBI Director Seeks Hill's Support As Hearings Get Under Way
Lawmakers weigh administration's request to let Mueller run restructuring • 85
By Bob Williams with Chuck McCutcheon

New Wave of Nuclear Weaponry Sure to Spur Explosive Conference
President's plan to develop powerful 'bunker busters' sharply divides parties amid fear of a new round of worldwide proliferation • 88
By Pat Towell

An Industry Called to Account
Will Enron collapse lead to new laws for auditors or more self-regulation? • 93
By Keith Perine

Analysts See a Seismic Shift In Health Policy Debate
With a patients' bill of rights 'barely on the radar screen,' focus is on cost • 97
By Mary Agnes Carey

Members Back Medicare Revamp But Are Not Unified on a Solution
Some lawmakers call for standardizing Medicare payment rates; others say more competition in the private market would help control costs • 102
By Mary Agnes Carey

Hill Contemplates Copyrights: Does Innovation Trump Piracy?
Bills must strike balance between creators' products and consumers' rights • 104
By Adriel Bettelheim

Bush Breaks With Position, Moves to Protect Steel Industry
President's action could affect midterm elections, fast-track legislation • 111
By Gebe Martinez

Welfare Overhaul Points Up Intra-Party Differences
Federal aid proposals focus on details of work hours, child care funds • 114
By Anjetta McQueen

Appendix • 118
The Legislative Process In Brief • 119
The Budget Process In Brief • 124
Glossary of Congressional Terms • 126
Congressional Information on the Internet • 150

Index • 152

Introduction

Guide to Current American Government is a collection of articles selected from the CQ Weekly, a trusted source for in-depth, nonpartisan reporting and analyses of congressional action, presidential activities, policy debates and other news and developments in Washington. The articles, selected to complement introductory American government texts with up-to-date examinations of current issues and controversies, are divided into four sections: Foundations of American Government, Political Participation, Government Institutions and Politics and Public Policy.

Foundations of American Government. This section examines issues and events that involve interpretation of the U.S. Constitution. This edition of the *Guide* explores the White House plan to create a Department of Homeland Security, proposals for resurrecting Congress in the event of a fatal attack, and the latest battle in an ongoing struggle for power between the legislative and executive branches of the federal government.

Political Participation. The articles in this section examine current issues in electoral and party politics, including incumbents' high reelection rates, the overhaul of the Democratic leadership in the House and the long-awaited passage of campaign finance reform.

Government Institutions. This section explores the inner workings of the major institutions of American government. Congress, the presidency and the bureaucracy are examined in light of recent events at home and abroad. In this edition of the *Guide*, the articles focus on changes in government caused by the Sept. 11, 2001, terrorist acts in New York City, Pennsylvania, and suburban Washington, D.C. Shifts in the balance of power between the major government institutions and new priorities in foreign policy and domestic security are some of the results of the war on terrorism.

Politics and Public Policy. These articles focus on major social policy issues, such as homeland security, health care, welfare, defense and technological innovation.

The *Guide to Current American Government* reprints articles largely unchanged from their original appearance in the *CQ Weekly*. The date of original publication is provided with each article to give readers a time frame for the events described. Page number references to related and background articles in the *CQ Weekly* and the *CQ Almanac* are provided to facilitate additional research. Both publications are available in many school and public libraries.

Foundations of American Government

This section presents coverage of issues that go to the heart of American democracy, including the balance of federal power and the composition of Congress. The focus here is on homeland security, both how to use the federal government to prevent terrorist attacks and how to keep the government running if terrorists strike the nation's capital.

The first two articles discuss President George W. Bush's plan to create a Cabinet-level Department of Homeland Security — and what this plan means for legislators and federal agencies. The first article puts Bush's actions in historical context — in times of trouble, many presidents have created new departments. Important examples include Lyndon Johnson's creation of the Housing and Urban Development Department in the 1960s and Harry S Truman's redesign of the War Department into the Department of Defense at the onset of the Cold War in the late 1940s. Although Republicans are better known for downsizing than for enlarging government, politically speaking, it's easier to add than to subtract.

What might this new Cabinet department mean for Congress? New committees and old committees with new jurisdictions. No fewer than 88 committees now have jurisdiction over some parts of the agencies and issues that Bush proposed for the new department.

The third article also discusses Congress and its makeup — but in a more sober context. What if a jetliner had flown into the U.S. Capitol on Sept. 11, 2001, killing hundreds of lawmakers? Could our government still govern? The Constitution allows governors to fill Senate vacancies, but House members must be replaced by special election — and that takes time. Legislators are now discussing alternatives.

The last article in this section ranges far from homeland security and disaster planning. On Feb. 22, 2002, the General Accounting Office — the investigative arm of Congress — filed a lawsuit to compel Vice President Dick Cheney to disclose documents regarding the actions of his energy task force, which had disbanded five months earlier. The inquiries preceding the suit began after newspapers published stories about meetings between the task force and contributors to Bush's election campaign. Although Cheney has disclosed the documents since this story was published, the fight for power between Congress and the executive branch continues as an American tradition.

Foundations of American Government

Bush's Swift, Sweeping Plan Is Work Order for Congress

White House proposal for security department goes beyond lawmakers' request

The phone calls from the White House began once Congress returned from its Memorial Day recess. They were almost casual inquiries to lawmakers who had sponsored homeland security legislation, and they bore no sign that President Bush was contemplating the most far-reaching reorganization of government agencies since World War II.

Someone phoned Rep. Jane Harman, D-Calif., to ask what she thought of moving the Transportation Security Administration, which Congress had just created last fall, into a new department. Over catfish and barbecue at a White House picnic a few days later, the subject came up again. Harman had her suspicions something was up, but the White House did not tell her.

Senate Governmental Affairs Committee Chairman Joseph I. Lieberman had a call from Tom Ridge, director of the White House Office of Homeland Security. "We've been looking at your bill; we have a few questions,'" Lieberman recalls him saying.

The Connecticut Democrat smiles. "I didn't realize how quickly they [were moving]."

Harman holds a copy of Bush's plan at a June 6 news conference with Rep. Ellen Tauscher, D-Calif., and Lieberman, whose homeland security bill may be combined with Bush's.

Once Bush and his closest advisers decided to propose creating a Department of Homeland Security to manage the domestic war on terrorism, rather than relying on Ridge's advisory office, they moved with the speed and stealth of a military strike force, catching nearly all of official Washington and even some Cabinet secretaries unaware.

Members of Congress from both parties did not seem offended. In fact, they welcomed the proposal because in its broad outline Bush's plan gives them what they have beseeched him for since last fall — a single homeland security agency headed by a Cabinet secretary answerable to Capitol Hill.

But Bush's proposal, released June 6 in a welter of briefings and color-coded charts topped off with a presidential address to the nation, is far broader than anyone in Congress contemplated. The plan not only would combine more agencies, such as the Transportation Security Administration, the Coast Guard and the Secret Service, but it calls for "significant flexibility" in the new department's rules on hiring, pay and personnel management. Some agencies and bureaus may be wiped out, others moved beyond Washington.

The challenge for lawmakers, particularly Democrats, will be how to reshape what they consider troublesome aspects of the homeland security plan or add their own ideas, without appearing to delay or defy a popular president on a national security issue.

"If they did this right after Sept. 11, there might have been quick passage," said James Thurber, professor of government at American University and an authority on Congress and the presidency. "Because the threat is there but it is now harder to define the problem, the process will be more deliberate and slower."

The administration is playing hardball, both to fashion the Homeland Security Department in its own image and regain control of the counterterrorism agenda after a month of unpleasant disclosures about intelligence slip-ups and investigative miscues before Sept. 11.

White House officials took pains to describe Bush's announcement as a logical step in a carefully reasoned, deliberative process that began last fall. But it was a clear departure for an administration that opposed the idea of creating a new fed-

CQ Weekly June 8, 2002

eral department until after the disclosure in March of mistakes within the Immigration and Naturalization Service. Ridge and White House Chief of Staff Andrew H. Card Jr. began meeting privately on the homeland security plan April 23.

Members of Congress, including some Republicans, have in recent weeks questioned whether the administration was in control of the domestic security front.

By proposing a sweeping plan that could wind up eliminating whole agencies and moving tens of thousands of workers, the administration is imposing a blueprint on Congress and ordering lawmakers to approve it by year's end. Congress will even have to draft the legislation because the administration has not submitted an actual bill. If the House and Senate bicker or engage in turf battles, the administration will accuse them of slowing down the war on terrorism and being unpatriotic.

The administration likens Bush's proposal to President Harry S Truman's reorganization of defense and intelligence agencies after World War II in preparation for the Cold War. Bush said the reorganization would both streamline bureaucracies and instill accountability in a homeland security net he acknowledged had allowed intelligence lapses before Sept. 11. (*History, p. 1502*)

"As we have learned more about the plans and capabilities of the terrorist network, we have concluded that our government must be reorganized to deal more effectively with the new threats of the 21st century," Bush said during a prime-time television address. (*Box, p. 6*)

Second-Largest Department

Bush has proposed combining 22 federal agencies, with just under 170,000 employees and a total budget of $37.5 billion, into what would be the second-largest Cabinet department after Defense, based on personnel.

The administration's plan would merge agencies and offices into four primary areas: border and transportation security; emergency preparedness; countermeasures against chemical, biological, radiological and nuclear weapons; and information analysis and infrastructure protection.

The department would include the Coast Guard, the Customs Service, the Immigration and Naturalization Service (INS), and the Border Patrol, as well as the Federal Emergency Management Agency (FEMA), the Secret Service and the new Transportation Security Administration (TSA).

The department also would absorb selected functions of other Cabinet agencies, including the Department of Agriculture's Animal and Plant Health Inspection Service, the Department of Energy's Lawrence Livermore National Laboratory and Nuclear Emergency Search Team, and the Department of Health and Human Service's National Pharmaceutical Stockpile.

The FBI and CIA would not be substantially affected, though the consolidation would create an intelligence and threat analysis division within the new department that would analyze material gleaned by multiple agencies.

The plan is far more ambitious than Lieberman's bill (S 2452) or a companion bill (HR 4660) by William M. "Mac" Thornberry, R-Texas. Both focus on consolidating agencies responsible for border security, including the INS, the Customs Service, the Coast Guard, FEMA, and infrastructure and domestic preparedness functions of the FBI. Thornberry said June 7 that he and other lawmakers probably will introduce Bush's plan in legislative form the week of June 10.

How Homeland Security Would Fit Into Cabinet

The proposed new department would be among the top five in terms of both size and number of employees:

Discretionary budgets (in billions of dollars)

Defense	$379.3
HHS	65.3
Education	50.3
Homeland Security	**37.5**
HUD	31.5

Civilian work force (end of fiscal year 2001)

Defense	647,000
Veteran Affairs	226,000
Homeland Security	**170,000**
Treasury	148,000
HHS	134,000

Source: Budget from Bush fiscal 2003 budget request; work force from FY2003 Budget of the United States Government, Historical Tables

Bush's proposal also is broader than a consolidation plan Ridge circulated within the White House earlier this year that was leaked to the press, then fell victim to bureaucratic infighting. (*2002 CQ Weekly, p. 1071*)

The White House says the reorganization would be essentially "budget neutral," requiring only some additional transitional spending. Administration briefing papers emphasize that the plan would eliminate overlap and overhead among agencies now doing the same or similar jobs, and that it would require no additional personnel. Briefing papers speak of "eliminating as many redundant and duplicative functions as possible."

Because the department would draw on the CIA, FBI and other agencies for intelligence, it would not have to pay to collect its own.

Stunning Turnabout

Some observers expressed surprise that Bush would propose such a sprawling department after repeatedly insisting that counterterrorism could be coordinated out of a small office within the executive office of the president.

"Here's a president who battled Congress to stop TSA from hiring federal employees as [airport] screeners, a president who wanted contractors but now points to the number of employees as proof that this is a good thing," said Paul Light, director of governmental studies at the Brookings Institution. "Here he comes forward with reorganization that's so dramatic, it dwarfs what Lieberman has been proposing."

Practically since Ridge was appointed last September, the White House has rebuffed congressional efforts to elevate his position to Cabinet-level status and even refused to allow him to testify before congressional panels in support of the White House's homeland security budget requests.

Administration officials cited Ridge's role as an adviser to the president, saying that to make him testify would violate the separation of powers between the executive and legislative branches. (*2002 CQ Weekly, p. 1159*)

Ridge will appear before congressional committees but only to explain and answer questions about Bush's plan, not to discuss homeland security actions or policies.

The administration said the decision to seek a new department was based on a continuing review of myriad terrorist threats and some apparent weaknesses in government or-

Foundations of American Government

Organization of the Proposed

BORDER AND TRANSPORTATION SECURITY

Division would unify all major federal security operations concerned with U.S. borders, territorial waters and transportation systems. Its mandate would be information sharing and linking compatible databases across the country. Division makeup:

■ **Border Security**
Controlling all aspects of crossing at more than 7,500 miles of border with Canada and Mexico.
■ **Transportation Security**
Securing all modes of transportation within U.S. borders.
■ **Coast Guard**
Moving the 212-year-old service from Transportation and giving it new powers to detain suspects at sea, along 11,000 miles of coastline and on inland waterways.
■ **Immigration Services**
Visa-issuing services are separated from the border patrol. This unit will process visas for foreign nationals wishing to legally enter the country while excluding suspected terrorists.

Moving Into Homeland Security Department

	FROM	PERSONNEL	BUDGET
INS / Border Patrol	Justice	39,459	$6.4 billion
Customs Service	Treasury	21,743	3.8 billion
Animal and Plant Health Inspection Service	Agriculture	8,620	1.1 billion
Transportation Security Agency	Transportation	41,300	4.8 billion
Coast Guard	Transportation	43,639	7.3 billion
FAA (some powers)	Transportation	TBD	TBD
Federal Protective Services	GSA	1,408	418 million

THE BOTTOM LINE
While the aim is to better secure U.S. borders and transportation avenues, the reality is that virtually the same number of people will be trying to patrol a massive territory. Some of the challenges:
■ Uninspected airline cargo
■ Just 2 percent of cargo containers are inspected in ports
■ Onerous visa tracking responsibilities

EMERGENCY PREPAREDNESS AND RESPONSE

Division would coordinate all federal assistance in the domestic disaster preparedness training of local first responders. Federal Emergency Management Agency would bring all its functions under the Homeland Security umbrella. A priority of the division would be to coordinate communications and integrate response plans between appropriate agencies. Division makeup:

■ **Preparedness**
Administering all grant programs for firefighters, police and emergency personnel currently managed by FEMA, Justice and HHS.
■ **Mitigation**
Mitigating risk and working with insurance and lending industries to promote community disaster resistance.
■ **Response**
Managing assets such as the Nuclear Emergency Search Teams (formerly of the Energy Department) and National Pharmaceutical Stockpile (from HHS).
■ **Recovery**
Merging all federal emergency programs to promote recovery from terrorist and natural disasters.

Moving Into Homeland Security Department

	FROM	PERSONNEL	BUDGET
FEMA	independent	5,135	$6.2 billion
Chemical, biological, radiological and nuclear response assets	HHS	150	2.1 billion
National Domestic Preparedness Office	FBI	15	2 million
Nuclear Incident Response	Energy	TBD	91 million

THE BOTTOM LINE
If this division comes together as planned, it will give states and local governments a true one-stop center for information, funding and training programs. Still, the first task will be to create a one-stop information center for the division itself, since all the incoming agencies have operated independently.

---

ganization. Most lawmakers praised the administration for taking a bold step.

"In this town, there's a lot of macho in never admitting you learned something," said Senate Intelligence Committee Chairman Bob Graham, D-Fla. "President Bush should be commended for studying the issue closely . . . it's a sign of reassurance to the American people."

At the same time it begins to assess Bush's reorganization plan, Congress is also expected to at least consider reorganizing itself to match the new lineup of agencies. The administration said pointedly that Congress should revamp its committee structure, and among its briefing materials was a chart showing 88 congressional committees and subcommittees with oversight over counterterrorism. (*Proposal, p. 9*)

Critical Timing

The timing of the announcement meant that, even as the administration was offering Congress an expanded role in homeland security, the White House was regaining the upper hand in an increasingly testy battle with the legislative branch over power and prerogatives.

The plan was unveiled the day the Senate Judiciary Committee was hearing testimony from FBI Director Robert S. Mueller III and a Minneapolis agent and whistleblower, Coleen Rowley, about security breakdowns before Sept. 11. News of the plan, and the president's speech, upstaged those events on the Hill and led some Democrats to speculate they were calculated to deflect attention from criticisms of the administration. (*2002 CQ Weekly, p. 1509*)

The plan, moreover, is expected to sap the momentum for establishing an independent commission to investigate the government's inability to detect terrorist activity before Sept. 11. (*2002 CQ Weekly, p. 1511*)

"My speculation is they have gotten

Reorganizing for Homeland Security

Department of Homeland Security

Chemical, Biological, Radiological and Nuclear Countermeasures

Division would oversee the nation's response to weapons of mass destruction. It also would create a system to identify and assess threats to the country. Division makeup:

■ **Science and Technology Development**
Focusing the energies of national scientific and technological institutions across several disciplines.
■ **Chemical**
Sponsoring and coordinating research and development of chemical vaccines, antidotes and diagnostics.
■ **Biological and Agricultural**
Developing, maintaining and deploying a national system to detect the use of biological agents within the United States.
■ **Radiological and Nuclear**
Preventing the import of any nuclear devices or material that could make such devices.

Moving Into Homeland Security Department

	FROM	PERSONNEL	BUDGET
Civilian Bio-Defense Research Programs	HHS	150	$2 billion
Lawrence Livermore Lab	DOE	324	1.2 billion
National Biological Warfare Defense Analysis Center	new	TBD	420 million
Plum Island Center	USDA	124	25 million

THE BOTTOM LINE
The most manageable division of the new department. Basically the scientists and researchers will continue what they are doing with a new mandate for better communication.

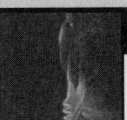

Secret Service

Presidential protection agency would move from Treasury with its 6,111 workers and $1.2 billion budget. None of its duties would change, including investigating counterfeit money.

Information Analysis and Infrastructure Protection

The centerpiece of the homeland security proposal, this agency would integrate and analyze all intelligence gathering by the CIA, FBI, National Security Agency, INS, DEA, Customs, Transportation and other organizations. Division makeup:

■ **Threat Analysis**
Creating a coherent system for conveying intelligence and threat information into action.
■ **Infrastructure Protection**
Coordinating efforts of federal, state and local authorities to secure critical infrastructure.
■ **Physical Assets**
Building a comprehensive assessment of the nation's critical infrastructure sectors.
■ **Telecommunications and Cyber-Security**
Placing a particular emphasis on the key cyber-security activities performed by multiple federal agencies.

Moving Into Homeland Security Department

	FROM	PERSONNEL	BUDGET
Critical Infrastructure Assurance Office	Commerce	65	$27 million
Federal Computer Incident Response Center	GSA	23	11 million
National Communications System	DoD	91	155 million
National Infrastructure Protection Center	FBI	795	151 million
National Infrastructure Simulation and Analysis Center	Energy	2	20 million

THE BOTTOM LINE
It is possible that information-sharing among intelligence agencies could have uncovered the Sept. 11 plot ahead of time, and that is the challenge for this new division. Possible roadblocks:
■ These agencies are dedicated to keeping secrets.
■ Congressional politics and turf concerns are likely to play a key role in whether all intelligence flows into one place.
■ Infrastructure in the United States is vast, involving buildings, roads, pipelines and monuments.

---

an indication from polling data that there's a concern of their grip of the situation with all the leaks coming out the CIA and FBI," said Rep. Barney Frank, D-Mass. "They're doing this as a defensive reaction that they no longer look omnicompetent to the public."

Senate Appropriations Committee Chairman Robert C. Byrd, D-W.Va., who for months unsuccessfully sought Ridge's testimony before his panel, responded to the announcement of the plan by criticizing the administration's "stubborn stonewalling" that may have undercut efforts to improve security.

"For many months, we have heard tales of little or no real direction from the federal government in assessing risk and pinpointing vulnerabilities," said Byrd. "I hope that this new status for the Office of Homeland Security amounts to more than just reshuffling the deck chairs on the Titanic."

The administration and its defenders said the reorganization was an acknowledgement that the current structure revolving around Ridge's office was unworkable because Ridge does not have direct authority over the agencies in question or their budgets.

Bush conspicuously did not say whether Ridge would lead the new department, though many in the administration believe he will. Bush has said he wants to retain an anti-terrorism adviser within the White House — a job akin to the one Ridge now holds. Ridge has not said whether he wants the Cabinet job.

The administration clearly sees the bills by Lieberman and Thornberry as starting points for fashioning its own legislation.

The president invited the lawmakers and some cosponsors of the legislation to breakfast at the White House on June 7. Afterward, Lieberman, the Democratic vice presidential candidate in 2000 and a potential presidential contender in 2004, said his committee will probably hold one or two hearings

Foundations of American Government

Expansion During Crisis
A Typical Response by Presidents

It is a pattern with modern presidents: In moments of national crisis, create an agency, or even better, a full-blown department.

With the onset of the Cold War, Harry S Truman redesigned the War Department in 1949, creating the sprawling Department of Defense. In 1939, the Great Depression prompted Franklin D. Roosevelt to form the bureaucratic precursor for the Department of Health, Education and Welfare, which since has morphed into the Health and Human Services Department.

Inner city blight drove Lyndon B. Johnson to create the Housing and Urban Development Department in 1965. And in 1977, Jimmy Carter responded to the oil crisis by establishing the Energy Department.

Now, amid congressional probes into the government's security failures before Sept. 11, President Bush aims to reshape a bureaucracy once again, this time merging Customs, Immigration, intelligence analysis, disaster relief and other functions under a new Homeland Security Department to guard against further terror attacks.

The White House calls its proposal the largest reorganization since the Defense Department combined the three armed services in 1947.

Some experts downplay the scope of the change, noting that the estimated $37.4 billion budget of the new department would be smaller, when adjusted for inflation, than those of the Health and Transportation departments when they were created in 1953 and 1966, respectively.

But if history is any guide, these experts say, a Homeland Security Department is likely to swell over time, despite Bush's insistence that he is merely consolidating existing agencies.

"If they follow the traditional design that we see in precedents, then we will end up with a hierarchy in Washington that will be 15 to 20 layers deep," predicts Paul Light, a government scholar at the Brookings Institution. "Bush can't be held to the promise that costs won't grow, because it's an impossible promise to keep."

For starters, a new Department of Homeland Security would require the hiring of at least 200 people, Light predicts. He cites the inevitable need to add a new oversight structure to the existing framework of disparate divisions.

"There is no one agency acting as a magnet for others, so you have to create that magnet from scratch," Light said.

Easier to Add Than Subtract

Some scholars have expressed surprise that Bush's plans are more far-reaching than those of congressional Democrats. This is because, historically speaking, modern Republicans are better known for their plans to dismantle government agencies than build them.

But in fact, Republicans have found it far more difficult to eliminate a department than to add one. Ronald Reagan campaigned on pledges to scrap the Education and Energy departments. But by the end of his second term, both remained. Meanwhile, Reagan surprised many of his conservative supporters by creating yet another Cabinet department, the Veterans Administration. (1987 Almanac, p. 374)

For Bush to create a Homeland Security Department, he will need congressional approval. This requirement reverses the practice of past years when presidents enjoyed wide latitude to reorganize the government as they saw fit.

Indeed, from 1949 through 1981, and for brief periods before, presidents did not need congressional approval to make many of the sweeping changes that Bush wants.

That power grew out of the 1949 Reorganization Act, which handed presidents broad authority to reshape government operations. The only limitation was a provision that gave the House or Senate the power to veto the president's plans, using a simple resolution. (1949 Almanac, p. 561)

The 1949 law was based on statutes going back as far as 1918 that gave the president greater authority to reshape the bureaucracy during times of crisis. That authority expired with the end of World War I.

But as the Depression posed new threats to the nation, Roosevelt revived some of those powers and famously used them to create an alphabet soup of new agencies by the time the law lapsed again in January 1941.

The version of law revived in 1949 gave the president more power than ever, broadening authority to reorganize agencies that had been protected under previous statutes. For the first time, Congress also allowed presidents to create Cabinet-level agencies, but took away that authority in 1964. In the 1970s, lawmakers also forced Richard Nixon to abandon plans to merge seven government departments into four.

The law expired in 1981, and any chance of renewing it evaporated two years later when the Supreme Court declared Congress' power to veto presidential plans as unconstitutional.

Today, as Bush urges Congress to approve his proposal, scholars say this history of governmental redesign has created promising precedents for Bush. "We've created new government agencies with some success," noted William T. Gormley Jr., a Georgetown University political scientist.

At the same time, Bush's plan reflects the nation's recent history. Says Capt. Rosemary B. Mariner, a visiting scholar at the Center for the Study of War and Society at the University of Tennessee: "It's a pretty typical political response to a crisis."

on the administration's proposal, then enter into negotiations with the White House to combine it with his bill if Senate leaders agree.

Thornberry indicated the House may move even faster. "All of us agree the president's plan is better than what we have been working on," he said.

No Rubber Stamp

But some lawmakers already have made it clear that they will not be a mere rubber stamp for the Bush administration. Rep. Henry A. Waxman of California, ranking Democrat on the House Government Reform Committee that likely would be the starting point for a reorganization bill, said he anticipated many changes will be made to Bush's plan.

"I certainly can't imagine it not being scrutinized, because this is an important issue," said Waxman. In particular, he stressed he wants to ensure that the new agency director would be required to report and testify before Congress.

Some observers suggested the administration still must lay out a comprehensive homeland security strategy to accompany the bureaucratic restructuring.

"We've had new budgets and now a new organization, but we still have not heard the president lay out his strategy for addressing the full range of threats we face or how he intends to make sure we are prepared and safe," said David Heyman, senior fellow in the technology and public policy program at the Center for Strategic and International Studies in Washington. "In the end, it's results, not organizational charts, that matter."

And even if the administration's plan becomes law before year's end, it could take years before it become reality. Sen. Robert F. Bennett, R-Utah, who as a Nixon administration aide in the 1970s helped preside over the organization of the Department of Transportation, praised Bush's plan but said the process of assembling such a large department is arduous. Bennett said merging agencies with different cultures and missions was possibly more daunting than combining several large corporations.

"Like any merger you face the question of redundancy: How many budget officers are coming together? Do you have jobs for everybody? That's no reason to put it off, but it's just a warning for everyone not to expect instant miracles," Bennett said.

Indeed, the reorganization plan hints at major structural changes for the agencies involved.

Only the Coast Guard and Secret Service would retain independent identities. The Customs Service and INS could be combined into one organization in the name of eliminating duplication at headquarters and inspection facilities at ports of entries, according to a White House fact sheet circulated to congressional offices.

FEMA would be given access to the latest threat information in order to quickly deploy resources to respond to potential terrorist attacks.

The largest components in the reorganization are the Coast Guard and TSA. Combined, they employ nearly 85,000 people, and Bush's fiscal 2003 budget request for both agencies totals $12.1 billion.

The reorganization raises new questions about the future operations of the TSA, which must federalize all airport passenger and baggage screeners by November and screen all baggage for explosives by year's end. The agency already has had numerous fights with congressional appropriators over its budget and staffing levels. (*2002 CQ Weekly, p. 1032*)

Coast Guard supporters in Congress, such as Young, say moving the agency makes sense. It has been under the Treasury and Transportation departments, and under the Defense Department in wartime. "I've always anticipated that the Coast Guard would be a lead agency in any homeland security department," said Rep. Bill Delahunt, D-Mass., one of the leading Coast Guard advocates in Congress. "It's a policeman for our maritime interests."

The White House said under its plan, agencies in the new Homeland Security Department that have missions other than security would continue to perform them. Customs would still collect duties and the Coast Guard would still rescue people.

However, some lawmakers, including Young, expressed concern that non-security missions might be played down under the new department.

While the Coast Guard is accustomed to moving around, the TSA is still being constructed. "What I worry about is already TSA is taking on a hard-core law enforcement attitude," said James L. Oberstar of Minnesota, ranking Democrat on the House Transportation and Infrastructure Committee. "This move would make it even more of a law enforcement entity, and less of a facilitating entity. Now, you can have both, but maintaining a more traveler-friendly culture is going to be difficult in that setting."

But Oberstar and Young believe committees of jurisdiction should maintain their oversight of various parts of the agency.

In general, the administration is asking for "significant flexibility in hiring processes, compensation systems and practices," a sign that it may insist on working outside of federal worker union pay scales and grievance procedures. A heated debate over whether airport security screeners should be federal employees or private contractors stalled last year's deliberations on creating the TSA. (*2001 CQ Weekly, p. 3055*)

Some unions of federal workers said the reorganization should focus instead on adding money for more personnel at borders, airports and seaports. The National Treasury Employees Union, which represents 12,000 Customs Service workers, said its employees are understaffed, with many having to work 12- and 16-hour shifts since Sept. 11.

"The administration has had adequate opportunity to strengthen border security," said the union's national president, Colleen M. Kelley. "It does not require the creation of a new Cabinet-level agency and a massive realignment that could well serve to be a distraction to those securing America's borders, airports and seaports."

T.J. Bonner, president of the National Border Control Council, another federal employees' union, said Bush's plan would create "a lot of inefficiency and confusion" over the next few years. Bonner said the administration should "work with what we have, tweak it and fix it.... We shouldn't be investing millions of dollars in schemes that won't work."

Not a Sure Thing

Questions about labor policies are one of the things that might slow down the plan in Congress, even though most lawmakers so far are throwing their support behind the reorganization. Different politicians have different definitions of homeland security and are apt to superimpose their pet causes on to the proposals.

Sen. Dianne Feinstein, D-Calif., for example, continues to press for a new director of intelligence to have formal

Foundations of American Government

control over the CIA and military intelligence agencies. Feinstein said she plans to introduce stand-alone legislation to that effect the week of June 10.

Rep. Edward J. Markey, D-Mass., is lobbying for enhanced security for nuclear power plants and weapons labs and liquid natural gas facilities. Markey wants enhanced protections in the event of a radiological emergency, including increased distribution of potassium iodide to protect people from radiation exposure.

The inclusion of the Department of Energy's Lawrence Livermore National Laboratory in the new department already is leading to calls for extra funding for other laboratories with expertise in nuclear and biological preparedness. Sen. Pete V. Domenici, R-N.M., is urging the administration to include the Los Alamos and Sandia national laboratories in his home state in the department's plans.

Furthermore, there are questions about why some agencies were left out of the reorganization. Lawmakers may try to include the Bureau of Alcohol, Tobacco and Firearms (ATF), the Centers for Disease Control and Prevention (CDC) and the Drug Enforcement Administration (DEA).

The White House has said such agencies are not primarily involved with border security or counterterrorism.

Behind Closed Doors

The private way in which the plan was assembled has not left hard feelings in Congress, which was just happy to get a plan at all. But even for an administration that exerts unusually tight control over information, the development of the reorganization was an unusually secretive process.

A group of senior White House aides working under Chief of Staff Card began melding organizational charts in late April. Secrecy was paramount, said administration officials, who feared that leaks would trigger turf battles among affected agencies.

House Speaker J. Dennis Hastert, R-Ill., and Majority Leader Dick Armey, R-Texas, were aware that the White House had been discussing the idea of creating a Cabinet-level homeland security department, and Armey said he spoke with Ridge about the idea a couple of times over the past three weeks. But no one in the leadership knew how or when the administration planned to roll out the plan.

Early in the evening of June 5, the White House left a message at Hastert's Capitol office. The Bush aide who called could have walked out the back door to the South Lawn where Hastert was standing in his shirtsleeves and suspenders at a White House picnic for members of Congress. It was not until later that night that a White House official told Hastert of the president's plan to reorganize the federal government and asked if Hastert could come to the White House for a briefing on the changes the next morning.

Card tried to deliver the news to Senate Majority Leader Tom Daschle, D-S.D., at 9:30 a.m. the day of the announcement but discovered he was in Boston attending the graduation of his son from Harvard University Law School. Card spoke to Daschle's chief of staff instead.

In advance, the White House quietly pressured the cancellation of a markup and a hearing scheduled for June 6 on the topic of homeland security. On May 31, a Bush administration official telephoned Rep. Christopher Shays, R-Conn., chairman of the Government Reform subcommittee on National Security, Veterans Affairs and International Affairs. Shays was not in the office but the official left a message that the administration "would be much better prepared to respond" to the committee's questions the week of June 10.

"That was fine with me," Shays said.

A Coast Guard helicopter patrols petrochemical facilities along Galveston Bay in Texas on May 10. In Bush's plan, the Coast Guard would be responsible for most maritime security.

"I knew something would happen since they were asking me to wait a week." Days later, Shays talked with a White House official and told him to "be bold" and not worry about what they thought they could get through Congress. Shays' hearing is now slated for June 11.

Since the beginning of the week of June 3, the White House had been in touch with Thornberry and Harman, respected legislators with security expertise who both have sponsored bills to create departments of homeland security. Graham was consulted as well.

"As [National Security Adviser] Condoleezza Rice would say, there was increased chatter," Harman said.

Lieberman said he does not resent the surprise announcement, chalking it up to presidential prerogative.

"Most important is that the president agrees that there should be a strong person in charge of Homeland Security," he said.

Lieberman was so "very pleased" with the Bush proposal he called a press conference outside of the Capitol building — in 92 degrees and 86 percent humidity — to hold what he called a victory press conference. Lieberman quickly noted the president's plan is close to his own. As for why the administration reversed itself, Lieberman said, "I don't know. I take it as a sign of strength when someone sees that something is not going as they wanted. I congratulate the administration." ◆

Reorganizing for Homeland Security

Proposal Presages Turf Wars

Committee chairmen bristle at notion of losing some jurisdiction

The point of President Bush's proposed Department of Homeland Security is to put lots of agencies under one roof and get them to put aside their turf wars. But it is Congress that faces the biggest challenge of all: getting its committee chairmen to halt their own jurisdictional battles long enough to make it happen.

If there is to be such a vast new Cabinet department, Congress is almost certain to have to rework the jurisdictions of its committees to oversee it, and possibly even create a new committee to put all of the oversight under one roof. Already, that prospect is igniting battles among committee chairmen who do not want to give up their oversight of powerful agencies. If those battles are not contained quickly, the petty rivalries between the FBI and the CIA that may have prevented investigators from uncovering the Sept. 11 plot could become a distant memory.

"Hell hath no fury like a committee chairman whose jurisdiction has been taken away," cautioned Sen. Robert F. Bennett, R-Utah.

"I would say that the war on terrorism has just expanded to the war on turf," said Rep. Jane Harman, D-Calif.

The political stakes will be enormous — especially for Senate Majority Leader Tom Daschle, D-S.D., who is already burdened with a long list of must-pass legislation and heckled by Republicans as a leader who cannot get things done. The expectations will be high not just because of the urgency of the war on terrorism, but because Daschle himself has been calling on Bush to make the Office of Homeland Security a Cabinet-level department.

Realistically, though, it will be tough for congressional leaders from both parties. House Speaker J. Dennis Hastert, R-Ill., says the task probably will require at least a reorganization of the jurisdictions of current committees. And there is already talk of a "supercommittee" that could gather the top members from various committees under one roof and

Don Young, speaking in his office, is emblematic of the committee chairmen who have vowed to defend their jurisdictions in the debate over homeland security oversight.

get them to talk to each other, much as Bush is trying to do with the agencies that would be placed under the Department of Homeland Security.

Such talk is already generating resistance from chairmen such as the House Transportation and Infrastructure Committee's Don Young, R-Alaska, who says he has "more involvement in this than any other committee" and is not about to give it up.

Lawmakers are not only marking territory over the right to oversee the new department, but also over the right to create it in the first place. Both House Government Reform Committee Chairman Dan Burton, R-Ind., and Judiciary Committee Chairman F. James Sensenbrenner Jr., R-Wis., already are staking claims to the jurisdiction over the legislation that would create the new department.

Those tensions could be just the beginning. Some Republicans say long-time Senate veterans such as Appropriations Committee Chairman Robert C. Byrd, D-W.Va., could present a similar challenge to Daschle if he tries to go the "supercommittee" route.

And powerful panel heads such as Senate Judiciary Committee Chairman Patrick J. Leahy, D-Vt., and House Ways and Means Committee Chairman Bill Thomas, R-Calif., all have jurisdiction over some piece of the proposed department. They can make it easy or difficult for Bush's proposal to get through Congress, depending on how badly they want to guard their ground.

Too Many Cooks

The only thing that could be a bigger headache than reorganizing the committees, however, is not reorganizing them. By the White House's count, no less than 88 committees and subcommittees in the House and Senate have jurisdiction over some part of the agencies and issues that would be handled by the new department.

Most lawmakers know the public will have little patience for a lengthy debate, and especially for turf battles. No matter how big a reorganizational challenge Bush has handed Congress — or how belatedly he reversed his opposition to making the Homeland Security office a Cabinet-level department — a failure to meet Bush's challenge by the end of the year would give

CQ Weekly June 8, 2001

Foundations of American Government

Bush's Plan Gives Appropriators Even More to Ponder This Season

No matter how — or even when — Congress produces legislation to create a new Homeland Security Department, President Bush will still be pressing this summer for $37.5 billion in fiscal 2003 spending on the programs that he now wants a new Cabinet secretary to control.

Increasingly, the GOP majority appropriators of the House and the Democratic majority appropriators of the Senate appear inclined to give Bush much of what he wants for homeland security in the next budget year.

Along the way, the appropriators will face important questions about their own structure. If Congress undertakes the massive governmental reorganization necessary to create the new department Bush desires, the chairmen of the spending panels — known as the "cardinals" — will need to decide whether to leave their homeland security jurisdiction as fractured as it is now, an unlikely scenario, or give one of the existing subcommittees responsibility for the new department. The most radical option would be to overhaul the entire structure of 13 subcommittees to reflect a comprehensive revamping of the executive branch flow chart.

As part of the president's campaign to keep development of his proposal secret, the leaders of the Appropriations committees were among those kept out of the loop, although their willingness to pay the bills will be a crucial hurdle the president must clear. And, indeed, the Appropriations committee leaders generally were enthusiastic about Bush's plan. "At last this administration has removed the veil from over its eyes and seen the light," said Senate committee Chairman Robert C. Byrd, D-W.Va.

Unwilling To Wait

But appropriators of all stripes made clear that they are unwilling to delay an already severely stalled spending agenda any further while authorizing committees haggle over the legislation necessary to enact Bush's plan. That consensus means that any department created along the lines of Bush's request will see responsibility for its first-year budget shared among 10 of the Appropriations subcommittees — a daunting congressional lobbying task for a nascent department if that fractured jurisdiction were to last into the debate on fiscal 2004 spending a year from now.

The Office of Homeland Security, created within the White House by executive order in October, falls under the domain of the Treasury-Postal Service Appropriations subcommittees because they have jurisdiction over the Executive Office of the President. "If you're going to create this agency, it makes sense to put it under our subcommittee," said Steny H. Hoyer of Maryland, the top Democrat on the House Treasury-Postal Service Subcommittee.

Commerce-Justice-State Subcommittee leaders see equally compelling reasons why they should oversee the new Homeland Security Department. Judd Gregg of New Hampshire, the top Republican on the Senate CJS subcommittee, said his panel handles a "huge" portion of the homeland security budget.

Gregg also floated the idea of a separate homeland security appropriations subcommittee — possibly a joint House-Senate venture.

Shuffling Jurisdictions

The Appropriations committees were created just after the Civil War, and their roster of subcommittees has fluctuated between nine and 15 since the end of World War II. For 45 years, ending in 1922, the panel ceded control of eight bills to relevant authorizing committees.

Senior House Appropriations aides say the new department may be a perfect excuse to restructure all of him the ultimate opening to rail against a "do-nothing Congress."

"The president made a comprehensive speech, but the real burden here, or the real responsibility, lies with Congress," said Sen. Pat Roberts, R-Kan.

In the Senate, the initial legislation creating the department most likely will be handled by the Senate Governmental Affairs Committee, which already has approved legislation (S 2452) by Chairman Joseph I. Lieberman, D-Conn., to create a Department of Homeland Security.

On the House side, the route for creating the department is more murky. Most lawmakers said they expected the legislation to go through the House Government Reform Committee, the counterpart to Lieberman's panel. But Hastert and House Minority Leader Richard A. Gephardt, D-Mo., also have discussed the possibility of a select committee that could assume that responsibility.

One Hastert aide said the select committee idea was "ill-defined," but could handle the creation of the new department, as well as the discussions over how committee jurisdiction might be reorganized.

That idea might not sit well with Burton. "The chairman is of the impression that both his committee and the [parallel] committee on the Senate side could handle this," said committee spokesman Blain Rethmeier.

At the same time, however, Sensenbrenner spokesman Jeff Lungren made it clear the Judiciary Committee has its own expectations. "We do expect we'll be right in the middle of it, given the broad new law enforcement part of this," he said.

Most Republicans endorsed Bush's call to get the legislation through Congress by year's end. "We'd like to have

Reorganizing for Homeland Security

One Difference of Opinion

Gregg, left, says the proper Appropriations subcommittee for a Homeland Security Department would be Commerce-Justice-State; he is the top Republican on that Senate panel. Hoyer, right, says jurisdiction should go to Treasury-Postal Service; he is the top Democrat on that House subcommittee.

the subcommittees before starting the fiscal 2004 appropriations bills.

The 13 subcommittees' jurisdictions have often changed as the government has grown and the federal reach has expanded. The result is that, for decades, the panels' scope of responsibility has been wildly varied: One handles only military construction, for example, while another handles two Cabinet departments and 20 federal agencies ranging from the EPA to the American Battle Monuments Commission.

To reshuffle jurisdictions in light of a new Homeland Security Department would be a decision for the committees to make. To create a 14th subcommittee would require a change in House and Senate rules.

A Rearrangement

Before making these decisions, appropriators say they need to begin writing the fiscal 2003 bills, which are languishing while they try to clear the anti-terrorism supplemental bill (HR 4775) while also settling on an overall spending ceiling for the coming year. *(2002 CQ Weekly, p. 1513)*

The $37.5 billion request for the new department simply rearranges items already requested by the president in February. While amounts for these programs will be set without regard for the possible creation of a single department, appropriators say they would be willing to adjust their bills in conference or allow some enacted appropriations to be shuffled — "reprogramming" is the congressional term — if the authorization process lasts into fiscal 2003.

Nearly two-thirds of the proposed budget, $23.8 billion, would go to border and transportation security, functions split among at least four Appropriations subcommittees. Emergency preparedness and response, mostly the domain of the Federal Emergency Management Agency, would get the next largest share of the funds at $8.4 billion.

The Secret Service's $1.2 billion budget, now a part of the Treasury, also would fall under the agency. Programs to defend against chemical, biological, radiological and nuclear attacks — spread throughout the departments of Health and Human Services, Energy and Agriculture — would be funded at $3.6 billion.

In announcing the proposal, Bush said the reorganization will neither create an entrenched bureaucracy nor increase the homeland protection costs. Any startup costs will be offset by new efficiencies, according to documents the White House sent to Capitol Hill. House Appropriations Committee Chairman C.W. Bill Young, R-Fla., disagreed. "I expect that it will cost more," he said.

The House's top Democratic appropriator, David R. Obey of Wisconsin, worried aloud that a new structure would not mean more funds for protecting the homeland. "The administration still is not supplying adequate funds for a whole range of items in homeland security," he said.

the work done before this Congress adjourns," said House Majority Leader Dick Armey, R-Texas. Others, however, warned against a rush job on a subject as crucial as homeland security.

"If we're going to be serious about this, we need to solve the problem, and it will not be solved by a single executive order or a single act of Congress," Bennett said.

Avoiding a War

The biggest challenge for Congress may be the one under its own roof: avoiding bitter territorial strife if congressional leaders decide to redraw the lines of committee jurisdiction, or even create a new committee, to oversee the new department.

"It's going to be one hell of a turf battle" in both the executive and legislative branches, said Sen. Jon Kyl, R-Ariz. "What committees here are going to be willing to give up jurisdiction?"

But some lawmakers favor a reorganization and suggest ideas that range from new Appropriations subcommittees to a massive new select committee. The current jurisdiction, they say, is so spread out over so many committees that it could be unworkable.

At a White House meeting June 7 with lawmakers who favor a new department, Bush suggested that Congress could sidestep the threat of turf wars by adding a new committee to create the department and possibly to oversee it afterward, according to GOP Rep. Saxby Chambliss of Georgia, chairman of the House Intelligence Terrorism and Homeland Security Subcommittee.

If that happens, it will be the first time Congress has added a new committee with an entirely new jurisdiction since the creation of the Budget committees in 1975 and the Intelligence committees in 1977.

Foundations of American Government

"It's going to be a decision that will have to be made by leadership," Chambliss said. "But the president wants to get the bill passed ASAP."

In public remarks before that meeting, Bush urged lawmakers not to let jurisdictional battles stand in the way of creating the new department. "There's nothing wrong with a good turf battle fight," the president said. "And one way to win that argument is to call upon the good services of effective members of the House and the Senate."

Bush noted, however, that Congress put aside its jurisdictional disputes in 1949 to enact President Harry S Truman's proposal that merged the armed services under the Department of Defense and created the National Security Council. "We need to do the same thing for the homeland," he said.

Daschle, who was in Boston attending his son's graduation from Harvard Law School and awaiting the birth of his first grandchild, was in no hurry to decide how to handle the legislation and whether a new committee would be needed.

"That's not our primary concern right now," said spokeswoman Ranit Schmelzer. "Our primary concern is to make sure we do a good job with it, and also, as we've been saying all along, to find out what went wrong with Sept. 11 and make sure it never happens again."

Indeed, in his one public statement June 6 about the Bush proposal, Daschle repeated his call for an independent commission to investigate the intelligence failures before Sept. 11.

The decisions on how the legislation should be handled will have to wait until the White House provides more details, Schmelzer said. "We've gotten one-pagers from the administration, but not much else," she said.

On the House side, Hastert began discussing how congressional committees might be reorganized at a late-afternoon meeting June 6 with Armey, Majority Whip Tom DeLay, R-Texas, and Republican Conference Chairman J.C. Watts Jr., R-Okla. Neither Hastert nor Armey would publicly endorse specific ideas, but Hastert and Gephardt discussed the select committee idea in a phone conversation, according to a Gephardt aide.

A House Republican leadership aide said GOP leaders hope to make decisions about how to proceed as early as the week of June 10.

But some of the committee chairmen and ranking members who have the most to lose are trying to shoot down the ideas before they get too far.

"It's going to be a battle on the floor here," Young warned. "It won't sail through Congress if Congress starts tampering with the committees of jurisdiction."

Young specifically warned against any efforts to strip his panel of oversight of the Transportation Security Administration, which his committee created in the aviation security bill (PL 107-71), and the Coast Guard. (*2001 CQ Weekly*, p. 2728)

Young is especially reluctant to give up oversight of the Coast Guard, which plays a large role in his home state of Alaska through environmental monitoring and search and rescue. "The Coast Guard is more than security," he said.

Other chairmen and ranking members issued their own warnings. Senate Commerce, Science and Transportation Committee Chairman Ernest F. Hollings, D-S.C., said he would resist giving up his panel's oversight of port and air transport security. Environment and Public Works Committee Chairman James M. Jeffords, I-Vt., said he was wary of losing his panel's jurisdiction over nuclear plant safety, hydroelectric dam security and drinking water safety.

And Rep. James L. Oberstar of Minnesota, the ranking Democrat on the House Transportation and Infrastructure Committee, was ready to back up Young in protecting their committee's jurisdiction. "Our committee is going to have to fight like hell to make sure that there's no new Homeland Security Committee created," Oberstar said.

Committee Ideas Take Shape

One of the most ambitious ideas is Roberts' proposal (S Res 165) to create a Select Committee on Homeland Security and Terrorism. The Senate majority and minority leaders would co-chair the panel, which would include the chairmen and ranking members of the committees that currently have jurisdiction over such issues, such as Judiciary. In addition, the majority and minority leaders would each get to appoint four other senators.

"Otherwise, you have 16 different committees and you won't know whose door to knock on," Roberts said. "It'll take you six months to do what should have been done in a week."

The select committee would have investigative power and be able to issue subpoenas. The panel would not meet regularly but convene only when intelligence briefings suggest a threat is imminent. Funding would not be an issue, at least initially, because the select committee could borrow staff members from existing committees, Roberts said.

Bennett suggested such a new select committee might be turned into a permanent standing committee later on.

Both Roberts and Bennett based their arguments on the experience of the Transportation Department, created by Congress in 1966. At the time, they said, Congress never revised the jurisdiction over all the agencies that were placed under the new department, so oversight of the department has been splintered ever since.

Meanwhile, Rep. Michael N. Castle, R-Del., called for new homeland security committees in the House and Senate and new Appropriations subcommittees to fund the new department. "Just as President Bush has recognized the need to reorganize and streamline government agencies to more effectively protect our nation from terrorism, Congress must do the same," Castle said in a June 7 letter to Hastert.

Some prominent committee chairmen were keeping quiet about their preferences. Leahy declined to say whether he would support the creation of a new committee, and Byrd said it was too early to take a position without more details of Bush's proposal.

Roberts, however, said there has been more resistance to his proposal from Democrats than Republicans in his previous efforts to generate interest.

Some lawmakers predicted the committee chairmen ultimately would not push their turf wars hard enough to block the creation of the new department.

"It's always difficult, but we're all patriots," said Castle. "Everyone understands the importance of national security. I would think this is a situation where chairmen will say, 'Hey, I've got to give it up.'"

Besides, Castle said, there could be a powerful consolation prize: a seat on the new committee that could easily become one of the most sought-after assignments in Congress.

"I think people would be vying for it almost immediately," he said. ◆

Preserving Congress

How to Resurrect Congress After a Debilitating Attack

Talk grows about ways to speed the filling of House vacancies if disaster strikes

Late on the afternoon of Sept. 11, about 100 shaken House members gathered at Capitol Police headquarters for a conference call with their two top leaders, under guard at a military bunker in Virginia. The subject: whether the House should formally reconvene inside the Capitol that night in a show of resolve after the terrorist attacks.

After a spirited discussion, Speaker J. Dennis Hastert, R-Ill., and Minority Leader Richard A. Gephardt, D-Mo., decided that a brief and heavily guarded appearance by House members and senators on the Capitol steps was the safer and more symbolically appropriate course. But for Rep. Brian Baird of Vancouver, Wash., the discussion raised this question: What would have happened had the Capitol been attacked that night, killing or disabling scores of lawmakers on the House floor instead?

It was not an academic concern. Although U.S. airspace had been shut down soon after hijacked airliners struck the World Trade Center and Pentagon, by that evening at least two international flights scheduled to fly to the United States were not yet accounted for. As a result, national security officials and Capitol Police could not guarantee to Hastert and Gephardt that the Capitol was out of danger.

And when Baird asked colleagues about the procedure for keeping Congress operating after suffering heavy casualties, he did not get a clear answer. That uncertainty prompted the second-term Democrat to make the creation of a straightforward response to that question his top priority. He has since been joined by several academics who are convinced that the 18th century constitutional system of filling congressional vacancies needs to be updated to handle 21st century threats.

Half a year after the attacks, the idea of creating a quicker means for filling House seats after a catastrophe is being taken seriously by a growing number of lawmakers. In the first months after the attacks, the topic did not generate much discussion outside of opinion pages in newspapers and the occasional think tank forum. Now, members of the House Republican and Democratic leaderships are expected to meet this spring to discuss options. Some of those options would require changing only House rules; others would require changing federal law; others would require a constitutional amendment. *(Box, pp. 14-15)*

In addition, 218 House members have signed a letter asking Hastert and Gephardt to create a task force of House and Senate members to discuss the issue. And prominent former members of Congress, including the two previous Speakers, Thomas S. Foley, D-Wash. (1965-95), and Newt Gingrich, R-Ga. (1979-99), have added their voices to the chorus of legal experts and constitutional scholars who say lawmakers should address the situation. *(2002 CQ Weekly, p. 791)*

The problem, all agree, is that the sole method for filling a House vacancy, set out in Article I of the Constitution, is a special election. If a terrorist strike destroyed the Capitol while Congress was in session — or if Washington were victim to a nuclear, chemical or biological attack — the Senate could be reconstituted quickly because the 17th Amendment gives governors the power to fill Senate vacancies, generally until the next regular election. The House, however, could be effectively shut down for months in a time of extreme national emergency until enough special elections were held to repopulate the chamber.

"People recognize that even though Sept. 11 is now six months ago, the potential for other actions is still there," said Baird.

Quick Contents

Senate vacancies are filled by governors, so reconstituting that chamber is somewhat straightforward. But special elections are the only available means of filling House vacancies, and those could take months after a catastrophe. Half a year since Sept. 11, House leaders are considering ways to assure that Congress continues after an attack.

Capitol Police officer John Lucas stands guard during last October's anthrax scare. The Capitol's vulnerability has fueled talk of altering the way Congress fills vacancies.

CQ Weekly April 6, 2002

Foundations of American Government

House Republican Policy Committee Chairman Christopher Cox of California, whom Hastert has asked to take the lead on the issue for the GOP leadership, agreed. "This is something that was not on anyone's radar screen pre-Sept. 11," he said, but since then the momentum to address the issue has become "significant."

Cox has sent a letter to Gephardt, who heads the House Democratic Policy Committee, proposing that the two policy panels work together to propose changes. A meeting has not been scheduled but seems to be inevitable, given that Gephardt has voiced his support for addressing the issue. "I'm sure we would welcome the opportunity" to hold a joint meeting of the policy committees, said Gephardt spokeswoman Kori Bernards.

Hastert and Gephardt have yet to respond to Baird's letter seeking creation of a task force. But Cox, who signed the letter, said he has talked to Hastert Chief of Staff Scott Palmer about the problems with the current system of House succession.

"I know the Speaker is supportive" of dealing with the issue, Cox said. Because of the sense of uncertainty and vulnerability all members of Congress have experienced since Sept. 11, Cox said, "there is a sense of reality" to the discussion that did not exist before.

Doomsday Scenarios

There have been other developments that have added to the growing urgency of the debate.

Closest to home, Congress last October was one of the targets of an anthrax attack. In addition, proliferation experts have long believed that some nuclear weapons may be missing from the Russian arsenal. President Bush has accused Iran, Iraq and North Korea of trying to create weapons of mass destruction. And there are reports that Osama bin Laden's al Qaeda network, the government's suspect in the Sept. 11 attacks, is trying to develop chemical or biological weapons of its own. (2002 CQ Weekly, pp. 316, 229)

"We live in a time of relatively available weapons of mass destruction and people who despise our country," said Baird. "The possibility that one of those groups could obtain a weapon of mass destruction is, I think, fairly high."

The danger of a devastating attack has prompted the Bush administration to create a team of senior officials and

Facing the Threat . . .

After the Sept. 11 attacks, Rep. Brian Baird, D-Wash., and a task force of academics called attention to the need for a faster system of replacing incapacitated House members following a disaster. But it took a March 17 op-ed article in The Washington Post by former Speakers Newt Gingrich, R-Ga., and Thomas S. Foley, D-Wash., to put the issue on the agenda of House GOP and Democratic leaders.

Gingrich

Foley

Baird

Specter

The most prominent proposals for replacement of House members under catastrophic circumstances have been submitted by Sen. Arlen Specter, R-Pa.,

station them at a pair of secret locations outside Washington. The procedure is designed to ensure that the executive branch, at least, could function uninterrupted despite a catastrophe. (2002 CQ Weekly, p. 630)

A Cold War bunker built for Congress in West Virginia was decommissioned a decade ago. To improve the chances for continuity in the legislative branch, former House members and constitutional scholars say, there must be at least a plan for filling House vacancies quickly.

The Constitution was designed to guarantee that the executive branch would be unable to run the federal government by itself, congressional experts point out. Even in the kind of crisis that would be created by the obliteration of Washington, they say, Congress still would retain the power of the purse — so both halves of Congress would need to function in order to appropriate the money required to keep the executive branch running, as well as to rebuild after or retaliate against an attack on the Capitol.

In addition, under the 25th Amendment, the House and the Senate must vote to confirm anyone picked by the president to fill a vice presidential vacancy.

Even setting a new location for meetings of Congress if the Capitol were destroyed would require votes by the House and the Senate, noted Norman J. Ornstein, a resident scholar at the American Enterprise Institute. If a new location were not chosen, the Senate could not meet to confirm presidential nominees or ratify treaties.

"This is not in competition with the executive branch," said Alton Frye, director of the Program on Congress and U.S. Foreign Policy at the Council on Foreign Relations, who has been working with Ornstein on the issue. "This is a vital supplement to make sure that the executive branch will have a congressional partner to work with."

The problem would arise if the House were unable to muster a quorum, or a majority of people who have been elected to and sworn in by the House. With all 435 seats filled, a quorum is 218. In theory, even if only a few lawmakers survived an attack, a majority of them could conduct the House's business.

But if a large number of House members survived but were incapacitated or too ill to go to work, it might prove impractical to obtain a quorum, Ornstein said. Even if survivors could assemble a quorum, he said, it would be wrong for the country if that meant a small percentage of the membership elected to a Congress made crucial decisions for the

Preserving Congress

... and Solving the Problem

Baird and the two previous Speakers. Here is how those proposals would compare with the current situation:

The Constitution: Under the 17th Amendment, Senate vacancies are filled by the state's governors. For the House, however, Article I proscribes that vacancies may be filled only by special election.

Baird (H J Res 67): The Constitution would be amended to allow a governor to name a temporary successor to a dead or incapacitated House member from his state. The replacement would leave after 90 days, or as soon as a special election had been conducted. The provisions would apply only when one-quarter or more of all House members had been killed or incapacitated.

Specter (S J Res 30): A constitutional amendment similar to Baird's, except the provisions would apply only when half the House seats were considered vacant. In addition, governors would be required to appoint people from the same political party as the members who were killed or incapacitated.

Foley-Gingrich: Alter the House rules, by simple majority vote, to allow members to name their own interim successors, who could serve until a special election. Such a rules change would be followed by a constitutional amendment to protect the arrangement from legal challenges.

---

entire House for an extended period.

"Nobody wants to confront the possibility of their own demise. The natural impulse is to say, 'Well, let's wait until something happens,'" Ornstein said. "If we wait until something happens, we could have a huge crisis of governance on our hands."

Options and Opposition

To Baird and Cox, the need for faster replacement of House members in a crisis ultimately will require a constitutional change.

In October, Baird introduced a resolution (H J Res 67) proposing a constitutional amendment under which governors would have to name temporary replacements for House members killed or unable to perform their duties. The replacements could serve for no more than 90 days, during which a special election would have to be held to fill the vacancy for the remainder of the Congress.

The House Judiciary Subcommittee on the Constitution held a hearing on the Baird proposal and others Feb. 28. Chairman Steve Chabot, R-Ohio, said he is still pondering the questions raised by that discussion and has no plans for additional hearings at the moment.

While Baird has won praise from Ornstein and others for being first out of the box with a plan, lawmakers and analysts say it does not address all of the concerns about such a situation.

There is, for example, the issue of partisan balance after governors appoint new House members. Even in a cataclysm that might kill hundreds of lawmakers, many members are so concerned about partisan battles that they want to make sure neither party would end up with a stronger margin in a post-disaster House.

"We have a certain political composition between Democrats and Republicans and independents now, that the people selected, and . . . it would probably be sensible to have that composition continued on that temporary basis again until the people could have special elections," Gephardt said at a March 22 news conference.

To address that issue, Sen. Arlen Specter, R-Pa., has introduced a resolution (S J Res 30) proposing a constitutional amendment similar to Baird's, but requiring governors to appoint interim House members of the same party as the members they would replace.

In addition, others are concerned that allowing governors to appoint House members would violate that chamber's 214-year history as the only branch of the federal government whose members always have been directly elected. (Presidents are chosen by the Electoral College; federal judges by presidents with the Senate's consent. Senators were chosen by state legislatures until the 17th Amendment was ratified in 1913.) And since a constitutional amendment could take years to ratify, they say an interim arrangement is needed to cover any emergencies in the meantime.

To address those concerns, Foley and Gingrich say a change in House rules — to be backed up later by a constitutional amendment — could allow House members to designate their temporary successors until special elections are held.

The other concern, raised by some lawmakers and legal experts whenever constitutional changes are discussed, is that it is inappropriate to amend the Constitution unless no other remedy will suffice. "We should always be very deliberate and very cautious before we amend the Constitution," Chabot said, and legislation or a change in House rules "would probably be the more prudent way to deal with the issue."

Charles Tiefer, a professor at the University of Baltimore School of Law who testified at Chabot's hearing, agreed. "Constitutional amendments tend to be hard to adopt," he said, and "are inflexible because there's no way afterwards to adjust them."

While the problem of House succession is a legitimate one, Tiefer said, there have been too many other movements of late to amend the Constitution — including the 1990s proposals to require a balanced budget and impose term limits on Congress — that faded after a rush of initial support.

Baird and Cox, however, believe the House succession issue cannot be solved permanently without a constitutional amendment because no other solution can cover all of the potential scenarios in which a faster method of succession might be needed.

Others who support a constitutional change conceded it would be a hard sell at a time when few outside Washington are paying attention. "There's not a groundswell of interest in pushing for a constitutional amendment," said James A. Thurber, director of the Center for Congressional and Presidential Studies at American University. "It's certainly not a grass-roots issue."

But Thurber says now is the time to start calling attention to the issue. "God help us if we have the problem," Thurber said. "But if we do, let's anticipate it and do something about it." ◆

Foundations of American Government

Risk Enough for All In *Walker v. Cheney*

GAO's document quest is a high-stakes game for Congress and White House alike

An inquiring letter from Henry A. Waxman or John D. Dingell is not an unusual event. One of the half-dozen House Democrats left from the post-Watergate "reform" Class of 1974, Waxman has made a career of needling Republicans and investigating tobacco companies and corporate polluters; his office wall of gray file cabinets bulges with related correspondence. During his 45-year tenure, fellow Democrat Dingell has transformed the Energy and Commerce Committee into one of Capitol Hill's premier investigatory arms; his "Dingell-grams" — blunt demands for information and tart rebukes to insufficient responses — have been penned at the rate of hundreds a year.

So last April 19, there was no fanfare when California's Waxman and Michigan's Dingell put their signatures on two more missives. Soon after newspapers published stories about meetings between Vice President Dick Cheney's energy task force and contributors to President Bush's 2000 campaign, they requested details from Andrew D. Lundquist, the task force's executive director. Expecting that Lundquist might be less than cooperative, they also wrote to ask the General Accounting Office (GAO) to scrutinize the task force.

The ensuing standoff has escalated far beyond what any of the congressional participants ever expected. The legal, political and institutional consequences are now potentially so great that Waxman and Dingell have unwittingly committed Congress to one of the highest-stakes balance-of-powers battles since Watergate. And in doing so, they have unintentionally put on the line the future of much of the very congressional investigative powers that have served them so well.

"If they prevail, they make useless the whole idea of a General Accounting Office as a nonpartisan watchdog agency," Waxman said of the Bush administration. "If they prevail, it would be a green light for them to do a lot of other things in secret, not just the energy task force."

As the investigative agency of Congress, the GAO filed a federal lawsuit Feb. 22 to compel the vice president to disclose which industry executives were consulted last year by the National Energy Policy Development Group, as Cheney's task force was called. It is the first time the GAO has ever gone to court to force the executive branch to disclose documents. Both sides are preparing for the case to end at the Supreme Court, where legal experts say the outcome is uncertain. (*2002 CQ Weekly*, pp. 566, 539, 396, 289)

If the GAO wins decisively, the ruling could strengthen the ability of Congress, or even a single lawmaker, to find out details not only about the policy deliberations of federal agencies, but also about discussions in the West Wing. If it loses decisively, the results could be an evisceration of the GAO's own reach and a crippling of congressional oversight powers. At the moment, it appears that only Comptroller General David M. Walker, the head of the GAO, views the stakes as minimal; the worst outcome in court, he said, would curtail less

CQ Weekly March 2, 2002

Presidents Often Win Document Fights with Congress

Capitol Hill has been seeking executive branch records for 210 years, with mixed success. No documents have ever been given to Congress in direct response to a federal court order.

GEORGE WASHINGTON

In 1792 he abided by a special House committee's request for documents about a disastrous military campaign against Indians in the Northwest Territories. Four years later, however, Washington refused to turn over correspondence about a treaty with Great Britain. The House dropped the issue when it passed a bill to implement the accord.

ANDREW JACKSON

In 1837 he defied a House resolution demanding names of people given administration jobs without Senate concurrence. Three months later the committee conducting the inquiry concluded it had overstepped its authority.

JOHN TYLER

In 1842 the House twice passed resolutions demanding War Department evidence of government fraud against the Cherokee Indians. Citing the need to protect his aides' confidential sources, Tyler withheld portions of the papers. Congress did not pursue the matter further.

GROVER CLEVELAND

In 1886 he defied a Senate resolution seeking records to explain why 650 office-holders had been replaced with his own political appointees. Cleveland maintained that the papers were private and confidential. He also asserted that federal agencies are beholden to the executive branch, because they carry out the president's policies, not the legislative branch, which writes the laws creating the agencies and annually pays their bills. In the end, the Senate passed an angry resolution but the president never handed over the papers.

The Legislature vs. the Executive

than 1 percent of his agency's work — concerning the operations of the Executive Office of the President.

The Bush administration, if it wins, could gain a substantial long-term and institutional advantage: A strongly written Supreme Court opinion allowing the White House to keep the names of meeting participants secret could set a precedent allowing future presidents to fend off all manner of congressional inquiries. The president and vice president say they are compelled to fight back for this reason: It is time to reclaim prerogatives that the presidency has lost, or ceded, in recent decades.

But politically, Bush seems to be playing with fire. Already the Democratic Congressional Campaign Committee, gearing up to assist House candidates in the midterm election, has established a "Hey Dick Cheney, Disclose the Documents" Web site (www.disclosethedocuments.com), relishing the opportunity to accuse the administration of concealing the involvement of top campaign contributors — especially executives from Enron Corp., the failed energy trading giant — in policy development.

By and large, the views of the fight from Capitol Hill fall along party lines, with Republican leaders supporting the president's position and Democratic leaders supporting the GAO. A prominent exception among Republicans is Dan Burton of Indiana. He is urging the administration to give the GAO what it wants, but his reasoning has nothing to do with his standing as chairman of the House Government Reform Committee, one of the main congressional oversight panels. In fact, he sees Cheney's legal position as stronger than the GAO's.

Cheney's accelerating the dispute into a balance-of-powers contest is a "big mistake," Burton said. "The American people want to believe that the government is open and above board. . . . I believe this will come back to haunt them, and us, in the fall."

"If they prevail, it would be a green light for them to do a lot of other things in secret, not just the energy task force."

— Rep. Henry A. Waxman, D-Calif.

Waxman and Dingell say they never intended such a fight. Asked to define the proper boundary for congressional inquiry into White House operations, Waxman concedes that he has not given the constitutional issues "a great deal of thought." Says Dingell, "This became a constitutional issue only because Mr. Cheney and the president made it so. . . . Now it is about the ability of the vice president to stiff Congress."

Considering the stakes, it is all the more remarkable that the fight is over a relatively small amount of information from a task force that disbanded in September. The GAO has scaled back its original demand for notes and transcripts of meetings and now wants to know only the names of lobbyists and industry officials who met with the task force, what topics were discussed and how the task force spent public moneys.

Yet the GAO has already received much of this information from the Energy Department, the Interior Department and the EPA. Officials from those agencies regularly attended task force meetings and largely complied with GAO's requests for information last year. It appears that the main information the GAO does not have is about the meetings that Cheney held without officials from those agencies, including a session with Enron Chairman Kenneth Lay last year, which the

---

Herbert Hoover

In 1930 he gave the Senate Foreign Relations Committee only some of the papers that the panel sought about negotiations on a naval treaty. The Senate adopted a resolution demanding the rest. Hoover refused — and the Senate ratified the treaty anyway.

Harry S Truman

In 1948 he refused to release the FBI files on a senior Commerce Department official to the House Un-American Activities Committee. The House then passed legislation to require all arms of the executive branch to comply with any congressional panel request for information "deemed necessary to enable them to properly perform the duties delegated to them by Congress." The bill was never considered by what is now called the Senate Governmental Affairs Committee.

Dwight D. Eisenhower

In 1954 he successfully limited the scope of testimony by Army Counsel John Adams at the anticommunist hearings chaired by Sen. Joseph R. McCarthy, R-Wis. (below). The president cited the "proper separation of power" and the importance of allowing candid and private communications within the executive branch.

John F. Kennedy

In 1962 he cited similar executive privilege in declining to tell a special Senate subcommittee who had edited speeches by senior military officials. Kennedy also decreed that such executive privilege could be invoked only by the president. Administration officials cited executive privilege, apparently without Kennedy's authorization, at least three other times in spurning requests from congressional committees.

Lyndon B. Johnson

He never personally invoked executive privilege, but at least two appointees of his administration refused to provide information to congressional committees.

Foundations of American Government

White House already has disclosed, along with five other task-force meetings with Enron executives.

The refusal to disclose more to the GAO is part of a larger pattern of tight information management during the Bush White House's first year. Journalists routinely complain they are unable to obtain answers they would have received easily from the Clinton, Reagan or first Bush White House. Leaks are exceedingly rare.

The lid has only been twisted down tighter since the Sept. 11 terrorist attacks on the United States, and Congress has often complained. Attorney General John Ashcroft has refused to provide the names of more than 1,000 people detained as part of the Justice Department's investigation or where they are being held, provoking anger from senators at a December committee hearing. Earlier in the fall, Bush moved to restrict attendance at classified briefings on Capitol Hill until he was told that more members of Congress were entitled to some of the information by law. Since then he and Cheney have pressed congressional leaders to limit the coming inquiry into intelligence-gathering failures before Sept. 11. (*2001 CQ Weekly, p. 2395; 2002 CQ Weekly, p. 311*)

The White House split a working group on Social Security policy in two so that its work would not be subject to federal sunshine law. And while partly complying with a subpoena from Burton's committee for some records from the Clinton administration, Bush has refused in at least two other instances to turn over other papers sought by House Government Reform. These include details of some Clinton pardons and some Reagan-era papers, even though their release has been sanctioned by the former presidents' advisers.

"This administration is trying to keep control of information and deliberative documents, even where there is an indication of illegal activity," Burton said.

His anger at the time stemmed from the Justice Department's refusal to turn over FBI records in a 30-year-old case that led to wrongful criminal convictions. On Feb. 27, Burton announced that his staff was preparing a resolution to hold the president in contempt of Congress in the matter. That evening, the White House handed over the documents the chairman sought.

Since Watergate, contempt citations have become a more frequently used tool of Congresses that have seen their demands for presidential records rebuffed. But they must have the support of the majority of at least one chamber at the Capitol, and there is no indication that such a move is being contemplated in the energy task force matter. (*Timeline, pp. 16-19*)

Fighting Erosion

Though Cheney's response to the lawsuit has been on narrow legal grounds so far, in public the vice president maintains he is fighting to strengthen the "principle" that the president has an expansive right to confi-

On NBC's "Tonight Show" on Feb. 19, Cheney won loud applause for his explanation to host Jay Leno that he was fighting the GAO in the hope of halting a slide in presidential power.

RICHARD M. NIXON

He formally invoked executive privilege only five times, including Watergate, though in at least 15 other instances his administration refused to provide Congress with documents or testimony, mostly on military and foreign policy matters. In 1973 the Senate passed a bill to require presidents to give written notice whenever their administrations withheld material from Congress; the legislation died in the House. In July 1974, the Supreme Court ordered Nixon to give a federal grand jury White House tapes subpoenaed by Leon Jaworski, a special prosecutor, and the clear evidence on the recordings about the president's coverup of the Watergate break-in hastened his resignation that August. Congress never received any of its subpoenas, however. In late 1973 Congress enacted a law without Nixon's signature designed to give more legal teeth to the demands of the Senate Watergate Committee for 500 tapes and documents, but Nixon still refused to comply. The next year, the House Judiciary Committee issued more subpoenas as part of its impeachment inquiry, and Nixon's rebuff of those became the basis for one of three articles of impeachment the Judiciary panel approved in July.

GERALD R. FORD

In 1975 the House Intelligence Committee voted to cite Secretary of State Henry A. Kissinger (right) for contempt of Congress for refusing, on the president's orders, to turn over records from the Kennedy, Johnson and Nixon administrations. The White House then provided many of the documents.

JIMMY CARTER

In 1980, he invoked executive privilege to withhold documents on his plan to impose an oil import fee. He relented after a House panel moved to hold Energy Secretary Charles Duncan in contempt.

The Legislature vs. the Executive

dentiality. He also says he is working to push the balance of power closer to the White House, further from the Capitol.

"I have repeatedly seen an erosion of the powers and the ability of the president of the United States to do his job," Cheney said on ABC's "This Week" on Jan. 27. "We saw it in the War Powers Act. We saw it in the Budget Anti-Impoundment Act. We've seen it in cases like this before, where it's demanded that presidents cough up and compromise on important principles. . . . That's wrong."

The vice president said he and Bush "feel an obligation . . . to pass on our offices in better shape than we found them to our successors. We are weaker today as an institution because of the unwise compromises that have been made over the last 30 to 35 years."

Waxman and Dingell emphatically disagree. "The power of the president is enormous, maybe more now than over any time in the last 20 years," Waxman said. "The power of the presidency has not eroded."

Some scholars share that opinion. "At the moment, the president is up and the Congress is down," said Stephen Hess, a Brookings Institution senior fellow. "After Watergate and Vietnam, it was the opposite. But I don't think it's been a steady decline like Cheney describes."

Lanny Davis, a White House lawyer throughout Bill Clinton's presidency, is on the side of the Bush administration in this case. "Congress has no right to know who the president consults with or what the subjects are, or else there is no such thing as executive advice and and candor from advisers," he said. "This is precisely the same argument I made on national television over and over again. . . . How in God's name can any Democrat criticize the Bush White House for taking the same position we took?"

John W. Dean III, President Richard M. Nixon's White House lawyer for three years, is on the side of Congress in this case. A court ruling in Cheney's favor, he wrote in an online law journal article in February, will create "a no-man's land where only the president and vice president can go, unobserved by the constitutional co-equals on Capitol Hill."

George Washington and most presidents since have refused demands by Congress for executive branch records. Sometimes presidents have acquiesced, often in the face of mounting political pressure. When they have resisted, Congress occasionally has abandoned its inquiries in deference to a president's public popularity. That pattern may argue in favor of the current administration's position, at least so long as Bush retains approval ratings in the range of 80 percent. Appearing on NBC's "Tonight Show" on Feb. 19, Cheney won a huge round of applause when he told host Jay Leno that he was fighting the GAO to restore presidential power after years of erosion.

Presidential popularity notwithstanding, the federal government's expansion during and since the New Deal has created many more areas for Congress to explore, and the pace of the tussles over records between the two branches has picked up since World War II.

Still, Congress has never obtained documents under the terms of a federal court order. Instead, lawmakers have historically either abandoned their quests or settled for less than everything they asked for. When a dispute between the Reagan administration and the 97th Congress over environmental policy files made it into U.S. District Court, for example, Judge John Lewis Smith Jr. wrote that he would not settle the matter because "courts have a duty to avoid unnecessarily deciding constitutional issues." The two sides came to agreement soon thereafter.

'Eighteen Acres Under the Glass'

Aside from the constitutional issues, competing values are at stake — the balance between transparency in government and efficiency of government, for example, especially at a time when expansive, round-the clock media coverage enhances the "fish bowl" nature of the venue for making public policy.

"The sort of confidentiality we absolutely took for granted under Eisenhower seriously chipped away under Nixon and is pretty much shredded now," said Hess, who served in both

RONALD REAGAN

In 1982, the House Energy and Commerce Committee started contempt proceedings against Interior Secretary James G. Watt, who then dropped an executive privilege claim and produced what the committee wanted. Later that year, the House held EPA Administrator Anne M. Gorsuch in contempt of Congress when, on Reagan's orders, she refused requests from two committees to turn over documents about the administration's plans to carry out the superfund hazardous waste cleanup law. The Justice Department refused to prosecute her and instead filed a lawsuit to block action on the contempt citation. U.S. District Judge John Lewis Smith declined to intervene, saying "courts have a duty to avoid unnecessarily deciding constitutional issues." A deal was struck under which the House voted to drop its contempt citation and the White House allowed committee members access to some papers.

BILL CLINTON

In 1996, he successfully invoked versions of executive privilege to resist giving Congress records detailing Haiti policy, the alleged shipments of Iranian arms to Bosnia, and the administration's drug interdiction efforts. But he relented to political pressure and handed over records related to the 1993 firing of White House travel office employees and the handling of FBI background files on officials in previous administrations. In 1998 the House Government Reform and Oversight Committee voted to hold Attorney General Janet Reno (above) in contempt of Congress for refusing to turn over internal Justice Department memoranda arguing for an independent counsel to investigate

1996 campaign finance abuses. She complied in part and the citation was dropped.

Also in 1998, Independent Counsel Kenneth W. Starr said one possible ground for impeaching Clinton was his abuse of executive privilege to obstruct the inquiry into his affair with intern Monica Lewinsky. The House did not pursue that charge.

SOURCE: CQ's Guide to Congress

Foundations of American Government

Either Side Could Prevail On the Legal Merits, Scholars Say

On its face, the lawsuit pitting Comptroller General David M. Walker against Vice President Dick Cheney concerns a relatively small universe of disagreements: whether a White House task force is considered an "agency," for example, or just how much public money must be spent for Congress to have the right to review the expenditure.

But both sides already are preparing for the suit to end up before the Supreme Court and for the key questions to be in the much grander constitutional realm of balance of federal power — the right of the executive branch to make policy against the right of the legislative branch to know how the policy was created.

At this stage in the process, legal scholars suggest the outcome could go either way.

Cheney's position is designed to "reaffirm the constitutional prerogatives of the president," said Douglas Kmiec, the dean of Catholic University Law School in Washington, who sees the Bush administration's case as legally stronger. "I think they've decided that the president has specific executive functions to perform, and he can't perform them if he's being constantly undermined with questions like this."

But Peter M. Shane, a law professor at Carnegie Mellon University in Pittsburgh, argues that the stronger legal precedents are being wielded by Walker, who is suing as head of the General Accounting Office (GAO), the congressional investigative arm. In the end, Shane said, the administration will need to advance a "theory of executive power last articulated by" Richard M. Nixon, who was unsuccessful in claiming executive privilege to hide the information that led to his resignation in the Watergate scandal.

In *Walker v. Cheney*, the GAO seeks to compel the vice president to provide the names of everyone who participated in meetings of the National Energy Policy Development Group. Cheney, who chaired that task force last year, maintains that the GAO lacks the statutory power to compel such disclosure. (2002 CQ Weekly, p. 539)

In a related case, U.S. District Judge Gladys Kessler on Feb. 21 ordered the Energy Department to turn over 7,500 pages of records related to the energy task force and demanded under the Freedom of Information Act by the Natural Resources Defense Council, an environmental group. She set a March 25 deadline, but it is unclear just how much of what the GAO wants to know will be revealed in those papers.

The GAO suit was filed Feb. 22 and assigned at random to Judge John D. Bates, a nominee of President Bush's who won confirmation only in December. Bates was a member of Independent Counsel Kenneth W. Starr's team and successfully convinced a federal appeals court that Hillary Rodham Clinton, as first lady, could not use attorney-client confidentiality to block the release of conversations she had with White House lawyers.

It is unclear what the next step in the lawsuit will be. Cheney has until the week of April 15 to formally respond to the suit, or he could file a motion to have it dismissed. The week of March 11, however, the GAO will be permitted to file a summary judgment motion, asking Bates to find in the agency's favor based on the initial complaint alone. And, at any time, the vice president could ask the president to use his authority to declare that the release of documents would unduly harm the workings of government.

Such a declaration would take the case of out of Bates' jurisdiction and, at least temporarily, end this particular fight. But observers do not believe either side wants to go to that extreme at the outset, instead preferring to fight it out in court and perhaps come up with a new rule to guide future administrations in their dealings with Congress.

The law authorizing the GAO (PL 97-258) says it may "investigate all matters related to the receipt, disbursement and use of public money" and "shall evaluate the results of a program or activity the government carries out under existing law."

Experts disagree on how that applies to the White House, if the task force was part of an established program, or if Cheney's group had minimal expenses.

"The plain wording of the GAO statute speaks broadly enough to cover the information they sought," Carnegie Mellon's Shane said.

The GAO may undertake "auditing and evaluative functions, countered Kmiec, and "neither of those are triggered by formulation of public policy by a constitutional officer."

Judge John D. Bates

Born: Oct. 11, 1946; Elizabeth, N.J.
Family: Married; three children
Education: Wesleyan University, B.A. 1968; U. of Maryland, J.D. 1976
Military service: Army, 1968-71
Career highlights: Law clerk, U.S. District Judge Roszel C. Thomsen of Maryland, 1976-77; associate, Steptoe Johnson, 1977-80; Assistant U.S. Attorney for the District of Columbia, 1980-97; deputy to Independent Counsel Kenneth W. Starr, 1995-97; partner, Miller Chevalier, 1998-2001; U.S. District Judge for the District of Columbia, 2001-present.

The Legislature vs. the Executive

administrations. "It's 18 acres under the glass. It never would have entered my mind in an earlier time not to send a president a memo of exactly how I thought about something. Now, it's not what do I think, but how will it look when it's commandeered by Congress or leaked to The Washington Post?"

Bush says his administration is resisting the GAO to enhance the likelihood that he will receive such unvarnished advice, not only from his aides but also from people outside government.

"In dealing with his own staff, the president has the right to absolute confidential conversations, even though we fund the salaries of every person in the meeting," said Waxman, who used a similar argument in 1998 when he warned Republicans to be "careful of the precedents" in what they were demanding to know about staff advice at the Clinton White House. But Waxman says that same protection should not apply to the lobbyists, contributors and others with special interests who advise the president on major policy questions. At a minimum, he said, their identities should be made public.

No Executive Privilege

The administration has not invoked the concept of executive privilege. There appear to be two main reasons for this. The first is that the Supreme Court's landmark 1974 ruling in *U.S. v. Nixon* held that the claim could be invoked only to resist a subpoena that could reveal military and national security secrets, and neither a subpoena nor that sort of information is at issue in the GAO case. The second reason is that the privilege would probably need to be asserted by Cheney, as the chairman of the task force, which would be an untested bid to expand vice presidential prerogatives. "Until I hear that Cheney is the president, executive privilege doesn't apply here," Dingell said.

In its dispute with Cheney, meanwhile, the GAO maintains that the degree of privacy the administration is seeking is far broader than the current reach of executive privilege. GAO is seeking victory on narrower grounds: that it has the statutory authority to get the information it wants. Cheney's lawyers, who have not formally answered the suit, say the GAO is seeking to apply its authority too broadly.

In addition, Cheney wrote to the GAO in August that a "president and his senior advisers must be able to work in an atmosphere that respects confidentiality of communications if the president is to get the good, candid advice and other information upon which wise decision-making depends." But there have been exceptions to the administration's insistence on such confidentiality — such as when the White House detailed the consultations Bush had in developing his embryonic stem cell research policy. (*2001 CQ Weekly, p. 2063*)

Will Senate Weigh In?

The GAO has long been a favored investigatory adjunct of the minority parties in Congress, in part because the most favored tool for congressional inquiries into the executive branch — the subpoena — as a practical matter is available only to the majority in each chamber. The House Republican majority has shown no signs of wanting to confront a president of their own party in this way. And the Senate Democratic majority has not taken much of an overt interest in the cause launched by their colleagues in the House. "It may still come to that point," said Waxman.

The only promised intervention so far has come from Senate Majority Whip Harry Reid of Nevada. Angry at the administration's plans to make Yucca Mountain in his state the nation's nuclear waste repository, Reid has vowed to file a "friend of the court" brief in support of the GAO's case. Beyond that, four other senior Senate Democrats — Ernest F. Hollings of South Carolina, Carl Levin of Michigan, Byron L. Dorgan of North Dakota and Joseph I. Lieberman of Connecticut — wrote the GAO to endorse its preparation of the lawsuit.

"A loss could be a real blow to the cause of open and accountable government," said Lieberman, who chairs the Governmental Affairs Committee, which has jurisdiction for oversight of the executive branch. "For decades, Congress has relied on the GAO to help it in that work," he noted.

The White House has declined to say whether it would abide by a Senate subpoena. "That's a hypothetical question, which we don't answer," said Cheney spokeswoman Jennifer Millerwise.

Given the unpredictable nature of the case, it would appear that both sides have powerful incentives to strike a deal. A settlement would presumably allow Walker to repair GAO's relations with congressional Republicans, and it would end the risk of seeing his agency's investigatory powers curtailed. At the same time, a settlement could allow the White House to limit the appearance that it is hiding something and the risk that its ability to resist Congress could be eroded.

"Every time the president goes to court, he takes the chance of chipping away at the authority that has been given to him in Article II of the Constitution. So many powers exist because they haven't been challenged, they have just been accepted," said Hess.

"It seems to me to be politically maladroit, no matter how it goes," said Peter M. Shane, a constitutional law professor at Carnegie Mellon University in Pittsburgh who sees the GAO as having the stronger case.

Were Bush to prevail, Shane said, it would only be after a long legal battle during which the Democrats could be expected to maintain their public posture that the administration must be trying to hide something. "They can't possibly win in the press, even if they win in the law," Shane said.

Both sides might see an advantage in the assignment of U.S. District Judge John D. Bates to the case. He was nominated by Bush last year. But in his prior life as a prosecutor, he won a case to limit confidential discussions with lawyers inside the Clinton White House.

Between capitulation by the White House and an abandonment of the claims by the GAO lie several options, one of which was offered by Davis, the self-described "damage control" adviser to Clinton. "In post-Enron Washington, my advice is to release the documents to the press, not Congress, so that you don't concede the separation-of-powers argument," he said.

Another possibility is that the lawsuit could be rendered effectively moot by the disclosure through other means of the material GAO wants. At least three public interest groups — Judicial Watch and environmental groups Natural Resources Defense Council and Sierra Club — are suing to obtain task-force details from the White House and the Energy Department under Freedom of Information and Federal Advisory Committee acts. Early rulings in those cases have gone against the administration.

No matter how *Walker v. Cheney* is resolved, Shane predicts, the material Waxman and Dingell went after 10 months ago "is not going to remain secret forever." ◆

Political Participation

The three articles in this section deal with campaigns, elections and their aftermath. On Nov. 5, 2002, an estimated 79 percent of House members will be reelected. To what do they owe such comfortable prospects? Over the years incumbency has become a formidable force. Through redistricting, the two major parties have carved up the country into districts that favor one party or the other and that are not likely to switch loyalties anytime soon. Incumbents also have an easier time of fundraising than their opponents do and enjoy other perks of office that make campaigning more productive. This article discusses the strategies that legislators use to keep their offices and considers what this inexorable incumbency means for our democracy.

The face of Congress may not change much this year, but the face of the Democratic leadership will. The second article in this section discusses the impending shakeup in the House's Democratic hierarchy. Nearly every leadership position will change hands when the party holds elections in December. Much depends on whether the Democrats win back the House, but term limits on lower-ranking positions will force a changing of the guard regardless of which party controls the chamber.

The last article details the odyssey of the campaign finance bill, which passed Congress with a decisive vote in late March. Pressure for reforming campaign finance had been building for years as soft money contributions grew exponentially. The bill's opponents have promised to fight on in court, and no one knows for sure what changes the measure will bring.

Political Participation

Safe House: Incumbents Face Worry-Free Election

Is glut of secure seats dangerous to nation's political health?

Re-election is now almost assured to a variety of House incumbents, including independent Sanders, shown left at a Capitol Hill news conference May 14, and Democrat Jackson, shown at a Cornell College lecture April 26.

Between now and Nov. 5, the two national parties will pour millions of dollars and immeasurable amounts of time and energy into congressional races across the country in a high-stakes contest for control of the House.

Yet the vast majority of House seats are not even in play this year. Most of today's incumbents will enter and win their races without even breaking a sweat.

As many as 342 of the 435 House members, or 79 percent, may be classified as "safe" for re-election, according to a Congressional Quarterly analysis, meaning they are virtually certain to win this year. Many do not have a major-party opponent at all or face only token opposition.

The increasing trend of incumbent security in the House can be traced to a number of factors, chief among them a redistricting process in which the two parties, behaving almost like a duopoly, have essentially carved up the nation into districts that favor one party or the other. Incumbents also benefit from the powers and perks of their office and from a fundraising environment that greatly benefits officeholders over challengers.

The result is a system in which the two parties, currently at near-parity in the House, are expected to stay that way for the foreseeable future, perhaps the next decade or so. Barring a major upheaval in national politics, such as those brought about by war or economic crisis, it will be next to impossible for either party to get the foothold necessary to end the stalemate that has existed in Congress for the past several years. (*Box, p. 32*)

Some political analysts believe the impact is even more profound, that the growing entrenchment of incumbents undermines the Founding Fathers' vision of the "people's House" as a place that registers and reflects the impulses of the voters at any given time.

In fact, the Senate, which the Founders envisioned to be the more stable of the two chambers — just one-third of its members face re-election every two years — has in some recent elections seen a much higher percentage of incumbents defeated than the House. In 2000, six of the 29 Senate incumbents who ran for re-election were defeated. That year, just nine of the 403 House incumbents who sought re-election lost.

"Shifts in opinion of the public electorate don't have the same impact," said John J. Pitney, a government professor at Claremont-McKenna College in Claremont, Calif. "In the past, if you had a lot of marginal seats, if there was shift in public opinion, it would register in the composition of the House. That is not necessarily the case now."

The Path to Safety

The House's safe incumbents represent districts from Maine to Hawaii. They are of both genders, many ethnicities and religions, and a wide variety of age groups. And they are

CQ Weekly May 18, 2002

Campaigns and Elections

House Incumbents Have Stellar Record: Vast Majority of Those Who Run Win

Since 1962, more than nine in 10 House incumbents running for re-election won. Incumbent winners and losers during the last 20 House elections:

All 7,921 races 1962-2000 — Won 93.3% | Lost 6.7%

YEAR	INCUMBENTS WINNING	LOSING	YEAR	INCUMBENTS WINNING	LOSING
1962	368	34	1982	354	39
1964	344	53	1984	392	19
1966	362	49	1986	385	9
1968	396	13	1988	402	7
1970	379	22	1990	390	16
1972	365	25	1992	325	43
1974	343	48	1994	349	38
1976	368	16	1996	361	23
1978	358	24	1998	395	7
1980	361	37	2000	394	9

SOURCE: Vital Statistics on American Politics, CQ research

practically evenly divided between Republicans and Democrats.

They include most of the top dogs, including Speaker J. Dennis Hastert, R-Ill., and Minority Leader Richard A. Gephardt, D-Mo., but also dozens of back-benchers.

And the avenues they take to safe incumbency are similarly varied.

Some of them inherit security by running and winning in districts drawn to strongly favor their party's candidates. Democrat Jose E. Serrano in New York has never fallen below 91 percent of the general-election vote in seven contests in his Hispanic-majority district, located in New York City's South Bronx; his district gave 93 percent of its 2000 presidential vote to Democrat Al Gore.

In Texas' GOP-dominated 7th District — located in the affluent suburbs of Houston — Republican John Culberson won an open-seat primary in 2000 and was so confident of general-election victory that he spent most of the rest of the year campaigning for Republicans in other congressional districts. Culberson went on to defeat a Democratic opponent with 74 percent in a district that gave 71 percent of its presidential vote to Texas Republican George W. Bush. (*Culberson, p. 31*)

In Nebraska, Tom Osborne would have been a shoo-in for the open 3rd District seat in 2000 as soon as he won the Republican primary — even if his legendary career as a University of Nebraska football coach had not made him perhaps the most recognizable man in the Cornhusker State. That is because Republicans have represented the sprawling Western district without interruption for 40 years. Osborne took 82 percent of the vote over his Democratic opponent in 2000. This year, he has no Democratic opponent.

Not all safe incumbents are safe just because of their districts' makeup, however. In Florida, 15-term Rep. C.W. Bill Young, a Republican who represents a Democratic-leaning district in St. Petersburg, maintains safe status partly because of his role as chairman of the House Appropriations Committee, clout so enormous that Democrats did not even field a challenger to him in 2000.

Others, such as Democrat Lois Capps in California, will run in "gerrymandered" districts that favor their party, a trend that appears to have intensified in the current round of redistricting, which sets the ground rules for elections this year and the remainder of the decade. In most states, protecting current incumbents has taken precedence over attempting partisan gains. (*Capps, p. 29*)

Some members have secured their positions simply by campaigning hard and tailoring their legislative agendas to constituencies that swing between the parties.

Democrat Rick Boucher would appear on paper to be potentially vulnerable in southwest Virginia's 9th District, a rural, socially conservative area that swung heavily for George W. Bush in the 2000 presidential election after narrowly supporting Democrat Bill Clinton in 1992 and 1996.

But Boucher has tended to the legislative interests of the coal miners, tobacco growers and cattle ranchers in his district, even as he pursues his passion for Internet issues as a member of the Energy and Commerce Committee. While Bush carried 55 percent of the 9th District vote in 2000, Boucher was breezing to a 10th House term with 70 percent.

Locked-In Advantage

Congressional Quarterly ranks each House, Senate and gubernatorial race by whether it is "safe" for the party that currently holds the seat, or "vulnerable" to a take-away by the other party. These risk rankings are continually updated during the year by the CQ Politics staff to reflect changing electoral conditions and developments, both national and local.

If this campaign year follows previous patterns, a number of currently safe House incumbents will face tougher than expected challenges and become vulnerable before the Nov. 5 elections. On the other hand, some members currently facing some level of serious competition could end up safe by November as challenges peter out.

It is quite possible that about 90 percent of all incumbents will be re-elected, despite the fact that 32 members are not seeking re-election and another handful will be displaced by the once-a-decade processes of congressional reap-

Political Participation

Wide Appeal Shores Up Independent

BERNARD SANDERS (I)
Popular Iconoclast

STATE AND DISTRICT:
Vermont at-large

Birthdate/Place: Sept. 8, 1941, Brooklyn, N.Y.
Hometown: Burlington
House terms: 6

2000 Election Outcome:
69% I – 18% R – 5% D

Closest House Outcome:
50%-46% (1994)

Average Vote Percentage:  59%

Unsuccessful House Campaigns:
1 (1988)

Previous Political Offices:
Mayor of Burlington, 1981-89

Vermont Rep. Bernard Sanders, a self-described socialist, is proof that even iconoclastic House incumbents can become virtually unbeatable.

Sanders, the former mayor of Burlington, was the first independent elected to the House in 40 years when he ousted Republican Peter Smith in a 1990 rematch of their close 1988 race.

Except for a 50 percent to 46 percent win in 1994, Sanders has run up progressively wider margins, and has become the de facto candidate of the Vermont Democratic Party — which has not endorsed a candidate against him in any of the past five elections.

Sanders is quick to say he does not take his 2002 election lightly, although he defeated his Republican opponent in 2000 by more than 50 percentage points.

While he has not abandoned his leftist roots, Sanders became a safe incumbent the old-fashioned way. He struck friendships at home and in Washington and campaigned hard. When one of his constituents calls with a question, he always has a staff member on the line with an answer.

"He is highly visible, and there's a sense that he will actually do something," said Sam Hemingway, a columnist for the Burlington Free Press. "He's the anti-politician politician."

Needing sponsorship to get committee assignments, Sanders talked his way into the House Democratic Caucus — despite having said that the Democrats failed to differentiate themselves from the Republicans on policy issues. "This is a very complicated institution," Sanders said. "You learn something new almost every day, so I am a better congressman than I was 10 years ago."

Every year, Sanders holds town meetings throughout the state on issues he thinks locals care about.

The agenda often reflects Sanders' ideological bent. His most recent town meeting was on "corporate control of the media."

As ranking minority member on the Financial Services Subcommittee on International Monetary Policy and Trade, Sanders voices liberal opposition to the policies of the International Monetary Fund.

But he has also sealed his popularity with his focus on home-state issues, such as dairy price supports. "He has made himself a person that appeals to people across ideologies," Hemingway said.

When Sanders first ran for the House in 1988, it appeared another quixotic effort for the often-rumpled populist, who failed to top 4 percent in four statewide campaigns in the early 1970s. Democrats complained that he was spoiling their chances to win.

But it was Sanders who held Smith to a 41 percent to 37 percent win, while the Democratic nominee got just 19 percent. Two years later, Sanders ousted Smith, 56 percent to 40 percent.

portionment and redistricting. That would prolong the trend that began in the 1998 and 2000 campaigns, when voters returned nearly 91 percent of all incumbents to office.

The underlying reality for Congress' safety in numbers is that most districts give one party or the other an overwhelming advantage.

Of the 435 House districts, 324 (74.5 percent) stayed in the same party's hands through the five elections from 1992 to 2000 — even though that period included the 1994 sea-change election, in which Republicans made a net gain of 52 seats to break the Democrats' 40-year control of the House.

The redistricting process this time appears to be creating even more rock-solid partisan strongholds.

Incumbent protection has become the dominant goal of both parties, relegating the days of redistricting as a political blood sport to increasing obscurity in all but a handful of states. (*Redistricting, 2001 CQ Weekly, p. 2627*)

Republicans overhauled district maps to their advantage in Pennsylvania and Michigan, while Democrats made a big strike in Georgia. But those states were the exceptions. More typical were the incumbent-friendly bargains struck by Republicans and Democrats in Illinois and California.

In Illinois, Hastert, who has represented the state's 14th District for eight terms, and 10-term 3rd District Democratic Rep. William O. Lipinski drafted a bipartisan plan that flew through the state legislature — the Democratic-controlled House and Republican-controlled Senate — and was signed by Republican Gov. George Ryan.

Campaigns and Elections

A Republican's Allure to Labor

PHIL ENGLISH (R)
Crossover Appeal

STATE AND DISTRICT: Pennsylvania (3)*
Birthdate/Place: June 20, 1956, Erie, Pa.
Hometown: Erie
House terms: 4

2000 Election Outcome:
61% R – 39% D

Closest House Outcome:
49%-47% (1994)

Average Vote Percentage: 56%

Unsuccessful House Campaigns: none

Previous Political Offices:
Erie City Controller, 1986-89

* Currently represents 21st District. Number changed in redistricting.

There were reasons to doubt Republican Phil English's political security after he first won his House seat in a politically competitive northwest Pennsylvania district in 1994.

English benefited from that year's big national Republican surge. He had top-of-the-ticket help from Republicans Rick Santorum, who won for the Senate, and Tom Ridge, English's predecessor in the House (1983-95), who in 1994 won his first of two terms as governor and now is the nation's homeland security chief.

Despite those factors, English won with less than 50 percent and with a margin of less than 3 percentage points.

But it did not take him long to become an entrenched incumbent.

Positioning as a Republican moderate — including outreach to organized labor — attention to his constituents, and a valuable seat on the House Ways and Means Committee that he received as a freshman helped move English from the ranks of congressional survivalists to those of the safest incumbents.

"After my first two years, I think it has become more clear to people in my district how much I'm doing, how central my committee assignments are and how I have been an advocate on their behalf," said English, who credited his safety to "political independence, which is something that is prized in western Pennsylvania."

After squeaking through his first re-election bid in 1996, English won by more than 20 points in each of his next two elections.

This year, with a modestly favorable redistricting design bestowed on English by state Republicans, Democrats did not even bother to field a candidate against him.

Representing a largely blue-collar district that includes the city of Erie, English takes a nuanced position on the global economy. He generally has supported trade but has sided with organized labor on a number of key issues, including safety regulations for Mexican trucks, a minimum wage boost and tariffs on imported steel.

The chairman of the Congressional Steel Caucus, English does not agree with the United Steelworkers of America on everything — the union endorsed his Democratic opponent in 2000 — but union officials say they have worked closely with him on a number of issues.

John P. DeFazio, District 10 director for the United Steelworkers of America, said, "Sometimes now you can overlook some of his views on other things because of his strong stand on tariffs. . . . I think that helps him a lot."

"English has tried to go out of his way to be supportive of the one group that really went after him the first time: organized labor," said political analyst Jon Delano. "While he is not one of their favorite congressmen, he is certainly trying to become one of their favorite Republicans."

Illinois, because of below-average population growth, is losing one of its 20 seats in the decennial reapportionment, so one incumbent has to go. The Hastert-Lipinski plan merged Republican John Shimkus and Democrat David Phelps in a redrawn 19th District that appears to favor Shimkus but could produce a competitive race.

But the other 18 incumbents — nine Republicans, nine Democrats — appear to have few worries about re-election. Only GOP freshman Mark Steven Kirk, who won suburban Chicago's 10th District in 2000 with 51 percent of the vote, appears to face any threat, though CQ still ranks him as favored to win.

Among those who appear safe under the new map is 10-term Democrat Lane Evans, who has endured a series of highly competitive Republican challenges since 1994. Evans had many Democratic voters added to his 17th District, which previously had only a slight Democratic lean.

Hastert and Lipinski — neither of whom has a major-party opponent this year in the districts they drew for themselves — bargained their compromise to avoid a possible stalemate between state House Democrats and the Republican governor. Such a stalemate could have thrown the remap into the courts, with the kind of uncertain outcome that makes incumbents of both parties very nervous.

Even so, the incumbent-protection theme was prevalent even in many states where one party had total control of the process, and the opportunity to target the other party's incumbents.

The tone was set early in the redistricting cycle by California, which at 53 seats remains the largest delegation

Political Participation

Powerful Name Secures Chicago's 2nd

JESSE L. JACKSON JR. (D)
Minority Star

STATE AND DISTRICT: ILLINOIS (2)
Birthdate/Place: March 11, 1965, Greenville, S.C.
Hometown: Chicago
House terms: 3 full (first elected Dec. 1995 special election)

2000 Election Outcome:
90%D-10%R

Closest House Outcome:
76%-24% (1995)

Average Vote Percentage: 87%

Unsuccessful House Campaigns:
None

Previous Political Offices:
None

As the son of a famed civil rights leader, Illinois Democratic Rep. Jesse L. Jackson Jr. bears a name that draws wide respect among the African-Americans on Chicago's South Side who make up most of his constituency.

Like most black and Hispanic House members, Jackson represents a district in which minorities make up a "supermajority" of the population. Most such districts were created beginning in the 1960s to address a dearth of minority members in Congress.

Running in a district in which blacks, an overwhelmingly Democratic constituency, make up more than two-thirds of the population, Jackson has been elected with as much as 94 percent of the vote.

Jackson says, though, that his highly recognized name was a boon in the 1995 special election that earned him his House seat at age 30.

"My first campaign cost about $750,000," Jackson said. "Had I not had this name and family that had been engaged in public service in Chicago for more than 30 years, it probably would have cost significantly more."

Jackson, who had never held office, won the crucial Democratic primary with a 9 percentage-point margin over 22-year state legislator Emil Jones, who was endorsed by nearly every Democratic leader in the district.

Jackson won the general election with 76 percent. He has coasted through three elections since and appears certain to do so again this year.

Jackson found himself a national celebrity from his first moments in Washington. The day before he was sworn in, he appeared on CNN's "Inside Politics," and his every move was reported in newspapers across the country during his first week.

Jackson said his security in office has given him more freedom to take chances and to lend his support to other candidates.

His success at the polls and growing influence in the House, where he is on the Appropriations Committee, has led to speculation on how far Jackson can go — including the possibility of following in the footsteps of his father, who twice bid for the Democratic presidential nomination.

Jackson, however, demurs when asked about his future. "What I promised the people of the 2nd District of Illinois is that I would represent them as long as they would have me," Jackson said. "Until I am confident that we are on our way to recovery, I am going to do my best to focus on what they've asked me to do."

Jackson, whose agenda focuses strongly on improving economic opportunity in his home district, is well-spoken and comfortable in public situations, even if he did not inherit his father's famous pulpit style of oratory.

A wag once described him as "the accountant for the Rainbow Coalition," the social action organization founded by the elder Jackson.

in the House, after getting one more seat through reapportionment.

Democrats have large majorities in both chambers of the California legislature, and Democrat Gray Davis is governor. National Democratic strategists hoped that this control of the remapping process would put at least some Republican incumbents in danger.

But rather than shift Democratic voters into Republican incumbents' districts to make them more vulnerable, California lawmakers shifted Democratic voters into the districts held by members of their own party — including Capps and six others who won with less than 55 percent in 2000 — to make them less vulnerable.

There was one odd man out: Los Angeles-area Republican Steve Horn decided to retire in expectation that his already Democratic-leaning district would be reshaped to elect a Hispanic Democrat.

But the only re-election-seeking California incumbent likely to lose this year has already done so: Democrat Gary A. Condit, seriously damaged by a scandal concerning his alleged affair with a Washington intern who subsequently disappeared, was ousted in the March 5 primary.

Solid Party Districts

Even before the redistricting process commenced, most incumbents were ensconced in seats that strongly favored their parties.

The 2000 election produced just 86 House districts that voted for a House member of one party and the presidential candidate of another party — the lowest total of crossover voting in a presidential election since 1952.

Campaigns and Elections

Redistricting Gurus Protect Incumbents

LOIS CAPPS (D)
Remap Beneficiary

STATE AND DISTRICT: California (23)*
Birthdate/Place: Jan. 10, 1938, Ladysmith, Wis.
Hometown: Santa Barbara
House terms: 2 full (First elected March 1998 special election)
2000 Election Outcome: 53% D – 44% R
Closest House Outcome: 53%-45% (1998 special)
Average Vote Percentage: 54%
Unsuccessful House Campaigns: none
Previous Political Offices: none

* Currently represents 22nd District. Number changed in redistricting.

As a result of the redistricting map employed for this year's elections, California's 23rd District is skinny as a snake — thinning at one point to span the distance between the ocean and the high-tide line.

But this elongated design broadens the political security of Democratic Rep. Lois Capps. After enduring three competitive contests in a slightly Republican-leaning constituency, Capps will run this year in a district that appears to have a Democratic tilt.

Protecting incumbents has been the most noticeable trend in the round of redistricting that has followed the 2000 census. California, where 50 of the 52 incumbents were made safer in the remap, is perhaps the most obvious example.

Capps' new district takes in coastal cities and Hispanic enclaves in its 220-mile stretch through San Luis Obispo, Santa Barbara and Ventura counties north of Los Angeles.

Capps currently represents a district, numbered the 22nd, that moves well inland from the coast to take in conservative, rural areas.

Capps has won all three of her House bids, beginning with the March 1998 special election to succeed her late husband, Walter Capps, who had broken a 52-year Republican winning streak in the district in 1996. But she has yet to crack 55 percent of the vote.

Like all other California House Democrats, Capps gave $20,000 to IMPAC 2000, a national Democratic redistricting group, which hired consultants to work with state legislators on an incumbent-protection redistricting plan.

Rather than press for greater gains in the heavily Democratic state, Democrats shored up all seven of their House incumbents who got less than 55 percent in 2000, including Capps. In the process, they guaranteed nearly all of California's incumbents safe seats until the redistricting that will follow the 2010 census.

"Lois had one meeting with those guys; it lasted 25 minutes, and frankly, there was pretty much a meeting of the minds," said a source close to the process.

While her old district favored GOP presidential nominee George W. Bush 49 percent to 45 percent, voters in the new district favored Democrat Al Gore by 53 percent to 40 percent — a 17 percentage point swing.

"It doesn't take a genius to see that this district politically will be more favorable to someone like Lois Capps," said her chief of staff, Jeremy Rabinovitz, though he insisted Capps would not take victory for granted.

The plan sliced off inland parts of Capps' district and gave them to Republicans Elton Gallegly and Bill Thomas. New to Capps are 227,000 voters in Ventura County. But this turf includes heavily Democratic and Hispanic Oxnard, population 170,358.

Redistricting brought that total down even further. Examples include freshman Michigan Republican Mike Rogers, who won the nation's closest House race in 2000, and four-term Illinois Republican Jerry Weller. Both currently represent districts that favored Gore, but are running this year in districts redrawn favor Bush.

To be sure, there will be a handful of incumbents across the country who will fall victim to redistricting. Democrat Tom Sawyer was upset in the May 7 Ohio primary in large part because a remapping plan gave him a district in which about 80 percent of the primary vote came from territory he does not currently represent.

Most redistricting-ousted members, though, will be those forced into showdowns with fellow incumbents in states that lost seats to reapportionment.

There are now eight such races, including the May 7 primary in Indiana's 4th District, in which Republican Rep. Steve Buyer defeated GOP colleague Brian Kerns.

Three more such races are expected in states that have not yet completed redistricting: two in New York and one in Oklahoma. The figures match each state's seat loss in reapportionment.

But otherwise in New York, the sluggish pace of redistricting may strongly benefit even those members whose destinies are not locked in by the district map.

Even if state legislative negotiations currently under way are completed soon, the remap is occurring so late in the cycle that prospective challengers will be hard-pressed to raise campaign funds and shape the political organization needed to topple an incumbent.

In Long Island's 2nd District, for ex-

Political Participation

Swing Votes Gives Ohioan the Edge

STATE AND DISTRICT: Ohio (1)
Birthdate/Place: Jan. 22, 1953, Cincinnati.
Hometown: Cincinnati
House terms: 4

2000 Election Outcome:
53% R – 45% D

Closest House Outcome:
53%-47% (1998)

Average Vote Percentage: 54%

Unsuccessful House Campaigns: 1 (1988)

Previous Political Offices: Cincinnati City Council, 1985-90; Hamilton County Commissioner, 1990-95

On paper, Ohio Republican Steve Chabot appears a potentially vulnerable incumbent. But after trying several times to defeat him in the Cincinnati-based 1st District, Democrats have given up — at least for 2002.

A talent for reaching out to his district's large constituency of socially conservative Democrats has provided Chabot a hardcore voting base. Democratic opponents managed to hold Chabot to under 55 percent of the vote in each of his three re-election races — but he never fell below 53 percent in any of those contests.

"He gets a lot of support from 'Reagan Democrats' and other Democrats in the district," said Gary Lindgren, Chabot's chief of staff. "And he knocks on every door."

Chabot was made somewhat safer by the redistricting plan enacted this year: 52 percent of voters in his redrawn district supported George W. Bush in the 2000 election, to 47 percent within the current lines.

But that fairly narrow change does not in itself appear to explain why Democrats utterly failed in recruiting a challenger this year — leaving write-in candidate Greg Harris as Chabot's opponent.

The district, which encompasses most of Cincinnati and some of its suburbs, had a 30 percent black population and a slight tendency toward Democrats.

Chabot, in fact, lost his first House bid, a 1988 challenge to Democratic Rep. Thomas A. Luken (1977-91).

But voter turnout tends to be much higher in the Republican-leaning suburbs than in the city, boosting Chabot in his subsequent House races. And even among Democratic voters, there is a large faction that is sympathetic to Chabot's conservative views on social issues. The area includes many Roman Catholics, and most residents oppose abortion rights.

Chabot also has repeatedly painted outside groups favoring his Democratic foes as trying to tell Cincinnatians what to think.

A former Cincinnati city councilman, Chabot benefited from the 1994 national Republican upsurge as he ousted one-term Democratic Rep. David Mann. Chabot then endured a pair of grueling contests in which local and national organized labor interests spent hundreds of thousands of dollars against him in the heavily blue-collar 1st District.

In 1996, he beat Mark Longabaugh, a former aide to House Minority Leader Richard A. Gephardt, D-Mo., with 54 percent. In 1998, he beat Cincinnati Mayor Roxanne Qualls — touted by national Democrats as one of their top recruits that year — with 53 percent.

Democrats in 2000 ran John Cranley, a lower-profile candidate, but the results were remarkably similar: Chabot won again with 53 percent.

ample, Republicans have yet to recruit a strong challenger to Democratic freshman Steve Israel, who won in 2000 with 48 percent in a five-candidate race. Republican Rick A. Lazio — Israel's House predecessor and Republican Senate nominee against Democrat Hillary Rodham Clinton in 2000 — declined to run despite heavy lobbying by GOP officials.

Minorities' Majorities

The ranks of safe incumbents include nearly every black and Hispanic member of the House. That is because those members tend to represent districts where the minority populations are highly concentrated — deliberately so, in most cases.

Most black and Hispanic members have gone an entire career without facing even a scintilla of real competition. The most senior black member, Michigan Democrat John Conyers Jr., has received at least 82 percent of the vote in each of his 19 House general elections.

Of the 37 black members of the House, just three took less than 60 percent of the vote in the November 2000 general election: Florida's Corrine Brown (58 percent); Georgia's Sanford D. Bishop Jr. (54 percent); and Indiana's Julia Carson (59 percent). All three represent districts in which black voters are less than a majority of the electorate.

Brown and Carson have mostly liberal voting records and represent reliably, but not overwhelmingly, Democratic-voting districts. Bishop represents a southwest Georgia district that voted for Bush, and his voting record is in line with his district's conservative-leaning electorate. He is a member of the Agriculture Committee and the "Blue Dog" coalition of conservative-leaning Democrats.

Campaigns and Elections

Unopposed Texan Steps Up for Others

JOHN CULBERSON (R)
Partisan Lock

STATE AND DISTRICT: Texas (7)
Birthdate/Place: Aug. 24, 1956, Houston
Hometown: Houston
House terms: 1

2000 Election Outcome:
74% R – 24% D
Closest House Outcome:
74%-24%
Average Vote Percentage: 74%
Unsuccessful House Campaigns: none
Previous Political Offices:
Texas House, 1986-2000

Republican John Culberson, a veteran Texas state representative, was nominated in April 2000 to succeed 15-term GOP Rep. Bill Archer in suburban Houston's affluent 7th District. He segued from his primary runoff win into the role of "safe incumbent" — nearly seven months before the November vote that would send him to Congress.

Culberson's confidence was well grounded: The 7th District is a Republican heirloom, one of many districts across the nation drawn to favor the nominee of one or the other major party.

When first created in the 1960s, it became one of the original Republican strongholds in the South. Its first representative was the elder George Bush; four years later, Archer won an open-seat race to succeed Bush and went on to dominate the district for 30 years as he moved up to become chairman of the House Ways and Means Committee.

Culberson knew that winning the primary to succeed Archer not only ensured him a November victory, but virtually guaranteed a long House tenure. So he developed a strategy to make himself a player in national GOP politics.

He hit the road almost immediately after the 2000 primary, campaigning for vulnerable Republican incumbents and strong challengers in several states and raising more than $250,000 for their campaigns.

In 2000, he had token opposition from Democrat Jeff Sell, who "held" Culberson to 74 percent of the vote. This year he has no Democratic opponent.

Culberson's fundraising has only accelerated since his January 2001 swearing-in. He held a fundraiser in Houston last month for four freshman House Republicans he deemed "most endangered" in this cycle — Mark Kennedy of Minnesota, Rob Simmons of Connecticut, J. Randy Forbes of Virginia and Shelley Moore Capito of West Virginia. The two-day event raised around $75,000.

"As an unopposed congressman from a safe Republican district, I want to be a political donation consultant to my constituents to help them filter the thousands of requests they receive, and help them identify the most worthy causes," he said. "I am hopeful that this model will be used by other Republican members in similar districts across the country to strengthen our majority."

Culberson knows that campaigning for others — and inviting members of Congress to his district — has rewards for his constituents as well.

He says he took his colleagues to see the traffic-plagued Katy Freeway in Houston, which he says needs to be expanded — with an infusion of federal money. "I made sure they all saw it," he said. "That's my No. 1 local legislative priority."

Because of their districts' overwhelming built-in advantages, most minority members are more vulnerable to challenge in primaries than in general elections.

Former California Rep. Matthew G. Martinez served 18 years (1983-2001) in a heavily Latino district just east of Los Angeles. But he was trounced by Hilda Solis, 62 percent to 29 percent, in the 2000 Democratic primary. Solis, who like Martinez is Hispanic, had no Republican opponent that November and took 79 percent against three minor-party candidates.

Neither Major Owens nor Edolphus Towns, black Democrats who have represented neighboring Brooklyn districts since 1983, has ever received less than 84 percent of the vote in a general election. But in their 2000 primary contests, Towns was held to 58 percent of the vote, and Owens garnered just 54 percent.

The Institutional Edge

For all incumbents who are trying to stick around — regardless of party affiliation, political geography or race — political security is closely linked to seniority.

Junior members are more likely to face serious electoral challenges because they have not developed the deep-rooted political organizations and name identification common to their more senior colleagues.

Of the six incumbents who were defeated in the November 2000 election, five had served four terms or fewer. Of the six who lost in the November 1998 election, all had served only one or two terms.

A leading factor in the re-election rate for House incumbents is the im-

Political Participation

Moderation on Endangered List As Safe Seats Breed Rigidity

By Karen Foerstel

For the past five years, efforts in Congress to fashion a bipartisan patients' bill of rights have been caught up in the question of legal liability for health insurance companies, an issue on which the two parties have deep philosophical differences.

In all that time, neither party has shown any willingness to bend, and it is unlikely they will be getting to "yes" anytime soon. Both the Republican House and the Democratic Senate passed patients' rights legislation last year (HR 2563, S 1052), but the two parties are so divided on the liability question that House and Senate leaders still have not even appointed members to a conference committee. (*Analysts, p. 97*)

The patients' rights measure is a prime example of legislation that has become a victim of the stalemate that has afflicted several high-profile legislative initiatives in recent years. Political scholars say this gridlock, especially on issues such as patients' rights that would otherwise appear to be a priority with voters, is one result of the return to office, term after term, of incumbents from safe districts that demand — and reward — ideological rigidity.

It can be seen on other issues, too: a long-term solvency plan for Social Security, a Medicare prescription drug benefit, and an overhaul of bankruptcy law, among others. Even the nation's response to Sept. 11, an issue that supposedly unified lawmakers, has not been immune to partisan paralysis. While a terrorism insurance bill (HR 3210) passed the House in November, largely along party lines, it is now mired in the Senate, where it will probably die. Once again, the issue is liability, with Republicans demanding a ban on punitive damages and Democrats adamantly refusing to go along. (*2002 CQ Weekly, p. 1320*)

The trend toward entrenched incumbents, congressional scholars say, has blocked any infusion of new blood, and new ideas, into the legislative debate. In addition, they say, lawmakers from safe political districts often find themselves insulated from diverse opinion, further reinforcing their partisan resolve.

"They go home to an echo chamber," says Norman J. Ornstein, an expert on Congress at the American Enterprise Institute, a conservative think tank.

Adds Gary Jacobson, a political scientist at the University of California in San Diego: "They get re-elected doing the same thing each year. It may make them inflexible. It doesn't invite innovation."

Fewer 'Swing Districts'

Aggravating that trend is the shrinking number of competitive races each year in so-called swing districts, where neither party commands a majority.

Congressional scholars say political moderates are the most likely winners of such seats. But increasingly, these experts note, redistricting is turning these moderates into endangered species. As more districts are redrawn to include overwhelming numbers of voters from just one party, partisan incumbents have less reason to reach out in an effort to draw cross-party support.

In the House, the result has been sharpened partisanship, amply illustrated by lawmakers' growing unwillingness to seek compromise.

"You've got few members in marginal seats, few members behind enemy lines," said John J. Pitney, a professor of government at Claremont McKenna College in Claremont, Calif. "The result is Republicans who can be very conservative, and Democrats who can be very liberal. And both can be very confrontational."

Perhaps the most dramatic illustration in recent years of how such institutional partisanship foments confrontation is the 1998 impeachment of President Bill Clinton. (*1998 Almanac, p. 12-3*)

Though national polls showed that most Americans opposed removing Clinton from office, impeachment remained highly popular in safe GOP districts. The result: Republican candidates pressed ahead with their impeachment drive, bringing much of the legislative agenda to a standstill.

On some issues this year, legislation made it into law despite partisan differences, largely because politicians from both parties feared that failure could influence a handful of competitive races whose outcome could determine control of Congress.

The recently enacted farm bill is a prime example. Concerned that rigid partisan positions could alienate farmers in those crucial districts, Democrats and Republicans loaded the measure with as many subsidies as possible. After the six-year, $248.6 billion farm bill (HR 2646 — PL 107-171) passed the House and Senate, President Bush signed it May 13. (*2002 CQ Weekly, p. 1222*)

"Knowing that it comes down to just a few seats, neither side wanted to be labeled as anti-farmer, so they got into a bidding war," says Ornstein. "Those few [competitive seats] wag the dog."

Seniority Rules

Veteran lawmakers point to the farm bill as an illustration of the institutional upside to incumbency: Their long years in Congress have given them the knowledge and experience to push through legislation that will improve the lives of their constituents and those across the nation.

"It's good," said Thomas M. Davis III of Virginia, chairman of the National Republican Congressional Committee, which is charged with getting Republicans elected to the House. "It brings continuity and experience."

Challengers Face Uphill Money Battle

Fundraising is much easier for congressional incumbents than it is for their challengers. During the past seven election cycles, the average sitting member spent more than twice his or her competition. General election spending:

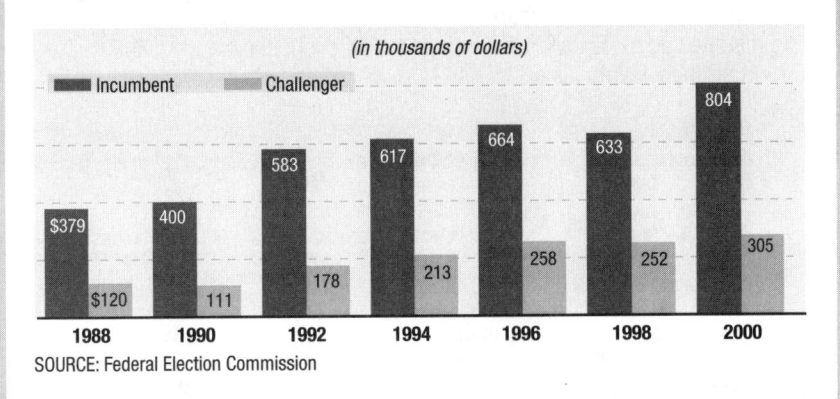

(in thousands of dollars)

Year	Incumbent	Challenger
1988	$379	$120
1990	400	111
1992	583	178
1994	617	213
1996	664	258
1998	633	252
2000	804	305

SOURCE: Federal Election Commission

Though Davis' argument may sound self-serving, independent analysts agree that such experience not only helps the legislative process but increases the power of the institution as a whole.

"One good thing is you get people who know what they are doing," said Jacobson. "If Congress is to be a viable and separate institution from the executive branch, it must have its own knowledge base."

And scholars point out that theoretically, once incumbents are given safe districts, they may be able to put politics aside and focus on their daily congressional duties. "They can spend more time on legislating rather than campaigning," Pitney said.

Cleaning House

Historically, prolonged periods of incumbent dominance in the House have periodically backfired on lawmakers, with voters tiring of the status quo and sending their representatives home in unusually high numbers.

The most recent examples were in 1994 — when 34 Democrats were defeated in the general election and not a single GOP member lost his seat. (1994 Almanac, p. 561)

In 1992, 24 incumbents lost their seats in their general elections. Another 19 that year were ousted in their primary bids, although redistricting also was a factor. (1992 Almanac, p. 15-A)

Often, such sweeps come after political scandal. The 1992 elections followed the "check bouncing" scandal, in which more than 200 lawmakers were found to have abused their accounts at the taxpayer-subsidized House bank. Of the members involved, more than one in four retired or were defeated in primary or general election bids for the House or other offices. (1992 Almanac, p. 23)

The post-Watergate elections of 1974 brought another sweep of incumbents. Then, 40 lawmakers lost their general election bids. (1974 Almamac, p. 839)

The Need for New Blood

Such sweeps have also prompted Congress to reform the way it operates, with an eye toward re-energizing the legislative process with new people and ideas.

Following the 1974 elections, Democratic leaders in the House instituted a number of internal changes, including a requirement to make committee chairmen subject to secret-ballot elections. That change resulted in the defeat of three senior chairmen and the end of the absolute seniority system for selecting chairmen. (1975 Almanac, p. 7)

The Republican class of 1994 was responsible for pushing through the House's "Contract With America" and implementing broad changes in House operations, including term limits for committee chairmen and the Speaker. (1995 Almanac, p. 1-4)

Supporters of term limits say such overhauls have been possible only when large numbers of new members take office, as in 1974 and 1994.

"With career politicians, the No. 1 priority is getting re-elected," said Stacie Rumenap, executive director of U.S. Term Limits. "Rather than legislation being drafted on the merits, they look out for their own best interests."

Rumenap also notes that term limits tend to revive voter participation. Faced with the all-but-certain return of incumbents to office, many voters stay away from the polls, adopting a "why bother" attitude, she says.

But in a sign of the enduring power of incumbency, the term limits movement has floundered of late. Since the House rejected a 1997 constitutional amendment to limit the service of congressional members, neither chamber has voted on any term limits proposal. Moreover, groups that support such limits say they have now shifted away from federal lawmakers to focus on state legislators.

In a reflection of how much the incumbency issue has faded since 1994, only three House freshmen came to office in 2000 with pledges to limit their terms: Republicans Jeff Flake of Arizona, Timothy V. Johnson of Illinois and Ric Keller of Florida.

That does not bother long-serving lawmakers. They point out that the nation's democratic process is designed to give voters the freedom to decide just how long their elected officials should stay in power.

"People have the choice, and they exercise the choice," said Rep. John D. Dingell, D-Mich., the most senior member of the House. "I don't think it's necessarily good or bad."

Because of redistricting, Dingell faces a serious primary challenge this year from incumbent Rep. Lynn Rivers. But with the new district carved from two of the safest Democratic strongholds in the country, whoever wins is virtually assured a permanent place in Congress.

Political Participation

Holders of 'Safe' House Seats

Congressional Quarterly currently forecasts that as many as 342 of the 435 House incumbents are "safe" for re-election this year. That figure includes estimates of safe seats in three states that have not completed redistricting — Kansas, New York and Oklahoma — based on preliminary redistricting proposals in those states.

Listed below are the 306 incumbents from the other states who are currently ranked as safe by CQ. Included are three districts in which incumbents of the same party are matched up in primaries because of redistricting; in each case, the winner of that primary will be ranked "safe" because the district strongly favors his or her party.

ALABAMA
2 Terry Everett (R)
4 Robert B. Aderholt (R)
5 Robert E. "Bud" Cramer (D)
6 Spencer Bachus (R)
7 Earl F. Hilliard (D)

ALASKA
AL Don Young (R)

ARIZONA
3 John Shadegg (R)
4 Ed Pastor (D)
5 J.D. Hayworth (R)
6 Jeff Flake (R)
8 Jim Kolbe (R)

ARKANSAS
1 Marion Berry (D)
2 Vic Snyder (D)
3 John Boozman (R)

CALIFORNIA
1 Mike Thompson (D)
2 Wally Herger (R)
3 Doug Ose (R)
4 John T. Doolittle (R)
5 Robert T. Matsui (D)
6 Lynn Woolsey (D)
7 George Miller (D)
8 Nancy Pelosi (D)
9 Barbara Lee (D)
10 Ellen O. Tauscher (D)
11 Richard W. Pombo (R)
12 Tom Lantos (D)
13 Pete Stark (D)
14 Anna G. Eshoo (D)
15 Michael M. Honda (D)
16 Zoe Lofgren (D)
17 Sam Farr (D)
19 George P. Radanovich (R)
20 Cal Dooley (D)
22 Bill Thomas (R)
23 Lois Capps (D)
24 Elton Gallegly (R)
25 Howard P. "Buck" McKeon (R)
26 David Dreier (R)
27 Brad Sherman (D)
28 Howard L. Berman (D)
29 Adam B. Schiff (D)
30 Henry A. Waxman (D)
31 Xavier Becerra (D)
32 Hilda L. Solis (D)
33 Diane Watson (D)
34 Lucille Roybal-Allard (D)
35 Maxine Waters (D)
36 Jane Harman (D)
37 Juanita Millender-McDonald (D)
38 Grace F. Napolitano (D)
40 Ed Royce (R)
41 Jerry Lewis (R)
42 Gary G. Miller (R)
43 Joe Baca (D)
44 Ken Calvert (R)
45 Mary Bono (R)
46 Dana Rohrabacher (R)
47 Loretta Sanchez (D)
48 Christopher Cox (R)
49 Darrell Issa (R)
50 Randy "Duke" Cunningham (R)
51 Bob Filner (D)
52 Duncan Hunter (R)
53 Susan A. Davis (D)

COLORADO
1 Diana DeGette (D)
2 Mark Udall (D)
3 Scott McInnis (R)
5 Joel Hefley (R)
6 Tom Tancredo (R)

CONNECTICUT
1 John B. Larson (D)
3 Rosa DeLauro (D)
4 Christopher Shays (R)

DELAWARE
AL Michael N. Castle (R)

FLORIDA
1 Jeff Miller (R)
2 Allen Boyd (D)
3 Corrine Brown (D)
4 Ander Crenshaw (R)
6 Cliff Stearns (R)
7 John L. Mica (R)
9 Michael Bilirakis (R)
10 C.W. Bill Young (R)
11 Jim Davis (D)
12 Adam H. Putnam (R)
14 Porter J. Goss (R)
15 Dave Weldon (R)
16 Mark Foley (R)
17 Carrie P. Meek (D)
18 Ileana Ros-Lehtinen (R)
19 Robert Wexler (D)
20 Peter Deutsch (D)
21 Lincoln Diaz-Balart (R)
23 Alcee L. Hastings (D)

GEORGIA
1 Jack Kingston (R)
2 Sanford D. Bishop Jr. (D)
4 Cynthia A. McKinney (D)
5 John Lewis (D)
6 Johnny Isakson (R)
7 Bob Barr (R) or John Linder (R) (Aug. 6 primary)
8 Mac Collins (R)
9 Charlie Norwood (R)
10 Nathan Deal (R)

HAWAII
1 Neil Abercrombie (D)
2 Patsy T. Mink (D)

IDAHO
1 C.L. "Butch" Otter (R)
2 Mike Simpson (R)

ILLINOIS
1 Bobby L. Rush (D)
2 Jesse L. Jackson Jr. (D)
3 William O. Lipinski (D)
4 Luis V. Gutierrez (D)
6 Henry J. Hyde (R)
7 Danny K. Davis (D)
8 Philip M. Crane (R)
9 Jan Schakowsky (D)
11 Jerry Weller (R)
12 Jerry F. Costello (D)
13 Judy Biggert (R)
14 J. Dennis Hastert (R)
15 Timothy V. Johnson (R)
16 Donald Manzullo (R)
17 Lane Evans (D)
18 Ray LaHood (R)

INDIANA
1 Peter J. Visclosky (D)
3 Mark Souder (R)
4 Steve Buyer (R)
5 Dan Burton (R)

KENTUCKY
2 Ron Lewis (R)
5 Harold Rogers (R)
6 Ernie Fletcher (R)

LOUISIANA
1 David Vitter (R)
2 William J. Jefferson (D)
3 Billy Tauzin (R)
4 Jim McCrery (R)
6 Richard H. Baker (R)
7 Chris John (D)

MAINE
1 Tom Allen (D)

MARYLAND
1 Wayne T. Gilchrest (R)
3 Benjamin L. Cardin (D)
4 Albert R. Wynn (D)

---

mense institutional advantage at their disposal.

Every franked piece of mail on which the member's signature is emblazoned, every case handled by the district director and every appearance on C-SPAN adds to the incumbent's advantage.

Going beyond the frequent communication with, and service to, individual constituents, members have the ability to accrue political capital and wield power through their committee work. House members regularly compete to be assigned to the committees that dovetail with their districts' needs.

Lawmakers can use the spoils of preferred committee assignments to help them win re-election, even in districts where voters of their party are not a majority.

Rep. John P. Murtha of Pennsylvania has long represented a west-central Pennsylvania district that backed Bush by 7 percentage points in 2000. But his prowess as the Appropriations panel's second most senior Democrat — and as the ranking Democrat on its Defense Subcommittee — has made Murtha politically invincible in general elections: He has amassed at least two-thirds of the vote in seven of his past eight such contests.

Murtha, who appears favored in a redistricting-spurred May 21 primary against fellow Democratic Rep. Frank R. Mascara, sells himself as a "congressman who delivers."

Committee assignments also allow House members to tap into rich sources of fundraising. They become known quantities with the political action committees (PACs) that contribute more heavily to incumbents.

Murtha's committee post has helped him raise well more than three times as much money as Mascara — about $1.7 million.

His benefactors include the PACs, and in some cases top executives, of major defense contractors such as

Campaigns and Elections

5 Steny H. Hoyer (D)
6 Roscoe G. Bartlett (R)
7 Elijah E. Cummings (D)

MASSACHUSETTS
1 John W. Olver (D)
2 Richard E. Neal (D)
3 Jim McGovern (D)
4 Barney Frank (D)
5 Martin T. Meehan (D)
6 John F. Tierney (D)
7 Edward J. Markey (D)
8 Michael E. Capuano (D)
9 Stephen F. Lynch (D)
10 Bill Delahunt (D)

MICHIGAN
1 Bart Stupak (D)
2 Peter Hoekstra (R)
3 Vernon J. Ehlers (R)
4 Dave Camp (R)
5 Dale E. Kildee (D)
6 Fred Upton (R)
7 Nick Smith (R)
8 Mike Rogers (R)
12 Sander M. Levin (D)
13 Carolyn Cheeks Kilpatrick (D)
14 John Conyers Jr. (D)
15 John D. Dingell (D) or Lynn Rivers (D) (Aug. 6 primary)

MINNESOTA
1 Gil Gutknecht (R)
3 Jim Ramstad (R)
4 Betty McCollum (D)
5 Martin Olav Sabo (D)
7 Collin C. Peterson (D)
8 James L. Oberstar (D)

MISSISSIPPI
1 Roger Wicker (R)
2 Bennie Thompson (D)
4 Gene Taylor (D)

MISSOURI
1 William Lacy Clay (D)

2 Todd Akin (R)
3 Richard A. Gephardt (D)
4 Ike Skelton (D)
5 Karen McCarthy (D)
6 Sam Graves (R)
7 Roy Blunt (R)
8 Jo Ann Emerson (R)
9 Kenny Hulshof (R)

MONTANA
AL Denny Rehberg (R)

NEBRASKA
1 Doug Bereuter (R)
2 Lee Terry (R)
3 Tom Osborne (R)

NEVADA
2 Jim Gibbons (R)

NEW JERSEY
1 Robert E. Andrews (D)
2 Frank A. LoBiondo (R)
3 H. James Saxton (R)
4 Christopher H. Smith (R)
6 Frank Pallone Jr. (D)
8 Bill Pascrell Jr. (D)
9 Steven R. Rothman (D)
10 Donald M. Payne (D)
11 Rodney Frelinghuysen (R)
13 Robert Menendez (D)

NEW MEXICO
3 Tom Udall (D)

NORTH CAROLINA
2 Bob Etheridge (D)
3 Walter B. Jones (R)
4 David E. Price (D)
5 Richard M. Burr (R)
6 Howard Coble (R)
7 Mike McIntyre (D)
9 Sue Myrick (R)
10 Cass Ballenger (R)
11 Charles H. Taylor (R)
12 Melvin Watt (D)

OHIO
1 Steve Chabot (R)
2 Rob Portman (R)
4 Michael G. Oxley (R)
5 Paul E. Gillmor (R)
6 Ted Strickland (D)
7 David L. Hobson (R)
8 John A. Boehner (R)
9 Marcy Kaptur (D)
10 Dennis J. Kucinich (D)
11 Stephanie Tubbs Jones (D)
12 Pat Tiberi (R)
13 Sherrod Brown (D)
14 Steven C. LaTourette (R)
15 Deborah Pryce (R)
16 Ralph Regula (R)
18 Bob Ney (R)

OREGON
1 David Wu (D)
2 Greg Walden (R)
3 Earl Blumenauer (D)
4 Peter A. DeFazio (D)

PENNSYLVANIA
1 Robert A. Brady (D)
2 Chaka Fattah (D)
3 Phil English (R)
5 John E. Peterson (R)
7 Curt Weldon (R)
8 James C. Greenwood (R)
9 Bill Shuster (R)
10 Donald L. Sherwood (R)
11 Paul E. Kanjorski (D)
12 John P. Murtha (D) or Frank R. Mascara (D) (May 21 primary)
14 Mike Doyle (D)
16 Joseph R. Pitts (R)
19 Todd Platts (R)

RHODE ISLAND
2 Jim Langevin (D)

SOUTH CAROLINA
1 Henry E. Brown Jr. (R)
2 Joe Wilson (R)

4 Jim DeMint (R)
5 John M. Spratt Jr. (D)
6 James E. Clyburn (D)

TENNESSEE
1 Bill Jenkins (R)
2 John J. "Jimmy" Duncan Jr. (R)
3 Zach Wamp (R)
6 Bart Gordon (D)
8 John Tanner (D)
9 Harold E. Ford Jr. (D)

TEXAS
1 Max Sandlin (D)
2 Jim Turner (D)
3 Sam Johnson (R)
4 Ralph M. Hall (D)
6 Joe L. Barton (R)
7 John Culberson (R)
8 Kevin Brady (R)
9 Nick Lampson (D)
10 Lloyd Doggett (D)
12 Kay Granger (R)
13 William M. "Mac" Thornberry (R)
14 Ron Paul (R)
15 Rubén Hinojosa (D)
16 Silvestre Reyes (D)
18 Sheila Jackson-Lee (D)
19 Larry Combest (R)
20 Charlie Gonzalez (D)
21 Lamar Smith (R)
22 Tom DeLay (R)
24 Martin Frost (D)
27 Solomon P. Ortiz (D)
28 Ciro D. Rodriguez (D)
29 Gene Green (D)
30 Eddie Bernice Johnson (D)
32 Pete Sessions (R)

UTAH
3 Christopher B. Cannon (R)

VERMONT
AL Bernard Sanders (I)

VIRGINIA
1 Jo Ann Davis (R)
2 Ed Schrock (R)
3 Robert C. Scott (D)
4 J. Randy Forbes (R)
5 Virgil H. Goode Jr. (I)
6 Robert W. Goodlatte (R)
7 Eric Cantor (R)
8 James P. Moran (D)
9 Rick Boucher (D)
10 Frank R. Wolf (R)
11 Thomas M. Davis III (R)

WASHINGTON
1 Jay Inslee (D)
4 Doc Hastings (R)
5 George Nethercutt (R)
6 Norm Dicks (D)
7 Jim McDermott (D)
8 Jennifer Dunn (R)
9 Adam Smith (D)

WEST VIRGINIA
1 Alan B. Mollohan (D)
3 Nick J. Rahall II (D)

WISCONSIN
1 Paul D. Ryan (R)
3 Ron Kind (D)
4 Gerald D. Kleczka (D)
5 F. James Sensenbrenner (R)
6 Tom Petri (R)
7 David R. Obey (D)
8 Mark Green (R)

WYOMING
AL Barbara Cubin (R)

The following non-incumbent seats also are considered safe: Arizona 2,7; California 21, 39; Georgia 12,13; Illinois 5; North Carolina 1; South Carolina 3; Tennessee 5,7; Texas 26, 31; Utah 1.

General Dynamics, Boeing, Lockheed Martin and Newport News Shipbuilding.

Murtha's special clout and fundraising prowess aside, he also embodies a principle advanced by many legislators, institutionalists and some academics: that there are positive aspects in well-placed incumbents' ability to deliver for their constituents.

A three-judge federal panel in Texas last year essentially enshrined that view as they invoked a congressional redistricting plan for the state that protected incumbents.

The judges, who took over the state's redistricting process after a legislative deadlock, drew a plan favored by Democrats over a sweeping overhaul that might have given Republicans big gains in the delegation.

The judges noted favorably that Texas has some of the top House leaders — including Majority Leader Dick Armey, Majority Whip Tom DeLay and Democratic Caucus Chairman Martin Frost. In their minds, incumbency was a good thing.

"It was plain that these members were not harmed in their re-election prospects by this plan and that, indeed, no incumbent was paired with another incumbent or significantly harmed by the plan," the judges wrote.

Committee Insiders

The House leadership has effectively acknowledged the incumbent advantage of a prime committee assignment by continually expanding the rosters of key committees.

In the 97th Congress (1981-83), three of the House's most powerful committees — Appropriations, Energy and Commerce, and Ways and Means — had a combined committee membership of 132, or about 30 percent of the House. Today, those same three panels have a combined membership of 163, or 37 percent.

But service on an elite committee is not always necessary for an incumbent

Political Participation

to achieve security. Getting a seat on the Agriculture Committee is as vital for a representative from a Farm Belt state as securing a post on Armed Services is for a representative with military installations back home.

Sometimes a confluence of such district needs and panel assignments make an incumbent untouchable.

The economy of southeastern Alabama's 2nd District is reliant on two things — peanut farms and military installations — and Republican Terry Everett tends to those interests as a member of the Agriculture and Armed Services committees.

Though Everett won with just 49 percent in his first election in 1992, his winning percentage since has been as high as 74 percent and never lower than 63 percent.

An increasingly popular panel is the Transportation and Infrastructure Committee, which authorizes billions of dollars in spending for highway and transit programs that are sluiced to House districts. Its membership has grown from 44 to 75 in the past two decades.

Mid-Course Corrections

One longtime member of that committee, Illinois Democrat Lipinski, also provides a model of how successful incumbents adjust to new contingencies back home.

First elected in 1982 in a district confined to Chicago's ethnic wards and its near-in suburbs, and consistently re-elected by wide margins, Lipinski was put at some risk in 1992 by redistricting. The new map removed many of his city constituents, moved him out into the more Republican-leaning suburbs, and forced him into a Democratic primary matchup with fellow incumbent Marty Russo.

But Lipinski tailored his political agenda to his new circumstances, both in 1992 — when he easily bested Russo and his Republican general-election opponent — and through the ensuing decade. Never one of the more liberal Democrats in the House, Lipinski became more vocal about his conservative views. He became one of the few Northern members of the Blue Dog Democrats.

On party unity votes — those on which Lipinski voted with a majority of his Democratic colleagues against a majority of House Republicans — Lipinski's average score from 1993 to 2001 dropped to 68 percent, down from an average of 76 percent during 1983-92.

Lipinski's political re-positioning earned him a series of easy wins in a district where Republicans initially thought he might be vulnerable.

That, in turn, enabled him to become the dean among Democrats in the Illinois House delegation — and chief negotiator with Republican leader Hastert on a redistricting plan that will give Lipinski back portions of Chicago that were stripped from him in the 1990s remap.

Georgia Democrat Bishop has a similar history. He represented a staunchly Democratic, black-majority district his first three years in the House (1993-95), and his "party unity" scores were 92, 92 and 84 percent, respectively. But his district in 1995 was struck down as an unconstitutional racial gerrymander, and the new map substantially lessened the black population and Democratic tilt of his district.

Bishop adjusted his voting behavior accordingly. By 2000, his party unity score had dropped to 65 percent.

Though Bishop won with 53.5 percent of the vote in 2000, he is currently ranked as safe because he received a more Democratic-leaning district and so far has no strong Republican challenger.

"Whether you're from a safe district or a marginal district, you always worry about the next election, and members of Congress have a very keen sense of what issues will stir up people who right now are perfectly contented," said Pennsylvania political analyst Jon Delano. "And it is the skilled politician who can anticipate how a particular bill might be used against him two years down the line that becomes the long-termer."

Money Matters

Sealing safety for most incumbents is the huge advantage they hold over challengers in campaign fundraising.

An analysis of House candidates' 15-month campaign finance reports for the 2001-02 cycle by the Campaign Finance Institute found that House incumbents raised a median of $414,000 over that period, compared with just $66,000 for non-incumbents — a ratio of more than 6-to-1.

One technique incumbents employ to boost themselves is collecting enormous sums of money early in the cycle to discourage potential challengers from entering the race. That is especially typical of incumbents who have had past competitive races that drained their campaign treasuries.

"So if you were in a close race, you start raising money right away," said Paul Herrnson, a political scientist and director of the Center for American Politics and Citizenship at the University of Maryland. "If you weren't in a close race, you have money left over."

Freshman Michigan Republican Rogers did not take a breather after winning his 2000 House race by 111 votes. His fundraising skill and the boost he got from redistricting have scared off all Democratic comers thus far: Rogers raised $716,000 in the first half of 2001 and currently boasts a campaign bankroll of $860,000.

The Democrats' only hope of dislodging Rogers appears to reside in their long-shot court challenge to the state's GOP-drawn redistricting map.

Rogers' strategy matches that of another Midwestern Republican elected two years earlier.

Though Rep. Paul D. Ryan had won an open-seat race in a politically competitive southeast Wisconsin district with 57 percent of the vote in 1998, he faced the possibility of a serious Democratic challenge in 2000.

But Ryan raised $734,000 for his campaign treasury in 1999 alone. It was enough to keep top-tier Democrats out of the race and help Ryan earn a sophomore term with two-thirds of the vote in 2000 — even as the district's voters favored Gore over Bush 49 percent to 47 percent.

Despite a trend towards safe incumbency, some observers believe American politics remains cyclical, and that a swing against incumbents is a matter of time.

"We've got pretty much an even divide between Democrats and Republicans," said Herrnson. "But things were not always like that, and times change. So I anticipate at some point, one of the parties will emerge with some level of dominance."

But for this year at least, the advantages of incumbency appear certain to break the momentum of any swing of the political pendulum. The faces of the 108th Congress next January will be very familiar. ◆

Campaigns and Elections

House Democratic Leadership To Undergo Complete Overhaul

Contentious races expected regardless of party control

No matter which party wins control of the House this fall, Democrats in that chamber can count on one thing: an entirely new slate of party leaders next year.

Competitive races are brewing for almost every seat in the party hierarchy in anticipation of the Democratic leadership elections in December, shortly after the midterm elections but before the 108th Congress begins.

So far, eight candidates are poised to run for leadership slots — including some posts that do not currently exist and that will open up only if Democrats capture the majority in the House. The elected leadership changes would span the entire line-up — from Speaker — if Democrats win control — down to caucus vice chairman.

If Democrats succeed in recapturing the House, party leader Richard A. Gephardt of Missouri will ascend to Speaker, causing a chain reaction of openings as others contend for his leader's seat and positions further down in the leadership.

But if Gephardt is unable — for the fourth time in a row — to lead his party into the majority, most in the caucus predict that he will leave the House. Such a departure also would prompt competition for the minority leader's slot.

Meanwhile, at the bottom of the elected leadership, term limits have created openings for the positions of caucus chair and vice chair.

Already, those who have officially entered the races are busy traversing the country, stumping for colleagues and raising money. Many used the Memorial Day recess to make campaign swings for endangered incumbents and challengers, hoping their help will reap dividends when their colleagues choose the new leadership next year.

As the leadership contests sharpen, party hopefuls have begun promoting themselves — and quietly slinging barbs at their rivals. Several candidates, in an attempt to scare off other challengers, also have released the names of colleagues who have pledged their support.

With the candidates including two African-Americans, three women, one Hispanic and two white men, the leadership elections highlight the Democrats' efforts to achieve diversity at the top. When casting their secret ballots, caucus members are likely to seek a range of ideologies, ethnicity and gender, ultimately producing a leadership whose competing factions are balanced and generally moderate in tone.

In the shorter term, the internal party races also could mean a flood of campaign contributions for members as leadership candidates court their allegiance. But as House Democrats maneuver against each other for the party's top slots, the races could draw candidates' attention away from broader party goals, deepen rivalries and sow divisions between Democratic factions in the run-up to the November elections.

"It can be reinvigorating in one sense and enervating in another," former Rep. Vic Fazio of California, who chaired the Democratic Caucus from 1995 to 1998, said of the looming leadership turnover. "Change is inevitable, and on balance, it's a net plus."

Pelosi vs. Frost

Perhaps the most contentious leadership race now brewing is for an opening that hinges on the outcome of the midterm elections.

Two candidates have positioned themselves for the majority leader's seat if Democrats win the House or if Gephardt steps

---

Quick Contents

The shape of the new House Democratic leadership will depend on whether the party recaptures the majority in November. But already rivalries could deepen party divisions.

As House Democrats plan for leadership elections, Gephardt, third from right on the Capitol steps May 23, is mulling whether to run for Democratic leader or president.

CQ Weekly June 1, 2002

Political Participation

down in the event Democrats remain in the minority.

Nancy Pelosi of California is next in line for the leader's seat, having won the No. 2 slot of whip last year. But she will face a challenge from Martin Frost of Texas, who must step down as chairman of the Democratic Caucus at the end of the year because of term limits.

Both lawmakers are proceeding carefully. Frost says he will not run for majority leader unless a Democratic victory in November opens up the slot. Pelosi says she is not yet thinking about the majority leader's position and is instead concentrating on her duties as whip. But her office says that on almost a daily basis, colleagues have expressed their support — should a race for the leader's position develop.

Pelosi became the highest-ranking woman in House history last October when she won the whip's seat in a long-fought race against Steny H. Hoyer of Maryland. Although she is one of the most liberal members of the caucus, Pelosi garnered support from across the party's ideological spectrum. (*2001 CQ Weekly, p. 2397*)

Her supporters argue that as a woman, a Californian and a prodigious fundraiser, Pelosi would do the most to broaden the party's appeal for the 2002 elections.

But Frost also has proven an effective campaigner, having chaired the Democratic Congressional Campaign Committee (DCCC) during the 1996 elections and helped Democrats whittle down the GOP majority that year. (*1996 Almanac, p. 11-23*)

During the Memorial Day recess, he hosted several fundraisers for the party in Texas, including a Dallas event that was expected to raise $300,000, party officials said.

Many predict that if Democrats remain in the minority next year, anger and pressure from the rank and file will force Gephardt from office within months. But rather than face an outright challenge, Gephardt and his rivals probably would negotiate a graceful exit that would allow him to resign to launch a bid for the White House, insiders say.

Fight for Caucus Chair

Another contentious race is shaping up for Frost's soon-to-be-vacated chairmanship of the caucus.

Rosa DeLauro of Connecticut is running for the post against Robert Menendez of New Jersey, who also must relinquish his position as caucus vice chair because of term limits.

Menendez promotes himself as the only Hispanic member in the elected leadership. Bolstered by the endorsement of the 18-member Congressional Hispanic Caucus, Menendez argues that Democrats need him for the midterm election campaign to court Hispanic voters and counter the growing appeal of President Bush.

Several Hispanic groups outside Congress have thrown their weight behind Menendez, warning that his defeat would send an insulting message to Hispanic voters and possibly threaten

---

WOULD-BE SPEAKER

Richard A. Gephardt, D-Mo.

Prospects: Failed three times to lead party to majority. Resignation likely if Democrats stay in minority next year.
House History: Elected in 1976 in Missouri's 3rd District (east — St. Louis, Jefferson and St. Genevieve counties); won 13th in 2000 with 57 percent.
Born: Jan. 31, 1941; St. Louis
Education: Northwestern U., B.S. 1962; U. of Michigan, J.D. 1965
Political Highlights: Sought Democratic nomination for president, 1988; House Minority Leader, 1995 to present
Committee: Minority Leader — no committee assignments

PARTY LEADER CANDIDATES

Nancy Pelosi, D-Calif.

Prospects: Won No. 2 slot in party in 2001; highest-ranking woman in House history; faces challenge from Martin Frost.
House History: Elected in 1987 in California's 8th District (San Francisco); won 7th term in 2000 with 84 percent.
Born: March 26, 1940, Baltimore
Education: Trinity College, A.B. 1962
Political Highlights: Calif. Democratic Party chairman, 1981-83, U.S. House Democratic whip, 2002
Committee: Appropriations, Select Intelligence, ranking member

Martin Frost, D-Texas

Prospects: Term-limited out of caucus chair, faces challenge from Nancy Pelosi.
House History: Elected in 1978 in Texas' 24th District (north — parts of Dallas and Tarrant counties); won 12th term in 2000 with 62 percent.
Born: Jan. 1, 1942, Glendale, Calif.
Education: U. of Missouri, B.A., B.J. 1964; Georgetown U., J.D. 1970
Political Highlights: U.S. House Democratic Congressional Campaign Committee Chairman, 1995-98; U.S. House Democratic Caucus Chairman, 1999 to present
Committee: Rules

Campaigns and Elections

Democratic chances in future congressional elections. "Having a Hispanic in the leadership is of incredibly important value to House Democrats," Menendez said.

He is also promoting his fundraising abilities. His New Millennium political action committee (PAC) so far has handed out nearly $200,000 to Democratic candidates this cycle and has another $315,000 cash on hand, according to the Federal Election Commission. Aides say he also has contributed $150,000 to the DCCC from his personal campaign committee.

DeLauro has not yet released the names of her supporters, but says she is leading Menendez two-to-one among caucus members — a number Menendez disputes. DeLauro also claims backing from a variety of Democratic factions, including members of the Black Caucus, the moderate New Democrats, and most of the ranking committee members.

She ran unsuccessfully against Frost for caucus chair in 1998. After the race, when women complained that they were not represented in the elected leadership, Gephardt created a position for DeLauro, appointing her "assistant to the leader." (1999 CQ Weekly, p. 951)

In that position, DeLauro says, she has successfully improved party communications, organizing "rapid response teams" to promote the Democratic message on various issues. Like Menendez, DeLauro also is touting her campaigning and fundraising efforts for colleagues. (2001 CQ Weekly, p. 818)

So far this cycle, she has traveled widely to campaign for Democrats. She notes that she has worked with each freshman class since 1997 to help newly elected colleagues return to office. And while DeLauro's PAC lists just $25,000 cash on hand, her supporters boast that she gave nearly $1 million to colleagues and candidates during the 1998 and 2000 election cycles.

But DeLauro could be hurt by Pelosi's election as whip last year, which some say filled the unofficial "woman's slot" within the leadership.

Another California Woman

Californian Zoe Lofgren is running for the open seat of caucus vice chair, the fourth-ranking slot in the party's leadership. She will face two members of the Black Caucus: James E. Clyburn of South Carolina and Gregory W. Meeks of New York.

There are currently no black members in the elected Democratic leadership — a factor that works against Lofgren. She could also be hurt by the fact that she, like Pelosi, is from California. Unlike the Republican House leadership, where Majority Leader Dick Armey and Whip Tom DeLay are both from Texas, some Democrats say their caucus may be reluctant to give two Californians that much power in the party leadership.

But Lofgren comes from a different political faction than Pelosi's liberal camp. One of the moderate New Democrats, Lofgren has worked to promote

---

WHIP HOPEFUL

Steny H. Hoyer, D-Md.

Prospects: Lost whip race to Nancy Pelosi in 2001. Faces no challenger so far.
House History: Elected in 1981 in Maryland's 5th District (south — outer Prince George's County); won 10th term in 2000 with 65 percent.
Born: June 14, 1939, Manhattan, N.Y.
Education: U. of Maryland, B.S. 1963; Georgetown U., J.D. 1966
Political Highlights: Md. Senate, 1967-79 (president, 1975-79; Md. Board of Higher Education, 1978-81; U.S. House Democratic Steering Committee co-chair, U.S. House Democratic Caucus chairman, 1989-94
Committee: Appropriations, Administration

SEEKING CAUCUS CHAIRMANSHIP

Robert Menendez, D-N.J.

Prospects: First and only Hispanic member of elected party leadership. Faces challenge from Rosa DeLauro.
House History: Elected in 1992 in New Jersey's 13th District (parts of Jersey City and Newark); won 5th term in 2000 with 79 percent.
Born: Jan. 1, 1954, Manhattan, N.Y.
Education: St. Peter's College, B.A. 1976; Rutgers U., J.D. 1979
Political Highlights: Mayor of Union City, 1986-92; N.J. Assembly, 1987-91; N.J. Senate, 1991-93; U.S. House Democratic deputy whip, 1997-98; U.S. House Democratic Caucus vice chair, 1998 to present
Committee: International Relations, Transportation

Rosa DeLauro, D-Conn.

Prospects: Lost bid for chairman to Martin Frost in 1998. Faces challenge from Robert Menendez.
House History: Elected in 1990 in Connecticut's 3rd District (south — New Haven); won 6th term in 2000 with 72 percent.
Born: March 2, 1943, New Haven, Conn.
Education: London School of Economics, attended 1962-63; Marymount College, B.A. 1964; Columbia U., M.A. 1966
Political Highlights: U.S. House Democratic deputy whip, 1995-98, U.S. House assistant to Democratic leader, 1999 to present
Committee: Appropriations

Political Participation

business interests, particularly those of her Silicon Valley district's high-tech industry.

Lofgren represents a safe Democratic seat and therefore says she can spend more time campaigning and fundraising for her colleagues. She has not released the names of any of her supporters yet, saying she first wants to sit down and discuss her candidacy with every member of the caucus before going public with endorsements.

Meanwhile, Clyburn recently released a letter signed by the 24 members of his campaign steering committee, touting his experience as a former chairman of the Congressional Black Caucus and president of his 1992 freshman class.

More than half of Clyburn's steering committee belongs to the 38-member Black Caucus, a group that Meeks is also expected to court in his campaign. An aide for Meeks said he hopes soon to release the names of some of his supporters for the race.

Clyburn is promoting a restructuring plan for the caucus, calling for the vice chairmanship to be split into several seats, allowing for more diversity in the elected leadership. Under his proposal, two seats would go to members whose sex and race were different from those of the caucus chairman. The chairman would appoint the third vice chairman.

Clyburn argues that by ensuring diversity in the party leadership, a variety of ideological voices will be heard.

Taking No Chances

The party whip's slot is the one position in the elected leadership that is currently uncontested, but Hoyer, the lone announced candidate, is taking no chances.

Last year, Hoyer lost the whip election to Pelosi after a bruising battle that enflamed rivalries and divisions with the party. (*2001 CQ Weekly, p. 2321*)

This time around, Hoyer has said he will run for the whip's seat if Democrats win the majority and Pelosi runs for party leader. Hoyer already has released the names of 157 names of colleagues who say they will vote for him if the whip's seat opens up.

"At this point, for somebody to get into the race would be very difficult," said Hoyer's spokeswoman, Stacy Farnen.

While many feared that the divisions exposed by last year's whip race would weaken the party, insiders say Pelosi and Hoyer have now mended their fences. And Democrats insist the internal races now shaping up also will not hurt the party. Rather, they say, the contests will force candidates to work harder to ensure that their party and their colleagues are victorious in November.

But some candidates admit their leadership ambitions are still the driving force. "If I was not running for vice chairman, would I be spending money and campaigning for my colleagues? Yes," said Menendez. "But would it be of the same degree and intensity? Possibly no." ◆

VYING FOR CAUCUS VICE CHAIRMAN

Gregory W. Meeks, D-N.Y.

Prospects: First-time candidate for leadership position. Faces challenges from Zoe Lofgren and James E. Clyburn, a fellow member of the Black Caucus.
House History: Elected in 1998 in New York's 6th District (southeast — Queens, Jamaica); won 2nd term in 2000 unopposed.
Born: Sept. 25, 1953, Harlem, N.Y.
Education: Adelphi U., B.A. 1975; Howard U., J.D. 1978
Political Highlights: N.Y. Assembly, 1993-98
Committee: Financial Services, International Relations

James E. Clyburn, D-S.C.

Prospects: Former chairman of Black Caucus, former president of 1992 freshman class. Faces challenge from Zoe Lofgren and fellow Black Caucus member Gregory W. Meeks.
House History: Elected in 1992 in South Carolina's 6th District (Florence, parts of Columbia and Charleston); won 5th term in 2000 with 72 percent.
Born: July 21, 1940, Sumter, S.C.
Education: South Carolina State College, B.S. 1962
Political Highlights: S.C. human affairs commissioner, 1974-92; sought Democratic nomination for S.C. secretary of state, 1978, 1986
Committee: Appropriations

Zoe Lofgren, D-Calif.

Prospects: First-time candidate for leadership position. Faces challenge from Black Caucus members Gregory W. Meeks and James E. Clyburn.
House History: Elected in 1994 in California's 16th District (Santa Clara County — San Jose); won fourth term in 2000 with 72 percent.
Born: Dec. 21, 1947, San Mateo, Calif.
Education: Stanford U. B.A. 1970; U. of Santa Clara, J.D. 1975
Political Highlights: San Jose-Evergreen Community College District Board of Trustees, 1979-81; Santa Clara County Board of Supervisors, 1981-95
Committee: Judiciary, Science, Standards of Official Conduct

Campaigns and Elections

Campaign Finance Passage Ends a Political Odyssey

Supporters and critics alike say legislation's effect will be unpredictable

Meehan, Feingold, Shays and McCain celebrated March 20 as their bill headed toward passage in the Senate. It took years, but momentum for their cause built inexorably as soft-money fundraising grew.

Quick Contents

Supporters of a campaign finance overhaul have pushed their legislation to passage after years of debate. The final vote was decisive, but no one knows for sure what changes the measure will bring. The opponents promise to fight on in court.

The safest bet in Washington had long been that Congress would never overhaul the campaign finance system.

The status quo logic of incumbency argued against it. Powerful outside interest groups, key to the base of each party, opposed it. With the courts leery of anything that might restrict political speech, the legal ground was uncertain.

But politically, the system finally became too difficult to defend.

By the time the Enron Corp. bankruptcy this winter embarrassed both major parties with revelations of the company's vast network of political giving and influence, the Senate already was on record supporting a broad rewrite of the nation's campaign finance laws. The legislation was in the House, where supporters blew past the last remaining opposition to send a fine-tuned bill (HR 2356) back to the Senate.

On March 20, a fight that had stretched over years, through one veto and hundreds of votes, ended almost anticlimactically, with a 60-40 vote that had been expected for weeks. (*2002 CQ Weekly, p. 838*)

President Bush quickly said he would sign the legislation into law.

Opponents, led by Republican Sen. Mitch McConnell of Kentucky, promise to fight on in court. Lawyers and political operatives already have laid out strategies for keeping the contributions flowing under the new rules of campaign fundraising, which include a ban on unregulated "soft money" contributions to national political parties.

Both parties are rushing to raise as much soft money as possible before the measure takes effect. The Democratic National Committee announced the week of March 18 that it had landed the biggest soft-money contribution in history: $7 million from a California entertainment tycoon.

Yet there is no denying the significance of this moment: Lawmakers have agreed to change the very system that elected them, and in so doing, they have stepped into the unknown. They have perhaps put their own careers at risk.

No one can say for sure how the changes they have approved, the first major rewrite of federal campaign finance laws in a generation, will affect American politics and the balance of power in Washington.

Years of Growing Pressure

The Enron scandal put the legislation over the top, but it was only the last push. The momentum for overhaul had been building at least since the 1994 elections, when a record-breaking $102 million in soft money, contributions from corporations, unions and

CQ Weekly March 23, 2002

Political Participation

How Campaign Finance Bill Alters Money Flow

HARD MONEY

INDIVIDUAL CONTRIBUTORS

Limit: $2,000 per election to candidates, $25,000 per year to national parties. Limits are indexed to grow with inflation.

What it means: GOP may gain major advantage. In the last full election cycle, Republicans out-raised Democrats in hard money $466 million to $275 million.

THE DONORS

ELECTION ADVERTISING

Limits:
- Broadcast "issue ads" that refer to a specific candidate, reach a candidate's electorate, and run 30 days before a primary or 60 days before a general election could only be paid for with regulated "hard money." As with all hard money, the names of contributors would have to be disclosed.
- The restrictions would not apply to groups running pure "issue adds" that do not refer to a specific candidate.

What it means: Close to Election Day, more money likely will go to other advertising, such as direct mail, print (magazine, newspapers), and telephone banks.

SOFT MONEY

NATIONAL PARTIES

Limit: Totally prohibited.

What it means: Parties lose a huge funding source. In the 2000 elections, the GOP raised $250 million in soft money; Democrats, $245 million.

STATE AND LOCAL PARTIES

Limit: $10,000 per year for voter registration and get-out-the-vote activities. State law determines who can give — individuals only, or corporations and unions as well.

What it means: State parties may play a larger role in congressional races.

SINGLE-ISSUE ORGANIZATIONS

Limit: None, as long as the money is not specifically used for federal election activity.

What it means: Experts say more money is likely to flow to groups, such as the NRA, NAACP or Family Research Council for issue ads or other activities that could have an impact on campaigns.

CQ GRAPHIC / MARILYN GATES-DAVIS

---

the wealthy, poured into the parties.

The amount of soft money flowing through the system more than quadrupled in the 2000 elections: $495 million for the two major parties together.

The tales of questionable fundraising tactics on both sides piled up.

Meanwhile, supporters of an overhaul were shaping and reshaping their legislation, making compromises, dropping some proposals as unworkable or politically unpalatable. The heart of the final legislation — a ban on soft money and restrictions on political advertising by outside groups — took shape gradually. *(Money, this page)*

The last pieces began coming together with the 2000 elections. Sen. John McCain, R-Ariz., a lead sponsor of the bill, made campaign finance the foundation of his presidential bid, boosting him and the cause to national prominence. Turnover in the Senate, where McCain and bill cosponsor Russell D. Feingold, D-Wis., had been blocked for years by filibusters, also shifted the balance of power in favor of an overhaul. *(Chart, p. 46)*

At the same time, Bush kept his distance from the fight. After Enron collapsed, news that the president's campaign was one of the primary beneficiaries of the energy trader's prolific giving made it politically impossible for Bush to oppose the bill's passage. During the final months of the debate, the White House rebuffed pleas from Republican leaders to help them fight the bill, sealing its victory.

Opponents said they were worn down, too weary for another round of parliamentary maneuvering to try to block legislation that now seemed inevitable.

"Sometimes even bad policy has a way of making it to the top," said Sen. Larry E. Craig, R-Idaho. "You just rub and rub and rub until people are sore. It's a wearing-down factor."

After the House approved the measure 240-189 on Feb. 14, McConnell, the staunchest of the critics, tried for a few more weeks to make changes to the bill, but about an hour before the final vote, he told reporters what by then was obvious: "We're going down to defeat," he said.

At about the same time, McCain and Feingold, who introduced the first version of their legislation in 1995, held a pep rally on the Capitol grounds, with banners and cheering crowds. The House sponsors, Republican Christopher Shays of Connecticut and Democrat Martin T. Meehan of Massachusetts, were there, too.

McCain told supporters, "At the end of this seven-year odyssey . . . I am somewhat speechless."

He and his cosponsors also promised to push for more changes to the system, including an overhaul of the Federal Election Commission (FEC) this year.

Bush Bows Out

Bush had opposed McCain's proposals as a candidate, but then said he too backed an overhaul of the system.

"Bush ended up saying, 'I'm for campaign finance reform. I'm the reformer with results,'" said Trevor Potter, a former FEC commissioner. "Bush did sense it was a winning issue."

When McCain forced a two-week

Campaigns and Elections

Bill Says Its Own Provisions May Be Challenged in Court Right Away

Mitch McConnell has battled campaign finance legislation for 15 years, but the coming court fight is expected to be comparatively quick.

The legislation the Senate cleared March 20 (HR 2356) specifies a quick path to the Supreme Court for any legal challenges to its own provisions. And the Republican senator from Kentucky's new priority is to take charge of the courtrooms campaign. Legal experts say the high court could rule on at least one aspect of the bills constitutionality by the end of its next session in June 2003 — lightning fast by the standards of most federal lawsuits.

The bill calls for an expedited judicial review, with a panel of three U.S. district court judges trying the case in Washington and their decision heading directly to the Supreme Court for review, thus bypassing the D.C. Circuit Court of Appeals.

On voice votes, the House on March 20 and the Senate two days later adopted a resolution (H Con Res 361) making several alterations to the campaign finance bill. One would give members of Congress legal standing to sue to stop enforcement of the law. Another would declare that judicial review could begin when President Bush signs the measure — not when most of it takes effect, on Nov. 6, the day after Election Day.

The president says he will sign the bill even though it presents some "legitimate constitutional questions," which he did not detail.

McConnell has not publicly mapped out his legal strategy, but as a first step, he could ask the district court to block implementation of the law, probably by asking for a temporary restraining order. To prevail, he would have to convince the judges that there would be "irreparable consequences" if the law took effect, such as preventing a candidate from getting enough money to run for office, said Gregory Magarian, a law professor at Villanova University in Pennsylvania.

McConnell on March 21 unveiled the legal team he has assembled to help him challenge the law. Led by former independent counsel Kenneth W. Starr, its other members are First Amendment scholar Floyd Abrams, Stanford University Law School Dean Kathleen Sullivan, James Bopp Jr. of the James Madison Center for Free Speech, and Washington attorneys Bobby Burchfield and Jan Baran.

They, like McConnell, say the bill's restriction on campaign contributions and broadcast advertising violate the First Amendment's protection of free speech - guarantees, they note, that were written by the framers with unfettered political speech in mind.

'Severable' Elements

"I fully expect the court to invalidate it, either in whole or in part," said Douglas Kmiec, dean of Catholic University's law school.

Even the bill's authors are not sure they have written something that can withstand scrutiny by the Supreme Court, which has typically been loath to restrict political speech. Sponsors were careful to make the bill's provisions "severable," meaning that if one section is held to be unconstitutional the rest may stay on the books.

"We're making our best effort to pass a law that is constitutionally viable," said Senate Majority Leader Tom Daschle, D-S.D. "But no one can say today with any authority that they know how the courts should rule or how the interpretation should be."

Congress has set up expedited judicial review procedures in other instances where all sides agree "that fast resolution of the issue is important," Magarian said. The telecommunications law (PL 104-404) enacted six years ago called for quick review of its limits on online child pornography, which were eventually struck down by the courts. The 1965 Voting Rights Act (PL 89-110) creates a means for expedited review of disputes over political boundaries. (*1965 Almanac, p. 533; 1966 Almanac, p. 3-43*)

While the trial court would likely review initial challenges to the law soon after they were made, few legal scholars expect the Supreme Court to review the new statute in its current term, which ends in June. More likely, the court will hear arguments in the term that convenes in October and issue its ruling by June 2002, still in time to affect most fundraising that would occur before the 2004 presidential and congressional elections.

McConnell, at microphones March 21, unveils the team that will help him challenge the campaign finance law in court: From left: Abrams, Baran, Bopp, Starr and Burchfield.

Political Participation

debate of his bill in March 2001, Bush released a list of "reform principles" that included a ban on soft money from corporations and unions, but not individuals.

Then Bush backed away. The White House told lawmakers not to count on Bush to veto campaign finance legislation if Congress cleared it.

Congressional Republicans who opposed the bill said they were angry with the administration for leaving them to fight the legislation on their own.

"I think there's some frustration in the party among those who fought against this for the past 10 years," Craig said. The House Republican Study Committee, a group of about 60 conservative lawmakers, released a statement saying they were "deeply disappointed" by Bush's promise to sign the bill into law.

Many give McCain a great deal of the credit for the legislation's passage. His popularity and tenacity, particularly after the 2000 elections, kept the measure moving forward.

Backers also say recent campaign finance scandals created broad support for overhauling the system. They point to the controversial "coffee klatches" and overnight stays in the White House's Lincoln Bedroom that the Clinton administration used to raise large amounts of soft money for the Democratic Party.

And they say the collapse of Enron Corp., with the subsequent reports of the millions of dollars it contributed to candidates and political parties, ultimately persuaded lawmakers to pass the overhaul bill.

Since 1990, Enron gave $3.6 million in soft-money donations to the Democratic and Republican parties. Overhaul supporters said Enron made their case perfectly: Huge contributions buy influence over legislation and create an impression of corruption.

Even without scandal, supporters say, the skyrocketing cost of federal elections was enough to prompt changes in the system.

The 2000 election cycle broke all spending records for congressional campaigns. Candidates spent a total of $1 billion, compared with $740 million during the 1998 cycle and $342 million in the 1982 cycle.

During the 2000 elections, both parties set new records for soft-money fundraising. Republican national committees raised $250 million in soft money, up 81 percent from 1995-96, the previous presidential election cycle. The Democratic national committees raised $245 million, up 98 percent from the 1996 elections.

Gradual Gains

In the House, Shays said, final victory was the result of incremental gains. Over the years, many members had gone on record by either voting for the legislation or signing "discharge petitions" to bring it to the floor. The House had passed versions of the bill twice before — in 1998 and 1999. (*1999 Almanac, p. 8-3; 1998 Almanac, p. 18-3*)

Many critics had said that House members, particularly Democrats, voted for the legislation in the past only because they knew it would die in the Senate. Some predicted that Democrats would bolt as passage grew more and more likely; and indeed, many raised new doubts about banning soft money, which they had come to rely on to stay competitive with Republicans.

But they had boxed themselves in. Politically, backing way from the legislation now was not an option.

"Putting people on record was very important," Shays said.

The turnover in the Senate after the 2000 elections also was critical, Shays said. Senators who had opposed the legislation were replaced by bill supporters. (*Votes, p. 46*)

Another five GOP senators who had opposed the measure in the past switched their position. The first to announce a change of heart was old-guard Republican Thad Cochran of Mississippi.

Cochran said he had watched his colleagues struggle against a tide of opposition money, and when it was over, he privately came to the conclusion that McCain was right.

"It became obvious to me that the influence of soft money and independent groups was overwhelming the effort of candidates," he said in January 2001. (*2001 CQ Weekly, p. 129*)

Another Senate Republican, Peter G. Fitzgerald of Illinois, said he

---

Bill Traveled a Very Long Road
Seven years separate proposal's introduction and passage

1995-1996

INTRODUCTION: McCain and Feingold team up to introduce a campaign finance bill. Shays and Meehan introduce similar legislation in the House.

MAJOR OVERHAUL: Both bills would eliminate soft money. They also include provisions later abandoned: a ban on contributions from political action committees (PACs) and incentives for candidates who agree to limit spending, such as free TV time.

OPPOSITION AND REJECTION: The Republican leadership in both chambers is opposed. The legislation is blocked in the Senate by filibuster. In the House, GOP leaders offer their own bill, equalizing contribution limits for PACs and individuals and raising contributions limits for candidates facing wealthy opponents. The house rejects both bills.

McCain and Feingold

1997-1998

RENEWED INTEREST: Another round of record-breaking election spending in 1996 and a series of fundraising scandals re-energize efforts to rewrite campaign finance rules.

ALLIANCE: McCain and Feingold decide to coordinate with Shays and Meehan. Their bills would ban soft money, lower PAC contribution limits, and provide incentives to candidates who abide by voluntary spending limits.

changed his mind because of new language that was added last year to double the amount of regulated "hard money" that individuals can contribute to candidates each election. The contribution limit is also indexed to inflation under the bill.

Republicans, who do better at raising hard money than Democrats, have long called for such an increase. "That dampened Republican opposition," Fitzgerald said. "Certainly Democrats are more reliant on soft money."

Changes and Compromises

The hard-money increase was just one of numerous changes made to the House and Senate bills over the years — changes supporters say were necessary to get enough votes for passage.

Some longtime supporters say the bill was watered down.

US PIRG, an environmental lobbying group that backed previous versions of the bill, now criticizes it as "riddled with loopholes" and said doubling hard-money limits would increase the power of the wealthiest Americans.

"Ordinary Americans [will] have their voices drowned out in the wave of cash," said Adam Lioz of US PIRG.

The first campaign finance bill introduced by McCain and Feingold in 1995 included provisions that would have given Senate candidates incentives to comply with voluntary spending limits. In exchange for keeping campaign costs down, candidates would have received free prime-time television advertising, reduced broadcast rates, and discounted postage rates. The bill also would have banned contributions from political action committees (PACs). (1995 Almanac, p. 1-44)

Neither of those provisions are in the current bill.

McConnell said that as some of the more controversial provisions in the bill were removed, it became more difficult to attack.

"It's a shadow of its former self," McConnell said. "Reformers kept stripping it back like peeling an onion."

However, he said the bill still violates political free speech, and vowed to be the lead plaintiff in a lawsuit challenging its constitutionality. (Story, p. 43)

Shays and others say that while the measure is not all that they had hoped for, the changes to the campaign finance system are substantial.

"This is 85 percent of what we wanted," Shays said. "This bill is a result of compromise to get the 60 votes [needed to end debate in the Senate]. But it's a strong bill."

Still, supporters of the legislation said it was only a first step.

This bill is "not anywhere close to what has to be done if we're seriously determined to change the laws in this country affecting the way we fund our campaigns," Senate Majority Leader Tom Daschle of South Dakota said.

Daschle said he would like to pass legislation mandating public financing of federal elections, although he said that Congress would never pass such legislation "in our lifetime."

In 1987, prompted by record spending in the previous election cycle, Oklahoma Democrat David L. Boren wrote legislation that would have, among other things, provided public funding for some candidates. After it reached the floor, Democrats failed a record seven times in their attempt to break a GOP filibuster, and the bill was pulled. (1987 Almanac, p. 33)

Daschle said he also would like to see a constitutional amendment that would allow Congress to set limits on how much money may be spent on elections. In previous rulings, including the landmark *Buckley v. Valeo*, the courts have said that restrictions on spending are unconstitutional. "That may be in our grandchildren's lifetime, but it won't be in our lifetime," he said.

Feingold said he will continue to push broader changes in the campaign finance system, including provisions that were dropped from earlier versions of his bill. "I would like to go back to the original McCain-Feingold bill," he said.

Feingold wants to reintroduce voluntary spending limits and free TV air time for candidates. He said he probably will not start a new push for changes this year, but could take up the battle in the next Congress.

And lawmakers on both sides of the issue say it is likely Congress will have to take action in the coming years to address unforeseen problems with the new campaign finance rules.

"Is today's effort pernicious?" Craig

1998 demonstrators support reform.

HOUSE PASSAGE: In the House, Shays and Meeham manage to force a vote in 1998. Speaker Newt Gingrich, R-Ga., puts it on the floor when they force his hand with a "discharge petition." The bill passes, 252-179

BLOCKED: In the Senate the legislation is blocked by filibuster.

1999 - 2000

ANOTHER WIN: Shays and Meehan force a vote in 1999. The bill, which mirrors the version the House approved the year before, passes, 252-177.

ANOTHER LOSS: In the Senate, McCain and Feingold are blocked again.

CLOSING LOOPHOLES: In 2000, McCain's bill to close a loophole favoring so-called 527 PACs clears Congress and becomes law (PL 106-230).

2001

COMBATANTS: McCain forces a debate of his bill. McConnell, a longtime opponent, leads the fight against it. The senate approves significant changes, many of which are incorporated in the bill that ultimately passes.

SENATE OK: In April, the bill passes, 59-41.

HOUSE DELAYS: The bill reaches the House floor in July, but then stalls in a fight over the rules for debate. When Congress adjourns in December, supporters are close to gathering enough signatures to force a vote.

McConnell, right, gave consistent opposition.

Political Participation

said. "None of us know yet. People will make the system fit to what are their political needs."

Daschle could not predict the impact of the new legislation. Asked how it would affect him as a politician, he said, "Well, that's a good question, and I don't know that anybody can give you a complete answer until we've experienced it. . . . I can't tell you how it's all going to play itself out."

FEC Overhaul

One issue that Congress may take up this year is an effort to overhaul the FEC, the agency charged with enforcing campaign finance laws.

McCain said he will begin working on legislation in the coming weeks. He said he wants to give the FEC more power to enforce campaign finance laws and reorganize the six-member commission, which he says too often deadlocks in tie votes.

FEC Chairman David Mason strongly opposed the campaign finance legislation and lobbied for its defeat, but he says he will do everything in his power to implement its provisions once it becomes law.

Mason added that his staff attorneys are now preparing to defend the law in the Supreme Court. The FEC — as the implementing agency —would be named as the defendant in the expected lawsuits.

Mason also said the commission's votes end in ties only about 5 percent of the time.

"I'm perfectly open and willing to discuss the composition of the commission, but the claim the FEC is ineffective because it locks up three to three too much of the time to me just doesn't hold up," he said.

Still, there does appear to be growing support for major changes in the commission this year.

"I think it's almost toothless," Daschle said about the commission. "If [McCain] is suggesting that perhaps we put some muscle and some real meaning behind the FEC, then I'm all for it."

Shays said he "absolutely" wants to take up legislation revamping the commission. Changes might be necessary to ensure that the new rules are enforced, he said.

"It's one thing to pass a good bill and another to make sure it's implemented properly," he said. "If they don't enforce it, we have to find someone who will."

Over the Top: Freshman Help

In October 1999, a cloture motion to break a filibuster of campaign finance legislation failed, killing the bill in the 106th Congress. But Membership changes since helped shift the Senate's attitude toward such a measure. Seven senators who voted to block the bill in 1999, for example, have been replaced by senators who voted for the bill (HR 2356) cleared March 20. Below are the senators who have arrived since October 1999 (in **bold**), their March 20 votes and their predecessors' 1999 cloture votes.

	1999	2002		1999	2002
George Allen, R-Va.		N	**Mark Dayton, D-Minn.**		Y
Charles S. Robb, D	Y		Rod Grams, R	N	
Maria Cantwell, D-Wash.		Y	**John Ensign, R-Nev.**		N
Slade Gorton, R	N		Richard H. Bryan, D	Y	
Jean Carnahan, D-Mo.		Y	**Zell Miller, D-Ga.**		Y
John Ashcroft, R	N		Paul Coverdell, R	N	
Thomas R. Carper, D-Del.		Y	**Bill Nelson, D-Fla.**		Y
William V. Roth Jr., R	Y		Connie Mack, R	N	
Lincoln Chafee, R-R.I.		Y	**Ben Nelson, D-Neb**		Y
John H. Chafee, R	N		Bob Kerrey, D	Y	
Hillary R. Clinton, D-N.Y.		Y	**Debbie Stabenow, D-Mich.**		Y
Daniel P. Moynihan, D	Y		Spencer Abraham, R	N	
Jon Corzine, D-N.J.		Y			
Frank R. Lautenberg, D	Y				

Four Republicans who had opposed such bills in the past have supported campaign finance legislation in the 107th Congress: Thad Cochran of Mississippi, Pete V. Domenici of New Mexico, Peter G. Fitzgerald of Illinois and Richard G. Lugar of Indiana. One other former opponent, John W. Warner, R-Va., voted "no" on the bills (S 27) the Senate passed last April but "yes" March 20. Ted Stevens, R-Alaska, voted "yes" last April but "no" March 20.

Potter, the former FEC commissioner, predicted that Congress will have to revisit the campaign finance laws regularly, and will probably have to make changes as problems arise and candidates find ways around the system.

"The laws break down as people break them down," Potter said. "Probably every 10 years Congress will have to re-address it." ◆

Government Institutions

The articles in this section provide insight into the inner workings of the major institutions of American government, focusing in turn on Congress, the presidency and the bureaucracy. The articles examine homeland security and the role of the United States in foreign affairs in an age of terrorism.

The section on Congress starts with an article on the investigation into the Sept. 11, 2001, terrorist attacks. Who knew what, and when did they know it? In trying to discern whether the attacks could have been prevented, and attempting to fix the intelligence system so nothing like this ever happens again, Democrats and Republicans alike face political roadblocks. As Congress seeks a balance between asserting its legitimate role as overseer and protecting sensitive intelligence from unwarranted prying — and tries to avoid accusations of political gain — the American people are unsure whether their legislators should launch a full-blown investigation.

At the beginning of the year a group of legislators traveled to Afghanistan and came back urging a hefty postwar role for the United States. The second article in this section is about how this role is being shaped. The legislators argue that it's not enough to fight and leave, that peacekeeping is crucial. The Bush administration contends that the U.S. has made its contribution in ousting the Taliban regime, and that our friends and allies need to take over postwar reconstruction.

The leaders of these debates between Congress and the administration are Senate Majority Leader Tom Daschle and President George W. Bush. The last article in this section analyzes the rivalry between the two men — the principles at issue, the history, the personalities and the victory tally.

Indeed, political tussles are a theme of the presidency section, which explores Bush's foreign policy and his influence on the federal budget deficit. The first article discusses the effects of growing warfare between Israelis and Palestinians. The once hands-off Bush administration has become hands-on in the Middle East, and this change has exposed dissension within Congress and even within the Republican ranks, all to the detriment of Bush's foreign policy. Bush's spending policy is the subject of the second article. Wartime needs and the recession that began in 2001 demand high levels of spending, and the days of budget deficits are certain to return.

The articles on the bureaucracy discuss this institution's relationship with Congress. The first story remarks on Secretary of State Colin Powell's positive dealings with legislators and contrasts this relationship with the less symbiotic ones between Congress and other departments. With important decisions being made every day in the war on terrorism, how much consultation is enough? The second article is about the Army's plan to modernize its weapons and tactics. Congress embraced the three-part plan in 1999, but now the budget is tighter, and other branches are clamoring for the same defense dollars. Legislators and Army personnel have their own opinions on where cuts will come from, and the spending battle wages on.

Government Institutions

Politics Muddies the Water Around Sept. 11 Investigation

Democrats nearly paralyzed by pressures on both sides of intelligence probe

Goss (left), speaking last week, prefers to leave an investigation to the Intelligence committees. But Pelosi and many Democrats want an independent probe.

Of all the investigations Congress has pursued in the past 30 years — the foreign policy scandals of the Iran-contra affair, the sex-and-lies scandal of President Bill Clinton, even the corruption of a government in the Watergate affair — none has had the same direct impact on people's lives as the upcoming challenge for lawmakers: finding out what went wrong before the Sept. 11 terrorist attacks and what must be fixed.

This also may be the investigation Congress is least prepared to handle.

The tangled, multilayered politics of the war on terrorism are making sure of that. Even as new details emerge daily about what President Bush was told in August about terrorist scenarios that an FBI agent predicted in July, Democrats are finding themselves in a no-win position: Make too much of whatever warnings the Bush administration received, and they are sure to be seen as opportunists. Pull punches, and they could be seen as abrogating the oversight that is Congress' job.

There are also election-year politics to navigate, as Democratic leaders try to call for an investigation without downgrading the domestic issues they consider their strengths. And then there are difficult internal politics. It is not clear that Senate

Majority Leader Tom Daschle, D-S.D., will have the support of all his Democratic colleagues for an independent commission that would investigate the administration's lack of preparedness before the Sept. 11 attacks. Even if he can win them over, he has to be careful not to call for a commission so strong it could overshadow the joint investigation that Sen. Bob Graham, D-Fla., and Rep. Porter J. Goss, R-Fla., already are leading as chairmen of the two congressional Select Intelligence Committees. *(2002 CQ Weekly, p. 1246)*

Meanwhile, Republicans have their own problems. The Bush administration may have undermined its arguments against releasing the Bush briefing and the FBI memo — which may contain sensitive national security secrets — by fighting so fiercely against congressional requests for less sensitive materials, such as energy task force documents. And Republicans are not necessarily united in their opposition to an independent commission. Prominent Republicans, such as Sens. John McCain of Arizona and Charles E. Grassley of Iowa, have endorsed the idea, with the support of conservative columnists George Will and Robert Novak.

Still, it is the Democrats who are spending the most time defending themselves and trying to find a consistent message. Under blistering attacks from Vice President Dick Cheney and other Republican leaders, they now insist the issue is not what Bush was told before Sept. 11 and what he

CQ Weekly May 25, 2002

did about it, even though their initial responses to the revelations of Bush's briefing in August suggested exactly that.

The issue, Democrats now say, is the need for an aggressive yet nonpartisan investigation that gives the nation a serious road map for how to guard against the next terrorist assault. But by attacking Bush, retreating under fire, and then sending Daschle out to suggest an independent commission "if Republicans will agree" — which they will not — the Democrats already have stirred a political atmosphere that could prevent such an investigation from going forward.

"It's pretty obvious that they don't want to dig, and they certainly don't want to dig deep," said Melvin Goodman, a former CIA analyst now teaching at the National War College. "If you don't want a serious investigation, you're not going to get a serious investigation."

Democrats clearly believe they need to do something — and not purely for political gain, but because it is their job. They said it became important to know what other information might be scattered throughout the administration after reports surfaced that Bush was told in August about Osama bin Laden's plan to hijack U.S. airplanes. Those concerns only intensified after reports that Attorney General John Ashcroft and FBI Director Robert Mueller were told after Sept. 11 about a FBI memo of July that raised concerns about Middle Eastern men attending U.S. flight schools.

Then, an FBI lawyer in the Minneapolis field office revealed May 23 that her superiors in Washington blocked agents from aggressively investigating suspected terrorist Zacharias Moussaoui before Sept. 11.

"If you were the family member of someone who was killed in the World Trade Center or at the Pentagon, and you found out that in June someone had warned that this could happen, you'd have questions about it," a Daschle aide said.

Still, some Democrats on the other side of the Capitol could not resist trying to score a few political points off the issue. House Appropriations Committee Democrats threatened to offer amendments to a supplemental spending measure (HR 4775) that would force the release of the July FBI memo, known as the "Phoenix memo," and force Ashcroft to explain reports that he used a "threat assessment" to justify leasing an expensive private plane two months before the Sept. 11 attacks. (*2002 CQ Weekly, p. 1377*)

Analysts say it is exactly those kinds of Democratic political antics that could corrode the credibility of any congressional investigation and let the Bush administration off the hook.

"They need to make sure what they're engaged in can be defended as not representing a fishing party," said Leon Fuerth, a former national security adviser to Vice President Al Gore. "They need to give every sign that they understand that the nation is in danger.

"Having made sure they've done these things," Fuerth said, "they need to stick to their guns and not allow the executive branch to try to intimidate them from the discharge of their legitimate responsibilities."

How to Investigate

There is certainly no guarantee that an independent commission will be created. Daschle insists the Intelligence committees can do only so much, since they do not have jurisdiction over some of the agencies that should play a role in preventing terrorism, such as the Federal Aviation Administration, the Justice Department and the Immigration and Naturalization Service. He says an independent commission should be created to take a broader view of the executive branch and make sure everyone is communicating.

"No one has said that the president could have prevented the tragedy of Sept. 11," Daschle said in a May 22 speech to the National Press Club. "But, by the same token, no one can take much comfort from the picture that has emerged of government agencies that seem totally out of sync with each other — or that it has taken eight months to begin putting that picture together."

But Bush and most congressional Republicans are taking a hard line against a commission, saying it essentially would reinvent the wheel because the Intelligence committees are already well into their own investigations and already have the security clearances and knowledge to handle classified information. Even before the disclosure of Bush's briefing in August, Cheney was lobbying Daschle to limit any investigation to the Intelligence committees, though Daschle says he never made Cheney any promises.

"There are committees set up with both Republicans and Democrats who understand the obligations of upholding our secrets and our sources and methods of collecting intelligence," Bush said May 23. "And therefore, I think it's the best place for Congress to take a good look at the events leading up to Sept. 11."

Congressional Republicans were even more adamant in their opposition to a commission. "Why would we want to tell Osama bin Laden what we knew about his organization, or even worse, what we didn't know?" asked House Majority Whip Tom DeLay, R-Texas.

Daschle has not necessarily closed the sale among his Democratic colleagues, either. Even as Daschle was preparing to go before reporters May 21 to endorse an independent commission, Graham and other Democrats on the Intelligence Committee questioned the need for such a commission before the committees had finished their own investigations. "Let us decide after that if we need a commission," said Sen. Dianne Feinstein, D-Calif.

And the reaction of Senate Foreign Relations Committee Chairman Joseph R. Biden Jr., D-Del., was not exactly a ringing endorsement: "I'm not sure it's necessary, but I'm not opposed to it."

Daschle does not see a problem winning Senate approval for a commission. He predicted the measure "would get at least 60 votes if we get to that point on the floor of the Senate." Part of the reason is he has promised Graham and other wary Democrats that any commission investigation would be done in addition to the Intelligence committees' probe, not in place of them.

Politically, Daschle has to allow the Intelligence investigations to proceed, but that is not because most lawmakers believe they are doing a spectacular job. Indeed, they may be the Bush administration's best hope for avoiding an aggressive investigation. They are often seen as too close to the CIA to conduct an impartial inquiry, and their credibility has been hurt by the resignation of the original staff director and a months-long delay in scheduling hearings.

Privately, some Democrats also fret that an all-out investigation could make it harder for them to refocus the country's attention on the domestic issues where they do best. Daschle's attempt May 22 to call up legislation to increase the minimum wage (S 2538), along with his efforts in his

Government Institutions

National Press Club speech to highlight core Democratic issues such as Social Security, education and Medicare, created barely a ripple in the press.

Publicly, however, top Democrats insist they are good at doing many things at once. They do not see a conflict between pursuing an aggressive Sept. 11 investigation while highlighting their differences with Bush over domestic issues. In the long run, the Bush administration could have more to fear from the timing. Any commission investigation would probably stretch well into 2003 — when Bush would be gearing up for his re-election campaign.

There is another reason Democrats may end up rallying behind a commission. Even as Bush and Republicans push the Democrats to back off, their Democratic supporters are grumbling that party leaders are not aggressive enough in challenging the Republican agenda. In a recent survey by the Pew Research Center for the People and the Press, one third of Democrats said congressional Democratic leaders are not speaking out enough against Bush's policies. The survey of 1,002 adults was conducted May 6-16.

Many Democrats are determined to prove those critics wrong.

"If we can spend so much time and money getting to the bottom of land sales in Arkansas and blue dresses in the White House, it would seem to me this could provide our country a little more value to prevent a future tragedy," said Rep. Patrick J. Kennedy, D-R.I., former chairman of the Democratic Congressional Campaign Committee. "It's a perfect example of where we do need to do an investigation."

Winging It

Finding the right balance between legitimate oversight and political gain, however, may be an impossible task in this case. If the Democrats appear to be winging it, it is because they are.

"I don't think anyone knows" where the line is, said David T. Canon, a political science professor at the University of Wisconsin at Madison. If there are more disclosures that the Bush administration withheld information, Democrats will be able to become more aggressive, Canon said. But if there are more attacks within the United States, he said, "the game changes entirely."

Democrats have been fine-tuning their message ever since the initial reports about the August briefing blanketed newspapers May 16. That morning, House Minority Leader Richard A. Gephardt, D-Mo., declared Congress should "find out what the president and what the White House knew about the events leading up to 9/11, when they knew it and, most importantly, what was done about it at that time."

Democratic political advisers braced for a Republican counterattack. It began when Cheney said the investigation should be conducted by responsible lawmakers, "not those who would seek short-term advantage." Other Republicans pounded away. (*2002 CQ Weekly, p. 1323*)

Since then, Democrats have backed away from the "what did the president know and when did he know it" questions and their obvious allusions to the Watergate scandal. Now, the blame has shifted to less popular officials, such as

---

Nation Divided on Investigation

Depending on how the question is asked, recent polls show widely differing views about whether Congress should investigate how the White House and the intelligence community handled information related to the terrorist attacks received before Sept. 11.

Do you think there should or should not be a congressional investigation into the fact that the Bush administration did not release this information sooner?

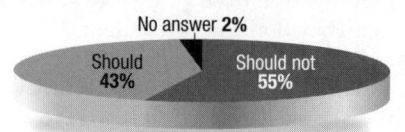

- Should: 43%
- Should not: 55%
- No answer: 2%

SOURCE: May 16 USA Today/CNN/Gallup Poll of 598 adults. Margin of sampling error: plus or minus 4 percentage points

Do you think it is in the national interest for Congress to investigate intelligence failures of the CIA and FBI in connection with the Sept. 11 terrorist attacks, or would such a public investigation at this time not be in the national interest?

- In the national interest to investigate: 68%
- Would not be in the national interest: 24%
- Don't know: 8%

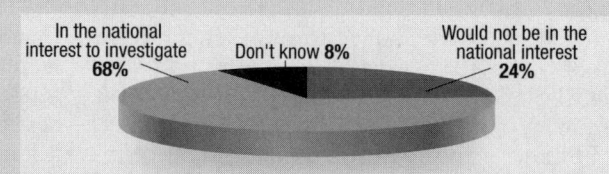

SOURCE: May 16-17 Newsweek poll of 1,002 adults conducted by Princeton Survey Research Associates. Margin of sampling error: plus or minus 3 percentage points

Do you think there should be a full-scale investigation into the handling of intelligence before Sept. 11, or do you feel this would be unproductive and too political?

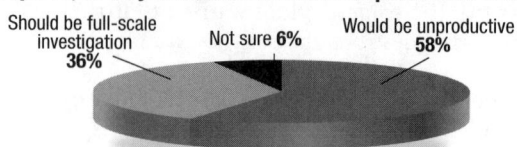

- Should be full-scale investigation: 36%
- Would be unproductive: 58%
- Not sure: 6%

SOURCE: May 18, 2002, NBC News/Wall Street Journal poll of 602 adults. Margin of sampling error: plus or minus 4 percentage points

Do you think the U.S. Congress should or should not conduct an investigation into what the Bush administration knew about terrorist threats before Sept. 11 and how it handled that intelligence?

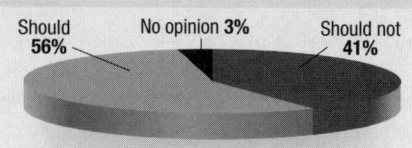

- Should: 56%
- Should not: 41%
- No opinion: 3%

SOURCE: May 18-19 ABC News/Washington Post poll of 803 adults. Margin of sampling error: plus or minus 3.5 percentage points

Ashcroft, and agencies such as the FBI.

"I don't think this is about what the president knew. I think this is about, 'What didn't the president know and why didn't he know it?'" Biden said.

Even Democrats who could use the investigation as a showcase for their own ambitions — such as Sen. John Edwards of North Carolina, who is gaining attention as a possible presidential candidate — are determined to stay on-message.

"We have to do it in a professional and nonpartisan way, getting the information in a way that doesn't blow it out of proportion but still gets the information to the American people in an accurate way," Edwards said.

But creating such a fair-minded commission would be difficult, if not impossible.

"You cannot remove politics from this process. Nobody would be that naive," said former Rep. Lee Hamilton (1965-99), who chaired the House select committee that investigated the Iran-Contra affair in 1987. "What you have to try to do is to let the facts drive the investigation. You pick members who are interested in finding out the facts; you develop staff that is highly professional [in] digging the facts out, and then you let the facts drive the investigation and the conclusions."

Supporters of the idea, both Democrats and Republicans, say the key to fairness is to allow members to be picked by the president as well as Congress. "We think it's important that the president gets to appoint members to this," said McCain, who is cosponsoring a commission proposal (S 1867) with Sen. Joseph I. Lieberman, D-Conn., that would allow Bush to appoint five of the 14 members, including the chairman.

Daschle has not committed to following the Lieberman-McCain model. Yet he does not appear to have a clear idea of what he does want. When Biden asked Daschle during a Democratic caucus meeting May 21 who the members would be and how much authority the commission would have, the majority leader indicated those issues were still being worked out.

Whatever he decides, most Republicans are not holding their breath for a commission that would be magically shielded from politics.

"Show me a commission that's going to work on a nonpartisan basis," asked Goss. "I think the good Lord is busy today, and I don't think He's going to come down and set that one up."

Goss, however, softened his tone by week's end and said he would not stand in the way of a commission. And supporters of the idea say a well-designed independent commission would be a better bet than leaving the investigation entirely to Congress.

"We're going into an election in five months, and it's one of the most closely contested elections in House history. The Senate is split by one vote," said Rep. Tim Roemer, D-Ind., a member of the House Intelligence committee who has introduced a proposal (HR 4777) for a 10-member independent commission.

"I'm confident that the Intelligence committees can do a good job," Roemer said, "but to have 10 independent experts who don't have to worry about running for re-election . . . to give us a second look is a very helpful consideration."

Information War

For Republicans, the risk lies in their appearance of hiding something by fighting so hard, in the name of national security, to prevent the release of the Sept. 11 documents.

Bush and Cheney have said that releasing the Aug. 6 briefing, for example, could betray sources and expose how the United States collects its information.

"Not only have we got to share intelligence between friends — which we do — but we're still at war, we've still got threats to the homeland that we've got to deal with," Bush said May 23. "And it's very important for us to not hamper our ability to wage that war."

Democrats agree it would be a mistake to release either the Aug. 6 briefing or the Phoenix memo in their entirety. But they say the documents could be released in redacted form, with names and other sensitive information blacked out. Some independent experts agree, and say Bush and Cheney are putting up an unnecessary fight.

"You're sanitizing documents all the time," Goodman said of his days as a Soviet affairs analyst for the CIA. "I was sanitizing documents to give to the Soviet Union. You're telling me we can give documents to the Soviet Union, but we can't give them to the Intelligence Committee?"

Already, some of the administration's accounts of the information it received have been called into question. In a May 16 briefing, National Security Adviser Condoleezza Rice said warnings the administration had through August generally pointed to overseas attacks. Two days later, The Washington Post reported that the Aug. 6 memo was actually about the possibility of attacks in the United States.

Democrats say that, at the very least, the Phoenix memo should be released in redacted form so the public will know what kind of information the FBI did not act on. "The first page and a half of the Phoenix memo is so explicit and so explosive that it should be released," said Sen. Richard J. Durbin, D-Ill., a member of the Senate Intelligence panel.

But the memo's author, FBI agent Kenneth Williams, reportedly has testified he did not believe the memo would have stopped the Sept. 11 attacks. And Republicans on the Intelligence committees say there is nothing to be gained by releasing it now.

Ultimately, however, the issue goes beyond whether to release or withhold documents, or whether the investigation should be done in the open or behind closed doors. The real question is whether Congress is capable of investigating the administration's performance in preventing past terrorist catastrophes while the threat of more outrages still exists. Beyond the Beltway, such a probe runs the risk of stirring patriotic anger, personal fear and eroding the public's confidence in their leaders.

But if lawmakers are worried about a public backlash for asking such questions in the middle of a war, they may be worrying too much.

History is replete with examples of Congress raising questions about presidents' handling of wars without paying a political price, according to Columbia University historian Alan Brinkley. From GOP attacks on Franklin D. Roosevelt during World War II to Democratic attacks on Lyndon B. Johnson and Richard Nixon during the Vietnam War, lawmakers have criticized their commanders in chief during wartime without inflicting political damage on themselves.

"War is no less political than any other time," Brinkley said. "Presidents have always been criticized for their conduct of wars. There is no inherent political liability in criticizing a president for his conduct of war — as long as the public is sympathetic to the criticisms." ◆

Government Institutions

Members Return From Afghanistan Urging Greater Postwar U.S. Role

Some in delegation see need for greater involvement in reconstruction, peacekeeping

Quick Contents

Estimates on the cost of rebuilding Afghanistan range from $15 billion to $25 billion over the next decade. How much will the United States contribute?

During the congressional recess, dozens of lawmakers traveled to Afghanistan to see first-hand the devastation from the U.S.-led military campaign to root out terrorism and the preceding two decades of civil war. The experience is fueling calls for the Bush administration to do more to rebuild the country and ensure peace in the region.

"We just can't say, 'We did the military, so we're out of here,' " said Frank R. Wolf, R-Va., chairman of the House Commerce-Justice-State Appropriations Subcommittee, after a nine-day visit to Afghanistan and neighboring countries. "Because if we do, you know the bad guys will come back into power."

In recent weeks, the Bush administration has tried to shift responsibility for Afghanistan's future to other countries, particularly the European Union, Japan and moderate Muslim states. Arguing that the United States already has made its major contribution by ousting the Taliban regime, the White House has said other countries should fund Afghanistan's reconstruction and provide policing until Kabul develops its own security forces.

Finding common ground on the question of a U.S. role in peacekeeping could prove difficult, reflecting the longstanding Republican and Democratic divide over the issue. Republicans believe that peacekeeping deployments hamper the ability of the military to carry out more essential missions, while Democrats argue that the U.S. presence is vital to ensuring their success.

In addition, budget constraints will make it tough for the administration and Congress to reach a consensus on an appropriate level of funding for Afghanistan. Observers estimate that as much as $25 billion in international aid will be necessary over the next decade to rebuild the war-torn country.

Senate Majority Leader Tom Daschle, D-S.D., speaking at a news conference Jan. 16 at the recently reopened U.S. embassy in Kabul, said, "We strongly believe that our country needs to be here for the long haul, that we aren't going to leave once the effort to defeat terrorism has been completed."

Secretary of State Colin L. Powell traveled to Kabul on Jan. 17, meeting with Afghanistan's interim leader Hamid Karzai. It was one of several Central Asian stops for Powell, who is headed to Tokyo for the Jan. 21 conference on coordinating assistance for Afghanistan.

Powell spoke in general terms about Washington's commitment to Afghanistan. "This country needs everything," he said in an interview with NBC's "Today" show. "It needs a banking system. It needs a health care system. It needs a sanitation system. It needs a phone system. It needs road construction. Everything you can imagine."

Powell provided no specifics on the amount of U.S. aid or a peacekeeping force.

Peacekeepers or 'Gap Fillers?'

In Washington, some Republicans say the administration's reticence is appropriate.

"The United States has borne the brunt, the overwhelming majority of the brunt and expense and risk in the conflict side," said Sen. John McCain, R-Ariz., upon his return. "And I think that it's very appropriate for the peacekeeping and a lot of the financial aid to come from our friends and allies."

That argument is likely to heat up as President Bush prepares his fiscal 2003 budget and presents his plan for a fiscal 2002 supplemental spending bill. The White House and Congress will have to shoehorn in aid for Afghanistan while the federal government

CQ Weekly Jan. 19, 2002

Daschle, foreground, and Sens. Robert C. Smith, R-N.H., and Richard J. Durbin, D-Ill., right, talk to reporters outside the reopened U.S. embassy in Kabul. A U.S. Marine looks on.

again operates with a budget deficit. Other countries are likely to press the United States to contribute more, as world leaders — including Powell — gather in Japan.

Looming over the money debate is the question of how to ensure peace and stability in Afghanistan. A British-led contingent of some 1,400 troops are helping the Afghan security forces.

Bush said Jan. 16 that he favors letting other countries carry out the peacekeeping mission in Afghanistan: "I've made it clear that our troops will be used to fight and win war, and that's exactly what they've done."

During the war in Afghanistan, the Pentagon largely left the task of ground operations to local allies, out of fear of incurring casualties such as those that drove U.S. forces from Somalia in 1993.

As it became clear that some type of international peacekeeping force would be needed in Afghanistan as that country strove to establish a new national government and rebuild its security forces, administration officials sought to keep their mandate — and U.S. participation in the operation — as limited as possible. Current plans call for a force of only 4,500 troops, largely limited to the capital of Kabul, until an Afghan security force can be trained.

At a Senate Foreign Relations Committee hearing Dec. 6, Richard N. Haass, who is coordinating the State Department's efforts on Afghanistan, said the administration sees the peacekeeping force as merely a "gap filler."

"We don't want to get involved in intensive nation-building," Haass said.

Said Sen. Chuck Hagel, R-Neb.: "We are doing exactly the right thing in the right amounts. I don't know what you would do with a division of troops."

But Senate Foreign Relations Committee Chairman Joseph R. Biden Jr., D-Del., said a more robust international force with a substantial U.S. presence would be needed.

"I'm not talking about peace, love and brotherhood and blue helmets," Biden said during his visit to Kabul, alluding to U.N. peacekeeping forces. "I'm talking about pursuers. Absent from that, I don't see any shot for this country. They have no army. They have no police force. They have no way to keep control."

Maurice D. Hinchey, D-N.Y., a member of the House Appropriations

Congress

Securing Nuclear Arsenals

Concerned that increasing tensions between India and Pakistan could lead to war or that terrorists may try to gain control of their nuclear weapons, lawmakers are advocating new steps to safeguard the countries' arsenals.

A bipartisan group of senators, including Majority Leader Tom Daschle, D-S.D.; Pete V. Domenici, R-N.M.; and Richard G. Lugar, R-Ind., are calling for extending to India and Pakistan the safeguard system and inspector access of a decade-old program initiated by Lugar and former Sen. Sam Nunn, D-Ga. (1972-97).

Those programs are aimed at preventing the theft of nuclear weapons and materials from the former Soviet Union and finding work for scientists to prevent them from working for terrorist groups or U.S. enemies.

At the urging of Senate Foreign Relations Committee member Christopher J. Dodd, D-Conn., lawmakers requested a report on the feasibility of expanding Nunn-Lugar in the fiscal 2002 defense appropriations bill (PL 107-117). The effort took on a new urgency after the Dec. 13 attack on the Indian Parliament by terrorists who want to free the disputed province of Kashmir from Indian control.

Instead of waiting for a report, lawmakers are urging President Bush to call for expanding the "Nunn-Lugar" program to India and Pakistan as part of his State of the Union address Jan. 29. Otherwise, they are expected to move forward with their own initiatives when Congress returns Jan. 23.

Last month, Lugar said that as part of the war on terrorism, "every nation which has weapons of mass destruction must account for what it has, spend its own money or obtain international technical and financial resources to safely secure what it has, and pledge that no other nation, cell or cause will be granted access or use.

"The closer ties that have developed since September with India and Pakistan offer new opportunities to discuss nuclear security with both countries, including safe storage and accountability," he added. "We must attempt to establish programs that respect their sovereignty and go far to help insure their security."

Experts disagree, however, over whether extending the Nunn-Lugar program to India would be wise.

Legitimize 1998 Tests

Some non-proliferation experts argue that efforts to improve the security and reliability of those countries' nuclear arsenals would wrongly legitimize their decision to test nuclear weapons in 1998.

In addition, it is unclear if the two nations, particularly Pakistan, would be willing to allow other countries to gain access to their arsenals as required by Nunn-Lugar.

"There is enormous reluctance to let foreigners get involved. Both nuclear programs are profoundly tied in with the countries' sense of survival and national pride," said Robert Templer, the Asia program director for the International Crisis Group.

Analysts say it will be difficult to transfer the Nunn-Lugar programs wholesale to India and Pakistan. Both countries have relatively small nuclear stockpiles and have expressed no interest in reducing them. In addition, neither country faces the problem of unemployed weapons scientists.

Experts say one aspect of Nunn-Lugar that could be transferred to India and Pakistan is a program under which U.S. experts help Russian facilities secure hazardous materials from theft and accidents.

But Stephen Philip Cohen of the Brookings Institution said there isn't much a Nunn-Lugar-style program could do to secure weapons. He noted that there is nothing to prevent either country from buying locks, seals and other safeguard materials. "If they want them, they've already got them," Cohen said.

Government Institutions

Committee who traveled to Afghanistan, said the U.S. presence has to be very visible for an extended time.

"I believe U.S. troops should be part of the international security force, and I believe the international security force will not be as successful if U.S. troops are not involved," Hinchey said at a news conference in Kabul on Jan. 15.

Containing the Warlords

A peacekeeping force of at least 30,000 troops would be needed to maintain a minimum level of security in Afghanistan's major cities and on its primary thoroughfares, said William Durch, a peacekeeping expert at the non-partisan Henry L. Stimson Center, a Washington think tank. The force also would need a substantial U.S. presence.

"If the U.S. isn't there, other countries will lose interest rather rapidly," Durch said. "Politically and on the ground, we have to be there."

That view won a surprising endorsement from the conservative editorial page of The Wall Street Journal on Jan. 15, which has opposed nation-building and peacekeeping operations under the Clinton administration, but has backed it for Afghanistan.

"We appreciate that the U.S. doesn't want to become a long-term peacekeeper," the editorial said. "But some American participation now would induce other countries to commit more of their own until local police can be reassembled."

How large an international force is needed, Durch said, depends in part on how much authority Kabul and its international allies are willing to cede to Afghanistan's warlords, who currently hold the real power.

Even some critics of a significant U.S. role, such as Jim Kolbe, R-Ariz., chairman of the House Foreign Operations Appropriations Subcommittee, say a more robust force is needed to curb the warlords.

"I think the key issue is where these peacekeeping forces are located," Kolbe told reporters in Pakistan on Jan. 15. "And I think they must be — let me repeat that — they must be more than in Kabul. And if we do not have them located in the other major cities, like Herat and Kandahar and Mazar-i-Sharif, we will find ourselves falling back into the same trap as before, where individual warlords take control of an area, and there's, kind of, a breakdown of law and order."

This argument also has spilled over into the economic arena, where experts differ over whether the United States and other international donors should devote more of their resources to the fledgling government in Kabul or to working through the warlords, who could fall prey to corruption but may also be more effective as conduits for assistance, at least in the short-term.

The Cost of Rebuilding

Substantial disagreements have emerged over exactly how much money will be needed to rebuild a society essentially from scratch and where those funds should come from.

Kolbe said $8 billion would be needed for Afghanistan over the next decade, including $1.5 billion from the United States. He has suggested that these needs could largely be met by taking money from other ongoing foreign aid programs.

Wolf disagreed, saying the funds should be in addition to current foreign aid spending and would have to be substantial.

"I don't think that's going to be enough," Wolf said. "We need enough to make progress. . . . You just don't have any choice."

Indeed, a "preliminary needs assessment" prepared for the Tokyo conference by the United Nations Development Program, the World Bank and the Asian Development Bank estimates that about $15 billion will be needed over the next decade. Some private analysts, such as the International Crisis Group, co-chaired by former Rep. Steve Solarz, D-N.Y. (1975-93), have said that even more money — as much as $25 billion — will be needed over that period.

The "needs assessment" indicates that much of the funds — about $5 billion — will be needed during the next two and a half years as Afghanistan makes the transition to an elected government in Kabul.

During that period, the report concluded, Afghanistan is expected to have little, if any, tax revenue. At the same time, funds are desperately needed for the basics of restoring a stable society: clearing land mines; restoring employment, particularly in agriculture; uprooting opium crops; resettling refugees, and providing health care and education, especially to women.

Bush is expected to take one step toward easing Kabul's immediate fiscal crunch by releasing $221 million in Afghan government assets that were frozen in 1999 to punish the Taliban.

Two key Democrats already have proposed more substantial programs of assistance to Afghanistan.

Tom Lantos of California, ranking Democrat on the House International Relations Committee, introduced legislation (HR 3427) in December that would authorize about $1.6 billion in aid to Afghanistan over the next four years. (2001 CQ Weekly, p. 3098)

Paul Wellstone, D-Minn., chairman of the Senate Foreign Relations Subcommittee on Near Eastern and South Asian Affairs, introduced a similar bill in December.

In presenting his legislation, Wellstone said on the Senate floor that "the United States should be the lead financial contributor to the rehabilitation and reconstruction effort in Afghanistan, and we believe should contribute as much as $5 billion to this effort over the next five years."

In addition to aid, lawmakers are looking for other ways to spur Afghanistan's economy.

Dana Rohrabacher, R-Calif., a member of the House International Relations Committee, has introduced legislation (HR 3440) that would grant normal trade relations to Afghanistan's government.

Members also are looking for the aid and peacekeeping operations in Afghanistan to be part of a broader regional effort.

Kolbe said Congress will have to appropriate aid for Afghanistan's neighbors, such as Pakistan, Tajikistan and Uzbekistan.

"No commitments have been made on the next year's budget to those countries, but I think there's no doubt that there will be more substantial support," he said.

In addition to his stop in Afghanistan, Daschle traveled to Pakistan, where he met President Gen. Pervez Musharraf. Following the session, Daschle indicated that more U.S. support for Islamabad was likely. The United States already has given the South Asian nation $600 million in aid since the Sept. 11 terrorist attacks.

"We expressed to the president as we met with him this afternoon a strong desire on the part of the United States to reciprocate as long-lasting partners, as partners who are not going to be fair-weather friends, but certainly as a country indebted and very grateful to the people of Pakistan for their extraordinary support," Daschle said.

Turkey, another key regional ally in the U.S. military campaign, also is seeking additional assistance from Washington, including a reduction of its $5 billion in military debt.

Turkish Prime Minister Bulent Ecevit met with Bush on Jan. 17 to discuss that issue and Turkey's potential leadership of the peacekeeping force in Afghanistan. Turkish officials have said their country, in poor economic straits, cannot carry out that task without significant U.S. assistance.

Additional aid to Pakistan and Turkey could encounter significant resistance in Congress as several powerful ethnic lobbies, including Indian-Americans, Armenian-Americans and Greek-Americans, oppose such efforts.

In a Jan. 14 speech at Georgetown University, Joseph I. Lieberman, D-Conn., a member of the Senate Armed Services Committee, suggested that greater trade ties were needed between the United States and Islamic countries, including Afghanistan.

Lieberman suggested that a two-year-old law (PL 106-200) that lowered import tariffs and removed quotas on certain goods from Africa should be seen as a model for future legislation dealing with Muslim nations.

"In Congress, we can help by adopting additional trade preference programs for countries that prove themselves to be good global citizens, including duty-free treatment and freedom from quotas for certain goods," Lieberman said.

Lieberman and other lawmakers also said a U.S. presence will be needed near Afghanistan for years to come to prevent rivals such as Iran, Pakistan and Russia from upsetting the region's balance of power. Lieberman likened it to the role the United States has played in East Asia since World War II.

Senate Armed Services Committee Chairman Carl Levin, D-Mich., expressed similar sentiments in a session with defense reporters Jan. 15. Levin also backed a "forward-leaning" U.S. presence in the region, including "both basing aircraft and pre-positioning equipment."

"I don't want to predict 10 years from now how the world's going to look, but I would say that for as long as I can see, there would be support," Levin said. ◆

Government Institutions

The Duel of Bush and Daschle: Men of Genteel Steel

Both men walk a fine line in power struggle over domestic policy

From the moment the Senate switched into Democratic hands last June, the political class has been waiting for the first really good public fight to erupt between George W. Bush and Tom Daschle. Such conflicts appeared inevitable between men who lead rival branches of the government, who steer opposing political parties and who may both seek election to the presidency in 2004.

So far, those who enjoy a Washington rhetorical set-to in the style of Bill Clinton and Newt Gingrich have been largely disappointed. Except for a flare-up this month over the consequence of last year's tax cut, the president and the Senate majority leader have cultivated an affability with one another, a style perhaps born of their 1950s childhoods on the Great Plains. Even when angry, they have been prone to hurl faint compliments, never mud.

With emphatic geniality, Bush says he understands how hard it is to run the Senate. With smooth mild-manneredness, Daschle says he appreciates the president's perspective. They eat breakfast together. They insist they want to work things out. Famously, they even embraced at the Capitol last fall for a national television audience.

It is not only the bipartisan commitment to fighting the war on terrorism that is holding these men back. It also appears to be, for each, a calculated passive-aggressive style. On the surface, all is genteel. But just underneath, Bush and Daschle are deep into a duel over domestic policy.

Already several rounds have been fought on issues as diverse as aid to the unemployed, farm subsidies and energy policy. A new spate of maneuvering came to the surface as the second session of the 107th Congress was called to order Jan. 23.

At times, the president and Senate leader enlist party loyalists as proxy warriors to do their bidding. Behind the scenes, the White House increasingly strategizes with Senate Republicans only, reaching out to Daschle and the Democrats far less often than in the weeks after the terrorist attacks, Democratic aides say. For his part, Daschle does not make it a practice to give the White House warning before unveiling a new initiative, presumably hoping to put administration officials off-balance with a skein of surprises.

"You got two pros, and it'll be interesting to watch," said Rodney Ellis, a leader of the Democratic majority of the Texas state Senate when Bush was governor. "They're each walking a tightrope. The White House has to be careful about demonizing the leader of the Senate. The Senate is a club and Bush could rile more than just the Democrats. Daschle has to lead the Democrats to victory, but also protect the institutional integrity of the Senate."

With the military campaign in Afghanistan now presenting no urgent questions for Congress to address, the tone of the congressional year — as well as its accomplishments — will probably be shaped primarily by the power struggle of these two men. At issue is not only who wins the upper hand on an economic stimulus package, the patients' bill of rights or managing the return of the federal deficit. It is also whether Congress is able to reassert itself against an unusually popular wartime president — who since Sept. 11 has been able to reclaim much of the power that ebbed out of the executive branch during Clinton's administration. (*2001 CQ Weekly, p. 163*)

The combat between Daschle and Bush seems sure to intensify after Bush's first formal State of the Union address, to a joint session of Congress Jan. 29, and to magnify again once the president unveils his fiscal 2003 budget proposal Feb. 4, the start of only 26 weeks of legislating that the lawmakers have arranged for themselves this year.

The winner, at least in 2002, will be settled Nov. 5, when the midterm election will not only determine control of the

CQ Weekly January 26, 2002

Congress

108th Congress but also send signals about the durability of Bush's popularity and the viability of Daschle's presidential aspirations.

Learning From Their Mentors

Both men appear to have learned much by studying their favorite predecessors. Bush watched from the anterooms of the White House while his father fell victim to George J. Mitchell's shrewd stewardship of the Senate Democrats a decade ago. It was during the 1990 budget summit that the 41st president agreed to abandon his "no new taxes" vow in exchange for the spending caps offered up by the Maine Democrat (1980-95). The disappointment that many Republicans felt about the deal contributed to the president's defeat for re-election in 1992. *(Box, p. 59)*

At the time, Daschle was a Mitchell protégé, the majority leader's handpicked co-chairman of the Democratic Policy Committee. That vantage point allowed the South Dakotan to observe his leader's laconic but determined style, especially the way Mitchell wore Bush down through a protracted summer and fall of negotiations. However, Mitchell sat in a stronger position than Daschle does now, because their party controlled both the House and the Senate with comfortable majorities that allowed Democrats not only to block presidential initiatives but also to pass their own. Daschle now operates at a comparative disadvantage. His party controls only the Senate, and he exercises that control with only one vote to spare.

The president has a multitude of tools for asserting his leverage over Congress. All presidents have the bully pulpit, and Bush's has been elevated by his wartime popularity. Bush has so far used his veto threat sparingly — his veto power not at all — while regularly trying to maneuver toward victory by wooing a handful of moderate Senate Democrats away from Daschle's side. Bush enjoys a high degree of loyalty from the fellow Republicans who hold a narrow majority in the House. When his priorities face long odds of being embraced at the Capitol, Bush exerts his power to bypass Congress altogether through executive order and administrative regulations.

"It's very difficult for a congressional leader to stand up to the president," said George C. Edwards III, a political scientist at Texas A&M University. "You can't really undermine a president. It was the recession, not Mitchell, that undid Bush 41," referring to the 41st president.

Daschle's standing as the Capitol's most influential Democrat offers him a podium from which to promote his ideas. More significantly, he can block many of the president's initiatives through the threat of a filibuster, compelling Bush and his allies — led by Minority Leader Trent Lott, R-Miss., and Minority Whip Don Nickles, R-Okla. — to find 60 senators to advance his agenda. With the Senate split so nearly down the middle, that has proven almost impossible because Daschle has brought to the duel an extraordinary ability to maintain party discipline.

As majority leader, he also has primacy over setting the Senate's legislative schedule. Off the floor, Daschle can set the Senate's agenda for oversight and investigatory hearings, calling presidential critics to the microphone or endeavoring to shift the public's attention to the collapse of Enron Corp., for example. *(2002 CQ Weekly, p. 234)*

Both Sides Claim Victory

During the first seven months of their quietly intensifying rivalry, both Daschle and Bush pulled out almost all the tools at their disposal on issues not purely defined as obligations of the War Congress. It has been problematic to assign victories and losses in their clashes so far, because the partisans of both men are quick to declare victory for their side and reluctant to concede defeat.

One example was last fall's tussle over spending for homeland security. Senate Democrats wanted to spend more than the $40 billion ceiling the president had set for last year's response to the terrorist attacks. They sought to reassert their power over the purse in terms of enhancing domestic protections against terrorism, and they moved to attach their program to the must-pass fiscal 2002 defense spending bill (PL 107-117) as the year came to an end. Office of Homeland Security Director Tom Ridge insisted that he was flush, Bush backed up that claim with a veto threat — and Senate Republicans in three test votes showed they would take his side even if that meant derailing the entire bill. In the end, Bush was able to claim a public victory for fiscal restraint, but in the legislative fine print the Democrats were able to reorder Bush's priorities for the $40 billion more to their liking. *(2001 CQ Weekly, p. 3029)*

"This was about the next three — perhaps seven — years, about how the appropriations process is handled," boasted one senior White House aide who had previously worked for the Senate Republicans. "It was a powerful test, and tough on our guys. The president said he didn't need the money. The Republican leadership, Lott and Nickles, held the conference together."

The farm bill was another area where it appeared, on the surface, that Bush outmaneuvered Daschle at the end of the year — but where the legislative substance, and events since, reveal a picture potentially more flattering to the senator. The president succeeded on one of his main objectives last year, which was delaying the debate on legislation to rewrite the farm law (PL 104-277)

Daschle, far left at a December press briefing, and Bush, at the Pentagon on Jan. 10, begin the year in a distant if not contentious posture with one another. That is a far cry from their embrace after Bush addressed Congress two weeks after the terrorist attacks.

PHOTO FOR CQ / DAVID SCULL (DASCHLE); AP PHOTO / RON EDMONDS (BUSH); REUTERS PHOTO / SHAUN BEST (EMBRACE)

Government Institutions

into this year. On policy grounds, the administration said Congress was moving too fast to expand a faulty crop subsidy regime; on political grounds, Bush was in no hurry to help Daschle advance legislation of enormous importance to his corn- and wheat-farmer constituents. As with the homeland security debate, Bush got GOP senators to take his side when the farm bill (S 1731) was debated in December. But after a four-week hiatus it now seems likely that Daschle will get the core of what he wants when the Senate returns to the bill: a big boost in commodity subsidies. (*2002 CQ Weekly, p. 238*)

Who's More Affable?

Bush uses his affable personality as a weapon, bringing the top four congressional leaders to a White House breakfast table each week to cut deals, talking powerful-man-to-powerful-man without the interference of even the most senior aides. (*2001 CQ Weekly, p. 2519*)

Ellis recalled how in the heat of a disagreement over hate crimes legislation in Texas he had scheduled a meeting in the governor's office. Less than 45 minutes before the meeting was to begin, Bush telephoned to ask if the two could meet instead in Ellis' office. "It was a great tactical ploy, especially if you're a weak-minded person and like to be stroked. It was such a disarming thing to do, for a governor to come to a state senator's office. Only one staffer came with him, who stepped out of the room once we started talking."

But Daschle, too, can be a master of affability. That has made it difficult for Republicans to pin him with the "partisan" tag. Republicans began learning that through trial and error last fall, when Vice President Dick Cheney and Republicans started labeling Daschle as an "obstructionist" who symbolized what was wrong with the return to politics as usual in Congress. (*2001 CQ Weekly, p. 2886*)

The GOP thought it had quality ammunition to make the label stick when, for example, Daschle refused to bring economic stimulus legislation before the Senate unless a majority of his caucus had endorsed it first — a requirement that thwarted White House attempts to pass the president's plan by picking off a dozen moderate Democrats. The campaign was dealt a publicity setback by overreaching when someone printed a flier comparing Daschle to Saddam Hussein.

"To the extent that people know Daschle in the country, they know him as the victim of anthrax — a symbol of attack on the United States," said Mark Mellman, who does polling for Daschle. Mellman suggested that the GOP demonization effort could paradoxically aid the senator's putative presidential candidacy because "they're turning him into a hero for Democrats."

Unlike Gingrich — the Georgia congressman (1979-99) who rose to be GOP House Speaker by appointing himself the loudest scourge of his political opponents — Daschle's style is to come off as the personification of reason, a trait which is difficult for his opponents to turn against him. Standing before the television cameras outside the Senate chamber Jan. 23, he demanded that Cheney disclose all his contacts with Enron and pushed to revive talks of an economic stimulus bill with unemployment and medical benefits for laid off workers, even punching his finger in the air for emphasis. But all the while his face was calm, his voice modulated and softly resonant.

"Very smooth. He's got the demeanor of Casper Milquetoast. Behind the scenes he's a good pol. Cut throat," said former House Appropriations Committee Chairman Robert L. Livingston, R-La. (1977-99). "That was the demeanor of George Mitchell, but Mitchell pulled it off. We won't know until Election Day if Daschle's successful."

To date, Daschle has made no move to disagree with the president over the war in Afghanistan, and Daschle went out of his way to limit criticism of the package of law enforcement enhancements (PL 107-56) Bush sought to prosecute suspected terrorists. Referring to the main strategist behind Clinton's 1992 campaign, Livingston described Daschle as taking "the [James] Carville approach. When campaigning against George Bush the elder, he realized he wouldn't win on foreign policy, so he concentrated on the economy. . . . But Daschle risks becoming the poster child for obstructionism if he keeps stonewalling the president's initiatives."

One of Daschle's defter victories so far was on the final form of aviation security law (PL 107-71) enacted in November. The key dispute was about how emphatically to make airport security Washington's responsibility. Bush did not want newly made federal employees at the passenger screening checkpoints and got the House to take his side; Daschle insisted on federalization and signaled he was willing to wait as long as it took to get his way. With the peak travel time of Thanksgiving approaching, Bush shifted his view and told Republicans in Congress to do likewise, allowing them to deflect blame if the new security system falls short. (*2001 CQ Weekly, p. 3055*)

Daschle is also savvy in taking on the White House media machine. He is fast on his feet in articulating positions for his party that Republicans find politically difficult to rebut. Aware that the president was about to travel the country to tout his economic vision for the year, Daschle pre-empted him Jan. 4 with the speech in which he blamed the tax cut (PL 107-16) for the evaporation of surplus in the near term. Bush fought back the next day with one of the most memorable sound bites of his first year in office: "Not over my dead body will they raise your taxes."

Again, on Jan. 22, the day before Congress reconvened, Daschle waited until 4 p.m. to make his latest stimulus package offer, which he described as simply accepting the narrow areas of current agreement between Republicans and Democrats. The White House, apparently unaware the offer was coming, allowed the Senate leader half a day's worth of air time to position himself as the repairer of the breach before spurning his offer. (*2002 CQ Weekly, p. 227*)

Is it the Economy or the War?

Until November, South Dakota will serve as a prime testing ground for the tactics that Daschle and Bush will employ against one another. That is because Republican Rep. John Thune is the president's hand-picked choice to run for the Senate this year against Daschle's Democratic colleague Tim Johnson.

Democratic consultants are split on how Daschle should maneuver against Bush. Peter Fenn, a political consultant whose clients include populist House Democrats such as David R. Obey of Wisconsin and David E. Bonior of Michigan, argues that Daschle should seek to force votes on issues that appeal to core Democratic voters — such as strong consumer protections in a patients' bill of rights and expansion of Medicare benefits to include prescription coverage — to help Democrats on the ballot this fall. Along the same lines, he is calling for Daschle to fight Republican domestic policy, such as drilling for oil in the Arctic National Wildlife Refuge.

Congress

The Previous Two Face-Offs

This year's duel between George W. Bush and Tom Daschle for pre-eminence over the legislative agenda is the latest in a long list of occasions when a president has squared off against a Senate majority leader belonging to the other party. In the two most recent examples, the public relationship was often quite different from what went on behind the scenes.

GEORGE BUSH AND GEORGE J. MITCHELL (1989-93)

The incumbent president's father spent all four years of his presidency across the negotiating table from Mitchell, the intellectual Maine liberal who preceded Daschle as the Democratic leader. For much of the first two years of their duel, Mitchell styled himself as an eager legislative mediator, working to pull factions together to pass legislation. In the second half, he transformed himself more overtly into a fierce partisan, structuring the Senate's business primarily to score political points. The one-two punch was delivered with the mannered politeness of the federal judge he once was, but it masked an intense political resolve that was widely seen as helping drive the 41st president from office after one term.

One of the biggest victories for Mitchell over Bush came at the midpoint of their professional relationship, when the senator held firm at the 1990 budget summit until the president agreed to break his "no new taxes" pledge in pursuit of deficit reduction. Passed over for a seat on the Supreme Court and commissioner of baseball, Mitchell retired from the Senate in 1994, afterward helping President Bill Clinton negotiate a peace accord in Northern Ireland.

BILL CLINTON AND BOB DOLE (1995-96)

Clinton had Mitchell on his side for the first two years of his presidency, but then Republicans won control of Congress and for the next 18 months the Senate majority leader was Dole. Although his acerbic wit often had been deployed as the point on a partisan spear, Dole positioned himself as the leading Republican pragmatist in Congress, a moderating influence to the GOP "revolutionaries" in the House and their Speaker, Newt Gingrich. Several planks in the House's "Contact with America" were cast aside by the Republicans as a result, and it was Dole who insisted that the GOP abandon its government shutdown strategy early in 1996 when the public turned against the idea.

Once Dole resigned from Congress that June to concentrate on his new role as the GOP candidate for president, he reconfigured his Senate persona and became more overt in his criticisms of Clinton. Dole's version of the one-two punch was credited with several of the period's biggest legislative achievements, including the bipartisan welfare overhaul. Dole and Clinton recently have teamed up on a new venture, helping to raise $100 million in college scholarship money for children who lost a parent in the Sept. 11 terrorist attacks.

On the economy, Fenn said, "The trick for the Democrats is going to be to balance a pro-growth economic policy which allows for stimulus tax cuts, like accelerated depreciation and tax breaks for companies who hire new workers, and puts off insane Republican policies."

Daschle's pollster Mellman, meanwhile, sees his client as largely unable to play much legislative offense because of his thin Senate majority and GOP control of the House and the White House. Still, Mellman suggests that Daschle may be able to avoid spending the year blocking legislation. "Bush has already done his tax cut and his education plan. We may find that there's not a lot this administration wants to get done this year except prosecute the war on terrorism. And Democrats will support him on that." (2002 CQ Weekly, p. 181)

Among Republicans, some from politically competitive states say they will push the White House to compromise with Daschle.

"There are only going to be 15 to 20 really competitive house seats. So most House members will want a track record of getting things done," said Rep. Fred Upton, R-Mich. During the recent recess, he said he heard "a lot of pressure from constituents to get something done. I did a two-hour radio show and a caller asked, in a nice way, 'What are you Republicans doing to help our families?'"

GOP conservatives appear more likely to press the White House to remain wary of the Senate leader. "Daschle will say to the end of the day he wants a stimulus bill, but that's a fraud," offered Rep. John Shadegg R-Ariz. "It's in his interest to have a slowing economy going into the elections. He wants the party in power to be damaged." ◆

Government Institutions

Indecision, Disagreements Hamper Bush's Foreign Policy

Conservatives lean toward taking more aggressive measures with Arafat

Quick Contents

The crisis in the Middle East has exposed the fault lines within Congress and the Republican ranks over U.S. policy. President Bush can now expect to spend some political capital keeping Congress behind him.

The growing warfare between Israelis and Palestinians that has forced a reluctant Bush administration to adopt a more engaged Mideast policy also has exposed fault lines not only within Congress but within the Republican ranks.

The combination of a spiraling death toll and the early hesitancy of the White House to intervene has altered the dynamics for Bush on Capitol Hill. Even members of his own party now say that the free hand Bush enjoyed on foreign policy is gone — and the high-polling president can expect to have to spend some of his political capital to build support for his ideas.

Since the Sept. 11 terrorist attacks, Bush has steered foreign policy with overwhelming support from Congress. The clarity of the situation — avenging the attacks by ordering U.S. forces to Afghanistan to root out al Qaeda terrorists — left little room for second-guessing. At the same time, Democrats and moderate Republicans praised the president's coalition-building overseas.

But the ambiguity of the Middle East crisis has shown the divisions in Congress, which

CQ Weekly April 6, 2002

in large part mirror the breaks within the administration itself. Hardliners have pushed to stand firmly with Israel and Prime Minister Ariel Sharon while moderates have called for maintaining an open channel with Palestinian President Yasser Arafat to ensure Arab support.

Bush quieted a great deal of the criticism April 4 when he announced that he was sending Secretary of State Colin L. Powell to the Middle East, but the continued uncertainty has shaken the president's political grip on international issues.

"Our foreign policy is in a state of paralysis because of the Middle East," Chuck Hagel, R-Neb., a member of the Senate Foreign Relations Committee, said after Bush's announcement.

A change in congressional support, even by degrees, could hamper Bush's ability to shape foreign policy as the international war on terrorism advances, with the administration pushing to rebuild Afghanistan and possibly confront Iraq.

"There will be a political element to this now. It won't be the united front we saw on Sept. 11," said Rep. Lindsey Graham, R-S.C. "When there's no clear course, Congress

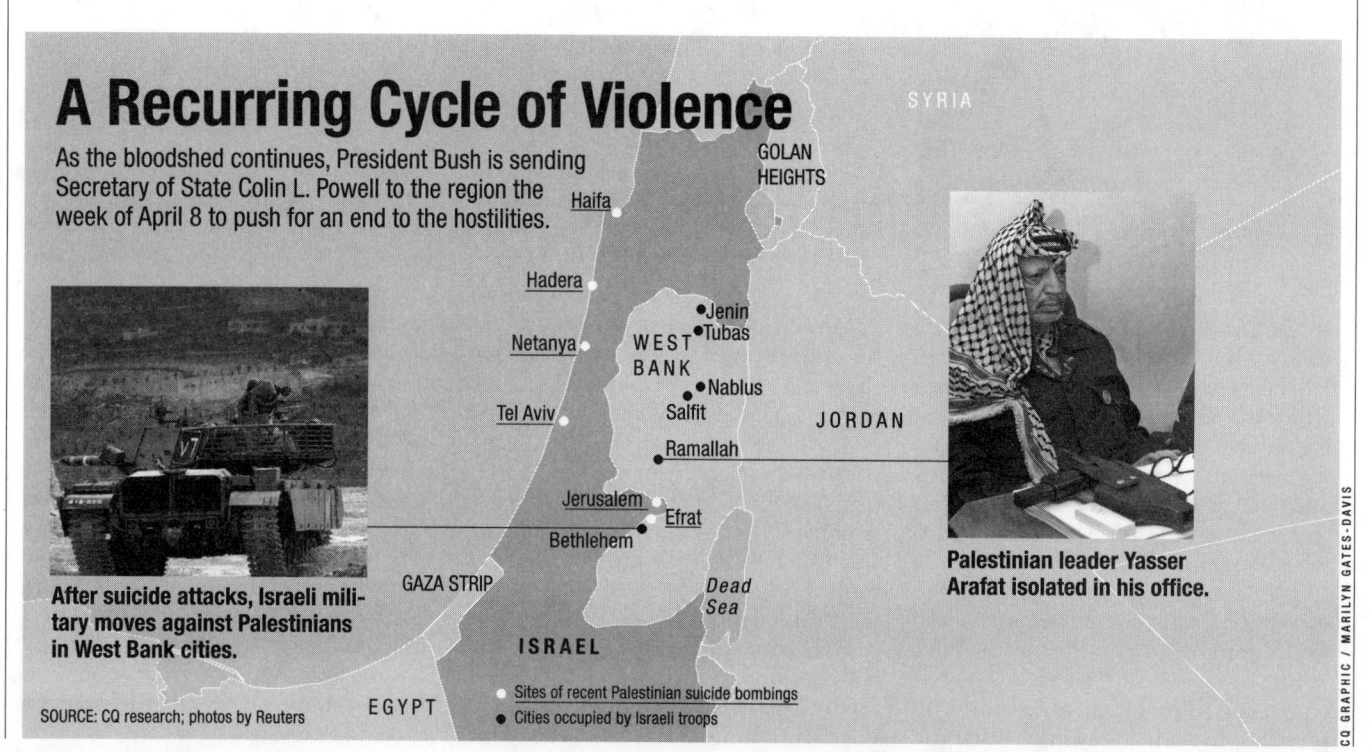

A Recurring Cycle of Violence

As the bloodshed continues, President Bush is sending Secretary of State Colin L. Powell to the region the week of April 8 to push for an end to the hostilities.

After suicide attacks, Israeli military moves against Palestinians in West Bank cities.

Palestinian leader Yasser Arafat isolated in his office.

- Sites of recent Palestinian suicide bombings
- Cities occupied by Israeli troops

SOURCE: CQ research; photos by Reuters

CQ GRAPHIC / MARILYN GATES-DAVIS

Presidency

Key Players in Mideast Policy Debate

Several Democrats and Republicans will be at the forefront of the debate over the Bush administration's Middle East policy.

TOM DASCHLE, D-S.D.
After urging the president to become more personally engaged in Middle East diplomacy, Daschle welcomed President Bush's announcement April 4, saying it was "rightly focused on results" and "puts the onus on Chairman Arafat."

TOM DeLAY, R-TEXAS
Based on a religious belief that Israel has a right to the disputed land, DeLay has rejected negotiations with the Palestinians, saying "Israel is resisting a campaign of death."

DIANNE FEINSTEIN, D-CALIF.
Feinstein urged the Bush administration to embrace a peace proposal by Saudi Crown Prince Abdullah, but she also championed legislation to cut U.S. ties to the Palestinians if they continue carrying out acts of terrorism.

NITA M. LOWEY, D-N.Y.
A strong backer of Israel and top Democrat on the House Foreign Operations Appropriations Subcommittee, Lowey has criticized Bush's commitment to diplomacy.

ARLEN SPECTER, R-PA.
The only Jewish Republican in the Senate, Specter urged Bush to send Secretary of State Colin L. Powell to the Middle East. But he criticized Bush for telling Israel to withdraw its troops before requiring Arafat to call for a halt to suicide bombings.

PATRICK J. LEAHY, D-VT.
Chairman of the Senate Foreign Operations Appropriations Subcommittee, Leahy has been a tough critic of Israel's military actions. He said the more than $2 billion in military aid to that country needs to be reviewed.

tends to weigh in. And there is a state of confusion in foreign policy matters."

Former House Foreign Affairs Committee Chairman Lee H. Hamilton, D-Ind., (1965-99) said Bush's support on international issues was bound to wane as the war on terrorism moved from the more clear-cut goals in Afghanistan to the more diffuse challenges of "phase two" of the war on terror.

"Phase one was the simple part," Hamilton said. "Political opposition was bound to rise as the president moved on to the next objectives in the war on terrorism, which were a little more murky, a little less clear."

Republican Divisions

Conservative Republicans, Bush's strongest allies, have urged the administration not to engage in talks with Arafat. Their views reflect those of Vice President Dick Cheney and Defense Secretary Donald H. Rumsfeld, who, it has been widely reported, have urged a more hawkish approach to the crisis than Powell.

"The time has come to drop the empty pretense that we can serve the region as a mere broker," House Majority Whip Tom DeLay, R-Texas, said in a speech April 3. "Israel is resisting a campaign of death."

DeLay had praised Bush for "resisting the constant calls to force Israel back to the negotiating table, where they will be pressured to grant concessions to terrorists."

But Bush came under fire from Democrats and moderate members of his own party, who urged the president to become more personally involved in resolving the crisis.

"You can't go to bat and expect to hit a home run every time," Arlen Specter of Pennsylvania, the only Jewish Republican in the Senate told CBS' "Early Show" April 3. "I believe it's the secretary of State's job to go and to try. And I don't think he ought to wait to have assurances of success."

Moderate Republicans argue that intervention is needed to maintain U.S. relations with moderate Arab states, prevent a larger terrorist war and preserve the international coalition formed after Sept. 11.

"We've got to move in and do something," said Amo Houghton, R-N.Y., a member of the House International Relations Committee. "In order to conduct a war on terrorism, we've got to have friends in the Arab world."

It is an argument many Democrats endorse.

"Diplomacy is not about trying, failing and going home," said Nita M. Lowey of New York, the ranking member on the House Foreign Operations Appropriations Subcommittee. "It's very delicate."

Until his April 4 announcement, Bush and his top officials had defended Israel's military incursions into Palestinian-controlled areas as self-defense following a wave of suicide bombings — a position DeLay supported.

But Bush clearly shifted tactics in announcing Powell's mission. He used strong words against Arafat, saying the Palestinian leader had "betrayed the hopes of the people he's supposed to lead" by not doing enough to crack down on terrorism and pressed for an immediate cease-fire in the region.

But the president backed a number of the Palestinians' key political demands in calling for the withdrawal of Israeli troops from Palestinian-controlled territories and a halt to the construction of new Israeli settlements in the West Bank and Gaza.

Buying Time

By dispatching Powell to the Middle East, Bush is likely to head off any immediate actions by Congress.

"I think there will be a lot of speechmaking but not much legislating," said Mitch McConnell of Kentucky, ranking Republican on the Senate Foreign Operations Appropriations Subcommittee. "Events are moving so rapidly I think most members of Congress are going to wait to see how it develops."

Government Institutions

But the volatile situation could quickly alter the legislative picture. Before April 4, McConnell had been working with Dianne Feinstein, D-Calif., to revive legislation that would effectively cut many U.S. ties to the Palestinian Authority, including closing its liaison office in Washington, designating the Palestinian Liberation Organization or one of its constituent groups a terrorist organization, and limiting aid to the Palestinians in the West Bank and Gaza to humanitarian assistance.

A version of the bill (S 1409), as contained in the fiscal 2002 foreign operations law (PL 107-115), urged but did not mandate sanctions against the Palestinian Authority — at the request of the White House. (2001 CQ Weekly, p. 3098)

Eliot L. Engel, D-N.Y., a member of the House International Relations Committee, also is drafting legislation that calls for the United States to impose sanctions on Syria.

The U.S. government has described Syria as a sponsor of terrorist groups that have attacked Israel, such as Hezbollah, Hamas and Islamic Jihad.

Bush in his April 4 remarks, said, "It's time . . . for Syria to decide which side of the war against terror it is on." On April 1, Rumsfeld had blamed Syria, Iran and Iraq for encouraging Palestinians to commit acts of terrorism.

Although U.S. claims of Damascus' complicity in terrorism has been around for decades, the United States has continued to maintain normal diplomatic and economic ties with Syria, seeing it as a key regional power.

The United States welcomed Syria as a valuable ally in the 1991 Persian Gulf War and recently it has credited Damascus with providing important intelligence information for the war on terrorism.

Engel's legislation, which he plans to introduce later this month, would require Bush to impose two or more sanctions on Syria, unless it ended its support for terrorism, military interference in Lebanon, development of chemical and biological weapons and violation of a U.N. embargo on Iraq.

The sanctions could include bans on U.S. investment and U.S. exports, elimination of U.S. government financing, a freeze of Syria's assets in the United States and the downgrading of its diplomatic status.

While some lawmakers have directed their attention to the Palestinians and Syria, others have questioned whether the United States should rethink its assistance for Israel.

Senate Appropriations Committee Chairman Robert C. Byrd, D-W.Va., and Foreign Operations Appropriations Subcommittee Chairman Patrick J. Leahy, D-Vt., have raised questions about whether the United States should continue to provide Israel with more than $2 billion in military aid while it carried out incursions into Palestinian areas. (2002 CQ Weekly, p. 720)

Amid the calls for Powell to travel to the Middle East, Reps. Jim Leach, R-Iowa, and Lois Capps, D-Calif., urged Bush to send three former presidents — his father, Bill Clinton and Jimmy Carter — to the region.

Ramifications in Iraq

The crisis also has raised questions about Bush's ability to carry out one of his key foreign policy goals: ousting Iraqi President Saddam Hussein.

Before the increased Mideast violence, Democrats and some moderate Republicans said Bush was too quick to threaten military action against Iraq, and he should put more effort into diplomacy. Proposed steps included reviving U.N. inspections of facilities where Iraq is suspected of developing nuclear, chemical and biological weapons, and enforcing international sanctions against Baghdad. (2002 CQ Weekly, p. 488; 2001 CQ Weekly, p. 2852)

"We should continue to push to get U.N. inspectors back on the ground," Daniel K. Akaka, D-Hawaii, chairman of the Senate Governmental Affairs Subcommittee on International Security, Proliferation and Federal Services, said at a panel hearing on U.S. policy toward Iraq last month. "Keeping Saddam Hussein bottled up and forcing him to confront obstacles in every direction is not a bad thing."

John W. Warner of Virginia, ranking Republican on the Senate Armed Services Committee, warned Bush that he needed to do some political spadework with Congress and the American people before conducting a military operation.

"The fact of the matter is, every day we pick up our paper we read that the president is directing a lot of thought to taking out Saddam Hussein militarily," Warner said at a March 19 panel hearing. "We've got to prepare the American people for the consequences."

But conservative Republicans, such as Sen. Fred Thompson of Tennessee, rejected such arguments.

"To me, the worst thing in the world that could happen is for Saddam to let the inspectors back in," Thompson said. "It just means another cat-and-mouse game, at which point he would run to the United Nations and get his friends there to protect him."

Moderate Republicans said the crisis in Israel now made it much less likely that such an attack could be carried out any time soon.

Hagel pointed to the fact that Cheney, while traveling in the Mideast last month, faced opposition from Arab leaders to any attack on Iraq. Arab leaders also criticized the administration for not doing enough to restrain Israel in its conflict with the Palestinians.

"We don't have any options on Iraq now because of Israel," Hagel said, arguing that the administration could not advance such a proposal in the current environment.

President Helped by Popularity

Still, key Democratic congressional aides said when push comes to shove, Bush ultimately would win support from Congress if he decided to carry out a military operation against Iraq. Recent polls show that the president remains extremely popular.

In fact, Bush's successful command of the military operation in Afghanistan has won him high marks in public opinion polls. Recently, however, approval of his handling of foreign policy has dropped slightly amid the current crisis.

Political analysts said he is likely to retain much of that support as long as U.S. troops are involved in conducting anti-terrorist operations. The terrorist attacks and the war have given Bush far greater control over foreign policy; the Middle East crisis complicates the direction.

"As long as there is a hot war going on, there will be a tectonic shift in power to the president that swamps the degree of criticism he will receive on any foreign policy issue, including the Middle East," said Jeremy Rosner, a former Clinton administration official and an expert on congressional-executive relations in foreign policy. ◆

Presidency

Will a New Era of Deficits Be Bush's Budget Legacy?

Conservatives troubled by red ink's return may fight spending plans

Stevens applauds Bush at the State of the Union address. He is among old guard appropriators likely to restore domestic cuts.

The collision of wartime spending needs and economic recession have provided President Bush with ample rationale for sending the federal budget back into the red for the first time in four years

Bush will deliver his fiscal 2003 spending plan to Congress on Feb. 4 as America's open-ended war against terrorism continues to require military action overseas and expansive security measures at home. And the loss of tax revenues from a nearly one-year-old recession has now erased recent surpluses. The budget that carries $48 billion in new military spending, $38 billion for homeland security and an election-year list of new or increased domestic spending would put the government in deficit by $80 billion next year.

But as economists and policy insiders offer only tempered warnings about running a modest deficit in a time of crisis, there is no apparent failsafe —in either budget politics or procedure — to prevent deficit budgeting from making a long-term return. Bush and his budget director last year found that reaching a deal with Congress meant going $6 billion beyond their spending target. Congressional Democrats have the leverage of a Senate majority to withstand Bush's proposed spending cuts. And congressional Republicans are split on whether to fight the deficit now or later.

And this is the year several influential budget laws, credited with helping tame the previous deficit, expire.

"We are unlocking the gates of fiscal discipline, and we are possibly going to see one of the biggest spending sprees in 30 years," said Stephen Moore, a senior fellow at the libertarian CATO Institute.

Bush's spending desires could come to define his budget legacy as much as his drive last year to cut taxes. The demands of fighting terrorism and protecting citizens appear destined to become a permanent and ever-growing portion of the budget — perhaps as sacrosanct as entitlement programs such as Social Security and Medicare, or the untouchable discretionary programs that include veteran's health care, farm subsidies and medical research.

All in all, spending on discretionary programs — those subject to the annual congressional appropriations process — would grow in Bush's 2003 proposal by about 9 percent.

Targeting for Cuts

To afford this without deviating too far from GOP principles of budget restraint, the president wants to cut or hold constant portions of the budget he believes are less critical. It is no coincidence that many of these cuts are planned in accounts favored by Democrats.

But Congress is sure to resist many of Bush's proposed cuts in the federal bureaucracy, and ignore again his call for curbing the congressional habit of earmarking federal dollars for parochial projects. Bush's plans for the Pentagon budget are so ambitious it seems inevitable that he will have to trade some military money for domestic programs — or accept appropriated spending even greater than the approximately

Government Institutions

$750 billion he is expected to call for.

Sen. Robert C. Byrd, D-W.Va., who is chairman of the Appropriations Committee, said he will not sacrifice other government operations to pay for Bush's defense request. "Before we rush headlong into massive increases in Defense Department spending, we ought to take a long, hard look at the priorities in the budget," he said. "I hope that this increase for the Pentagon does not come at the expense of education, health care, Social Security and job training initiatives that are so critical in these difficult economic times."

Byrd is likely to have allies among Republican spenders such as Sen. Ted Stevens of Alaska, the top Republican on the Appropriations Committee.

Bush's plan is undergirded with an optimism that fiscal discipline on domestic spending will be enough to return the budget to balance.

"To win the war, protect the homeland and revitalize our economy, our budget will run a deficit that will be small and short-term, so long as Congress restrains spending and acts in a fiscally responsible way," Bush said in his Jan. 29 State of the Union address.

But failing that, conditions are aligned, to some degree, against other remedies. During the deep deficits of President Ronald Reagan's administration, budgets were guided by the belief that fiscal policy could sufficiently stimulate economic expansion to grow the federal budget out of debt. Bush makes the same case about the value of the tax cut last year and the need for a stimulus package this year. But unlike Reagan's military build-up paired with domestic spending cuts, Bush's budget contemplates a new, higher baseline for spending to accommodate a long-term war footing.

In addition, the loss of surpluses can put upward pressure on long-term interest rates, which inhibits economic growth. Although rates are affected by a host of other factors, high levels of federal debt can push up interest rates by increasing the competition for investment capital.

"There is no question that my basic desire is for maintaining as low a level of the national debt as we can, because I think it has very great economic advantages," Federal Reserve Chairman Alan Greenspan said at a Jan. 24 Senate Budget Committee hearing.

A Republican Fight

Of course, it remains true that the deficits expected in the coming years do not look at all like those of 10 to 20 years ago, when interest payments on the debt had become a significant burden on the budget.

Economists such as Robert D. Reischauer, president of the Urban Institute think tank and director of the Congressional Budget Office from 1989 to 1995, say that running deficits in the range of $100 billion a year for the next several years is not a fiscal catastrophe. Such deficits are actually relatively small when calculated as a percentage of the size of the U.S. economy, which many economists believe is the most appropriate way to measure deficits and the debt.

"The deficits that we're experiencing today are not even close cousins of those structural imbalances that we faced in the 1980s and in the early part of the 1990s," Reischauer said.

Despite the relatively modest size of the deficits in Bush's budget, conservative Republicans in Congress are not willing to accept the return of red ink without a fight. Although House Speaker J. Dennis Hastert, R-Ill., and Budget Chairman Jim Nussle, R-Iowa, support Bush's deficit budget, the party's fiscal hawks are not on board.

"I think you can balance the budget by identifying programs that are wasting money right now and programs that don't work," said John Shadegg of Arizona, the chairman of the Republican Study Committee, a group of the most conservative GOP members in the House. "I'm simply not ready to surrender on that issue yet."

The looming deficits were a topic of anxious debate at a House GOP strategy retreat Jan. 30-Feb. 1 at the Greenbrier resort in West Virginia. "The discussion was how do you balance the expense of fighting a war with the desire of many people to keep to the promise of a balanced budget," said Rep. Rodney Frelinghuysen, R-N.J., of a Jan. 31 session on the budget.

A powerful ally for those opposing a deficit budget is Majority Whip Tom DeLay of Texas. "A balanced budget is the right thing to do, philosophically and politically," a DeLay aide said.

Yet even the conservative study group would support deficits caused by tax cuts in an economic stimulus plan, and another group that typically presses for fiscal restraint, the "Blue Dog" coalition, might step back from the debate given the limited range of realistic options for balancing the budget. The Blue Dogs, a group of fiscally conservative House Democrats, typically offer on the House floor a centrist budget alternative that falls somewhere between the primary Democratic and Republican budget blueprints.

By ruling out future tax increases or even a repeal of tax cuts slated to go into effect in the years ahead, the president has so narrowed the nation's fiscal options that a realistic debate over solutions to the deficit is unlikely, said Blue Dog Jim Turner of Texas. As a result, the group might not offer a budget alternative this year. "The president has to chart that course," said Turner.

The Remaining Agenda

Bush took office promising not only to cut taxes but also to overhaul Medicare and Social Security to prepare for the retirement of the Baby Boom generation. But like his predecessor, Bill Clinton, who was elected after promising middle-

> "Before we rush headlong into massive increases in Defense Department spending, we ought to take a long, hard look at the priorities in the budget."
>
> — Sen. Robert C. Byrd, D-W.Va.

Presidency

Deficits (or Surpluses) as a Percentage of GDP

The return of budget deficits is unwelcome political news for President Bush. But the economic news is not nearly as bad. White House projected deficits of $106 billion in fiscal 2002 and $80 billion in fiscal 2003 would be about 1 percent of the size of the gross domestic product. By that standard, such deficits would be far smaller than the deficits of the 1970s, 1980s and 1990s.

(federal budget deficits or surpluses as a percentage of gross domestic product; fiscal years)

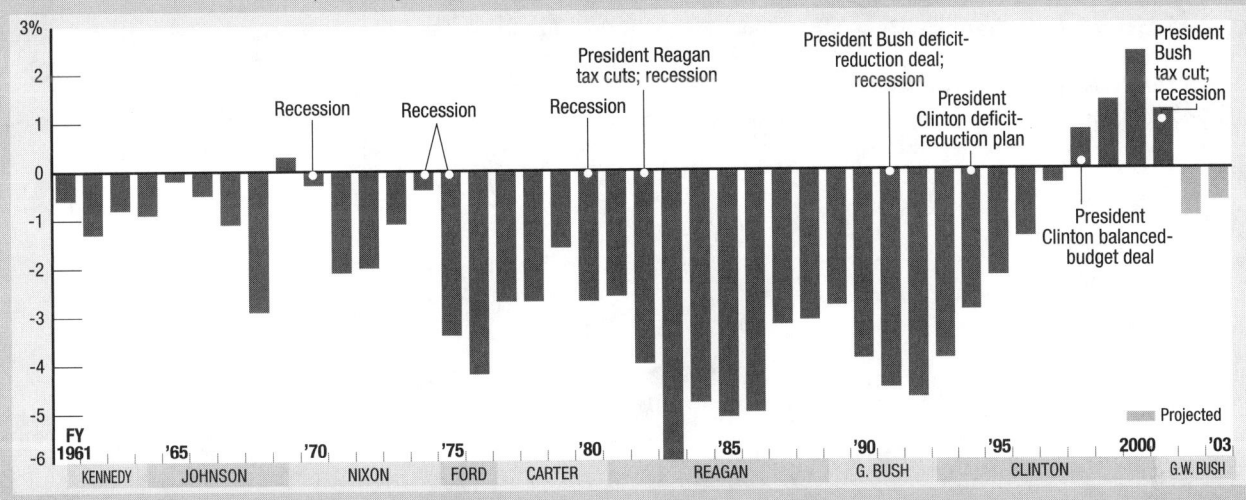

Note: Before fiscal 1977, federal fiscal years began on July 1.
SOURCE: Office of Management and Budget

---

class tax cuts but whose plan soon was abandoned to fight a spiraling budget deficit, Bush's goals could very easily be threatened by the deficit.

"We gave away a once-in-a-lifetime opportunity to address the very large challenges in dealing with restructuring Social Security and Medicare," Reischauer said.

The return of deficits makes it much more difficult to transform Medicare and Social Security in any meaningful and politically achievable ways, all of which will entail some transition costs, Reischauer said. Plans for a prescription drug benefit for seniors, which Bush has proposed in a significantly slimmed-down form, are iffy at best, and broader assaults on systemic problems in federal retirement programs appear to be off the table altogether.

In his widely watched State of the Union address, Bush tried to reassure the nation that some of the things Washington promised during the heady days of budget surpluses have survived. *(2002 CQ Weekly, p. 285)*

He spoke of plans to help the unemployed, strengthen education and spend more on veterans' health. He has proposed expanding food stamp eligibility for legal immigrants at a cost of about $2 billion over 10 years, and he announced the creation of a new "USA Freedom Corps" to organize a wide range of volunteer activities. The program is slated to cost $560 million in fiscal 2003.

The National Institutes of Health also would get a hefty spending increase, and Bush has proposed allocating about $100 billion over 10 years to help improve access to health insurance, primarily through tax credits.

In addition, the administration agrees that it still owes New York at least $9 billion for cleanup and rebuilding efforts in lower Manhattan, and probably even more.

And Bush reiterated his pledge to pursue a Medicare prescription drug program, pledging $190 billion over the next decade, starting with the neediest seniors. That is a far cry from last year's budget, in which Bush stated that "Medicare should assure that all seniors have affordable access to prescription drug coverage." Democrats blasted the $190 billion plan as insufficient, and even Republicans had budgeted $300 billion for a similar plan as part of the fiscal 2002 congressional budget resolution.

The White House has thus far kept a lid on the elements of the budget that require sacrifice. But when the document is released Feb. 4, it will contain much bad news for Cabinet departments and agencies that quickly grew accustomed to increasing budgets during the brief surplus period.

The shift in focus is reflected in the bottom line for departments including Commerce, Interior and Labor, whose budgets would freeze or shrink under Bush's blueprint, say congressional sources familiar with his plans.

Cuts of about $9 billion also are in store for federal highway spending, because of a reduction in federal gas tax receipts and other revenue sources for the Federal Highway Trust Fund. *(2002 CQ Weekly, p. 247)*

Last year, Bush's efforts to hold back spending were relatively modest. His fiscal 2002 budget proposed a boost in appropriated spending of about 7 percent, fueled in large part by a $27 billion increase in the Pentagon budget.

But a confrontation with Congress over spending never materialized after Sept. 11. Instead, the White House and Congress swiftly agreed to a $40 billion emergency supplemental appropriation and a $6 billion add-on to ease passage of the remaining 2002 domestic spending bills. It took veto promises by Bush to hold the line even there, as lawmakers such as Byrd pressed for ad-

Government Institutions

Daniels' Domestic Austerity Drive May Further Strain Relations With Hill

Davis Stockman. Richard G. Darman. Leon E. Panetta.

All three former budget directors still loom large in Washington's collective memory. Stockman helped President Ronald Reagan sell the novel notion that he could cut taxes and greatly expand military spending while balancing the budget. Darman was a key figure behind the 1990 budget deal that broke President George Bush's "read my lips" tax pledge, which improved the nation's balance sheet but cost Bush re-election. Panetta helped engineer a politically costly budget bill that helped President Clinton balance the budget on his watch.

The man currently in the role, Mitchell E. Daniels Jr., has yet to elevate himself in similar fashion. Last year, other officials in the administration took the lead on the central feature of President Bush's first budget, a $1.35 trillion tax cut (PL 107-16). Meanwhile, Daniels' impolitic efforts to restrain spending thoroughly alienated appropriators. Asked last year what the Hoosier-born Daniels could do to repair his relations with Congress, top Senate Appropriations Committee Republican Ted Stevens of Alaska snapped: "Go back to Indiana."

The presentation of the administration's second budget Feb. 4 will present a fresh opportunity for Daniels to make his mark. With major changes in tax law unlikely, Daniels' spending blueprint will take center stage. His promises to squeeze a wide range of domestic programs will sorely test his already strained relations with Capitol Hill.

"Daniels has been taking a beating, no doubt about it," said Allen Schick, a University of Maryland professor of public policy and an expert on the federal budget. Part of Daniels' problem, Schick said, is that it is typically easier to be a budget director for a Democratic president than a Republican one. With few exceptions, a person pushing for more spending will be better-liked — particularly within his own administration — than one trying to take money away.

Daniels' difficulties last year may have been compounded by inexperience. Although he was a top policy and political aide in the Senate and the Reagan administration in the

"A person pushing for more spending will be better-liked — particularly within his own administration — than one trying to take money away."

1970s and '80s, he had almost no experience with federal budgeting before taking the helm of the Office of Management and Budget (OMB). *(2001 CQ Weekly, p. 184)*

Good Cop, Bad Cop

While Bush has spent the last few weeks touting the big increases in his budget for the military, "homeland security" and a handful of domestic programs such as medical research, Daniels has been warning of the lean times ahead for many other agencies under the president's proposal. It will be Daniels' job to try to make the tough decisions stick. "The president needs people who are willing to take the heat," Schick said.

Even last year's relatively modest administration effort to restrain domestic spending generated considerable ill will between Daniels and the appropriators on Capitol Hill.

One of Daniels' first priorities was an attempt to curb lawmakers' appetite for earmarking taxpayer funds for parochial projects back home. If anything, the practice got worse.

Still, Daniels pressed ahead, despite enduring severe criticism from members of both parties. He made a series of comments — some of which he now says he regrets — complaining about the entrenched ways and pro-spending mindset of congressional appropriators. "Their motto is, 'Don't just stand there, spend something,' " Daniels told The Wall Street Journal late last year. "This is the only way they feel relevant."

James W. Dyer, chief of staff of the House Appropriations Committee, took issue with that. "As an employee of the Appropriations Committee, I bitterly resented his comments," Dyer said in an interview. "He may have just been trying to be cute, I don't know. But it wasn't taken that way."

Daniels has suggested that he will try a less confrontational approach with Congress this year, although he has vowed to continue fighting earmarks.

If OMB has not yet instilled fear on Capitol Hill, the same may not be true elsewhere. Daniels continues to deride federal agencies for seeking extra funds by reclassifying routine expenditures as homeland defense.

And despite the cuts he will propose in the budget, not a single federal department appealed OMB's funding decision to the president, Daniels said. "This was a very, very collaborative operation," Daniels said. "I was surprised at how few disagreements there were."

In fact, given Bush's talk on the budget, agency heads probably assumed it would have been futile to appeal to the president. But when appropriations season rolls around, the federal bureaucracy is certain to find much more sympathy on Capitol Hill than they are getting from Daniels.

Presidency

Budget Chairman Nussle, speaking to reporters after Bush's Jan. 29 State of the Union address, is among those willing to accept short-term deficits. Some conservatives in his party want immediate balance, an uphill task given the demands of war and homeland security.

ditional emergency spending for New York and for homeland defense.

Deficits as Leverage

The central question is whether the emergence of deficits will help the White House enforce Bush's 2003 budget or give license to a spending spree. The point man in the debate is Office of Management and Budget Director Mitchell E. Daniels Jr., whose attempts to rein in appropriators last year were met with outright hostility. (*Box, p. 66*)

One problem for Daniels as he tries to push the budget through Congress is that Bush has undercut him at times by saying "yes" to members of Congress not long after Daniels sent a different message. Such was the case recently with farm programs, when Bush promised farm-state Republicans — over Daniels' objections — that the administration would support $74 billion in farm payments over the next 10 years.

And in last year's spending negotiations, Vice President Dick Cheney trudged to the Hill to try to settle fights between Daniels and the appropriators. He sealed agreement to add the $6 billion to domestic appropriations after the relationship between Daniels and the appropriators had become too poisoned. On another occasion, when appropriators were pushing the administration to increase the size of the $40 billion supplemental, Bush stood firm — but appropriators nevertheless felt they needed to hear it from a higher source than Daniels to be sure they were getting the final word from the administration.

The red ink arrives as several budget laws are about to expire. Those laws — year-by-year discretionary spending caps and pay-as-you-go requirements (PAYGO) — were created as part of the 1990 deficit reduction law (PL 101-508) and were extended in 1993 and 1997 (PL 103-66, PL 105-33). PAYGO requires that tax cuts or spending increases beyond those in budget targets must be offset with revenue increases or spending cuts elsewhere. (*1990 Almanac, p. 161; 1993 Almanac, p. 124; 1997 Almanac, p. 2-48*)

The expiration of those laws means the jobs of Senate Budget Committee Chairman Kent Conrad, D-N.D., and his House counterpart Nussle will be more significant this year.

Their fiscal 2003 congressional budget resolution would set a limit on the amount of money available to appropriators. But if the Democratic Senate and the Republican House reach an impasse and no budget resolution is adopted, appropriators can bring bills to the floor without having to live within any overall limits set by the full House and Senate.

"If Mr. Nussle and Mr. Conrad can't come to an agreement . . . then there is no allocation to the Appropriations Committees, and Katie bar the door," said G. William Hoagland, Republican staff director for the Senate Budget Committee.

No Budget Resolution?

Lawmakers and staff aides, as well as outside observers, say the House and Senate will be unable to reach consensus on a budget resolution. Hoagland, however, is more optimistic.

Bush's budget allows so much additional money for defense that Democrats may go along with the overall total for the opportunity to reallocate resources more to their liking later.

Indeed, the president's budget contains several pots of money that might be tapped for domestic programs. The administration's proposal for missile defense will be highly controversial, Hoagland said, and some of that money might be reallocated elsewhere.

The same is true of Bush's proposed $10 billion "war reserve," an idea one key Democrat was quick to reject. "To put in $10 billion based on nothing — that's without precedent," Conrad said.

James W. Dyer, GOP chief of staff for the House Appropriations Committee, also indicated his doubt that Congress will approve the full measure of Bush's proposed $48 billion increase in defense spending. "If there's going to be more money, I think they're going to have to have reforms," said Dyer. He was reiterating a complaint lodged by both Democrats and Republicans early last year that the administration had failed to fully explain and justify the increases Bush was requesting for defense.

The events of Sept. 11 erased those criticisms in an instant, and Congress quickly approved the president's defense requests. But such concerns could rise again as Congress returns to a more routine fight over spending priorities, particularly in an election year.

Dyer said Daniels is not likely to get support on Capitol Hill for his budget by using performance evaluations on federal agencies, since many of them have strong advocates in Congress.

Dyer, who has had a rocky relationship with Daniels, said he expects OMB's performance evaluations to have little impact on appropriators. "We have a system in place for doing this, and despite all its warts, I can't find a way to improve on it," Dyer said. "My thinking is we'll do business this year the same way we did it last year, when all the smoke clears." ◆

Government Institutions

Powell's Congressional Army Guards His Flank

Moderate in Bush administration courts allies on the Hill

Netanyahu told senators April 10 that military action is the only way Israel can defend itself against Palestinian attacks. "There is no political solution for terror. You have to defeat terror militarily in order to have a political process," he said. Attending the session were (left to right) Feinstein, Fred Thompson, R-Tenn.; Mike DeWine, R-Ohio; Ben Nelson, D-Neb.; Joseph I. Lieberman, D-Conn., and George Allen, R-Va.

It was a moment when politics ignored the proverbial boundary of the waters' edge. After appeals from world leaders and Congress to get more deeply involved in the Israeli-Palestinian conflict, President Bush on April 7 dispatched Secretary of State Colin L. Powell to the Middle East in a bid to end the fighting.

But as Powell huddled with Arab and European leaders of Morocco and Spain, an unexpected critic of the Bush administration surfaced on Capitol Hill on April 10. Former Israeli Prime Minister Benjamin Netanyahu, speaking to a gathering of 20 senators, pummeled Bush for abandoning the "moral clarity" of his war on terrorism by pressuring Israel to halt its military offensive in the West Bank and by initially approving a Powell meeting with Palestinian leader Yasser Arafat. That meeting was postponed after a suicide bombing April 12.

"Until last week, I was absolutely certain that the United States would adhere to its principles and lead the free world to a decisive victory," Netanyahu told the lawmakers in remarks broadcast on cable television. "Today, I, too, have my concerns. I am concerned that when it comes to terror directed against Israel, the moral and strategic clarity that is so crucial to victory is being lost."

For supporters of Powell's peace efforts, it was a crude show of disrespect at a time when the secretary was attempting to conduct some delicate diplomacy. But, as it turns out, it could have been worse. Netanyahu was denied a grander platform before the Senate Foreign Relations Committee. Jesse Helms of North Carolina, the panel's ranking Republican, had sought to bring Netanyahu to testify before the committee, but Chairman Joseph R. Biden Jr., D-Del., nixed the idea out of deference to Powell. Sen. Jon Kyl, R-Ariz., extended the invitation for the informal session.

Biden's willingness to guard Powell's flank on this matter grew out of a concerted effort by the secretary and his top advisers to aggressively cultivate congressional allies. Under Powell, a former chairman of the Joint Chiefs of Staff, the State Department has worked hard to develop a warm relationship with both Republicans and Democrats on Capitol Hill, hearing out their concerns and seeking their counsel at critical times. Biden is Powell's closest ally on the Hill.

These efforts have come in a year in which relations between the administration and Congress are increasingly testy, with lawmakers complaining that the president is attempting to run too much of the government without seeking congressional permission or even guidance. For more than a month, Congress and the White House have been tussling over the seemingly innocuous question of whether Homeland Security Director Tom Ridge should explain Bush's domestic security plans in formal congressional testimony.

But on matters of foreign policy, the implications of a Congress with wounded sensibilities could be enormous. Whatever next step the president decides to take in the war

CQ Weekly April 13, 2002

Bureaucracy

on terrorism, Bush is going to need congressional backing. And questions such as whether Ridge testifies, or whether the White House provides records of energy task force meetings, pale in comparison if lawmakers spurn Bush's efforts in the Middle East to protest what they view as the administration's lack of respect for Congress.

In the case of Netanyahu, Congress was using the event to express once more what many lawmakers feel is the administration's repeated failure to consult with them.

Some of Israel's strongest allies on Capitol Hill already have mobilized to make sure Bush does not push Israeli Prime Minister Ariel Sharon too hard. In the Senate, Dianne Feinstein, D-Calif., and Mitch McConnell, R-Ky., are threatening to advance legislation (S 1409) that would sever ties between the United States and Arafat's Palestinian Authority. In the House, Gary L. Ackerman, D-N.Y., has prepared a similar measure (HR 1795) that would force the president to punish the Palestinian Authority with sanctions.

Rice generally has limited her contacts with Congress, prompting criticism on Capitol Hill.

The White House, with the help of moderate congressional leaders, for now has persuaded Israel's allies to hold off action on these measures while Powell is in the Middle East, but administration officials are clearly on the defensive. With the Netanyahu visit, for example, the White House chose not to block him from speaking, fearing that doing so would only further highlight the deep divisions on Capitol Hill over Bush's policies.

"We decided it would be a bigger story if the White House canceled the meeting," a senior White House official said. "There are certain realities on Capitol Hill when it comes to Middle East policies."

Consultation Complaints From the Hill

Powell's warm relations with lawmakers mark a dramatic change from past administrations when simmering hostility was the norm. This was partly the fault of lawmakers who saw little benefit to their districts or states from State Department programs and partly the fault of career diplomats who regarded lawmakers as provincial.

But that has changed. Today, thanks to the efforts of Powell and his deputy, Richard L. Armitage, the State Department enjoys an often symbiotic relationship with Capitol Hill. Powell has granted his friends in Congress a say in foreign policy before final decisions have been made, rewarding them with prestige among their colleagues in a field that had lost its cachet. (Box, p. 70)

At the same time, Powell and Armitage have won congressional support for increasing the department's budget and substantially boosting foreign aid, despite longstanding Hill skepticism. And with the help of their congressional allies, they also have managed to reclaim the State Department's role as a moderate national security player in an administration more inclined to take hardline stands on issues regarding Iraq, North Korea and the Middle East.

While the State Department wins praise from lawmakers for its new willingness to cooperate, both parties have criticized the White House for what they consider its inaccessibility.

Senate Majority Leader Tom Daschle, D-S.D., complained April 10 that he had not talked to National Security Adviser Condoleezza Rice during the previous three weeks — even as fighting between Israelis and Palestinians escalated into a crisis.

And Rice only met with House Democrats on April 11 after they complained about being excluded from a briefing she gave to their Republican counterparts the day before.

The result is free-agent moves, such as the Kyl-sponsored invitation to Netanyahu, that have the potential to be embarrassing for the president.

Daschle warned reporters April 11 that such episodes were bound to recur unless Rice made it a habit to consult with Congress. He called for "continued briefings, continued information from the administration . . . on a daily basis, given the extraordinary importance and complexity" of foreign policy issues.

"Where I think the administration could do better is in consulting with the congressional leaders on major security issues, including the president and the national security adviser," agreed Senate Armed Services Committee Chairman Carl Levin, D-Mich. "In terms of seeking input, or reaction to proposed courses of action, there's been very, very little of it." In the House, Minority Leader Richard A. Gephardt, D-Mo., echoed the call.

But it is not only Democrats who are complaining. Senior Republican lawmakers have groused to Rice that they cannot properly brief their colleagues on the administration's national security policies because they have been unable to communicate with her or her aides.

"I had better relations with the Clinton White House than I do with these people," grumbled one senior Republican senator. He recalled regular discussions with former national security adviser Samuel R. Berger, as well as several lengthy meetings he had attended with former President Bill Clinton during the Kosovo and Bosnia conflicts.

The White House has responded defensively to these complaints. "Sometimes, you just have to recognize that in Washington no amount of consultation is ever enough for the Hill," White House spokesman Ari Fleischer said April 11.

The spokesman then shifted blame to lawmakers, suggesting that their complaints were disingenuous. "There's often an issue where people go up to the Hill to brief and very few members of Congress even show up," he said.

Moreover, the White House argues that it is not the job of the National Security Council to keep Congress informed. That, says NSC spokesman Sean McCormack, is primarily the job of the State Department and the Pentagon.

McCormack said that when Rice took office, she deliberately cut the role of the agency's congressional liaison office. He said Rice wanted the NSC, which had ballooned in size

Government Institutions

As International Issues Heat Up, Foreign Affairs Panels Regain Prestige

When Nebraska Republican Chuck Hagel was elected to the Senate in 1996, one of his first committee choices was the Foreign Relations panel. Friends told him he would be wasting his time.

"Everybody questioned why I wanted to be on it. They said, 'Are you crazy? That's a throwaway committee,'" Hagel recalled in an interview. "We actually had to persuade people to agree to come on it because we couldn't fill all the slots."

Just over a decade ago, assignment to the congressional committees focused on foreign policy was a prestigious posting that made statesmen of former Sen. Arthur Vandenberg, R-Mich. (1928-51), who forged bipartisan support for the Marshall Plan and NATO, and former Sen. J. William Fulbright, D-Ark. (House 1943-45; Senate 1945-74), who used it as a forum to rally opposition to the Vietnam War.

But the end of the Cold War and a sharp drop in the public's interest in foreign policy turned the respective committees into second or third choices, with lawmakers favoring Appropriations or Budget.

The numbers tell the tale. Between 1948 and 1990, 12 senators voluntarily left the Senate Foreign Relations Committee, according to George W. Grayson, a professor of government at the College of William & Mary. During the 1990s, that number rose to 18.

Lawmakers on the foreign policy panels, however, have noticed a change in attitude since the Sept. 11 terrorist attacks and the Bush administration's campaign against terrorism. Those events have sparked an interest in foreign policy among the American people and when constituents care, so do lawmakers.

"The war on terrorism is going to keep this [interest] long-lasting," said Sen. Dianne Feinstein, D-Calif., a former Foreign Relations member who left for a seat on Appropriations.

The determining factor for Congress will be the response to openings on the committees in the next year.

"Things are going to reverse because of the new relevancy of world affairs," Hagel said. "I predict that in a couple of years, you're going to see Foreign Relations become one of the most hotly sought-after committee assignments."

Another measure will be the number of overseas trips. During the 1990s, lawmakers showed little interest in foreign travel, reflected in the sharp decline in the number of congressional delegations, or CODELs — travel groups authorized by leaders or committee chairmen. The trips were derided as costly taxpayer-funded junkets. But during the recent congressional recess, lawmakers traveled to Afghanistan and Africa.

A renewed interest could prove a mixed blessing for the executive branch. On many foreign policy issues, lawmakers have deferred to the White House.

"The potential [for greater confrontation] will be there, because you'll have a better-informed Congress and a more powerful Congress in terms of expertise," said Sen. Fred Thompson, R-Tenn., a former Foreign Relations member now on the Intelligence Committee.

To be sure, the surge in interest could prove episodic — a reaction to the explosiveness of the current Middle East situation and lawmakers' natural inclination to focus on front-burner issues.

"I've seen this happen on other issues — interest usually abates when some other issue emerges," said Sen. Christopher J. Dodd, D-Conn., a longtime Foreign Relations member.

Increased GOP Interest

An increasing number of Republican candidates for the Senate have mentioned a desire to tackle foreign policy matters if they are elected in November, said Bill Frist, R-Tenn., chairman of the National Republican Senatorial Committee.

"The interest in international relations and intelligence is much heightened," Frist said. "People are saying that in the Senate you have an opportunity to deal with these issues and to have an impact, more so than in the House."

Lawmakers who acknowledged they never had much interest in the and responsibility under Berger, to be pared back and focused on advising the president, not reaching out to the public or Congress.

Rice's Narrow Circle

Rice generally has limited her contacts with the Hill to a brace of trusted lawmakers, including several GOP congressional leaders, Biden, Sen. Chuck Hagel, R-Neb., House Intelligence Committee Chairman Porter J. Goss, R-Fla., and Rep. Tom Lantos, D-Calif. (*Chart, p. 72*)

One of Rice's most unheralded but perhaps most important contacts is Goss. Intelligence committee chairmen typically enjoy warmer relations with the White House than other lawmakers because of their need to be informed on highly classified matters. But Goss, a former CIA agent, has an unusually trusting relationship with CIA Director and former Hill staffer George J. Tenet, which has given him a broad role in the administration's decision-making process. (*2001 CQ Weekly, p. 2621*)

"Sometimes I feel I work for the executive branch more than Congress," Goss said, pointing out how he spent half of the congressional recess carrying out administration missions in Morocco, Malta and Crete.

Likewise, House Republican Policy Committee Chairman Christopher Cox, R-Calif., said Bush had invited him and other members of the House leadership for a weekend at Camp David in February to hash out national security issues with the president, Vice President Dick Cheney and Tenet.

Bureaucracy

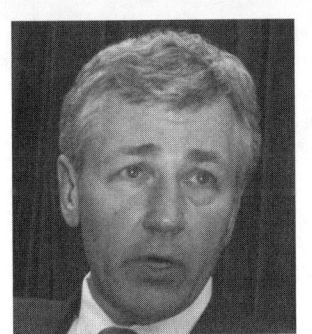

> "I predict that in a couple of years, you're going to see Foreign Relations become one of the most hotly sought-after committee assignments."
>
> — Sen. Chuck Hagel, R-Neb.

subject suddenly are drafting legislation. Evan Bayh, D-Ind., introduced a bill (S 2066) in March that would prohibit U.S. financial assistance and commercial arms exports to countries that do not support the war on international terrorism.

"We may actually see a perceptual change [about foreign policy] on the part of the American people," said Bayh, an Intelligence Committee member who has been mentioned as a potential Democratic presidential candidate in 2004.

House Intelligence Committee Chairman Porter J. Goss, R-Fla., said the list of lawmakers wanting to join his committee has grown since Sept. 11 — and that a number of current members have let him know they want to stay on the panel.

"At any given moment, I probably have two dozen or so people who are seriously interested" in a committee slot, Goss said. "And I get a lot of other people hearing that there's a list to get on and asking about it."

Goss attributed the increased popularity to the growing realization among colleagues "that you can't do your job only knowing Fortress America."

A test of the renewed interest will come in January. Jesse Helms of North Carolina, the ranking Republican on the Senate Foreign Relations Committee, has announced he will retire after five terms. Whether a line forms to fill that vacancy remains to be seen.

A spokesman for Richard G. Lugar of Indiana, who would become the committee's top Republican in the 108th Congress, said he was not aware of any lawmakers approaching Lugar about the opening.

"People are waiting until the dust settles" from the November elections, spokesman Andy Fisher said.

Institutional rules play a key role in committee popularity with lawmakers. Party practices limit senators to service on only one of the so-called elite or "Super A" committees, which include Appropriations, Armed Services and Finance, in addition to Foreign Relations.

From the 1940s through the 1970s, the firsthand experience that many U.S. residents had with the world — through military service in World War II, Korea and Vietnam — helped keep foreign policy as a primary concern.

"Members of Congress had substantial parts of their constituency that had fought and served in the European theater and elsewhere," Dodd said. "They came back home personally involved and committed to those questions."

Senators periodically have discussed downgrading the Foreign Relations Committee to make it more attractive to those wanting to serve on other "super A" committees.

Thompson served on Foreign Relations after he was first elected to the Senate in 1994 but later left to join the Finance Committee, the tax-writing panel that vies with Appropriations for being the most popular with lawmakers.

"I would have kept [the Foreign Relations seat] if I could have, but I had to give it up to do some other things I wanted to do," he said.

Thompson has stayed active on foreign policy matters. But other current and former lawmakers lament that few of their colleagues have developed the persistence needed to work on international issues.

"It just takes a lot of determination — you need people who are going to stick with it for a year or two," former Majority Leader Bob Dole, R-Kan. (House 1961-69; Senate 1969-96), said in an interview. "I loved foreign policy when I was here, and I did a lot of it — maybe more than I should have."

Outside experts also point to the role of two senior Republicans on the Senate Foreign Relations Committee, Hagel and Richard G. Lugar of Indiana.

"The leadership in the Senate in foreign policy is gradually moving toward people like Hagel, who, for a relative freshman, is becoming more of a voice they can talk to," said retired Gen. Brent Scowcroft, national security adviser to Bush's father and now chairman of the President's Foreign Intelligence Advisory Board.

But if Rice has deliberately limited herself to a narrow circle of confidants in Congress, Powell has cast a wide net on Capitol Hill, using the same inclusive style that made him so popular among lawmakers as chairman of the Joint Chiefs of Staff.

John W. Warner of Virginia, ranking Republican on the Senate Armed Services Committee, likes to boast, "I have known Powell since he was a major."

Helms is fond of reminiscing about an exchange of notes he quietly conducted with Ronald Reagan while Powell, then the president's national security adviser, was conducting a briefing.

Impressed, Helms scribbled a note to Reagan that suggested a promotion for Powell. "Joint Chiefs?" he wrote. Similarly wowed, Reagan wrote back and underlined "Chairman."

Still, Powell has not solely relied on his reputation and personal charm to sway Congress. Using the discipline he learned in the military, he has mobilized many former Pentagon aides there and deployed them to Capitol Hill to improve the State Department's poor standing.

71

Government Institutions

"Traditionally relations between Congress and the State Department have been awful," said a key House foreign policy aide who also has worked in the executive branch. "We have never had better relations with the State Department than we do now."

Powell's Troops

Powell's principal weapon has been his deputy, Armitage, a muscular former Marine who is so close to Powell that he will refer to the secretary as "homeboy" in private conversations. Unlike previous deputies, Armitage, who also served as an aide to former Sen. Bob Dole, R-Kan. (House 1961-69, Senate 1969-96), has made keeping a strong relationship with Congress one of his primary responsibilities.

Armitage talks to Biden and his House counterpart, International Relations Committee Chairman Henry J. Hyde, R-Ill., as often as three times a week. But he also talks regularly with other lawmakers who do not oversee his department, such as Warner and Sen. John McCain, R-Ariz.

Armitage's blunt style and barracks vocabulary, his many longstanding friendships with lawmakers and his willingness to engage with even the most junior lawmaker have made him extraordinarily popular on Capitol Hill.

"He knows how to stroke people," McCain said.

Lugar pointed out that Armitage volunteers a much-appreciated service to lawmakers. He will call to brief them on foreign policy issues before they appear on national television, helping them sound informed and, not incidentally, ensuring that Powell's agenda receives maximum exposure.

These efforts at outreach are part of a broader strategy by Powell and Armitage to build a constituency on the Hill for a department that has little pork to offer as an enticement. By engaging lawmakers at an early stage, the two top diplomats have successfully won crucial congressional support for their policies and programs.

Specifically, Powell and Armitage broke the stranglehold on State's relations with Congress that had traditionally been exercised by the department's bureau of legislative affairs. Paul V. Kelly, who now heads that bureau, said Armitage contemptuously referred to the office as the "Stasi," which was the onetime East German secret police.

White House Communications

The Bush Administration is often accused of going its own way without consulting Congress on key issues. Still, there are members of the House and Senate who have regular communication with the executive branch. They include:

Leadership
Democratic and Republican leaders in the House and Senate:

Sen. Tom Daschle, D-S.D.
Sen. Trent Lott, R-Miss.
Rep. J. Dennis Hastert, R-Ill.
Rep. Richard A. Gephardt, D-Mo.
Rep. Tom DeLay, R-Texas

Hastert    Gephardt

Inner Circle
Lawmakers in constant contact with the State Department, Pentagon and the White House:

Sen. Joseph R. Biden Jr., D-Del.
Sen. Ted Stevens, R-Alaska
Sen. Richard G. Lugar, R-Ind.
Sen. Chuck Hagel, R-Neb.
Rep. Porter J. Goss, R-Fla.

Biden    Goss

Stovepipe
Lawmakers whose dealings with the Bush administration generally are limited to the Cabinet secretary or agency head based on the members' committee service:

Senate Armed Services:
Sen. Carl Levin, D-Mich.
Sen. John W. Warner, R-Va.

Senate Intelligence:
Sen. Bob Graham, D-Fla.
Sen. Richard C. Shelby, R-Ala.

Senate Foreign Relations:
Sen. Jesse Helms, R-N.C.

House International Relations:
Rep. Henry J. Hyde, R-Ill.
Rep. Tom Lantos, D-Calif.

House Appropriations:
Rep. Jerry Lewis, R-Calif.
Rep. Jim Kolbe, R-Ariz.
Rep. Nancy Pelosi, D-Calif.

Specialists
Lawmakers who speak to administration officials when the issue for which they have expertise is on the front burner:

Sen. Jon Kyl, R-Ariz. (missile defense)
Sen. Sam Brownback, R-Kan. (Central Asia)
Sen. Bill Frist, R-Tenn. (bio-terrorism)
Rep. Doug Bereuter, R-Neb. (Asia)

Brownback    Bereuter

SOURCE: CQ research

Bureaucracy

Armitage, center, shown here testifying before an Appropriations subcommittee April 11 with his undersecretary, Grant S. Green, left, has been known to call lawmakers before their national television appearances to brief them on foreign policy issues.

Kelly handled congressional relations for Powell at the office of the Joint Chiefs. Like Armitage, he brings a plain-spoken military style to a job that had traditionally been dominated by the careful formulations of diplomats.

Kelly has ensured that Powell's senior lieutenants — the undersecretaries and assistant secretaries of State — stay in frequent contact with the subcommittee chairmen who oversee their areas of responsibility.

The effort has paid off. Powell won an 11 percent increase in the State Department budget in fiscal 2002 and recently secured Bush's commitment to increase foreign aid by $5 billion beginning in fiscal 2004. (*2001 CQ Weekly, p. 3021; 2002 CQ Weekly, p. 833*)

Lawmakers and aides said Powell also has gained a receptive audience in Congress as he pushes the administration to pursue diplomatic, rather than immediate military solutions, to trouble spots around the globe, from Iraq to North Korea.

"Even though the gut instincts of the president are probably closer to hardliners like [Defense Secretary Donald H.] Rumsfeld and Cheney, Powell has ended up winning on a lot of these issues," said a senior Republican congressional aide.

Powell and Armitage's careful tending of Congress was evident before Bush's decision April 4 to send Powell to the Middle East. (*Indecision, p. 60*)

In the weeks leading up to that decision, Powell allies Biden, Lugar and McCain had been publicly pushing Bush to take that step.

As soon as the decision was reached — but before Bush's announcement — Armitage and Powell rushed to inform their supporters so they could communicate a consistent message.

By contrast, the White House notified only selected Republican leaders. Daschle and Gephardt learned about Powell's trip on television with the rest of the country.

Adding to the confusion about Bush's policy on the Middle East, the White House also allowed House Majority Whip Tom DeLay, R-Texas, to deliver a speech April 3 criticizing a Powell mission to the region only a day before it was announced. While DeLay later endorsed the trip, his criticism, coming from one of Bush's closest political allies, left a muddled picture of the administration's foreign policy.

White House officials argue that their tendency to be upstaged by members of their own party partially reflects Rice's intense focus on the minute-by-minute management of the Middle East crisis, including conversations with foreign officials and efforts to draft the president's remarks.

But critics say the failures also reflect deeper structural problems at the NSC. Unlike her predecessor, Rice has not asked her senior director for legislative affairs, George Michael Andricos, to sit in on the meetings of the principal national security deputies, who include Armitage, Deputy Secretary of Defense Paul D. Wolfowitz and Deputy National Security Adviser Stephen Hadley.

Rice also has cut the number of NSC aides who work primarily with Congress, making it harder for lawmakers to obtain information.

Congressional aides and lawmakers said this lack of involvement has sometimes led to slip-ups in the policy process, encouraging the State and Defense departments to fight out their battles on the Hill rather than behind closed doors.

For example, House Foreign Operations Appropriations Subcommittee Committee Chairman Jim Kolbe, R-Ariz., and his Senate counterpart, Patrick J. Leahy, D-Vt., recently objected to a Pentagon request for $130 million in military aid in fiscal 2002 to unspecified foreign countries or "indigenous forces." Such spending authority traditionally has rested with the State Department.

Testing Powell's Skills

Until now, Powell and his allies have saved Bush from considerable embarrassment on the Hill, while using their new army of supporters to push the administration's Mideast policy toward the diplomatic approach they favor.

Last fall, Powell used some of the political capital he had accumulated to largely head off legislation that Feinstein and McConnell had wanted to include in the fiscal 2002 foreign operations appropriations law (PL 107-115).

The measure would brand the Palestinian Liberation Organization or one of its constituents groups a terrorist organization, close down its Washington office, deny visas to its top officials and limit aid for Palestinians in the West Bank and Gaza to humanitarian assistance. The foreign aid spending bill ultimately urged but did not require the president to impose the sanctions. (*2001 CQ Weekly, p. 3098*)

But the limits of Powell's coalition-building efforts on Capitol Hill may soon become apparent.

As tensions rise over Bush's policy, Feinstein and McConnell are threatening to push again for the legislation if Powell's mission does not succeed. ◆

Government Institutions

Army's Three-Part Plan Causes Budget, Hill Disharmony

Military seeks faster, lighter, smarter weapons of tomorrow

Quick Contents

The Army's three-phase transformation plan has galvanized congressional skeptics who question whether the modernization plan can become a reality with the services competing for budget dollars.

In the Pentagon's planning model war game "Vigilant Warriors 2002," the Army responds immediately to the invasion of oil-rich Azerbaijan by dispatching four U.S. divisions. The game assumes that new technologies have transformed the force into a radically lightweight one that is just as lethal as current tank units but can move rapidly from U.S. base to battleground. The deployment of thousands of troops is measured in hours, not weeks.

This is what the Army calls its "objective force," the culmination of its plan to modernize to an agile, fast-moving military capable of decimating an enemy. It is also still a simulated conflict, played on the computers at the Army War College in Carlisle, Pa. The year is 2020, when technology will make this force a reality.

To get to that point, the Army has laid out a three-stage plan. It will upgrade its current "legacy force" of weapons, while building an "interim force" of six brigades that will serve as a bridge to the "objective force."

This approach has galvanized congressional skeptics, who question whether the modernization vision can be realized, and pushed some to latch on to a single phase. It also has had the unintended consequence of splintering budget resources.

"We could be ending up with an unmodernized legacy force, an objective force that isn't ready and interim brigades that may or may not work, and then where are you?" asked Rick Santorum of Pennsylvania, the ranking Republican on the Senate Armed Services Airland Subcommittee.

Congress embraced the Army's three-part modernization plan when the service unveiled it in 1999, praising its willingness to rethink long-held assumptions and its commitment to transformation.

Now, the ambitious plan has raised fears among several lawmakers of a looming budget crash, especially with the Navy and Air Force clamoring for the same dollars.

For the third straight year, Army Chief of Staff Gen. Eric K. Shinseki informed the congressional defense committees that the fiscal 2003 budget request from the White House was at least $9 billion short of what the Army believes is needed.

"Even though we're giving the Army more money, we're not giving them enough to do what we're asking them to do," said Joseph I. Lieberman, D-Conn., chairman of the Airland Subcommittee.

Convinced that the Army cannot afford all three components, some senators are trying to force the service to choose — or face the possibility that Congress will do it for them. The Senate Armed Services Committee begins work on its version of the fiscal 2003 defense authorization bill the week of May 6, and there are serious reservations about the Army's three-part plan.

"It appears to me that the Army has to make some very hard decisions to free up their resources to make that transformation happen," Lieberman said.

But the Army is resisting the call from some lawmakers that it make choices among the three phases or at least cut back on the projected spending for the interim force.

"There are no priorities among essentials," Undersecretary of the Army Les Brownlee, a former staff director for the Senate Armed Services Committee, told Congress on March 14.

While the Army is reluctant to choose,

CQ Weekly April 27, 2002

"We have a long way to go, but the promise is good," Riggs told a House panel April 11 of the Army's goal to develop a lightweight, lethal force incorporating new technology.

lawmakers are not. Lieberman prefers to reduce spending on the legacy and interim forces to steer more money to the objective force. Santorum believes the Army is shortchanging the needs of the legacy force.

Outside analysts wonder if the objective force is too ambitious, with the Army counting on high-tech developments that may not occur.

"I don't think that the technology is going to be there to do a lot of the things they want to do as fast as they want to do them," said Andrew F. Krepinevich, a retired Army lieutenant colonel who is now a defense analyst.

The director of the Army's Objective Force Task Force defends the service's approach. Lt. Gen. John M. Riggs said the plan is to field the new force in successive "blocks," with new capabilities phased in as the technology matures.

"We're talking an era, not an end state," Riggs said in an April 4 interview.

The task force director acknowledged that some of the technologies may take a while to mature, but Riggs stressed that they were being pursued because of their potential payoffs. For example, the Army is trying to condense water from vehicle exhausts to reduce the high volume of water that has to be shipped to combat units.

Riggs concedes that it is "a little far flung," but a worthy pursuit.

"We know where we are today, we know where we project to be, and we know what's in the art of the doable in subsequent blocks," he said. "We have a long way to go, but the promise is good."

Improved Mobility

During the Cold War, the Army worried less about getting its forces to the conflict because it expected the conflict to come to the forces.

Four heavy divisions were stationed in Germany, while at least one remained in South Korea — two places where attack by a large armored force seemed plausible. Meanwhile, the tanks and other heavy gear for three additional divisions were stored at depots in and around Germany. In the event of a crisis, troops en route from U.S. bases would be able to pick up what they needed.

In 1979, that orthodoxy was shaken when Islamic fundamentalists in Iran threatened U.S. oil supplies from the Persian Gulf. The looming question for the Army was how quickly it would be able to move a large force to the region to fend off tank divisions.

Within months, then Army Chief of Staff Gen. Edward C. Meyer tried to equip the 9th Infantry Division with better communications and other innovations, including missile-armed dune buggies, to ensure that units could be flown to the Gulf quickly and be better equipped.

But that effort bogged down after Meyer retired in 1983. Seven years later, when Iraq invaded Kuwait, the only significant improvement in the Army's ability to get heavily armed units to Saudi Arabia was the acquisition of eight high-speed cargo ships to carry tanks and other vehicles of one heavy division from U.S. ports.

Within three days of President George Bush's order on Aug. 6, 1990, to defend Saudi Arabia, soldiers of the 82nd Airborne Division began arriving in the desert kingdom. One of the division's 3,000-man brigades was on the ground within a week; a second arrived within 15 days.

But that rapid deployment was risky. Despite the arrival over the next few weeks of air squadrons and Marine Corps units, the situation was "tenuous in the extreme," according to the official Army history of the Gulf War. Pentagon leaders worried that if Iraq quickly invaded Saudi Arabia, thousands of enemy armored vehicles would overwhelm the lightly armed U.S. units and seize the airfields and seaports required to land reinforcements.

"All of us held our breaths," Shinseki told Congress years later when the newly appointed Army chief of staff testified on the service's rationale for the transformation plan.

Not until late August 1990, when the fast cargo ships began unloading 70-ton M-1 tanks and 35-ton Bradley troop carriers of the 24th Mechanized Infantry Division at Saudi ports, did U.S. planners feel that the defenders could hold their own.

After the war, the Army tried to solve the problem of rapid deployment the same way it had planned to move in Europe: Pre-position the necessary equipment for battle-ready troops in allied countries or on nearby ships.

But in the 1990s, the Army's role in U.S. defense plans came under increasing scrutiny. Krepinevich and other analysts argued that more potential adversaries could acquire chemical and biological weapons that would shut down the air and sea bases overseas.

In addition, the Army took on missions in Bosnia and Kosovo in which its units that were designed to fight fast-moving armored battles had to improvise, sometimes swapping their tanks for "Humvees" that could better negotiate town streets and small bridges.

From the critics' perspective, the unwieldiness of Army combat units was encapsulated in April 1999, when 24 Apache helicopters were sent to Albania for possible use against Serbian forces in neighboring Kosovo. The addition of construction engineers to build the necessary facilities and combat units to protect the site increased the size of the force, Task Force Hawk, to more than 5,300 personnel.

Two months later, Shinseki began his four-year stint as chief of staff. In October 1999, he launched the three-track transformation plan, stressing the importance of a light and lethal force.

"We must be able to project power anywhere in the world. . . . The Army must change because the nation cannot afford to have an Army that is irrelevant," he warned last fall in a speech.

Keeping a Step Ahead

The objective force plan calls for the Army's 10 active-duty divisions to be equipped with the new weapons by 2020.

In the meantime, Army officials insist that the existing forces must be upgraded to stay a step ahead of traditional adversaries such as Iraq and North Korea. Some of the current equipment, such as helicopters and digital communications links among the troops, need to be kept up to date because they will remain in service with the next generation of units.

"By selectively modernizing . . . we will guarantee the Army's near-term war fighting readiness through the transformation process," Army Vice Chief of Staff Gen. John M. Keane told the Senate subcommittee March 14. "A portion of this force will be with us until 2020."

Two years ago, the Army had planned to "recapitalize" 26 types of equipment that would remain in service for at least two decades, but to free up funds, the service plans to upgrade

Government Institutions

Updating Today's Army...

Over the next decade, the Army will be seeking funds from Congress to transform itself into a different type of fighting force. Along the way it will seek money to upgrade and extend the life of its current force. If funded, the transition will come in three stages:

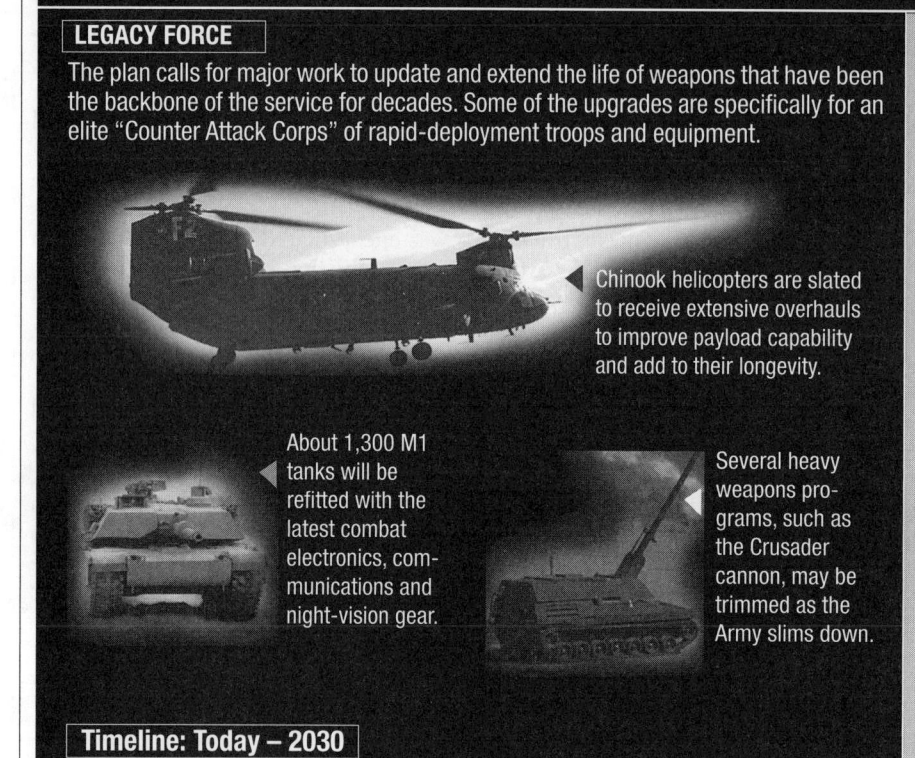

LEGACY FORCE
The plan calls for major work to update and extend the life of weapons that have been the backbone of the service for decades. Some of the upgrades are specifically for an elite "Counter Attack Corps" of rapid-deployment troops and equipment.

Chinook helicopters are slated to receive extensive overhauls to improve payload capability and add to their longevity.

About 1,300 M1 tanks will be refitted with the latest combat electronics, communications and night-vision gear.

Several heavy weapons programs, such as the Crusader cannon, may be trimmed as the Army slims down.

Timeline: Today – 2030

INTERIM FORCE
This 20,000-soldier unit was created to bridge the gap between today's heavy units and the "Objective Force" of the future.

Units are built around the use of Stryker eight-wheeled vehicles outfitted for a variety of assignments from infantry carrier to mobile guns and medical evacuation.

All units of the interim force will be able to fit into C-130 cargo planes and deploy anywhere in the world within 96 hours.

Timeline: Today – 2031

---

17. Some improvements will be limited to the three divisions of the so-called counterattack corps.

"We've very judiciously effected some terminations and let some programs dry up . . . and we'll be doing some more of that," Riggs said. "We've been very selective in where we've put our money into the legacy force."

Some of the changes in the 17 programs are intended to reduce the cost of aging equipment. For example, the fiscal 2003 budget request includes $141 million to continue rebuilding artillery rocket launchers. The overhauls should reduce the annual cost of operating and maintaining the launchers by 31 percent, according to the Army.

Planned improvements to the M-1 tank, on the other hand, are aimed at reducing annual operating costs and significantly improving the combat power in the counterattack corps. The budget request includes $691 million to upgrade the M-1. More than three-quarters of that amount is earmarked to equip 134 tanks with the most advanced night-vision equipment and digital communications gear. In future years, however, the lion's share of the tank modification budget is slated for safety and reliability improvements. Only about 1,300 of some 8,000 M-1s will be equipped with the most sophisticated combat electronics.

Similarly, the Army decided two years ago to assign the Crusader mobile cannon to select units only, cutting from 1,138 to 480 the number of guns it plans to buy. The big gun remains controversial because its 40-ton weight runs counter to the thrust for easy deployment, but Shinseki insists that the cannon's long range and accuracy would be invaluable if enemy anti-aircraft defenses interfered with precision bombing. (2002 CQ Weekly, p. 624)

Lieberman has suggested that the Army might have to forgo some of the planned improvements. Santorum, however, contends that the budgetary lid on improving the current force is too tight, with needed weapons canceled to free up funds for speculative development programs.

For instance, the Army may revive a recently canceled program to protect helicopters against shoulder-launched anti-aircraft missiles.

"I suspect by the time we get to the fall, that list will be longer," Santorum said.

'Interim' Brigades

In the near term, the Army plans to spend nearly $10 billion to bridge the gap between its heavy and light forces, using existing technology. The money would equip six brigades of 3,500 soldiers each with more than 2,100 eight-wheeled armored cars. The vehicles are based on a Swiss design that the Marines have been using for two decades.

The fiscal 2003 budget request includes $936 million to continue developing the so-called Stryker and to buy 332 for the planned brigades.

Because variants of the same chassis will be used as troop carriers, mobile command posts, missile-armed tank-hunters and other vehicles, Army officials hope the new units' supply and maintenance needs will be reduced. They insist that all versions of the vehicle will fit onto C-130 cargo planes, though the fit will be snug. These "interim" brigades will meet Shinseki's

Bureaucracy

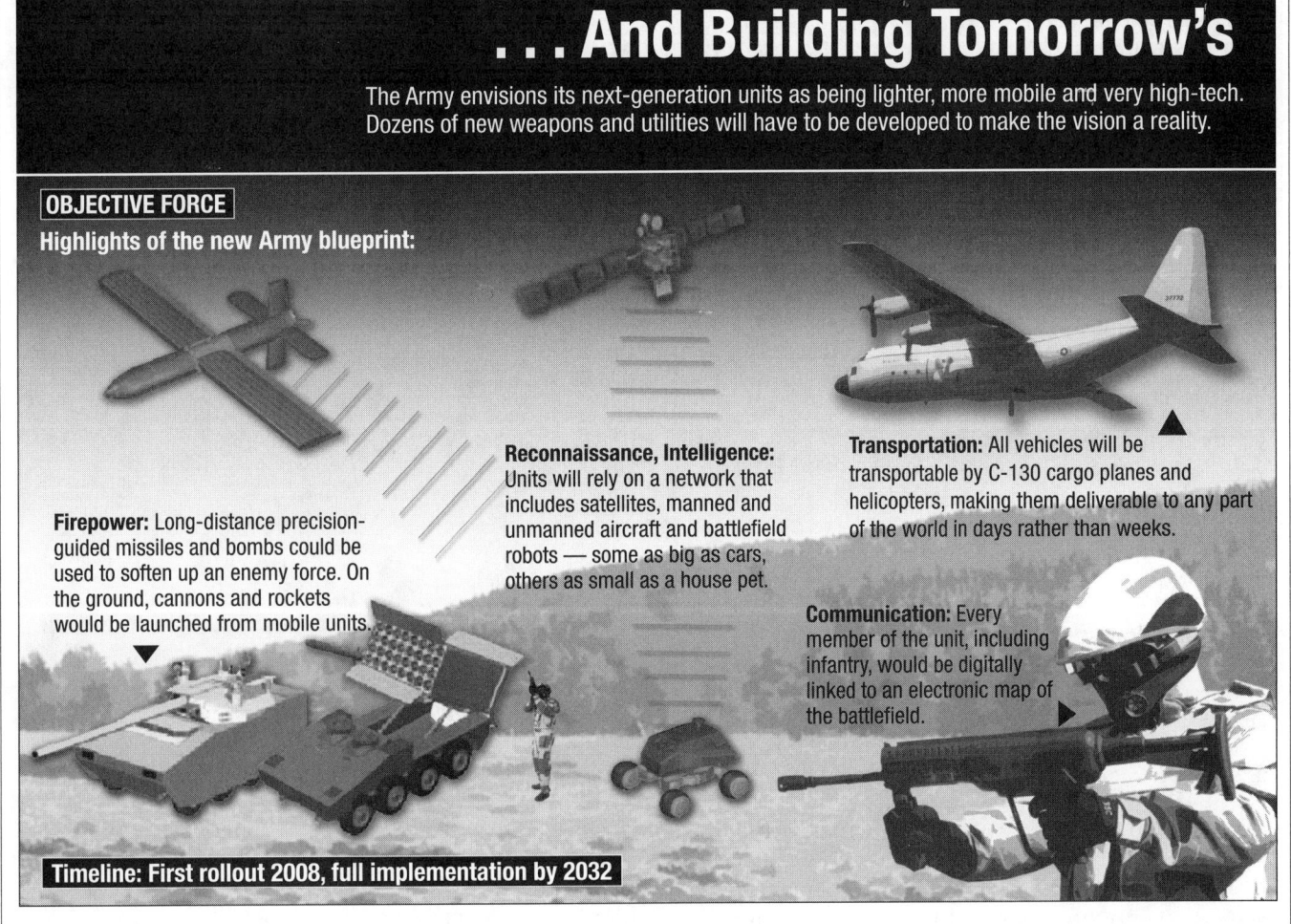

...And Building Tomorrow's

The Army envisions its next-generation units as being lighter, more mobile and very high-tech. Dozens of new weapons and utilities will have to be developed to make the vision a reality.

OBJECTIVE FORCE
Highlights of the new Army blueprint:

Firepower: Long-distance precision-guided missiles and bombs could be used to soften up an enemy force. On the ground, cannons and rockets would be launched from mobile units.

Reconnaissance, Intelligence: Units will rely on a network that includes satellites, manned and unmanned aircraft and battlefield robots — some as big as cars, others as small as a house pet.

Transportation: All vehicles will be transportable by C-130 cargo planes and helicopters, making them deliverable to any part of the world in days rather than weeks.

Communication: Every member of the unit, including infantry, would be digitally linked to an electronic map of the battlefield.

Timeline: First rollout 2008, full implementation by 2032

goal of deploying practically anywhere within four days. All told, an interim brigade's equipment would add up to less than half the 30,000 tons of a conventional tank brigade.

Army officials believe the brigades could play a useful role as the early-arriving vanguard of a heavily armored force. The units also will be part of the strategy for the objective force.

But the Army's decision to build the interim units around a wheeled vehicle rather than one that moves on tracks has been controversial. Critics insist that the Strykers cannot match the off-road mobility of tracked vehicles, while proponents say they will be faster on roads and easier to maintain.

Like the planned objective force, the interim force is intended to rely more on information than on armor to survive on the battlefield. While the Strykers are designed to fend off machine gun fire, they lack the massive armor that allows an M-1 tank to handle large cannon shells — and drives its weight to nearly 70 tons. To compensate, the interim brigades will have a 400-man intelligence-gathering squadron designed to

let the unit find the enemy first and launch a surprise attack.

In 2000, the Senate Armed Services Committee, based on the advice of Santorum and Lieberman, balked at the cost of buying a new vehicle to equip the planned interim brigades. The fiscal 2001 defense authorization bill (PL 106-398) ordered the Army to conduct field tests comparing an interim unit equipped with the new wheeled vehicle and one equipped with the M-113 tracked personnel carrier, of which the service has about 17,000. (*2000 Almanac, p. 8-15*)

In 2001, that requirement was repealed at the Army's request, though congressional skeptics salvaged a requirement that the Defense secretary review the plan to equip the units with the wheeled vehicle before spending the money to equip more than three brigades.

Fighting Smarter

The projected future force would build on the Army's decade-long effort to leverage information for combat. Most of the Army's current combat vehicles are being equipped to plug into a digital communications network in which soldiers can see an electronic map of the battlefield showing the location of friends and enemies. A related project called Land Warrior, which would give individual soldiers the same information through a helmet-mounted eyepiece, has had some development problems but now is slated to enter the service in 2005.

The objective force is intended to exploit a broader range of information sources: orbiting satellites, drone airplanes or unmanned aerial vehicles (UAVs), small robots designed to climb stairs and check out the upper floors of buildings, and even sensors to see through walls. Simply plugging a combat unit into a reliable, worldwide network would allow field commanders to reduce the size of their headquarters.

"Right now, it's a very cumbersome process, vacuuming every bit of information they can get and then putting that information into something that is usable for the commanders," Riggs said.

Commanders of the new units, while traveling in their vehicles to the

Government Institutions

front, would be able to reach back to staffs who can digest raw data into relevant information and radio it forward.

The plan is for the new force to find the enemy first and strike with long-range precision munitions before maneuvering for a surprise attack. In addition, the force would rely on the communications network to isolate targets for other U.S. forces. That would reduce the weight of ammunition that a unit would have to carry and the chance that the force would get involved in a head-to-head shoot-out requiring heavy armor.

The centerpiece of this project is the Future Combat Systems (FCS), which calls for developing an array of troop carriers, light tanks, mobile rocket launchers, robot "scouts," UAV launchers and other vehicles, all plugged into this communications web and none weighing more than 20 tons. In fiscal 2003, the Army has requested $717 million for FCS. An additional $37 million has been requested for a companion program, Objective Force Warrior, intended to let individual soldiers make greater use of the information network.

The commander and crew, in the vehicles, will rely chiefly on their superior view of the battlefield to avoid a head-to-head attack. The vehicles also may have ultra-hard but lightweight ceramic plates or electromagnetic armor that slows down incoming bullets before they hit, and automated grenade launchers to deflect approaching missiles.

Instead of the massive cannon tanks to fire heavy projectiles to penetrate thick armor, the FCS may use lighter guns of a novel design that can punch through the same armor with a smaller projectile.

The effort to slash the weight of the equipment is matched by an effort to reduce significantly the amount of fuel, water and other supplies needed to keep a unit operating.

"If you take a gallon of gas and say, 'I want to get it to the soldier on the battlefield,' what you wind up doing is consuming two-thirds of that gallon just getting the remainder to him," Riggs said. "So we're looking at how we can cut today's fuel consumption rates phenomenally."

The lighter weight vehicles would use less fuel, but the Army is considering the use of hybrid-electric engines that could yield savings of 50 percent or more. ◆

Training, Environment Clash

The military is seeking an exemption from many of the nation's longstanding environmental laws to conduct training exercises, but the controversial, last-minute request may not be resolved for months.

The House Armed Services Military Readiness Subcommittee took an initial step April 25 by approving provisions that would limit the impact of two environmental laws as it began work on the fiscal 2003 defense authorization bill. The full committee will revisit the issue when it marks up the bill May 1.

Several panel members backed the Pentagon's plea, but others indicated they will challenge the request as the bill moves forward.

In addition, other House committees, including Resources and Energy and Commerce, may claim jurisdiction over any effort to change environmental laws.

Under one provision, the Pentagon would be allowed to get a permit from the Fish and Wildlife Service to hold exercises though migratory birds could be killed. On March 13, a federal judge ruled the Navy was violating the 1918 Migratory Bird Treaty Act by using a small island near Guam as a bombing range.

Another provision would amend the Endangered Species Act of 1973 (PL 93-205) to bar the Interior Department from designating a "critical habitat" on bases governed by an agreement the military made with federal and state environmental officials. Activities in critical habitats are tightly restricted by law. (*1973 Almanac, p. 670*)

Pentagon officials, with the backing of several Armed Services Committee members, argue that it is increasingly difficult for military units to conduct realistic training because of the combination of environmental laws and restrictions imposed by urban development.

But subcommittee member Jim Maloney, D-Conn., insisted the panel's action was unnecessary. In many cases, he pointed out, environmental laws already allow exemptions for military training.

Military Readiness Subcommittee Chairman Joel Hefley, R-Colo., assailed the Pentagon for submitting its exemption request late in the day on April 19, giving his subcommittee little time to consult with other House panels with authority over environmental laws.

In response, the subcommittee acted on only two provisions even though the Pentagon had requested

> *"The Pentagon would be allowed to ... hold exercises though migratory birds could be killed."*

changes to numerous environmental laws, including those dealing with clean air and clean water.

Twenty-one environmental groups sent a letter to House members April 24 objecting to any congressional move to give the Pentagon special leniency in complying with environmental laws.

The subcommittee also voted 13-3 against a proposal by Gene Taylor, D-Miss., to cancel a round of military base closings slated for 2005. Although most of the panel agreed with Taylor, Hefley and others warned against reopening the issue from last year. (*2001 CQ Weekly, p. 2990*)

Politics and Public Policy

The term *public policymaking* refers to action taken by the government to address issues on the public agenda; it also refers to the method by which a decision to act on policy is reached. The work of the president, Congress, the judiciary and the bureaucracy is to make, implement and rule on policy decisions. Articles in this section discuss major policy issues that came before the federal government in the first half of 2002.

The first three articles tap into the theme of homeland security that is so prominent in this book's other sections. As the opening story observes, the federal budget has an entirely new category dedicated to protecting the nation from terrorists — and organizations small and large are lobbying aggressively for a piece of the pie. The second article talks about the proposed reorganization of the FBI and the support that agency is seeking from Capitol Hill. Also new on the defense front is a wave of nuclear weaponry. The third story describes President Bush's plan to develop powerful "bunker busters" and notes that the proposal has sharply divided the parties amid fear of a new round of worldwide proliferation.

The next six articles cover a variety of topics, revealing that business as usual is still a viable concept even during a war on terrorism. One story investigates the financial collapse of Enron Corp., the energy giant whose sudden bankruptcy jilted thousands of employees out of their retirement savings and launched a congressional inquiry into the accounting industry.

Stories on health policy and Medicare show a shift in the way the nation is approaching the health care debate. The cost, not the quality, of health care is now the number one concern among policymakers. And although Medicare needs revamping before the baby boom generation reaches its golden years, policymakers are divided on what to do.

The next story looks at copyrights. How do policymakers balance the intellectual property rights of creators against the economic imperative to let technological innovation run its course? As Congress debates the issue and the courts consider the definition of property in the digital age, consumers wait to see how the outcome will affect their use of the Internet, personal computers and other digital devices.

The story on steel imports analyzes Bush's decision to protect the steel industry by setting tariffs. The decision, which won Bush friends in the domestic steel industry but may have alienated global trading partners, will have implications for free trade.

The article on welfare, the last in the section, discusses the planned overhaul and the divisions that fall along party lines. Hot topics include the length of the mandated work week for welfare recipients, bill provisions that promote marriage and a waiver program for states.

Because many of the topics discussed here will remain at the top of Congress' agenda in the months ahead, the articles are valuable contributions to issue studies, predictors of legislative outcomes and primers on the policymaking process.

Politics and Public Policy

New Pot of Federal Dollars Has Admirers From All Over

Homeland Security spending could threaten other programs

Beside the Kickapoo River in southwestern Wisconsin, LaFarge is a hamlet where hunting, fishing and snowmobiling are among the favorite pastimes. It is unlikely that the 775 residents have been thinking much about the threat of local terrorism this spring, while the high school girls' basketball team made a run at a state championship.

But in April — not long after the team lost the regional final to Hillsboro — the chief of LaFarge's Volunteer Fire Department was on Capitol Hill, imploring the Senate Appropriations Committee to think more broadly about how the nation should prepare its citizens and institutions to respond to terrorism.

"It isn't going to happen from Washington," said Philip C. Stittleburg, who also is chairman of the National Volunteer Fire Council. "It's going to happen from the grass roots, and it's going to happen because you train us and equip us at the local level."

The sudden appearance on the federal budget books of an entirely new category of spending — under the amorphous label of "homeland security" — has set off a remarkably broad-based and aggressive wave of lobbying, much of it by organizations that previously had little input on the nation's spending priorities. President Bush has proposed $38 billion for homeland security in fiscal 2003. But whole new clusters of line items in appropriations bills do not materialize often, so substantial pressure is building to spend billions of dollars more than that. One consequence is that homeland security spending appears destined to become a permanent, growing and politically untouchable part of the federal spending baseline.

And, at a time when Bush and the congressional leadership of both parties all are pledging to hold down the pace of growth in discretionary spending, the arrival of such a powerful force on the appropriators could have a profound impact on other — particularly domestic — programs, from special education to wetlands protection.

That might mean tough times ahead for those and other government entities unable to tie their mission somehow to the broadly defined concept of defense of the people, places and infrastructure of the United States. But it has energized those who believe they have a legitimate claim on federal anti-terrorism spending. Stittleburg's Volunteer Fire Council, which represents fire departments and a long list of companies that make firefighting equipment, is setting aside past internal squabbles and pulling together in an unprecedented way this year. The group's message, which Executive Director Heather Schafer said is winning attention from Congress, is that small-scale emergency response units across the country need better training and equipment because they, not federal agencies, often will be the first on the scene of major disasters.

"We've been working on these issues for years, but now the momentum is there, the awareness is there and we have to take advantage of it," she said. "It's a good time for the fire service."

Hers is among dozens of groups that the 107th Congress will be hearing from in the weeks ahead, as work intensifies on the bills that will dictate all discretionary spending for the fiscal year beginning Oct. 1. Appropriators are coalescing around a $768 billion ceiling for those 13 bills; if that figure holds, Bush's homeland security request would eat up 5 percent of the total.

Divvying Up the Cash

Many of the new wave of supplicants go by unfamiliar acronyms such as NACCHO, for the National Association of County and City Health Officials, and AMWA, for the Association of Metropolitan Water Agencies. Though they are far from familiar names at the Capitol, these types of organizations represent millions of private and public-sector workers.

Their requests, along with the more high-profile demands of the Defense Department and other federal agencies, means the definition of homeland security potentially stretches from providing cellular telephones for "first responders," such as ambulance drivers in the nation's most rural areas, to fueling the Air Force fighter jets patrolling the skies over Washington and New York.

Last year, Bush set a hard limit on how much emergency spending he would accept in response to Sept. 11, and he threatened to veto any spending beyond that $40 billion, itself a record for such a supplemental spending request. This year, Bush has vowed to use vetoes if necessary to avoid a repeat of Vietnam-era budgeting, when "increased spending required by war was not balanced by slower spending in the rest of government." But so far he has not tied his veto threat to a specific monetary figure, in effect giving Congress ample latitude to spend what it views as expedient in this election year. (*Background, 2001 CQ Weekly, p. 3018; 2002 CQ Weekly, p. 1019*)

The early signs are that Bush might not have to take a hard line on the spending level for homeland security. Many inside and outside Congress describe the president as having been generous in that area, at least for the coming year, so the major spending fights are likely to come in other areas.

James W. Dyer, the staff director for the House Appropriations Committee, says he thinks the president has allocated enough, at least for homeland security — to make Congress happy. "The pot is so big that most of this should be accom-

Homeland Security

Fire Chief Philip C. Stittleburg of LaFarge, Wis., is one of the new faces crowding Washington in search of "homeland security" spending this year. Third from left, below, he testified on a panel of public safety officials to the Senate Appropriations Committee on April 11.

modated by the president's request," he said. "This is one of the few areas where we're awash in cash."

Not so for the rest of the budget, however. An analysis by Republicans on the Senate Budget Committee found that, in order to fully fund Bush's homeland security proposals, appropriators would need to cut $11 billion, or 3.3 percent, below the amount being spent in fiscal 2002 on other nondefense programs. That is because Bush divides his own homeland security proposal as $7 billion for the Pentagon and the other $31 billion for non-defense programs. That latter figure represents 8.3 percent of the probable non-defense starting point for the appropriators — to be sure, a problematically large slice of the proposed pie.

A Pleasant Surprise . . .

I. Michael Greenberger, a University of Maryland law professor who directed a counterterrorism project at the Justice Department in the Clinton administration, said Bush's homeland security proposal came as a pleasant surprise to many counterterrorism experts, who worried that Bush would underfund homeland security programs in the name of overall fiscal discipline. "There is just a phenomenal amount that needs to be done," he said.

He credits Homeland Security Director Tom Ridge with persuading Bush to call for such a large amount of new spending. Such praise has been heard less lately. Ridge has lost a series of recent turf battles within the administration, state and local officials question his approach to homeland security and his balance-of-power tussle with Congress has never gone away. (*2002 CQ Weekly, p. 1071*)

Still, Michael Scardaville, a homeland defense policy analyst for The Heritage Foundation, a conservative think tank, praised the $38 billion request as a "significant improvement across the board" and called it a tenfold increase for local police, firefighters and other first responders. Still, he urged Congress not to spend more without a comprehensive plan. "Throwing money at this issue is not going to make Americans secure," he said.

But it is a sign of the pressures for more spending that Scardaville also predicted that Congress might have to commit itself to a significant spending increase in the homeland security budget for fiscal 2004 as well as move a supplemental spending package this year solely dedicated to homeland security.

In addition, Bush's $27 billion midyear spending request, one-fifth of which is for homeland defense, may well be plumped up by Congress to provide an early down payment on its own homeland spending desires. The first step in that process will come when the House Appropriations Committee marks up its supplemental bill, now unlikely before the week of May 6.

The biggest wild card in the debate is another report due this summer from Ridge, in which he is supposed to describe the administration's long-term homeland security strategy. A spokeswoman said the White House Office of Homeland Security has not decided whether to attach spending recommendations to its plan. If it does not, it might not take long for lawmakers and businesses to put their own price tags on their views of the unmet needs.

. . . A Philosophical Dilemma

A number of needs that are clearly federal in scope have made headlines, such as border and port security. In some cases, members of Congress have found what they consider potential vulnerabilities without a request for funding. For example, Edward J. Markey, D-Mass., and other lawmakers have called for federalizing the security staff at nuclear reactors, a move the industry and federal regulators have resisted.

But in many cases, requests are rolling in for federal funding of intensely local activities that are being redefined as anti-terrorism measures. Contra Costa County in California, for example, recently hired a lobbyist to work on, among other things, "emergency response communications." The water agencies' association has warned that the tens of thousands of small municipalities need training and infrastructure improvements to help prevent and detect attempts to contaminate their treatment plants. And local health officials say they lack the facili-

81

Politics and Public Policy

Pie chart: Bush's Homeland Budget
- Supporting first responders: 9%
- Information-sharing and technology: 2%
- Securing our borders: 28%
- Department of Defense: 18%
- Defending against bio-terrorism: 16%
- Other non-defense programs: 14%
- Transportation security: 13%

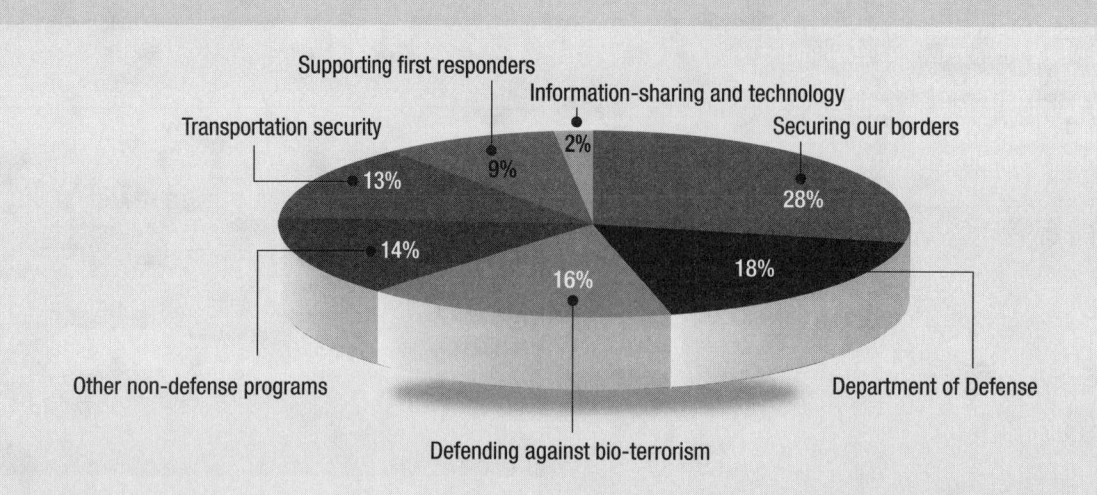

Bush's Homeland Budget & Congress' Response

The administration unveiled this summary of its fiscal 2003 homeland security budget in February, and Congress has been considering its response since. (The Congressional Budget Office says it cannot produce an independent analysis of Bush's plan, so well-marbled are his homeland security proposals within a vast array of federal agency budget requests.)

Supporting first responders
Bush: $3.5 billion would be spent providing local firefighters, police and emergency medical technicians with equipment, training and planning expertise. The Federal Emergency Management Agency (FEMA) would create a streamlined process for getting federal money to local authorities.

Analysis: Appropriators have held several hearings to take testimony from local emergency response officials, a signal that spending could grow as lawmakers seek to steer resources back home. Local officials lament that Bush is rolling a $900 million FEMA grant program for firefighters into his "first responder" budget; they want the two kept separate.

Defending against bio-terrorism
Bush: $5.9 billion would be spent to prepare for the "deliberate use of disease as a weapon." The emphasis would be on developing vaccines and diagnostic testing, in addition to establishing a communication infrastructure that links federal, state and local health authorities.

Analysis: Congress added $2.5 billion for bio-terrorism preparations to the fiscal 2002 defense spending law (PL 107-117) and is now in conference on a bill (HR 3448) to authorize at least $2.9 billion. But that measure includes provisions on food and water supply security, which the administration categorizes elsewhere, and is caught in a debate with Bush over proposed cuts to the Centers for Disease Control budget.

---

ties and personnel needed to prevent an infectious disease outbreak from turning into a raging epidemic.

Such a broad array of pressures could cause a philosophic dilemma for Republicans in the administration and in Congress over their view of the proper limits of federal governance. Throughout Bill Clinton's presidency, the GOP fought efforts to embrace and expand Washington's role in education, arguing that it was primarily a local responsibility. The party largely has given up that fight and decided instead to challenge Democrats on which party has a better education track record at the federal level.

A similar transformation could be occurring in other areas because of homeland security needs. Recent reports that captive members of al Qaeda — the group being held responsible for the Sept. 11 terrorist attacks — have cited shopping malls and supermarkets as possible targets will bolster the case of those arguing for a greater federal role in local affairs. Bruce Shirk, a government contracts attorney with Powell Goldstein Frazer & Murphy in Washington, predicted that "billions and billions and billions" of new federal dollars soon will be flowing to state and local governments.

David Keating, executive director of the Club for Growth, which advocates low taxes and reduced federal spending, said Congress and Bush should reject the idea that any security needs arising from Sept. 11 are automatically a federal responsibility. "The states have a certain responsibility for basic security," Keating said. "I think it's clear they're going to have to decide who's best at doing what."

The temptations will be great for Congress to add to the president's request when pet parochial projects can be construed as vital to homeland security, Keating said. "I'm sure they're all eager to show they're helping to make sure people are more secure through their efforts in Congress," Keating said. "That's going to be even more appealing than the normal pork."

Corporations on the Hunt

In addition to the intense lobbying by local entities, more traditional corporate arm-twisting is under way. In particular, many high-tech firms, fueled in the 1990s by an influx of cash from the Internet boom, are experienc-

Homeland Security

■ Securing our borders
Bush: $10.6 billion would be spent on improved screening of people and cargo entering the country by land, sea or air. This includes an improved visa system, additional Customs and border patrol personnel and improved ship tracking and surveillance systems for the Coast Guard.

Analysis: The House is set to clear a bill (HR 3525) to boost border security and on April 25 passed a measure (HR 3231) to break apart the Immigration and Naturalization Service — measures that may put pressure on appropriators to spend more than Bush wants. The Coast Guard, plagued by an aging fleet and an unclear mission, is coming under increasing scrutiny as it is asked to play a larger role in homeland defense.

■ Information-sharing and technology
Bush: $722 million to improve information sharing among federal programs and among federal, state and local agencies. One focus would be improved tracking of short-term visitors to the country.

Analysis: Telecommunications companies and other high-tech industries are gearing up for a big year on Capitol Hill. Congress likely will face considerable pressure from those industries and local agencies that want federal help in improving their communications infrastructure.

■ Transportation security
Bush: $4.8 billion to fund the newly created Transportation Security Administration within the Transportation Department. The agency will coordinate federal, state and local efforts to protect pipelines, bridges and aviation infrastructure.

Analysis: Aviation security costs are exceeding expectations, and the installation of new baggage screening devices is behind schedule. With the airline industry still in recovery, the federal government is being pressed to ensure that security demands do not siphon funds from airport expansion plans.

■ Department of Defense
Bush: $6.8 billion for security at the Pentagon and other Defense Department facilities, to maintain combat air patrols over parts of the United States that are the likeliest terrorist targets and for research into fighting terrorism. Other funds also would support specialized teams to respond to domestic terrorism-related disasters.

Analysis: Congress is likely to give Bush anything he requests for the Pentagon, particularly in areas where there is an overlapping homeland security issue.

■ Other non-defense programs
Bush: $5.4 billion for security at numerous federal agencies — including the Agriculture, Commerce, Energy and Interior departments — and for federal law enforcement activities. The amount also includes funding for security research at the National Science Foundation and for emergency planning in the Washington area.

Analysis: This encompasses numerous line items where members of Congress likely will press for additional funding, in part because many government agencies have field offices across the country. In addition, growing numbers in Congress say the Bush proposal is deficient in two areas that lawmakers see as top priorities: protecting the domestic food supply and improving security at nuclear power plants.

---

ing another burst of growth because they can market themselves as capable of helping governments solve their communications challenges.

"It's generating a cottage industry of high-tech specialists," Dyer said. "It's fertile territory for entrepreneurs."

One of those entrepreneurs is K. Narayanaswamy, co-founder of Cs3 Inc., which wants some of the $50 billion Bush would spend on computer security in the next year. Cs3 offers ways for the government to block cyberterrorists from swamping its Web sites and networks with bogus users and causing them to crash. "We're not sure in dollar terms exactly what this will mean, but the government is a very strategic market for us," Narayanaswamy said.

Grant E. Seiffert, a top lobbyist for the Telecommunications Industry Association, said the nation's homeland security needs undoubtedly will benefit Lucent Technologies, Nokia and Motorola and the other telecommunications equipment manufacturers he represents. "When the government starts talking about homeland security, starts talking about redundancies in the system, that requires our help," Seiffert said.

Seiffert said he is taking a cautious approach in an effort to avoid appearing insensitive to the tragedies that created the current budget situation. "It's a sensitive issue," Seiffert said. "No one wants to be running up to Capitol Hill with their hands out." Still, he predicted, the pressures on Congress will be enormous. "There's going to be a mad dash up there," he said.

Entities that have registered lobbyists recently specifically to work to obtain a piece of the counterterrorism and homeland security pie include:

• Sensatex Inc. of New York, which is trying to persuade public safety agencies to buy its SmartShirt, which it maintains is capable of monitoring a rescue worker's vital signs and emitting homing signals to locate a wearer trapped under rubble.

• Focal Communications Corp. of Chicago, which wants to win contracts to maintain government and other telecommunications networks during emergencies.

• HydroGeoLogic Inc., a consulting firm based in Herndon, Va., that has done work for several local water management districts, as well as major corpo-

Politics and Public Policy

rations and the Defense Department. It wants federal agencies to purchase software that can simulate a "catastrophic release" of water on a community.

• The American Society for Industrial Security, whose members provide security for banks and other businesses.

Shifting Expenses

The pressure is being applied, initially, on the fiscal 2002 emergency supplemental spending bill set to begin moving in the House in May. Appropriators are eyeing the bill as a way to make work on the fiscal 2003 spending bills easier by shifting some expenses in those bills to the supplemental and boosting its price tag. The $5.3 billion in the president's package for homeland security would go mostly to fund the new Transportation Security Agency. (2002 Weekly, p. 1032)

Budget Committee Chairman Jim Nussle, R-Iowa, is urging the House to resist efforts to push the supplemental's price tag above Bush's request. "If we cross that line now, there will be nothing to keep the appropriations process from exploding," he said April 25. That night, Speaker J. Dennis Hastert, R-Ill., instructed the Appropriations Committee to produce a bill that stays under Bush's ceiling.

Nussle also said he will work to include provisions in the supplemental to set new spending caps and extend expiring budget enforcement mechanisms. (2002 CQ Weekly, p. 280)

Separating security from other programs endangers the traditional labor, environmental, health, transportation and water programs that lawmakers will want to tout while campaigning this fall. This will be particularly true if Bush makes good on his pledge to force Congress to live with the overall spending totals he has proposed, and if deficit hawks such as Nussle get spending restraint mechanisms enacted.

For example, Sen. Pete V. Domenici of New Mexico, the top Republican on the Budget Committee as well as the Energy and Water Appropriations Subcommittee, said his fiscal 2003 spending bill may reflect a tension between those who want more for nuclear safety, now a hot homeland security topic, and water projects, which for decades have served as a way for lawmakers to bring federal cash to their constituents. Bush proposed a deep cut in water project spending, an approach House appropriators are likely to reject. Absent a generous overall spending ceiling, appropriators will be hard-pressed to dedicate the billions of dollars for security that power plant operators desire.

That has led House Appropriations Committee Chairman C.W. Bill Young, R-Fla., to conclude that he cannot realistically abide by Bush's program. Young wants to spend about $9 billion more for domestic programs outside homeland security than Bush has proposed. Top GOP Senate aides make a similar case, saying the arrangement would allow Congress to hold non-defense, non-homeland security spending constant with the cost of doing business this year. (2002 CQ Weekly, p. 953)

Though the White House argues, as do many Republicans, that regular spending should be cut back during wartime, senior GOP aides at the Capitol see no political will to make those cuts. "At a time of war, history is not on the side of this argument, particularly now, given the blurring of distinctions between categories of defense and non-defense in protecting the homeland," said G. William Hoagland, Republican staff director of the Senate Budget Committee.

Former Rep. Tillie Fowler, R-Fla. (1993-2001), who sits on Defense Secretary Donald H. Rumsfeld's Policy Board, said the budget squeeze is tighter because of the proposed $31 billion military buildup to fight the war on terrorism abroad. "We're beefing up homeland security, and we're also fighting a war, so you've got two different fronts you're trying to fund," she said. "They definitely need the extra money, and they're going to need more."

Whether members of Congress can swallow cuts to earmarked projects during an election year remains to be seen.

"Being a former member, I understand totally the need to bring home the bacon," Fowler said. She said the war on terrorism gives members a reason for their list of projects to be shorter this year. "It's an answer that I think my constituents would pretty much relate to, though they may not want to hear it every year for several years."

Making 'Cardinals' Happy

Appropriators are still in the early stages of matching homeland security needs with potential funding levels. So far, the assessment of subcommittee chairmen, or "cardinals," varies widely.

"I am very concerned that the administration has not requested enough for airport security, port security, Amtrak," said Patty Murray, D-Wash., chairman of the Senate Transportation Appropriations Subcommittee. "Everything I've seen is that it's going to cost a lot more than they've requested."

For example, Murray's aides noted, a grant program offering $93 million to ports to upgrade their security elicited $700 million in requests.

Sen. Ben Nighthorse Campbell, R-Colo., said Congress has focused so much attention since Sept. 11 on fixing security lapses in commercial aviation that it has slighted the risks to general aviation. The top Republican on the Treasury-Postal Service Appropriations Subcommittee, Campbell said current spending estimates are, at best, guesses. "Frankly, who knows if it will do what's necessary, because it's an evolving process," he said.

Lawmakers also worry about the threat posed by biological or chemical weapons — or even terrorists themselves — transported in large containers. To reduce the risk, lawmakers from port districts say containers must be inspected, sealed and watched.

Some appropriators are comfortable with the funding levels they expect. Mary L. Landrieu, D-La., chairman of the Senate's District of Columbia Appropriations Subcommittee, said the $200 million approved last year will keep the city safe for the time being. "They had a huge plump-up last year, and we don't want to just throw money at it. We want to make sure that the money is being spent well," she said.

Likewise, Senate Legislative Branch Appropriations Subcommittee Chairman Richard J. Durbin, D-Ill., said assured funding for the Capitol Visitor Center will solve most of his immediate homeland security concerns.

Judd Gregg, the top Republican on the Commerce-Justice-State Appropriations Subcommittee, said they not only have enough money for border and law enforcement programs, but he also sees the focus on homeland security invigorating some agencies. "We're getting more dollars on top of traditional dollars. The biggest plus from this exercise — to the extent there's any plus — is that it has refocused agencies like the FBI," he said. "We were giving them all sorts of things to do, from fighting Internet crimes to bank robberies, you name it. Their focus was getting blurred as a result. Now they've got a purpose." ◆

Law and Judiciary

FBI Director Seeks Hill's Support As Hearings Get Under Way

Lawmakers weigh administration's request to let Mueller run restructuring

Lawmakers intend to push ahead with hearings into the FBI's mishandling of intelligence before Sept. 11 despite a sweeping reorganization plan from Director Robert S. Mueller III.

The question now is whether they will let Mueller lead the way in reshaping his troubled bureau, or insist that Congress take charge — as they have in the debate over restructuring the Immigration and Naturalization Service, another agency widely criticized as dysfunctional and ill-prepared to face terrorist threats. (*2002 CQ Weekly, p. 1155*)

Politically, Mueller starts on solid footing. He is relatively new to the job, taking office only a week before the Sept. 11 attacks, and he continues to enjoy good will from members of both parties in Congress. He was confirmed unanimously by the Senate. He also has the strong backing of the White House, a point driven home by Attorney General John Ashcroft's comments at a news conference announcing the reorganization May 29.

Mueller also may have helped defuse criticism by admitting that the bureau made mistakes and needs an overhaul. He thanked an FBI agent-turned-whistleblower for a critical memo, leaked last month.

But a recent string of embarrassing revelations about evidence and opportunities missed in the months before Sept. 11 has energized the FBI's critics and drawn intense scrutiny from lawmakers. Congressional criticism of the FBI and demands for a broader investigation intensified May 24 with the disclosure of the memo from Minneapolis FBI agent Coleen Rowley, who complained that superiors in Washington hindered, rather than helped, agents in the field assemble a picture of the terrorist plot and stop it.

Mueller's statements just after the attacks, in which he said he knew of no warning signs of the plot, also have come back to haunt him, threatening to undermine his credibility.

And with the public unnerved, members of Congress are under considerable pressure to show voters they will be tough on security lapses and will push hard to prevent future terrorist attacks.

Lawmakers have any number of ways to weigh in on Mueller's plans and even override him, should they choose. For example, Congress could pass a reauthorization bill for the Justice Department, setting policy for the FBI and other agencies — something lawmakers have not done since 1979. They also could draft new legislation ordering their own overhaul of the agency.

For now, closed-door hearings are set to begin June 4 as part of the joint inquiry being conducted by the House and Senate Intelligence committees. Those hearings are expected to run through September, with some later meetings open to the public. (*Box, p. 87*)

Sens. Joseph I. Lieberman, D-Conn., and John McCain, R-Ariz., may offer a bill (S 1867) this month to authorize an independent commission to scrutinize the government's ability to detect and deter terrorist plots. House Intelligence Committee member Tim Roemer, D-Ind., plans to offer a similar plan as an amendment to the fiscal 2003 intelligence authorization bill (HR 4628). (*Politics, p. 48*)

The Senate Judiciary Committee plans to begin its own hearings on the FBI's performance June 6.

"Congressional oversight committees are partners in the effort to sharpen and refocus the FBI and the Justice Department," said Chairman Patrick J. Leahy, D-Vt. "And we will continue to assess and prescribe the

Quick Contents

The director of the FBI needs Congress' approval to proceed with his plan to overhaul the bureau. But faced with a steady drumbeat of questions about the FBI's ability to protect the public, will lawmakers let him run the show?

Ashcroft gave Mueller (pictured) his unqualified support, saying the FBI director is up to the task of overhauling the bureau. But reaction from Congress has been mixed.

CQ Weekly June 1, 2002

Politics and Public Policy

changes needed to make the bureau as effective in the war on terrorism as the nation needs it to be."

Republican Charles E. Grassley of Iowa, a member of the Judiciary Committee and a longtime FBI critic, wants Rowley to testify in open session.

In the House, Judiciary Committee Democrats also are pushing for hearings. However, Chairman F. James Sensenbrenner Jr., R-Wis., said he is inclined to give Mueller time to work. He has not scheduled hearings.

New Rules for the FBI

Mueller's reorganization plan, unveiled at a news conference May 29, would shift resources away from the agency's traditional crime-fighting divisions to intelligence-gathering and analysis.

Mueller said the FBI is making counterterrorism its top priority and revamping its staff accordingly.

He also admitted to earlier misstatements about what the bureau knew before the attacks, saying he made mistakes in his public comments based on bad or missing information.

Ashcroft made it clear Mueller has the full backing of the White House.

"There is a difficult job ahead," said Ashcroft. "Bob Mueller is the right man for that job. He has a mandate for change from this administration."

Also the week of May 27, Ashcroft announced he was loosening 25-year-old guidelines that restrict the FBI's surveillance of religious and political organizations. The rules, adopted after Watergate in response to evidence that the FBI was monitoring civil rights protesters and others, were intended to strictly limit domestic spying.

Relaxing them will allow field offices to initiate counterterrorism investigations without approval from headquarters in Washington. It also will allow agents to mine databases and tap into the Internet and e-mail to help spot suspected terrorists.

The announcement could further complicate Mueller's efforts to sell his reorganization plan to Congress, reopening the debate about the proper balance between security and civil liberties. The new rules drew immediate criticism from civil liberties groups and some members of Congress.

"Any government effort to institutionalize the same powers that allowed the FBI to wrongfully spy on the activities of civil rights organizations and dis-

Changing the Focus of the FBI

On May 29, Attorney General John Ashcroft and FBI Director Robert S. Mueller III announced a series of changes to the "structure, culture and mission" of the FBI that they said would refocus the bureau on fighting terrorism. They plan to:

- Shift 480 agents from drug and other criminal investigations to counterterrorism. In all, the bureau would devote about 2,400 agents to counterterrorism, up from 1,644 before Sept. 11.
- Hire 990 additional agents by September, with a focus on computer experts, linguists, scientists and engineers to improve the bureau's intelligence-gathering and analysis.
- Develop closer ties to the CIA, with CIA analysts working within the FBI.
- Create a new Office of Intelligence, under the FBI's top official for counterterrorism and counterintelligence.
- Establish a national Joint Terrorism Task Force that includes state and local law enforcement agencies and other federal agencies, including the CIA.
- Create special Washington-based "flying squads" to coordinate national and international terrorism investigations.
- Upgrade the bureau's computer technology, with new units focused on combing through bank records, documents and e-mail for clues.
- Develop closer working relationships with state, local and foreign agencies.
- Improve counterterrorism training for FBI agents and partners in other agencies.

close information on the private affairs of Martin Luther King Jr. would constitute an embarrassing step backwards for civil liberties in this country," said John Conyers Jr. of Michigan, the House Judiciary Committee's ranking Democrat.

The FBI must have the blessing of Congress to implement much of the reorganization plan. First and foremost, Mueller needs money to hire new agents and upgrade computers, and Congress holds the purse strings.

He enjoys fairly broad, bipartisan support. One of his staunchest supporters is Dianne Feinstein, D-Calif., a member of the Senate Judiciary Committee. Even the agency's critics in Congress say they think Mueller is trying his best to overhaul the agency.

But some members said the plan does not go far enough. Grassley envisions a bureau operating exclusively as a domestic intelligence agency, giving up its traditional role of investigating bank robberies and other crimes.

"The FBI needs to let go of these areas and recognize that we've got a Drug Enforcement Administration, a Bureau of Alcohol, Tobacco and Firearms, a Coast Guard, a Customs Service, the Secret Service, a Border Patrol and others at the federal level, along with state and local law enforcement nationwide, to handle these kinds of criminal investigations, arrests and prosecutions," Grassley said. "The FBI has to concentrate on terrorism to get the job done."

Others praised Mueller's plan. "I believe it reflects a dramatic reallocation of resources to terrorism prevention without abandoning traditional law enforcement," Sensenbrenner said.

Congress' Role

House Intelligence Committee Chairman Porter J. Goss, R-Fla., said members involved in the joint House-Senate intelligence investigation will develop their own proposals for the FBI. But Mueller's plans, particularly his proposed Office of Intelligence, are a "fine start," he said.

"The devil's going to be a little bit in the details on whether you create an office that does anything," Goss said. "You need fusion between law enforcement and intelligence, and just setting up an office doesn't make that happen."

Observers from the intelligence community itself are divided about lawmakers' role.

The former head of the FBI's counterterrorism office, Robert Heibel, said lawmakers will have to be involved in the plan if it is to be successful.

"Congress will have to supply the money and will probably have to back

Law and Judiciary

Ex-Federal Prosecutor Eleanor Hill Leads Staff of Intelligence Probe

The new staff director for the joint House-Senate investigation of intelligence failures starts with considerable good will based on her work in Congress and at the Pentagon. The absence of a spy-gathering background will force her to be a quick learner.

Leaders of the House and Senate Intelligence committees announced May 29 that Eleanor Hill would lead the bipartisan inquiry. She had been the top candidate for several weeks, but her hiring was delayed because her security clearance had expired. (2002 CQ Weekly, p. 1370)

A former federal prosecutor, Hill served as the Pentagon's inspector general during the Clinton administration. She worked for the Senate Governmental Affairs Permanent Select Subcommittee on Investigations. She also served as counsel to former Sen. Sam Nunn, D-Ga. (1972-97) during the Iran-contra inquiry.

Hill is a partner with Nunn at the law firm of King & Spalding.

She replaces former CIA inspector general L. Britt Snider, who resigned in April after hiring someone who had once failed a CIA polygraph test. His selection drew criticism from conservatives who feared he was too close to CIA Director George J. Tenet to look aggressively at the CIA's performance. (2002 CQ Weekly, pp. 1174, 485)

Lawmakers strongly praised Hill for her impartiality and familiarity with the mechanics of conducting congressional investigations.

"I believe that our objective is to produce a credible product which will help prevent a third Pearl Harbor," said Richard C. Shelby of Alabama, the Senate Intelligence Committee's ranking Republican and a critic of Snider. "I am hopeful that Ms. Hill's extensive national security and law enforcement experience, coupled with her professional detachment, will help our joint inquiry achieve that objective."

Outside observers such as Steven Aftergood, a senior research analyst at the Federation of American Scientists, have noted Hill's lack of direct experience at the CIA or other spy agencies and said she will have to learn quickly. House Intelligence Committee Chairman Porter J. Goss, R-Fla., said Hill is up to the task.

She will oversee a staff of two dozen investigators who have been reviewing documents and interviewing witnesses since February. Although lawmakers complained that the Justice Department had blocked access to some documents and witnesses, they are confident those problems have been worked out.

The committees are planning to begin a series of closed hearings June 4. Open hearings will follow later in the month.

The probe will coincide with consideration of the fiscal 2003 intelligence authorization bill (HR 4628). House leaders plan to take up the bill the week of June 3, hoping the clamor for an independent commission will have subsided.

this plan very aggressively in order for it to work," he said. "Mueller can't possibly pull this thing off unless Congress is fully on board with him."

Another former top Justice Department counterterrorism official, Victoria Toensing, said Congress will only do damage if it tries to oversee the agency's reorganization too closely. Toensing, who helped start the FBI's first terrorism unit in 1984, during the Reagan administration, said no one in Congress is up to aggressively managing such a reorganization.

"They will summon Mueller to the Hill and make a lot of noise, but in the end it will have to be up to him to make this whole thing work," she said.

An FBI overhaul bill (S 1974) is already awaiting a Senate vote. That measure, approved by the Judiciary Committee on April 25, was written largely in response to earlier scandals, including the discovery that longtime agent Robert Hanssen was a spy. (2002 CQ Weekly, p. 1085)

The measure would require FBI employees and contractors with access to sensitive information to undergo periodic lie detector tests. It would mandate that the bureau report to Congress on the legal justification for all of its programs and activities — a provision meant to lay the groundwork for a congressional review of its responsibilities.

The bill also would clarify that the Justice Department's inspector general is responsible for overseeing the FBI.

The bill has been blocked by an anonymous hold by a Republican senator. Leahy said the legislation would be a good step forward. Strengthening the powers of the inspector general to root out problems is long overdue, he said.

Senate Judiciary aides say that bill will probably not be used as a vehicle for a more ambitious congressional restructuring package for the FBI. More likely would be a new bill, drafted by either the Intelligence or Judiciary committee.

Another vehicle could be a reauthorization bill for the Justice Department. The House and Senate passed competing versions of that measure (HR 2215) last year. (2001 CQ Weekly, p. 3092)

Without a reauthorization bill, the programs have been continued for the past 23 years as part of the annual appropriations bills for the departments of Commerce, Justice and State.

If they chose to, lawmakers could use a reauthorization to mandate changes in policy and funding for the FBI. ◆

Politics and Public Policy

New Wave of Nuclear Weaponry Sure to Spur Explosive Conference

President's plan to develop powerful 'bunker busters' sharply divides parties amid fear of a new round of worldwide proliferation

In writing a defense bill, the Republican-controlled House not only echoed, but elaborated on President Bush's view that nuclear weapons are more versatile tools of war and diplomacy than has been the case in recent U.S. policy.

That perspective gives Senate Democrats pause, especially lawmakers who believe that the Bush administration, by treating nuclear weapons as a useful instrument, provides other countries with a powerful incentive to acquire them.

The argument guided the Senate Armed Services Committee, which in drawing up its version of the fiscal 2003 defense authorization bill (S 2514) took the opposite tack from the House, cutting Bush's request for some nuclear programs.

And if the slim Democratic majority can maintain those nuclear positions against promised Republican challenges when the Senate takes up the defense bill later this month, the stage will be set for a fierce showdown in a House-Senate conference.

The House bill (HR 4546) not only would approve of Bush's request to develop a new nuclear "bunker buster," capable of digging out deeply buried chemical, biological or nuclear weapons, it also would order the Energy Department to lay the groundwork for speedy resumption of nuclear weapons testing — if the president called for it.

In its report on the bill, the House Armed Services Committee also urged the Pentagon to consider using nuclear warheads on anti-missile interceptors, even though such weapons do not figure in the administration's wide-ranging missile defense plan.

The Senate panel, in its bill, denied the $15 million that Bush sought for the bunker buster, which is certain to be a focal point of a conference in either July or September. (*2002 CQ Weekly, p. 1207*)

These craters in the Nevada desert, in 1992, are the result of underground nuclear tests. The United States has observed a nuclear test moratorium since September of that year.

The significance of the nuclear arms issue belies the relatively small fraction of the $393.4 billion authorization measure that is at stake.

Conferees also will have to wrestle with a high-priced dispute over Bush's $7.8 billion missile defense request, which the House bill would fully fund but the Senate committee would cut by $812 million — barring any successful GOP amendments on the Senate floor to restore the money.

Price Tag Could Be Trouble

In the coming months, Senate Armed Services Committee Chairman Carl Levin, D-Mich., and his allies will have to decide how hard to push on nuclear weapons and missile defense issues. Bush has made it clear that he holds the high card — the veto card, to be exact.

Despite the prestige of the House and Senate Armed Services committees, the annual defense authorization bill — their chief legislative product — is not a must-pass bill; the defense appropriations measure, one of the 13 annual spending bills, can cover the military's expenses.

Since 1988, when President Ronald Reagan vetoed the first version of the fiscal 1989 authorization bill over Democratic-sponsored provisions that restricted anti-missile defense, presidents of both parties have vetoed, or threatened to veto, authorization bills to dispose of what they see as onerous provisions. (*1989 Almanac, p. 399*)

Even President Bill Clinton, whose problematic draft record made some in his administration hesitant about challenging the military, vetoed the first version of the fiscal 1996 defense bill at no apparent political cost. (*1995 Almanac, p. 9-3*)

Last fall, Bush threatened to veto the fiscal 2002 bill to force reluctant Republicans to approve additional base closings. This year, he already has made one veto threat, warning Congress that he would spike the bill if it blocked the Pentagon's decision to cancel development of the Army's Crusader cannon. (*2002 CQ Weekly, p. 1326*)

Beyond specific issues such as nuclear arms and missile defense, the conferees face a major challenge in simply agreeing on the total amount of spending they can authorize.

CQ Weekly June 1, 2002

Defense

On paper, the Senate committee version would authorize about $10 billion more than the House bill — $393.3 billion. But in fact, the $383.4 billion House plan is the larger of the two because the Armed Services Committee used creative bookkeeping, drawing up a second bill of $10 billion and adding $3.4 billion to Bush's budget request. The move allowed the House Armed Services Committee to ensure that the defense bill remained in compliance with a House-passed budget ceiling.

This reflects the insistence of House Republican defense hawks that despite the $48.1 billion defense budget increase Bush has proposed for 2003, the amount is not enough. The defense hawks believe that at least an additional $20 billion is needed annually to maintain the force and field new high-tech weapons under development. (2002 CQ Weekly, p. 1410)

Though many congressional Republicans share this view, it is at odds with the approach of Defense Secretary Donald H. Rumsfeld, who insists that the services' long-range modernization plans are simply unaffordable and must be cut back.

Rumsfeld's first major initiative in that direction was his May 8 decision to cancel the Crusader. Consistent with that step, the administration sent an amended budget request to Congress May 29 seeking to reallocate the cannon's funds.

In his budget-driven push to modernize the force, Rumsfeld also has ordered the services to draw up alternative plans that would cancel or scale back the planned purchase of several major programs, including the Air Force's F-22 fighter, the Marine Corps' Osprey tilt-rotor aircraft, the Army's Comanche scout helicopter and the Navy's plan for a new type of aircraft carrier.

$10 Billion Contingency Fund

Further complicating the defense budget process are bookkeeping differences between Bush's request and the congressional measures.

Under the president's plan, the budget would provide $3.3 billion to cover the cost of anticipated changes in pensions and medical care for retired civilian employees. Congress has not approved the proposed changes, and neither version of the defense bill includes that money.

Bush also sought a $10 billion contingency fund for the future war on terrorism. The Senate committee would provide those funds, while the House-passed measure does not, which accounts for most of the disparity in the two bills.

The House Armed Services Committee dipped into the $10 billion fund to pay for $3.4 billion worth of defense programs. It drafted a second bill (HR 4547) that would authorize the $10 billion fund and then transferred costs totalling $3.4 billion out of the regular bill into HR 4547.

The House committee said the costs it shifted to the smaller bill were all associated with the ongoing war against terrorism, including $900 million to cover the cost of Air Force patrols over U.S. territory. But the budgetary maneuver also allowed the panel to add to its bill funds for long-term investments, such as $1 billion for shipbuilding and $550 million to increase by nearly 1 percent (12,652 personnel) the size of the active-duty force.

Eyeing Modifications, Upgrades

The bunker buster, also known as the robust nuclear earth penetrator, would be an air-dropped bomb designed to dig out deeply buried command posts and installations that manufacture or store chemical, biological and nuclear weapons. In addition to the $15 million requested, the project is expected to cost $46 million in future years.

The Clinton administration developed a modified version of the B-61 nuclear bomb for this purpose, placing the warhead in an extremely strong casing with a pointed nose. But the new version did not dig very deep, even when dropped from a high altitude. The Energy Department's current plan is to try other modifications of the B-61 or reconfigure a larger nuclear weapon, the B-83, as a penetrator.

Critics argue that developing a nuclear weapon to deal with a non-nuclear threat — in this case, chemical and biological weapons — will weaken the psychological barrier against the use of nuclear weapons. Another element to that argument is the view from proponents of nuclear earth penetrators, who maintain that if they are small enough, they could destroy their targets without creating widespread damage or nuclear fallout.

But the current plan makes no such promise; the weapons to be modified would have an explosive power equivalent to 300,000 tons of TNT (300 kilotons).

The House bill would require the Energy Department to draw up a plan to reduce to one year the time it would take to conduct an underground nuclear explosion, once a decision to test was made. Current estimates show it would take two to three years to resume testing.

The United States has observed a nuclear test moratorium since September 1992, relying on periodic inspections and computer simulations to monitor the effectiveness of its nuclear stockpile. However, many conservatives insist that test explosions would have to be resumed to check the condition of the stockpile and to develop new warheads, such as the earth penetrator.

The House bill would make relatively minor changes to Bush's request for $7.8 billion to develop and deploy a missile defense system. The bill would add $52 million to that effort to modify the Navy's Aegis cruisers to intercept long-range ballistic missiles in midflight.

But the House committee has its doubts about the administration's plan to equip a 747 jetliner with a missile-killing laser. The Pentagon has placed a greater emphasis on the program in which the laser would destroy a missile in the first few minutes of flight, the so-called boost-phase, when the missile's rocket engine is fired and is easy to locate.

The bill would authorize $521 million of the $598 million requested for the airborne laser, a reduction that the committee said would delay the purchase of some equipment without affecting the pace of development.

The panel stressed that 30 years of efforts to develop a militarily useful anti-missile laser had shown "singularly unimpressive" results.

A more promising alternative, the committee argued, would be for the Pentagon to consider using drone airplanes armed with guided missiles that could catch a missile as it accelerates from its launch site.

House Republicans remain optimistic about the Pentagon's long-term budget outlook, evident in the way their bill deals with major Army weapons programs. The legislation would authorize the amounts requested

Politics and Public Policy

Where the Money Would Go

President Bush requested $393.4 billion for the military in fiscal 2003. The House version of the defense bill (HR 4546) and the Senate Armed Services Committee bill (S 2225) would cut spending for some programs while increasing the funds for others.

(in millions of dollars)	BUSH REQUEST	HOUSE BILL	SENATE COMMITTEE	
GROUND COMBAT				
Comanche helicopter	$915	$915	$915	House limits development to $6 billion
Interim armored vehicles	812	812	812	Pentagon plans to buy 332 wheeled vehicles for third of six brigades
Future combat system	836	836	941	Goal is to field several types of 20-ton vehicles beginning in 2008
Crusader cannon *- amended request	0*	476	476	Rumsfeld wants to shift funds to other artillery weapons
Armored vehicle upgrades	947	1,053	947	House would add $106 million to improve equipment for National Guard units
NUCLEAR ARMS AND MISSILE DEFENSE				
Small nuclear warhead	$15	$15	$0	Aim is to develop earth-penetrating weapon to destroy underground stocks of chemical and biological weapons
Weapons plants	950	995	990	Energy Department program maintains currently inactive facilities to manufacture nuclear bomb components
Ballistic missile defense	7,763	7,784	6,951	Bush's goal is to develop an array of anti-missile systems. Also procures the Army's short-range PAC-3
Former Soviet arms disposal	1,218	1,179	1,218	Nunn-Lugar and related programs to dispose of nuclear, chemical and biological weapons
ELECTRONIC WARFARE				
Joint STARS radar plane	$279	$279	$279	Pentagon plans to buy 17th of the ground-surveillance planes
Global Hawk and Predator unmanned aerial vehicles	283	309	283	House bill would add to Bush's request to buy long-range, armed Predators
Prowler radar jammer plane	224	328	338	Both bills accelerate modernization of jamming gear and aging airframes

Comanche helicopter

Global Hawk

to develop lighter, more easily deployable forces for the future, and it would add to the money sought for modernizing the current force.

As Bush requested, the bill would provide $836 million to continue developing the Future Combat Systems, a family of lightweight vehicles, including tanks, troop carriers, mobile cannons and reconnaissance robots. None of the items would weigh more than 20 tons — less than a third of the weight of the M-1 tank.

But when it comes to upgrading the current so-called legacy force, the House bill is more generous than the administration.

The Army insists that it has to continue upgrading some of its current equipment to keep up while the new, high-tech units are being created. But it plans to install the most expensive of these modifications in only a portion of the existing force.

The House bill would provide the $500 million requested to equip some M-1 tanks with advanced computers and night-vision equipment. The measure also would add $60 million to the $397 million requested to upgrade Bradley troop carriers, while it would add $46 million to the $50 million requested to upgrade caterpillar-tracked tow vehicles intended to recover 70-ton M-1 tanks that break down or are damaged on the battlefield.

Court Ruling Could Affect Bill

Consistent with the president's request, the House bill would authorize construction of two Aegis destroyers ($2.3 billion) and one nuclear submarine ($1.5 billion), as well as $706 million to buy components to be used in future submarine construction. It also would authorize $825 million to convert four large subs to carry conventionally armed cruise missiles instead of the long-range Trident nuclear missiles they were built to launch.

In total, the bill would add $1.1 billion to Bush's $8.2 billion shipbuilding request, including $229 million to reverse an administration decision that would have delayed by one year the

Defense

	BUSH REQUEST	HOUSE BILL	SENATE COMMITTEE	
AIR COMBAT				
F-22 fighter	$5,248	$5,248	$5,248	Air Force plans to continue flight testing and buy 23 planes
Joint Strike Fighter (F-35)	3,471	3,471	3,471	Pentagon wants to continue development with first procurement in 2008
F/A-18 E/F	3,073	3,073	3,313	Senate-committee bill would add four planes to the 44 requested
B-2 modifications	297	346	356	Aim is to improve communications and durability of "stealthy" surface
NAVAL FORCES				
Aircraft carrier	$244	$473	$473	Both bills would enable construction to begin in 2006, reversing administration decision to delay work for one year
DD(X) destroyer	960	960	960	Navy envisions designing new family of warships, with construction of first vessel to start in 2005
Aegis destroyers	2,296	3,180	2,296	In the House bill, the outcome of pending litigation will determine how many Aegis destroyers would be funded
Missile submarine conversion	825	825	825	Pentagon plans to convert four nuclear Trident submarines to carry conventional cruise missiles
AIR AND SEA TRANSPORT				
C-17 long-range jet	2,694	2,694	2,705	Senate committee would add $11 million for training equipment
Blackhawk helicopter	$438	$626	$534	House bill would add 12 helicopters, Senate committee nine to the 27 (of various versions) budgeted for the Army and Navy
Army and Navy V-22 Osprey	1,046	1,046	1,046	Pentagon wants to continue flight testing and buy 11 aircraft to keep production line intact
LPD-17 transport ship	596	596	596	Navy plans to buy fifth ship of the class

SOURCE: House, Senate Armed Services Committee bills
PHOTO CREDITS: Global Hawk, Blackhawk — Department of Defense; F-22 fighter — U.S. Air Force

start of construction of the next nuclear powered carrier.

But when it came to dividing up the rest of the increase, the House Armed Services Committee was caught between the competing demands of shipyards in Maine and Mississippi that build destroyers and yards in Connecticut and Virginia that build submarines. Ultimately, the bill stipulated that the allocation of $810 million in shipbuilding funds would depend on the outcome of pending litigation.

At issue is an 11-year-old legal challenge by Boeing and General Dynamics to the government's cancellation of the A-12 attack plane. Last August, the U.S. Court of Claims ruled in the government's favor, making the companies liable for $2.3 billion — $1.3 billion that they were paid on the contract before it was canceled in January 1991, plus $1 billion in interest.

The companies instead offered a package of discounts and other contractor-provided sweeteners for several defense programs. Included in the proposed deal was an offer of $385 million that General Dynamics would spend to buy submarine components that would allow the Navy to start buying two subs a year as early as 2005. Under current budget projections, the Navy would buy only one sub a year until 2007, when it would start buying two annually.

The Justice Department has rejected that offer, but the companies still are negotiating for an in-kind settlement with the government. Meanwhile, the House bill would authorize $810 million to buy a third Aegis destroyer if the submarine builder committed to spending $385 million for sub components in fiscal 2003.

If there was no deal, the bill would parcel out the $810 million among three programs — $415 million for sub components, $210 million to begin modernizing older Aegis cruisers and $185 million to refuel a sub.

More Hardware

The bill would authorize the $12 billion requested for the services' three

Politics and Public Policy

main jet fighter programs: the Air Force's Lockheed Martin F-22; the Navy's Boeing F/A-18 E/F; and the Lockheed Martin F-35, formerly the Joint Strike Fighter. The latter will be built in three versions for use by the Navy, Air Force and Marine Corps.

The House bill would add $49 million to the $297 million requested to develop and make improvements in the B-2 stealth bomber. The additional funds would equip the plane with better communications links and various modifications intended to make it easier to maintain its radar-evading surface.

As requested, the House bill would authorize $279 million to buy the 17th Joint STARS ground-surveillance radar plane, the last one the Pentagon plans to fund. The bill also would authorize the $679 million requested for the prototype of a new ground-surveillance plane that would be based on Boeing 767 jetliners, rather than the aging 707s that were converted into Joint STARS.

The House Armed Services Committee went along with the $784 million requested to continue developing the Global Hawk long-range reconnaissance drone and to buy three of the planes, which have the wingspan of a medium-sized jetliner. But the panel shifted $65 million for one of the three planes to the companion bill, HR 4547, authorizing a total of $719 million for Global Hawk in the main authorization bill.

The House panel approved the $113 million requested to continue production of the smaller Predator drone and to buy Maverick guided missiles, which have been fired from Predators at targets over Afghanistan. However, the bill would shift $61 million of this amount to the companion bill. In the main defense bill, the House would add $26 million to the Predator authorization to begin buying a larger version of the aircraft that could remain in the air longer and carry more weapons.

The bill also would add $114 million to the $224 million requested to upgrade the Navy's aging fleet of Prowler radar jammer planes. The additional money would accelerate the replacement of wing sections that are wearing out and the installation of more versatile jamming equipment.

As requested, the bill would authorize $2.7 billion to buy 12 additional C-17 cargo jets and $1 billion to buy 11 tilt-rotor Osprey troop carriers, the minimum number that would keep the assembly line intact while the craft undergoes at least 18 months of additional flight tests, which began May 29. The aircraft was grounded in December 2000 after two fatal crashes.

As has become routine, the bill would authorize more than was requested to buy the Army's Blackhawk troop carrying helicopters and the Navy's similar Seahawks, which are built in Connecticut by United Technologies. Bush requested $438 million for 27, aircraft and the bill would authorize $626 million for 39.

As requested, the bill would authorize $243 million to continue construction of a large helicopter carrier for Marine Corps landing forces, being built in Pascagoula, Miss., by Northrop Grumman. It also would provide the $10 million requested to begin work on the next ship of this type.

The bill would add to the requested $9 million to continue experimenting with a high-speed Australian-designed catamaran that the Army, Navy and Marine Corps have tested.

Pensions vs. Disability Payments

In response to the outcry from service members and veterans, the House bill would begin the process of substantially eliminating by 2007 the law that bans "concurrent receipt" of military pensions and disability payments.

Under the existing law, retirees' pensions are reduced to offset any disability payments they receive from the Department of Veterans Affairs. Congress has tried to compensate veterans who are more than 60 percent disabled by awarding them a special monthly payment. The House bill would increase those payments through 2007, at which point retirees with 60 percent or more disability would receive both their full military pensions and their full VA disability benefits.

The Congressional Budget Office estimates that the cost of this provision would rise from $516 million in 2003 to just under $2 billion in 2007. ◆

Bush Strips Crusader's Budget

If any doubts existed in Congress as to whether President Bush is serious about cancellation of the Crusader cannon, the administration has made it official.

The White House on May 29 formally amended its initial fiscal 2003 budget request that called for funding the program at $476 million. Now, Bush wants to reallocate all the funds for the Crusader to other Army programs.

Defense Secretary Donald H. Rumsfeld announced May 8 that he was canceling the program, the first step in his effort to transform the military to a lightweight, mobile force. (CQ Weekly, p. 1202)

But there is strong resistance to the decision on Capitol Hill. The House defense bill (HR 4546) would provide the $476 million and report language states that work on the 40-ton cannon cannot be shelved until a review is done.

The Senate Armed Services Committee also would fully fund the program in its bill (S 2514), but the panel's leaders said the committee would decide on the program's fate after receiving the amended budget request. That decision could be made as early as the week of June 3, when Congress returns from its Memorial Day recess.

As Pentagon officials had promised, the amended request keeps much of the money in the Army's budget with all but a small amount directed to projects designed to field highly accurate, long-range artillery.

The largest piece ($310 million) would go to the Future Combat Systems to accelerate work on a highly mobile guided-missile launcher. Other projects that would receive significant slices of the Crusader money are the Excalibur artillery shell ($48 million) and a guided version of the Army's standard artillery rocket ($45 million), both of which would use global positioning system satellites to steer the weapon within 10 yards of its target.

Finance

An Industry Called to Account
Will Enron collapse lead to new laws for auditors or more self-regulation?

Energy and Commerce Committee investigators pore over Enron documents Jan. 17. Revelations from the scandal have revived a debate about stiffening oversight of corporate auditors to restore public confidence in corporate financial statements.

Only a year and a half ago, Rep. Billy Tauzin was one of many lawmakers who helped block a plan by Securities and Exchange Commission (SEC) Chairman Arthur Levitt Jr. to bar accounting firms from taking consulting payments for some extra services from corporations whose books they audited.

Many members of Congress, ranging from the conservative Tauzin, a Louisiana Republican, to liberal New York Democratic Sen. Charles E. Schumer, wrote Levitt to protest the proposed rule, which the accounting industry feared would choke off their increasingly lucrative consulting businesses.

"At the time, he felt it was premature," said Tauzin spokesman Ken Johnson. "But none of us has a crystal ball."

Tauzin is not the only lawmaker rethinking old policy questions in the wake of the spectacular collapse of Enron Corp., the Houston-based energy giant whose December bankruptcy is the largest in U.S. history.

"It's inevitable we will see a requirement that you can't audit and consult for the same clients," said senior House Energy and Commerce Committee Joe L. Barton, R-Texas.

Critics of the industry — which is responsible for maintaining the integrity of corporate financial statements — are pressing for tighter regulation.

Not only are lawmakers rethinking their opposition to a ban on consulting fees, but the new chairman of the SEC has proposed a plan to tighten oversight of the loosely regulated accounting industry, reversing his own pledge to take a "kinder and gentler" approach to regulation.

Fueled by a drumbeat of revelations the week of Jan. 14 of mistakes by Arthur Andersen LLP, which was Enron's outside auditor, SEC Chairman Harvey Pitt unveiled plans Jan. 17 to create a new oversight body funded by the private sector but "dominated" by public members, to regulate accounting firms under the SEC's continuing oversight.

The new body would replace the current clubby system of peer review, in which accounting firms take turns reviewing each others' work, with the SEC focusing on investigations of illegalities.

The accounting scandal stirred up by Enron is just the latest example of a big corporation having to revise its financial statements, with resulting losses to investors. Despite many prior auditing mishaps, the industry easily beat back Levitt's efforts to impose a new rule that would have banned accounting firms from performing some types of other services for their auditing clients.

Accountability Crisis

But with the Enron scandal in the national spotlight, at least eight congressional committees have launched investigations and even the accounting firms are signaling a willingness to accept oversight they have successfully resisted in the past.

"The industry does see the need to do something," said John C. Coffee Jr., a law professor at Columbia University. "They understand that they have an

CQ Weekly Jan. 19, 2002

Politics and Public Policy

accountability crisis."

The political elements of the emerging scandal are tinged with partisanship. Some Democrats are eager to exploit Enron's numerous ties to the Bush administration to seek a tactical advantage in the midterm elections in November. Republicans and the White House insist there is no evidence of wrongdoing by administration officials.

But there is also a bipartisan sense of outrage over allegations that Enron executives played a fast-and-loose accounting game that enriched company officers but left investors and employees holding the bag.

To date, the accounting industry has used its considerable clout on Capitol Hill to avoid not only legislation, but more stringent regulation, such as Levitt's attempt to impose new restrictions. Now, the Enron/Andersen debacle has revived Levitt's proposal, which was aimed at preventing conflicts of interest between the accountants' duties as auditors and their increasingly profitable work as consultants for the same clients.

The key question for the accounting industry is whether the unraveling chain of revelations about the conduct of both Enron and Andersen will lead to new legislation mandating stricter standards.

Pitt said the SEC has all the authority it needs under current law to tighten oversight of the beleaguered accounting industry. Some powerful lawmakers, however, are eager to get directly involved.

"We're definitely going to do a bill," said Tauzin.

Enron filed for bankruptcy Dec. 2, weeks after revealing that accounting errors had forced it to revise financial statements for the past several years.

Renewed Scrutiny

Since then, there has been a flood of revelations about the many private investment partnerships that Enron engineered to keep debts totaling hundreds of millions of dollars off its balance sheet. The SEC, the Justice Department and several congressional committees are examining whether Enron complied with existing accounting standards in constructing the partnerships, and what role Andersen's auditors might have played in signing off on erroneous financial statements.

To put it mildly, the affair has renewed scrutiny of the regulatory regime for the accounting industry.

At the least, changes likely are on the way for the industry's self-regulatory peer review process. Critics say the system, in which the large firms essentially take turns every three years reviewing each others' work, gives them little incentive to issue negative reports.

Federal securities laws give the SEC the authority to police accounting and auditing standards. In practice, the commission has always delegated that authority to several privately funded standards-setting bodies, such as the Financial Accounting Standards Board and the American Institute of Certified Public Accountants (AICPA). The SEC investigates potential legal violations and brings civil enforcement cases.

"The history for a long time is that there's been no discipline in the accounting profession," Coffee said, adding that the peer review process was "noteworthy because of the lack of censure or discipline."

At a Jan. 17 news conference, Pitt unveiled the concept of a new oversight body for the accounting industry, funded by the private sector but "dominated" by public members. The details of the new body are being worked out in discussions with the accounting firms — discussions that began before Enron filed for bankruptcy. But Pitt

Policy Debates From the Ashes of Enron

As congressional committees and criminal investigators sort through the puzzle of Enron Corp.'s finances, the epic collapse of an economic giant has sparked substantive debates that could occupy Congress all year. The issues include:

PENSION SECURITY

Enron employee retirement savings were lost in the company's collapse, triggering a prompt re-examination of the rules governing retirement plans. Congressional Democrats are calling for new legislation that would limit the amount of employee assets in employer-sponsored retirement plans that could be invested in employer stock, and would require firms to allow workers more flexibility to trade their stock. And new life has been breathed into a bipartisan bill (HR 2269) that would give workers access to third-party investment advisers. President Bush launched a retirement security task force, which Treasury Secretary Paul H. O'Neill says will examine the rules while being careful not to "create a chilling effect that reduces incentives that people have to create retirement security plans."

ENERGY POLICY

Many analysts were already skeptical about the prospects for enactment of a broad new energy policy this year, and the bankruptcy of Enron can only add to the difficulty. This election-year debate was expected to be more political than policy-oriented, making Enron's trouble ripe for possible exploitation by Democrats who say Bush is too cozy with the energy industry. And an electricity deregulation bill pushed by Joe L. Barton, R-Texas, chairman of the Energy and Commerce Subcommittee on Energy and Air Quality, now seems even less likely to move through the House with the loss of a major deregulation champion, Enron.

DERIVATIVES REGULATION

The Commodity Futures Modernization Act of 2000, which largely exempted trading in over-the-counter derivatives from federal scrutiny, is likely to be the focus of lawmakers' efforts to require more transparency in these financial instruments. Derivatives are financial contracts based on the value of an underlying product, such as stocks, commodities or currencies. After a debate over the need for disclosure, the 2000 law codified a level of secrecy in the growing derivatives market, permitting parties to enter into contracts without having to report details of the deal to their investors.

Tauzin-Dingell Cooperation Gets Results in Enron Probe

Before launching his investigation of power marketing giant Enron Corp., House Energy and Commerce Committee Chairman Billy Tauzin, R-La., sought assistance from an old ally, Democrat John D. Dingell of Michigan.

"I wanted his help to get the facts on the table," Tauzin said.

And so he has. Dingell, whose take-no-prisoners investigative style became legendary during his 14-year tenure as committee chairman, agreed to make the probe a bipartisan one.

So far, the investigation has produced more detailed information about Enron's collapse than any other Capitol Hill probe. It was as a result of requests for documents by the committee's staff, for example, that Enron auditor Arthur Andersen LLP acknowledged that some relevant paperwork had been shredded, and that a senior executive at Enron had written a letter warning that accounting irregularities could destroy the company.

When Tauzin took over the committee in 2001, he pledged to be more of an activist chairman than his predecessor, Thomas J. Bliley Jr., R-Va. (1981-2001). But the new chairman was not expected to wield the oversight as aggressively as Dingell had. (2001 CQ Weekly, p. 258)

With Enron, however, that perception is changing quickly. Under an unusual deal cut last year to expedite the investigation during the recess, Dingell and Tauzin agreed to pool investigators and share a treasure trove of documents and interviews with whistleblowers.

On Jan. 16, eight staff aides of both parties grilled the chief auditor of Enron after he had been fired by Andersen. While Tauzin stalked deer on a hunting trip with Rep. Sonny Callahan, R-Ala., and tended to constituents that week, committee investigators interviewed sources in Houston and made preparations for a hearing the week of Jan. 21.

Under Tauzin, shown here in 2001, Energy and Commerce is regaining its old reputation for investigative activism.

Now, Tauzin is developing a legislative outcome for his Enron probe: a draft bill that would increase disclosure requirements for power marketing companies.

"We're going to deal with accounting standards. And I want to look at how energy markets function," Tauzin said.

One of Tauzin's close allies, Joe L. Barton, R-Texas, said the committee's bill would probably require a company's auditors and consultant to be independent. "There's clearly a conflict of interest if one company is filling both roles," Barton said.

This issue could rekindle a rivalry between Tauzin's panel and the Financial Services Committee, but Tauzin said he would try to work out an agreement on jurisdiction. The committees have jostled with one another for turf on matters of corporate regulation since Speaker J. Dennis Hastert, R-Ill., worked out a deal to move securities issues from Tauzin's panel to Financial Services.

Hastert's compromise gave Tauzin control over rules set by the Financial Accounting Standards Board, which sets standards for the industry, but ensured that Financial Services Chairman Michael G. Oxley, R-Ohio, would have jurisdiction over the Securities and Exchange Commission, which oversees some accounting mandates. (2001 CQ Weekly, p. 261)

Committee members say Tauzin's inclusiveness — he brings both subcommittee chairmen and ranking Democrats into his trust — is part of his management style. But his relationship with Dingell is a complex one.

Dingell was a mentor to Tauzin before the Louisiana lawmaker left the Democratic Party in 1995.

'Wherever It Leads'

"John is my model," Tauzin said. "He showed us that you must be aggressive. You follow the investigation wherever it leads, friend or foe."

The two are known for their collaboration on a bill (HR 1542) to deregulate the high-speed data market. But they have clashed on Tauzin's efforts to repeal the Public Utilities Holding Company Act of 1935, which Dingell staunchly backs.

Barton and other Republicans say Tauzin's media blitz on Enron and his push for new product safety disclosure standards after the Firestone tire recalls in 2000 have helped the committee regain the reputation it built under Dingell.

"There's a different chemistry now," Barton said. "Who's a whistleblower going to call? Billy Tauzin. Our committee has been getting all the facts."

Politics and Public Policy

said the new organization would be empowered to investigate and discipline individual firms.

"Somehow we have got to put a stop to a vicious cycle that has now been in evidence for far too many years," Pitt said.

Pitt also called for more frequent financial disclosures, and "plain English financial statements."

Pitt said he was seeking to change the peer review process "to avoid firm-on-firm review." The SEC chairman is pushing for more frequent monitoring of accounting firms by a "permanent quality control staff" hired by the prospective new oversight body.

Whether the move to establish the new oversight board will head off new legislation to regulate the accounting industry may depend on how satisfied Congress is with the SEC's final product.

"The ultimate need for legislation is a determination Congress should make," Pitt said, adding that he intended to work closely with Capitol Hill in further developing his proposal.

The evolving SEC proposal came under fire from Sen. Jon Corzine, D-N.J., a former Goldman Sachs co-chairman who has urged Pitt to recuse himself from the SEC's Enron investigation. In a Jan. 17 statement, Corzine said Pitt's plan was fundamentally flawed and called on the SEC to assume direct responsibility for hands-on oversight of the accounting industry. Corzine said he is prepared to introduce legislation mandating new rules for auditors if the SEC "cannot handle the task through its own administrative actions."

Questions also have been raised about whether Pitt, who represented the Big Five accounting firms as a private lawyer before assuming the SEC chairmanship last year, is the right person to trust with a regulatory overhaul of the profession. Pitt on Jan. 17 forcefully rejected such concerns.

"There is no way that I would ever do anything to compromise the integrity of this agency's actions," Pitt said.

Rep. John D. Dingell of Michigan, the ranking Democrat on the House Energy and Commerce Committee and a longtime advocate of auditor independence, called Pitt's plan "useful" and said the SEC chairman "should anticipate vigorous Congressional assistance with the all-important details."

The accounting industry responded to Pitt's announcement with cautious optimism.

"We support the plan and the principles he's laid out," said Barry C. Melancon, president and CEO of the AICPA. "It's a constructive step to focus on the public's confidence in the capital markets."

Auditing vs. Consulting

Lawmakers are likely to turn a skeptical eye on the accounting industry's increasing habit of making money by selling other services to their clients.

Critics charge that the objectivity of auditors is compromised by the fact that, in many cases, the audit firm also gets paid for performing other work, such as internal auditing, tax services, and information technology consulting.

In recent years, such revenues have become a steadily larger share of the auditing companies' overall income. In 2000, Andersen earned $25 million from Enron for its auditing services, and an additional $27 million for other services it performed.

In June 2000, Levitt proposed eliminating possible conflicts of interest with a new SEC rule that would have banned auditing firms from performing certain kinds of other services for their clients, such as installing financial information systems.

The large accounting firms, along with AICPA — all of whom have considerable clout on Capitol Hill — swung into action to block Levitt's proposal. Collectively, the six entities donated more than $4.2 million to federal candidates and political parties in 2000, according to Common Cause, a public watchdog group. Andersen spent $1.6 million on lobbying in the last six months of 2000 alone, according to the Center for Responsive Politics, another watchdog group.

"I don't think it ever pays to bet against the accounting industry when you're talking about the Hill," said Barbara Roper, director of investor protection for the Consumer Federation of America.

In the end, Levitt's SEC bowed to pressure from Congress and the accounting firms, especially Andersen, which vigorously fought the new rule. The accounting firms and the SEC struck a compromise in November 2000 that restricted some non-audit services and boosted disclosure requirements.

The final rule was a "modest, weak substitute for what was originally proposed," Coffee said. "I was never really happy with this modest tinkering with the deck chairs on the Titanic."

One target of lawmakers' ire could be the "special-purpose entities" Enron established to move debt off its balance sheet.

"I never had heard, until Enron, of a special-purpose entity," groused Sen. Ernest F. Hollings, D-S.C., at a Senate Commerce Committee hearing Dec. 18 on Enron. "In fact, I'm determined to put in a bill to eliminate that thing; I don't know what it is."

The House Energy and Commerce Committee, chaired by Tauzin, raced out in front of the congressional pack, with a series of letters to Enron, Andersen and the SEC, demanding untold reams of documents related to Enron's business practices, Andersen's auditing work, and the SEC's oversight of Enron. The committee's investigators have been responsible for a string of explosive revelations regarding Andersen's audits of Enron's books.

The committee discovered several Enron and Andersen documents. Among them are an August 2001 memo from an Enron executive to Kenneth L. Lay, the company's chief executive, raising accounting concerns about several of Enron's partnerships. Tauzin's committee also has publicized two internal Andersen memos from February and August of 2001 that suggest the auditor was aware of Enron's shaky financial underpinnings.

Critics of the status quo also have pointed to the Private Securities Litigation Reform Act of 1995 (PL 104-67) Among its provisions, the law changed the standard for auditors' exposure to damages in securities lawsuits. Auditors previously were accountable for joint and several liability, whereby auditors were held equally responsible with their clients. Under the new regulation, auditors are held for proportionate liability, under which they are responsible only for a certain fraction of damages, with some exceptions. (1995 Almanac, p. 2-90)

Regardless of whether the Enron scandal will lead to new rules or laws governing the accounting industry, observers, including Pitt, say the system is so flawed that a shake-up is necessary.

"There have to be some major structural changes," said Howard M. Schilit, president of the Center for Financial Research and Analysis. "Or in three years, we'll be talking about something else bigger than Enron." ◆

Health Care

Analysts See a Seismic Shift In Health Policy Debate

With a patients' bill of rights 'barely on the radar screen,' focus is on cost

What happened to the great health care debate? After years of high-decibel arguments over the patients' bill of rights, prescription drugs for the elderly and the need to overhaul Medicare before the Baby Boom generation retires, the issue seems to have gone underground.

One obvious answer is that Sept. 11 and the war on terrorism have rearranged the nation's priorities and overtaken some of the most contentious issues of the past.

But there is another, perhaps more powerful, dynamic at work. The burgeoning cost of health care is eclipsing quality of care as the No. 1 concern among policymakers. Politicians who once were able to paint their health care positions in black and white terms — for or against a patients' bill of rights, for example — now face the much more complicated question of how to deal with surging costs at a time when the nation is slipping back into a budget deficit.

This shift in focus puts lawmakers in a difficult position in an election year. Many of them know that as employers pay more for health care, they will pass those costs on to employees, scale back coverage or even phase it out completely. They also know that as costs rise and as more people lose their insurance, they look to Washington for an answer. Already governors are seeking more money for Medicaid, the federal-state health insurance program for the poor. And in Medicare, doctors, hospitals and other providers are increasing pressure on lawmakers to reverse scheduled cuts in payment rates.

Lawmakers are acutely aware of the cost issue, even though they are not yet certain how exactly it will play out in Congress. Most of them think soaring costs are of major concern to voters, but the solutions — finding efficiencies in the system or getting Americans to examine their own expectations about care and its costs — are fraught with political risks.

"We're not going to deal with it in an election year, that's for sure," said Sen. John B. Breaux, D-La., a moderate who is a main player in many health policy debates, including Medicare's future, patients' rights and prescription drug coverage. He said even though costs are rising, lawmakers do not yet feel pressure to do something and therefore "keep putting it off."

For the insurance companies and large employers that have been lobbying against new regulations on managed-care plans and health maintenance organizations (HMOs), it is just as well that the cost issue has taken on new urgency. It underlines the case they have been making for years about the need to avoid doing anything that will increase costs for employers and their workers. *(Box, p. 100)*

"People are more concerned about costs than clamoring over a patients' bill of rights that socks it to the HMOs," said Dan Danner, chairman of the Health Benefits Coalition, a group of large employers that opposes new federal regulation of the plans. "Patients' bill of rights is barely on the radar screen at all."

The cost projections also may help business beat back other bills they can argue would drive costs even higher, such as "mental health parity" legislation (S 543). That bill would ban employers who offer mental health coverage from putting tighter restrictions on it than on coverage for physical illnesses — such as allowing fewer doctor visits or charging higher co-payments.

The Rise of Managed Care

After a decade of slow growth in health insurance premiums, some analysts now are predicting that rates will rise as high as 16 percent this year. The trend is expected to continue, with health spending reaching $2.8 trillion, or 17 percent of the gross domestic product by 2011, up from its current share of 14 percent, according to a recent study by the Centers for Medicare and Medicaid Services (CMS).

The increases are reminiscent of those that hit the nation in the 1980s, when premium increases of 15 percent to 20 percent per year were common. By 1990, "it was considered good news when rates for employer-sponsored group health coverage increased only 14 percent; the year before, premium increases had averaged 24 percent," wrote Walter A. Zelman and Robert A. Berenson in "The Managed Care Blues and How to Cure Them."

That growth in costs was curtailed by the acceptance of managed care, which reduced the amount businesses pay for health insurance and employees' out-of-pocket costs. Premium increases were limited to the single digits over the last decade, and for three consecutive years in the mid-'90s they were lower than the rate of inflation.

"The American [health care] system was so rife with inefficiency, there were so many things to be done," said Mark A. Peterson, editor of the Journal of Health Politics, Policy and Law. Managed-care plans could easily squeeze out inefficiencies and place limits on how much providers charged and how much patients paid.

More than 90 percent of people in private health insurance plans are enrolled in managed care. But managed care's ability to control costs may have reached its limit, Peterson and other experts say. Higher prices for drugs and

Politics and Public Policy

technology, hospital procedures and doctors' fees are among the factors making it more difficult to keep a lid on cost increases. Consumers also are willing to pay more to have a broader choice of doctors, hospitals and other health care providers, which in turn drives up health insurance premiums.

The seemingly never-ending spiral must be contained or costs will continue to climb, says Robert D. Reischauer, president of the Urban Institute and former director of the Congressional Budget Office. "We have to come to grips with the fact that not everyone can afford to have the care they would like or that the medical profession would like to provide to them," he said.

According to the Center for Studying Health System Change, a nonpartisan private research organization, health care spending rose 7.2 percent in 2000, the largest jump in a decade. The center also found that premiums for employer-sponsored coverage increased 8.3 percent in 2000, followed by an 11 percent increase in 2001.

Hewitt Associates, a management consulting firm, last fall predicted health insurance premiums would rise an average of 13 percent to 16 percent this year, following an average rate hike of 10.2 percent in 2001. A recent survey from Towers Perrin, a management and human resources consulting firm, projected that health costs for 2003 would rise between 14 percent and 22 percent depending on the type of plan offered, with that trend continuing into next year and beyond.

Rich Ostuw, a senior Towers Perrin health care consultant, said companies may ask employees to pay a larger share of these costs. "Employers should look ahead to the years 2004 and 2005 and ask themselves how much are they willing to spend on health care benefits at that time," he said.

The CMS study projects more modest increases, with premiums rising 10.4 percent for 2002 after a 9.6 percent increase in 2001. The researchers, whose findings were published in the March/April issue of the journal Health Affairs, also found that employers would likely pass on much of the cost increases to employees in the forms of higher premiums, co-payments or deductibles.

Covering the Uninsured

Analysts predict that if costs continue to rise, the result will be an increase in the number of uninsured, now at approximately 39 million. Employers may find it too expensive to offer health insurance as a benefit, or they may pass on premium increases to employees. Workers may not be able to afford a higher share of premiums, deductibles and co-payments, and they might drop their coverage.

"If we have more years of double-digit increases, people will be priced out of the market," said Paul B. Ginsburg, president of the Center for Studying Health System Change. More uninsured people also could trigger an increase in hospital emergency room costs, where people without health insurance often seek medical care.

The weak economy also has added to the problem. According to a study released in February by the advocacy group Families USA, more than 2 million Americans lost their health insurance in 2001, the largest one-year increase in nearly a decade. Approximately half of the increase occurred from September through December, reflecting the impact of Sept. 11 on the economy.

In addition, those who have coverage are worried about

No Relief From Health Care Costs

According to recent projections, spending per enrolleee on private health insurance will continue to climb through 2011.

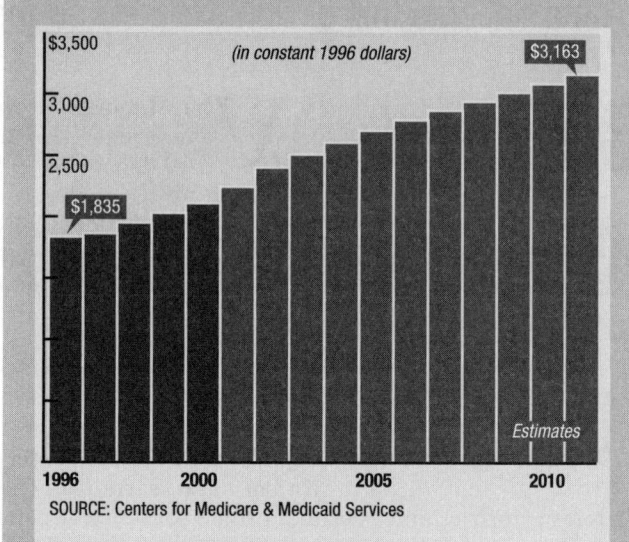

(in constant 1996 dollars)
1996: $1,835 — 2011: $3,163
SOURCE: Centers for Medicare & Medicaid Services

Premiums Far Outpace Cost of Living

Inflation: 45.5%
Premiums: 72.3%

Projections 1996-2011
SOURCE: Centers for Medicare & Medicaid Services

Where Increases Have Come From

Changes in per capita costs for these health care sectors, 1900-2000:

Prescription drugs	206.6%
Hospital outpatient treatment	153.4%
Physicians	45.5%
Hospital inpatient treatment	-3.9%

SOURCE: Milliman & Robertson

losing it, according to a survey conducted for Covering the Uninsured, a coalition representing unions, insurers, business groups and the elderly. Forty-three percent of those questioned said they believed their employer or their spouse's employer might cut back or eliminate certain health care benefits and coverage options sometime over the next year.

The question of how to help the uninsured is especially complicated in the context of higher costs. Congress has focused on two main approaches to reduce the number of people who have no insurance, and both strategies are expensive. One, expanding public health programs such as Medicaid and S-Chip, the State Children's Health Insurance Program, would require both the federal government and the states to contribute, unless the federal government picked up the whole tab. Democrats generally favor this approach because they think it is the fairest, most comprehensive way to ensure that the most vulnerable people get the coverage they need. Opponents say broad expansions of such entitlements will set a precedent for simply adding money to programs whenever a need presents itself.

Republicans generally prefer using tax credits to help the uninsured buy coverage on their own in the private insurance market. Proponents cite recent studies that say Bush's plan of $1,000 credits for individuals and $3,000 credits for families is enough to buy coverage.

But opponents say tax credits would leave the uninsured in the lurch. Critics say the credits do not provide enough money to buy coverage in the individual market, where policies are often more expensive than those purchased at group rates.

Public pressure to act on the uninsured could help end the disputes, said Mark McClellan, a member of Bush's Council of Economic Advisers.

"I think this year is different. . . . A lot of the country is very worried about health care costs and the affordability of their own insurance," he said, adding that many people who previously may have believed their health care coverage was secure may not feel that way now.

Political and philosophical battles aside, Gail Shearer, director of health policy analysis for Consumers Union, sees momentum on the uninsured that neither party will be able to ignore.

"I think the rising unemployment rate and the growing awareness among everyone that they could lose their health insurance, that could move us toward that tipping point and Congress is going to have to pay more attention," she said.

As people lose their health insurance, they may turn to Medicaid for their coverage. Governors complain that their share of Medicaid expenditures are already a burden on state budgets and having to give more people health coverage will only worsen the situation.

"Our challenge is to find a way to not cut services when we have less money than we had the year before," Kentucky Gov. Paul E. Patton, a Democrat, told the Senate Special Committee on Aging at a hearing on March 21. "There is absolutely no way we can absorb a 10 percent increase in Medicaid with a zero increase in revenue."

Moderate Democrat Breaux, who is deeply involved in health care policy issues, does not expect Congress to tackle the most challenging health care questions in an election year.

The National Governors' Association, of which Patton is vice chairman, is calling for a Medicaid Commission to recommend fundamental long-term improvements to the program.

The states also hope Congress will give them more money to help pay for rising Medicaid costs. The weak economy has reduced tax revenues for many states, making it difficult for them to cope without making huge cuts in other programs, such as education.

The federal budget deficit should not stop lawmakers from spending more money on federal health programs, said Sara Rosenbaum, director of the Center for Health Services Research and Policy at George Washington University.

In 1984 and 1990, for example, Congress voted to expand Medicaid even though the government faced budget deficits. Using higher healthcare costs as an excuse to not spend additional funds or create new regulations is "a rather extreme approach to policy making," Rosenbaum said. (*1984 Almanac, p. 24; 1990 Almanac, p. 569*)

The Medicare Squeeze

As costs rise, lawmakers will also find it even more difficult to develop a way for Medicare, the federal health program that covers nearly 40 million elderly and disabled people, to include prescription drugs.

The two parties already have deep philosophical differences over how to structure a benefit that has great public and political support. Republicans typically favor allowing the private market to offer prescription drug coverage to seniors, and many Democrats want the government, rather than private insurers, to oversee it.

But the reality both parties face is that prescription drug coverage is the fastest-growing component of health care spending, and seniors use more prescription drugs than any other age group. So implementing a prescription drug benefit that compares with those offered by private insurance plans would involve huge costs to taxpayers.

"Medicare prescription drugs is pricing itself off the table," Reischauer said.

Both parties have struggled with the challenge of giving senior citizens drug coverage that program recipients would find satisfactory and affordable.

In past years, they have attempted to find a way around the cost issue by proposing plans that would delay the start of drug coverage and required monthly premiums and hefty deductibles for seniors.

This year, the parties appear to be taking a more modest approach. The president's fiscal 2003 budget proposal would set aside $190 billion over the next 10 years to overhaul Medicare, including funding for prescription drugs. Bush health adviser McClellan said that the program, along with the president's proposal for a discount prescription drug card, "reflect the urgency of health care costs" and are solid first steps that could be broadened later.

Politics and Public Policy

But some Republicans and many Democrats believe the president's game plan is too narrow and that Congress should take broader action. (*2002 CQ Weekly, p. 376*)

To that end, the House voted 221-207 on March 20 to pass a fiscal 2003 budget resolution (H Con Res 353) that includes $350 billion over 10 years to create a prescription drug benefit for seniors and "modernize" Medicare. The budget resolution is only a spending blueprint, however. Republicans are expected to introduce their plan for Medicare prescription drug coverage soon after the spring recess, and the full House could act on the bill as early as May.

In the Democratic-led Senate, the Budget Committee's fiscal 2003 budget resolution, approved March 21, calls for $500 billion over 10 years for a Medicare prescription drug benefit, expanded health coverage for the uninsured, and to give higher payments to Medicare health care providers.

These fairly modest proposals reflect the reality that a more comprehensive bill probably would be more than lawmakers would be willing to pay for. "Politicians put forth what they can afford," Reischauer said, referring to the current proposals.

The largest effort lawmakers have made to control Medicare came in the 1997 balanced-budget law (PL 105-33), which was designed to trim Medicare spending by $112 billion over five years.

At the time it was hailed as a bipartisan success, but twice since the law was enacted, providers have successfully fought back to receive higher reimbursements and stop some scheduled cuts. There is pressure to do so again this year. (*1997 Almanac, p. 6-3*)

Some lawmakers point to that experience when arguing that the only way to really get a handle on costs in Medicare is by redesigning it from the ground up. But any sort of program overhaul is unlikely in an election year.

In the meantime, the White House and Congress are at odds about how much — if any — additional funding should be given to the Medicare providers. Bush officials have told House Republicans that any increases must be done in a "budget-neutral" fashion, which would mean making cuts in other areas of Medicare spending.

Insurance Liability Stalls Talks

Patients' rights legislation is back to where it has been so many times before: staffers wrestling over the details that will matter only if their bosses have the political will to cut a deal.

Sometimes meeting each week, sometimes not, health policy experts working for the White House and for Sen. Edward M. Kennedy, D-Mass., are trying to come together on the question of health plan liability, an issue that has long divided the two parties.

The talks appear to be stalled over whether to cap the amount an individual could collect from his or her insurer in a lawsuit, and whether such suits should be tried in state or federal courts.

Both sides are keeping details of the talks private, with participants aware that they have a better chance for success if there are no leaks.

There is no set deadline at which the negotiations would stop, but the goal is to cut a deal "as quickly as possible before the election year politics take over," said Kennedy spokesman Jim Manley.

Opponents of the broad patients' rights legislation say they believe the dilemma will be resolved only of Democrats feel they cannot get any more political mileage on the issue.

But a resolution also would help Republicans by allowing them to take credit for a popular initiative and eliminate an issue that Democrats have used to their advantage for years — and can be expected to use again in this year's campaigns.

"I don't think the president would mind having a point in that column. . . . Republicans would like something to run on," said Robert D. Reischauer, president of the Urban Institute and former director of the Congressional Budget Office.

Liability Questions

President Bush and Kennedy initiated the discussions in January in an attempt to find common ground between competing bills (HR 2563, S 1052) that Congress passed last summer. (*2002 CQ Weekly, p. 241*)

The Senate bill would allow patients to sue their health plans in state courts when they believed they had received poor quality of care because of a plan's coverage decision, and in federal court when it was question of whether a plan covered a specific service. Punitive damages in federal court would be capped at $5 million.

Under the House bill, patients could sue in state court for cases involving medical judgment, but they would be subject to federal caps of $1.5 million for "pain and suffering" damages and $1.5 million for punitive damages, which would be allowed only if a health plan ignored the decision of an independent review panel.

The House bill also would permit patients to sue health plans in federal court if the issue concerned an administrative question, such as whether a particular service was covered by a contract. Patients would be required to exhaust appeals before filing a lawsuit.

As the Senate's lead negotiator with Bush, Kennedy will have to decide whether to embrace the liability provisions of the House bill, which Bush negotiated with Rep. Charlie Norwood, R-Ga., last year.

But that might anger supporters, such as patient groups that do not want insurers' liability capped. In addition, other Kennedy allies — physicians, hospitals and other health care providers that face unlimited liability — think insurance companies should bear the same risk.

The idea of caps could be attractive for lawmakers who fear that the legislation will drive up the cost of health insurance. Such caps are designed to provide reasonable compensation to victims but prevent jury awards of millions of dollars, which many legislators and health care experts worry would ultimately make health insurance even more expensive.

Health Care

"We have no compelling evidence that there is a problem with the overall adequacy of provider payments," Health and Human Services Secretary Tommy G. Thompson and Office of Management and Budget Director Mitchell E. Daniels Jr. wrote in a March 14 letter to Ways and Means Committee Chairman Bill Thomas, R-Calif., and Health Subcommittee Chairman Nancy L. Johnson, R-Conn.

Thompson and Daniels acknowledged that a scheduled 5.4 percent cut this year for Medicare doctors is "substantial," and signaled that lawmakers should reduce hospital payments to give doctors more money, a suggestion that hospitals reject.

The American Medical Association is lobbying Congress to reverse that cut, and many lawmakers want to. House Energy and Commerce Committee Chairman Billy Tauzin, R-La., and John D. Dingell of Michigan, the panel's ranking Democrat, have endorsed legislation (HR 3351) that would reduce the scheduled rate cut and give lawmakers time to rewrite the fee system. Similar legislation pending in the Senate (S 1707) has 75 cosponsors.

At a Feb. 28 Ways and Means Health Subcommittee hearing on Medicare physician payments, Congressional Budget Office Director Dan L. Crippen reminded lawmakers that, in spite of the scheduled cut, CBO is projecting that total Medicare payment to physicians will rise by 5.9 percent in fiscal 2003, with total Medicare payments to physicians continuing to increase.

Patients' Rights

For years, insurers and employers have argued that if patients' rights legislation were enacted, it would drive up health care costs. They especially have opposed bills that would expand patients' rights to sue their health insurer, arguing that the mere threat of liability would expose employers to lawsuits and drive premiums higher.

With health care costs on the rise, business lobbyists are raising those concerns again, hoping they will have more punch, especially in an economy emerging from recession.

But for some lawmakers eyeing various policy initiatives, a patients' rights bill now might be one of the cheapest to do, because it would have minimal direct cost for the government — and further, it would dispose of an issue that has plagued Congress and the White House for years.

According to numbers in CBO analyses of the bills passed by the Senate and House (S 1052, HR 2563), the legislation would be far less expensive than other health care initiatives such as a Medicare prescription drug benefit.

"It's one of the few things they can afford to do monetarily," said Kenneth E. Thorpe, professor of health policy and management at Emory University.

Discussions on how to merge the two bills are ongoing between the staffs of Bush and Sen. Edward M. Kennedy, D-Mass., a leading cosponsor of the Senate bill. It is not clear whether the negotiations will produce a bill that would satisfy both parties in Congress.

For years, employers and insurers have complained that patients' rights legislation would drive up costs because of the bills' numerous coverage mandates and provisions that would give patients new power to sue their health insurers.

"In particularly slow economic times, people are worried about what will happen to their coverage if their employer is forced out of the system because they can't sustain rising costs," said Karen M. Ignagni, president and chief executive officer of the American Association of Health Plans, a group representing managed-care insurers.

Employers feel "a sense of disbelief that anyone could be considering additional cost increases" that are bound to come if patients' rights legislation becomes law, said Doug Badger, the former chief of staff to Senate Republican Whip Don Nickles, R-Okla., and now a partner with Washington Council Ernst & Young.

Neil Trautwein, health care lobbyist for the National Association of Manufacturers, said the health spending estimates have added "new urgency to our message to Congress: Help, don't hurt. . . . Employers are upset about health care costs and they don't want Congress to make it worse."

Proponents of patients' rights legislation say the cost argument is an old one that should not persuade anyone, especially since premium increases are already in the double digits without Congress taking any action.

"It's a little like the story of the boy who ran around yelling, 'The sky is falling,'" said Dingell, who cosponsored a patients' rights bill passed by the House in October 1999. "They've been playing that game for years. This is not a new approach." (1999 Almanac, p. 16-3)

Kennedy points to the CBO analysis, which estimated that the bill would increase costs by 4 percent over the next five years.

"The cost of a Big Mac a month," Kennedy said, adding that states that have expanded patients' ability to sue their health plans for damages have not seen large increases in premiums.

Consumers may even view the increase in premiums as well worth the extra money because a patients' rights law would give them greater power with their health insurers, especially in an era of rising costs that might tempt insurers to cut back coverage, said Ron Pollack, president of Families USA.

"The insurance companies are stone-cold silent when it [a premium increase] pads their bottom lines," Pollack said. "But when a tiny fraction would go to the benefit of consumers, then they yell."

Pollack said he doubts the efforts by business and employer groups to tie future premium increases to enactment of patients' rights legislation will have any influence.

"I don't think anyone in Congress is rethinking their position on this issue," Pollack said, referring to the lengthy debate that has given members plenty of time to establish — and defend — their positions, .

Many members of Congress share that view. "I think the votes are where the votes are," said Sen. Maria Cantwell, D-Wash.

Focusing on the patients' rights legislation will do little, however, to address the cost issue, said Brian R. Klepper, a co-founder of the Center for Practical Health Reform, a non-partisan, health care policy group composed of business groups, insurers, hospitals and other health care providers.

"The real issue is that if health care if unaffordable, patients' bill of rights doesn't matter," Klepper said. "People who do policy have a very poor understanding of how life works in the field. Saving the system is about cost, period." ◆

Politics and Public Policy

Members Back Medicare Revamp But Are Not Unified on a Solution

Some lawmakers call for standardizing Medicare payment rates; others say more competition in the private market would help control costs

It is becoming a tradition on Capitol Hill: doctors, hospitals and other Medicare providers fighting to roll back payment cuts approved as part of the 1997 Balanced-Budget Act (PL 105-33).

For the third time, lawmakers are expected to hand out billions of dollars in so-called givebacks, raising payment rates for providers.

Some say the repeated fights over payment rates are unavoidable with a program as huge and complicated as Medicare, which treats nearly 40 million elderly and disabled.

But by simply tinkering at the edges of the system, lawmakers are shaping the program year by year, allowing the demands of health-care providers rather than larger policy goals to drive them.

Many lawmakers say they could end the continual disputes if members would focus on a broader, long-term overhaul of Medicare.

"The larger lesson is we need fundamental reform," said Sen. Jon Kyl, R-Ariz. "We have to reform the reimbursements for Medicare so they more accurately reflect real costs and their reimbursement."

With midterm elections approaching and lawmakers divided over how to add prescription drug coverage to the program, a full-scale overhaul is unlikely this year. But some hope it will happen in 2003 when politics might be distant enough to focus on policy.

House Ways and Means Health Subcommittee Chairwoman Nancy L. Johnson, R-Conn., said she hopes Congress will resolve the ongoing dispute over Medicare drug coverage this year "so next year we can begin to look at some of these systemic problems." (2002 CQ Weekly, p. 1219)

"The fundamental structure on which Medicare payments is based is so outmoded," she said. "It just doesn't work anymore."

Democrats and Republicans alike

Medicare is a staple at events such as the May 15 rally with Senate Majority Leader Tom Daschle, D-S.D., center. But Congress has focused on short-term fixes to the program.

are eager to move beyond the reimbursement fights that cast one provider group against another.

"They're robbing Peter to pay Paul, but Paul doesn't have any money," said Sen. John B. Breaux, D-La., who co-chaired the Bipartisan Commission on the Future of Medicare, created by the 1997 law. "Decisions are being made on the politics, who's getting gored."

Searching for a Way Out

Sen. Paul Wellstone, D-Minn., said the answer is to devote more money to Medicare to meet the needs of the millions of Baby Boomers who will enter the program over the next decade.

"None of this can really be done on the cheap," Wellstone said. "We have to come to terms with it. Our heads are in the sand when it comes to understanding the expense of this."

Some want to revisit the provider rate cuts established in the Balanced-Budget Act and look again at how to control Medicare's costs. (1997 Almanac, p. 6-3)

Rising health care costs will make it more difficult to take money away from providers, especially since private insurers also are cutting their payments.

"There's no place to cost-shift to," said Mark A. Peterson, a political science professor at the University of California-Los Angeles and editor of the Journal of Health Politics, Policy and Law.

Breaux is one of several legislators who believe that private-market competition would help Medicare deliver better benefits for less money.

It also would take lawmakers out of the political minefield of setting reimbursement rates for nursing homes, home health agencies and other providers, groups they would rather not alienate.

"It would be nice to get out of the game [of deciding among provider reimbursements]," said Republican lobbyist Mark Isakowitz.

The Balanced-Budget Act launched an initiative called Medicare+Choice to encourage more private managed-care insurers to offer coverage to Medicare beneficiaries.

But Democrats point to the number of Medicare+Choice plans leaving Medicare as proof that the program must remain one whose benefits are de-

CQ Weekly May 18, 2002

Health Care

signed and administered by the federal government, not the private sector.

Proponents of Medicare+Choice say the federal government does not pay insurers enough to stay in the program.

Another issue for Congress to confront is wide disparities in payments to providers in rural and urban areas. Members representing rural areas have long complained that their provider payments are far beneath those in urban areas.

Many providers are dropping Medicare patients or leaving rural areas altogether, some lawmakers say.

"If we lose our doctors and our hospitals, a prescription drug benefit certainly has a lot less value," said Rep. Jerry Moran, R-Kan., who co-chairs the Rural Health Care Coalition.

Others say the payment struggle between Medicare providers and the government is to be expected, just as it is in the private sector, where hospitals, doctors and others seek higher reimbursements from insurers.

"This is a time-honored tradition," said Tricia Neuman, director of the Medicare Policy Project for the Kaiser Family Foundation, an independent, nonprofit research organization. "It's what happens when you have a payer and you have a provider. . . . The tensions are likely to remain."

Health care groups are lobbying hard for more money.

Karen M. Ignagni, president of the American Association of Health Plans, which represents managed-care insurers, helped lead 170 Medicare+Choice beneficiaries around the Capitol on May 15 and 16 as they met with members to make the case for higher reimbursements.

The group also has launched an advertising campaign featuring senior citizens praising their Medicare managed-care plans.

Making the Case

The American Hospital Association is sponsoring a series of print ads extolling the many services hospitals — which rely heavily on Medicare funding — perform, such as emergency medical care, delivering babies and caring for the elderly.

The American Health Care Association, which represents nursing homes, released a study May 14 that said the care given to Medicare beneficiaries could decline if reimbursements are cut as scheduled Oct. 1.

To help members make the case for more money to providers, the groups are providing statistics about the number of hospitals that may close in their districts, or the number of home health agencies that may have to shut down.

"I'm seeing the fruits of our providers educating people much more carefully about this situation," said Johnson.

Johnson has her own parochial concerns over the Medicare reimbursement issue. Redistricting has put her in a tough race against Rep. Jim Maloney, D-Conn., who has accused Johnson and other Republicans of cutting payments to hospitals and nursing homes to help fund a drug benefit for seniors.

"I have my own problems in my district, and I'm chairman of the committee," she said. "It's A, humiliating, and B, it's infuriating."

One way or another, providers are expected to receive higher Medicare reimbursements this year.

New York House Republicans are pushing for more money for their hospitals and have told House Speaker J. Dennis Hastert, R-Ill., it would be "very difficult" to support Medicare legislation that did not accomplish that goal.

Moran said he has 76 signatures on a letter asking that hospitals and home health agencies receive higher reimbursements.

"I think there are a significant number of members that, absent rural America needs being met, they're willing to not support the legislation," he said.

Concerns from rank-and-file Republicans over proposed payment cuts included in drafts of the House Republican prescription drug bill helped push action off until June.

Hastert had said he planned to bring up the legislation before Congress leaves town for the Memorial Day recess. ◆

Giveback Timeline

August 1997: President Bill Clinton signs the Balanced-Budget Act (PL 105-33), which includes $112 billion in savings from Medicare, the largest spending reduction since the program was created in 1965. *(1997 Almanac, p. 6-3)*

October 1998: Home health care agencies complain that the 1997 law cut their reimbursements too deeply. They persuade lawmakers to delay a scheduled across-the-board 15 percent payment cut and to revamp a payment formula so that 65 percent of the agencies actually get an increase. *(1998 Almanac, p. 14-16)*

November 1999: Citing lower-than-expected Medicare spending, hospitals, managed-care plans, home health care agencies and other Medicare providers push Congress to pass a $16 billion, five-year package of "givebacks" to help restore payment reductions made in the 1997 bill. *(1999 Almanac, p. 16-31)*

July 2000: Medicare providers step up the pressure for a second Medicare giveback bill with television and print advertising campaigns. Hospitals say they want another $25 billion over five years, while managed-care companies seek an additional $15 billion. *(2000 Almanac, p. 12-25)*

September 2000: The House Commerce Committee approves a $21 billion bill, the same amount proposed by Clinton.

October 2000: House Republicans push through a package of about $35 billion.

Clinton says the bill gives too much money to managed-care plans and threatens a veto. Lawmakers combine the changes with appropriations measures and then clear it all as an omnibus package (PL 106-554) on Dec. 15.

May 2002: Medicare providers lobby lawmakers for a third giveback package. Some House GOP leaders want to include the payment changes in the same bill with a plan to add drug coverage to Medicare, which Hastert, above, wants to pass soon. Other Republicans push to split the two.

Politics and Public Policy

Hill Contemplates Copyrights: Does Innovation Trump Piracy?

Bills must strike balance between creators' products and consumers' rights

The year was 1908, and songs such as "Shine On Harvest Moon" and "Memphis Rag" were all the rage. Rather than just play them on conventional pianos, though, Americans were turning to a new technology: the player piano, which pumped out renditions using a vacuum device that read rolls of perforated paper.

Because copyright protection at the time only extended to sheet music, frustrated songwriters and publishers received not a nickel from this new use of their works. The aggrieved appealed to Congress and the courts for help, setting off almost a century of painstaking debate over copyright law and intellectual property.

Each subsequent advance in communications and entertainment technology — records, radio, "talkies," tapes and television — has led to long negotiations among industries and with Congress. One debate lasted 20 years before legislation was finally abandoned on the eve of World War II.

In today's computer age, books, movies or music can be reduced to millions of digital information packets that course through electronic transmission lines and are reassembled into flawless copies at the other end. The copyright issue has become the illegal downloading and copying of entertainment and other fare on the Internet. Musicians, authors, publishers and entertainment powerhouses such as The Walt Disney Co. are demanding a legislative remedy for the unauthorized and near-perfect reproduction of their work.

But the fundamental question remains the same: How do policymakers balance the intellectual property rights of creators against the economic imperative to let technological innovation run its course?

Congress appears ready to start talking about the issue and a series of legislative proposals this spring, and at the same time federal courts are considering the definition of property in the digital age. The outcome is expected to influence how consumers use personal computers and other digital devices and even the shape of the Internet in the future.

The debate will determine who really controls the architecture of the Internet, said James Boyle, a Duke University law professor and authority on copyright issues. "The property rules, in the long run, will have a bigger effect than rules on Internet taxation or censorship or filtering."

For Congress, these copyright questions reveal fault lines between those who want to protect the creators and those who fear stifling technology. It used to be easy for Congress to focus on the needs of the creators, but now there is a compelling counterpoint: the needs of computer and consumer electronics users.

"The way I see it, this is Napster times 10," said Sen. Dianne Feinstein, D-Calif., referring to the dispute last year between major record labels and the free music file-swapping network later shut down. (*2001 CQ Weekly, p. 715*)

Limited but Exclusive Rights

Copyright is one of the nation's fundamental doctrines. Article I of the Constitution empowers Congress "to promote the progress of science and useful arts, by securing for limited times to authors and inventors the exclusive right to their respective writings and discoveries." The concept of copyright has been expanded repeatedly over the years to accommodate new developments in the marketplace; printed music, for example, became protected in 1831.

For Congress, the task of making copyright laws accommodate new technology has always been a headache. Lawmakers have been drawn into bitter clashes over recording rights, licensing fees and what constitutes "fair use" of copyrighted material — limited copying without the owner's permission, usually for research or other non-commercial purposes.

After the Supreme Court ruled in 1908 that copyright protection did not extend to piano rolls or other mechanical reproduction of songs, content creators appealed to Congress, which revised the law and enacted a licensing formula requiring makers of piano rolls and phonographs to pay royalties. Lawmakers spent the 1920s and 1930s vainly trying to solve how music could be performed for profit in motion pictures and on the radio. It went though similar contortions in the 1950s and 1960s to address the growing popularity of jukeboxes, television and even Muzak, creating a Copyright Office of experts to provide advice on how to draft laws. (*Timeline, p. 106*)

Many in Congress are only beginning to sort through the

Technology and Communication

intricacies of the Internet and intellectual property law that form the core of the current debate, and virtually no one expects sweeping legislation to pass this year. But lawmakers who regularly deal with such issues by virtue of committee assignments or interests appear to be gathering forces in two distinct camps.

One group, including Sen. Ernest F. Hollings, D-S.C., chairman of the Senate Commerce, Science and Transportation Committee, backs tougher measures to protect content creators. It argues that rampant piracy is destroying the business model of some industries and discouraging entertainment companies from releasing their most popular fare through new media. Lawmakers in this camp cite Hollywood executives who estimate they lose at least $3 billion a year to illegal copying and are withholding digital versions of first-run films from widespread release. Such arguments generally have prevailed in congressional revisions of copyright law over the past 25 years.

"When Congress sits idly by in the face of these [illegal downloading] activities, we essentially sanction the Internet as a haven for thievery," Hollings said recently.

No one in Congress condones Internet piracy. But lawmakers such as Rep. Rick Boucher, D-Va., an authority on high-tech issues, believe bills proposing digital locks to control software could trample basic consumer rights to unlimited personal use of legally purchased material. These lawmakers are allied with consumer electronics and information technology companies that fear new copyright laws could restrict the functions of computers and other digital devices.

"Over the years, there has been a historic shift in favor of the copyright community at the expense of [consumer] use rights," Boucher said. "The time really has come for a rebalancing."

Congress will have to perform that rebalancing across several fronts.

Hollings has written legislation (S 2048) that would use the established remedy of requiring industry leaders to meet and work out a solution — this time to develop a technology that would discourage or block illegal copying of digital material, which Congress could then codify as a new technical standard. The bill comes largely at the behest of Disney and News Corp., which complain that movie studios are victimized by 350,000 to 400,000 illegal downloads a day and that the technology sector has been slow to respond. High-tech companies say the rapidly changing nature of their industry makes a quick fix elusive.

The House Judiciary Committee separately is set to debate revisions (HR 2724) proposed by Boucher and Christopher B. Cannon, R-Utah, to the 1998 Digital Millennium Copyright Act (PL 105-34), which clarified rules for placing copyrighted material on the World Wide Web and extended protection to software and compact discs. (1998 Almanac, p. 22-3)

Among the questions being considered by the House committee is whether to create a system to ensure that Internet music services can gain access to copyright-protected music at a fair price. The debate also is expected to take up the music industry's recent practice of releasing CDs that cannot be copied or played on computer hard drives.

Court cases, meanwhile, will test how much control Congress has over Internet content.

The Supreme Court later this year will hear the case of *Eldred v. Ashcroft*, in which a New Hampshire book publisher is challenging 1998 legislation (PL 105-298) that added 20 years to the life of copyrights. Some users of protected materials, such as libraries and universities, contend lawmakers overstepped their authority. The case has major ramifications for electronic publishing and consumer electronics. (2002 CQ Weekly, p. 536)

A U.S. District Court in San Jose is taking up the question of whether the Digital Millennium Copyright Act is unconstitutional because it bans technology that can circumvent copyright protection. Critics say it is so focused on putting technological locks on material that it infringes on the public's right to make "fair use" of materials they legally can purchase.

Congress as Referee

Lawmakers confronted with difficult copyright issues more often than not have held hearings, failed to agree on a single solution and summoned the warring parties to work out a compromise among themselves. This practical "conference process," which led to such breakthroughs as the creation of music performance royalties, has relieved Congress of having to pick winners. But some scholars say it creates overly specific laws that leave no room for future innovation and do not consider the needs of the public.

"The unspoken premise of the conference process was that Congress would enact any bill that everyone else could agree on," Wayne State University law Professor Jessica Litman writes in her book "Digital Copyright," an examination

Disney CEO Michael Eisner, right, talks with Motion Picture Association President Jack Valenti, left, and News Corp. executive Peter Chernin at a Senate hearing Feb. 28 on digital copyrights.

Politics and Public Policy

Technology Forces Changes in Protection Rules

Policymakers have attempted to adapt copyright law to new forms of entertainment for nearly a century, with mixed success.

1905-1909

Early recordings: The advent of piano rolls and gramophones prompts a fight over the reproduction of copyrighted sheet music.

In Congress: In the 1909 Copyright Act, lawmakers accept an agreement between the makers of new products and the music industry, requiring a license for mechanical reproductions of music. Coin-operated devices are exempt, later giving rise to the jukebox industry.

1910-1912

Movie mayhem: The Kalem Company produces a motion picture based on Gen. Lew Wallace's novel "Ben Hur" without getting a license from Wallace or his publisher. The Supreme Court rules that the film company infringed on the copyright.

In Congress: Rep. Edward Townsend, D-N.J., introduces legislation limiting the motion picture industry's exposure in copyright infringement cases. It quickly becomes law.

1914-1940

ASCAP uprising: The American Society of Composers, Authors and Publishers (ASCAP) attempts to pool members' copyrights and force businesses to buy performance licenses. Focus of the action is on the radio industry and Hollywood "talkies."

Backlash: Broadcasters and motion picture theater owners respond by seeking legislation to abolish ASCAP.

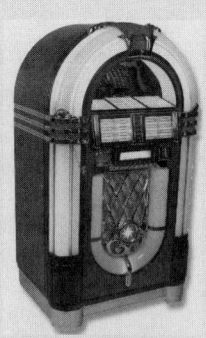

In Congress: Legislation is proposed to bring U.S. law into agreement with the international Berne Convention mandating automatic copyright protection without requiring notice or registration. Decades of industry negotiations fail to produce a bill acceptable to all sides, and talks end with the start of World War II.

1956-1961

Changes needed: The growth of radio, jukeboxes, sound motion pictures and television complicate industry efforts to abide by laws with no provisions for new technologies.

In Congress: In 1956 Congress appropriates money for an advisory committee of copyright experts called the Copyright Office. Six years of study yield a report, but little consensus among industries on how to proceed.

1961-1976

More meetings: The Copyright Office continues to sponsor meetings of industry representatives.

In Congress:
1967: The House passes a general revision of the copyright system but controversy over cable television retransmission and other issues prevents Senate action.
1971: Congress passes a stopgap bill (PL 92-140) establishing a limited copyright to prevent unauthorized duplication of sound recordings.
1976: Congress passes a broad rewrite (PL 94-553) that raises music royalties, extends new protections to writers and imposes copyright liability on public broadcasters, cable television systems and jukebox operators. The legislation also extends copyright protection from 56 years to the lifetime of the author plus 50 years.

1988

Satellite beams: The growing satellite television industry wants to sell to individual homeowners, not just to cable systems, but local TV stations complain that beaming in distant signals would infringe on their copyright franchises.

In Congress: The Satellite Home Viewer Act, part of a trademark bill (PL 100-667), allows satellite carriers to serve homeowners out of range of local TV stations and requires them to pay copyright fees.

1992

Recording blues: Copyright owners attempt to block the sale of digital recording devices and threaten claims against consumers for unauthorized copying of recorded music.

In Congress: In the Audio Home Recording Act (PL 102-563), manufacturers agree to pay a royalty on every digital recording device or digital tape sold.

MP3 player

1998

Update: International software piracy and other issues force the first major copyright law overhaul since 1976.

In Congress: The Digital Millennium Copyright Act (PL 105-304) implements two international treaties aimed at protecting computer software and compact discs, limiting the liability of Internet service providers for certain copyright infringements and banning the sale, use or manufacture of devices primarily designed to circumvent technology that protects copyrighted works.

SOURCE: *Digital Copyright,* by Jessica Litman, "Copyright and Compromise," chap. 3 (Amherst, N.Y.: Prometheus Books). Copyright © 2001 by Jessica Litman.

of intellectual property in the digital age.

The current deliberations may be different. Digital technology enables vast amounts of voice, video and text to be compressed into packets of data that can easily be stored on hard drives or blasted along the backbone of the Internet at the speed of light. The information can be copied endlessly without any degradation in picture or sound quality, unlike older forms of media, such as videocassettes.

Many people legally manipulate digital entertainment by downloading CDs onto their computer hard drives, then transferring the files to portable MP3 players.

But that process is not appreciably different from what anyone with a personal computer and the right software can do at Napsterlike file-sharing services such as Australia-based KaZaA, where the Oscar-winning film "A Beautiful Mind" can be downloaded for free. With a digital copy of the film in hand, one person can become a de facto worldwide distributor of the film, which is not yet commercially available in DVD format.

Mass production has been taken out of the exclusive control of content creators and has created a countervailing force in the copyright debate. While the movie and music industries insist on greater protection, end-users are wary of anything that could inhibit the creative capacity of the electronic gadgetry they buy. Already, there are hints of a backlash against existing technological restrictions, such as the electronic "must watch" flags on DVDs that prevent users from fast forwarding through movie previews.

"I believe Hollywood is using the legislative process to create new lines of business at consumers' expense," Joe Kraus, founder of DigitalConsumer.org, told a Senate Judiciary Committee copyright hearing on March 14. His group is made up of high-tech executives and venture capitalists.

Hollywood's goal, Kraus said, "is to create a legal system that denies consumers their personal use rights and then charge those consumers additional fees to recoup them."

Kraus and others contend that entertainment companies are bent on cutting off consumers' copying options, then creating their own commercial services that control the flow of popular fare.

Technology and Communication

Courts Next to Enter the Fray

While Congress mulls the future of digital entertainment, several pending court cases are taking up fundamental questions about copyright and congressional oversight of the Internet:

Napster Clones
The Recording Industry Association of America and the Motion Picture Association of America are suing Consumer Empowerment BV, a Dutch company that created file-sharing technology, and two of its licensees, MusicCity.com and Grokster, in U.S. District Court in Los Angeles. The entertainment industry charges that the three file-swapping entities help people steal music, movies and other copyrighted fare. The case is scheduled to go to trial Oct. 1.

E-Book Security
A Moscow software company, ElComSoft Co. Ltd. is facing charges in U.S. District Court in San Jose that it violated the 1998 Digital Millennium Copyright Act (PL 105-304) by creating software, legal in Russia, that disables digital restrictions on Adobe Systems Inc.'s e-book reader.

Copyright Extensions
The Supreme Court later this year is set to hear arguments in *Eldred v. Ashcroft*, in which a New Hampshire book publisher charges that Congress overstepped its authority by passing a 1998 law (PL 105-298) that added 20 years to existing copyright protections. The law aligns U.S. law with protections available in Europe.

Content creators say they do not want to inhibit a consumer's right to copy a movie or song for use in the home. But they say that lawmakers must use the upcoming hearings to rein in the freewheeling, almost anarchistic mindset of the Internet.

"Part of the reason this is becoming more political is there is a kind of populism that says everything should be free . . . that if you buy an online service, it's like candy that can be harvested," said former Rep. Pat Schroeder, D-Colo. (1972-96), president and chief executive officer of the Association of American Publishers, which supports stronger copyright protections but is not directly involved in the online entertainment debate.

"People went out on the Internet, found a lot of information was not valid and started wanting high-quality content," Schroeder said. "If you lose the rights to that, you lose a terribly important and vital part of the economy."

The tension between these lines of thought is being felt in the debate over Hollings' bill between Hollywood studios and the high-tech industry. The stakes for each side are huge: Consumer electronics and technology companies are leery of including copy protection devices in digital players, recorders and computers because it would limit the devices' capabilities and raise prices. Entertainment companies do not want to release premium fare unless it is fully protected.

The rhetoric escalated after Disney Chairman and CEO Michael D. Eisner told a Feb. 28 hearing of Hollings' committee that many technology companies had been slow to address piracy that is carried out by their electronic devices and develop common standards to discourage illegal copying.

"High-tech companies have simply lectured us that they have no obligation to help solve what they describe as 'our problem,'" Eisner said. "We are confident the government can act to facilitate the needed technology standards."

Hollings' bill attempts to do this by requiring content creators, consumer electronics makers and consumer groups to meet and, within one year, develop encoding rules and other unspecified technologies to protect digital content. If they could not agree, the Federal Communications Commission

Politics and Public Policy

Debate Over Illegal Copying Focused On Type of Data, Length of Protection

House Judiciary Committee Chairman F. James Sensenbrenner Jr., R-Wis., and Energy and Commerce Committee Chairman Billy Tauzin, R-La., agreed early in the 107th Congress to set aside their jurisdictional claims on copyright issues and draft one joint bill that would legally protect commercial caches of data, such as real estate listings or legal reference materials.

Now, a year later, an agreement has emerged on the framework of the bill, but deep differences remain on the substance. Recent draft versions would establish civil penalties for a new federal offense: misappropriation of information.

The key dispute has been over just what collections of data should be protected, and for how long.

Tauzin and a staunch supporter of the bill, Howard Coble, R-N.C., said talks would intensify this month. "I'm hoping that it's possible to get something done. But I don't know yet how we get there," Coble said.

Supporters such as Reed Elsevier, a publisher of scientific, legal and research material, and the National Association of Realtors, whose members provide real estate listings, have argued that protection is vital to preserve the investment they have made in collections of information and to allow them to distribute information on the Internet without fear that rivals will reap some benefits.

(Congressional Quarterly also collects, compiles and analyzes data on Congress and provides the information to subscribers.)

Critics of the bill argue that protection should be tailored to fit different types of information. They contend that long-term protection should not be applied to certain kinds of information, such as live stock quotes distributed by the New York Stock Exchange that are used by investors and brokers to make timely investment decisions.

One compromise has been floated that would create a category of "hot news" — data that has high value for a brief period — that would be protected for only a short time.

Another key unresolved issue is the degree of protection needed for information displayed by live auction services, such as eBay Inc., a strong supporter of the bill. The company wants to fend off online rivals that want to market goods and services to eBay's customers and divert online shoppers from eBay's Web site to their own. A draft version of the bill would bar an online vendor from diverting online traffic from another vendor's Web site.

Cautious Optimism

Drafts of compromise language have been traded back and forth by committee staff members in recent weeks. Proponents are calling for Sensenbrenner and Tauzin to make choices and finish the wording.

"We are cautiously optimistic," said Edward Miller, a spokesman for the National Association of Realtors. "We hope the two committees will reach a compromise that will quickly move through the House."

The impetus for a bill grew out of a 1991 Supreme Court ruling in *Feist Publications Inc. v. Rural Telephone Service Co.* that copyright protection could be applied to original schemes for displaying facts, but not to names and telephone numbers.

Rather than rely on the Copyright Clause of the Constitution, which protects creative works and inventions, Tauzin and Sensenbrenner's draft would bar misuse of commercial data — in which companies have made a substantial investment — under the Commerce Clause, which empowers Congress to regulate interstate trade.

Critics question whether the bill would effectively circumvent — or violate — the Constitution by attempting to protect factual information that is not covered under the Copyright Clause. "We are concerned that the bill would give database owners almost complete control over facts," said Will Rodger, director of public policy for the Computer and Communications Industry Association.

But Rodger says his group, representing 40 high-tech and communications companies including AOL-Time Warner Inc. and Oracle Corp., is still open to compromise.

High-Tech Opposition

Rodger and other critics of the bill argue that penalties for data misuse would hurt high-tech companies by slowing the flow of information on the Internet and the growth of online commerce. And they question whether the bill might lead to more Internet regulation.

High-tech companies strongly oppose adding criminal penalties of up to five years in prison and $250,000 in fines. Supporters of the bill say they mainly want victims to be able to sue for damages.

Negotiators in recent months have considered exemptions for libraries and universities, Internet service providers, and consumers who copy data for personal use, not for distribution or resale.

Staff aides say both committees will focus on the issue in coming weeks. Tauzin said he is determined to complete a bill, but he deflected rumors that he would make concessions to Sensenbrenner to repay him for agreeing not to block House action on a separate bill (HR 1542) to deregulate the high-speed data market. That bill passed, 273-157, on Feb. 27. (2002 *CQ Weekly*, p. 585)

"There was no quid pro quo," Tauzin said. "We've been at odds, but we're still talking. . . . It's a delicate balance between protecting the work product in these collections of information and not shutting off the availability of information."

Technology and Communication

Copyright Protection Requires Complex Fix

The Problem
Open architecture allows users to record virtually any content from a variety of sources

Content providers: music, movies, etc.

Content typically goes to consumer via cable, DVD, CD or satellite

Without controls, consumers can download or record digital content

Personal computer

DVD or CD player

Once digital content is recorded, user can redistribute or sell high-quality copies

The Fix
All manufacturers must include digital decoders to block unauthorized recording of content

Content providers: music, movies, etc.

Digital "flag" or "watermark" — invisible to the user — is embedded into content

Personal computer

DVD or CD player

In order to block illegal copying and distribution, new consumer electronics must be equipped to detect the flags or watermarks.

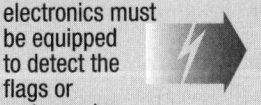

SOURCE: CQ research; movie scene: "Training Day" from Warner Bros.

CQ GRAPHIC / MARILYN GATES-DAVIS

(FCC) would have to dictate solutions after consulting with the same parties.

The legislation would outlaw the sale of digital media devices that did not contain government-approved copy protection standards. It also would be unlawful to import software or hardware that did not adhere to the standards or to transmit copyrighted material that had been purged of its copy-protected code.

Hollings' bill, introduced March 21, has attracted support from a powerful group of colleagues, including Ted Stevens, R-Alaska; Daniel K. Inouye, D-Hawaii; John B. Breaux, D-La.; Bill Nelson, D-Fla.; and Feinstein, who represents both Hollywood and Silicon Valley.

Feinstein said she really began to appreciate the copying problem after a staffer, at her request, demonstrated how to use file-swapping services to download copies of the feature films "A Beautiful Mind" and "Shrek" and then copy them onto CDs.

Techies Seething

The Hollings bill has left technology executives seething over the potential of a government mandate influencing how they design equipment.

Information technology companies maintain there is no single technology that can plug all the leaks in the digital world and is hacker-proof. The technology sector says it takes piracy seriously because billions of dollars of software is pilfered online each year. But those companies also say that affected industries should be given time to work out solutions through private negotiations. And they note that the prospect of the government selecting a single technology to discourage theft will instantly make that technology the target of hackers worldwide.

"We care about piracy, we are providing solutions to solvable problems, and those solutions come best through a voluntary, consensual process — not regulatory mandates," said Craig R. Barrett, chief executive officer of chipmaker Intel Corp.

Tech executives are not the only ones upset with Hollings' bill. Senate Judiciary Committee Chairman Patrick J. Leahy, D-Vt., is said to be incensed over the Commerce Committee dabbling in copyrights and intellectual property — generally the domain of the Judiciary panel.

"Certainly, no legislation will pass this year," Leahy said tersely during the Judiciary Committee's March 14 hearing on copyrights.

During the hearing, Leahy termed Hollings' approach "wrong-headed" but called on senior entertainment and high-tech executives to get more involved in finding a solution.

The two industries are, in fact, already collaborating on some copy protection technologies. A body called the Copy Protection Technical Working Group, also consisting of Internet service providers and various user groups, meets monthly in California to discuss the design of new digital locks. But the technical task of plugging all of the gaps has been difficult because of the multilayered architecture for distributing digital media.

Movie and television executives, for example, are concerned that unprotected over-the-air broadcasts of digital fare can be captured with digital recording equipment and redistributed without permission over the Internet. The copy protection group is developing a standard digital marker called a "broadcast flag" that would be read by computers and other digital media players and block distribution of the files containing the programming without permission. Industry participants think the standard could be introduced this summer.

A second gap occurs when digital

Politics and Public Policy

video signals are converted into unprotected analog format so the material can be viewed on the millions of analog home TV sets. This so-called analog hole concerns content creators because pirates can capture copyrighted material from the analog outputs of DVD players or digital televisions.

The answer could lie in "watermarking" technology that is embedded in the content to prevent unauthorized copying but is imperceptible to users. However, efforts to develop a watermark standard have been hampered by patent disputes between owners of the technology and by questions about what programs would be eligible for protection and what rules would apply to digital recording and display devices.

Congress may eventually be called on to endorse standards agreed upon by the industry for broadcast flags and watermarking. But the most difficult gap to police is the so-called peer-to-peer file-sharing services such as Napster and the second-generation Morpheus, Grokster and KaZaA.

Regulating these services is practically impossible because they are decentralized, operating with software that automatically links users without having to go through a computer server that could track what works are on subscribers' computers. KaZaA says it is more protected from legal challenge because it cannot control or even know what people trade with each other.

Technology company officials say the only way for entertainment companies to block piracy in such an environment is a costly scrambling of digital entertainment from the source using encryption software — something studios probably will do when they go to full digital distribution of movies. The file-sharing services more broadly illustrate how new technologies can render laws obsolete almost as soon as they are passed.

The Digital Millennium Copyright Act tried to address the ease and frequency with which copyrighted works can be stolen, but it did not envision the rise of Napster and its clones. Instead, the law tried to close specific loopholes lawmakers envisioned, for example by banning the use of technology to crack encryption software or other copy protections used for digital works. The act is an example of how narrowly written provisions can quickly become inapplicable to reality.

"If Congress moves too quickly, you get a situation where you're protecting the buggy whip while Henry Ford is moving the Model T off the assembly line," said Dan L. Burk, professor at the University of Minnesota Law School. "The other option is to devise more flexible rules, leave it to courts to sort out how they should be applied to different circumstances and avoid trying to anticipate everything and making the law look like the tax code."

In Tune With Music

The House Judiciary Committee this spring may attempt to clarify how the 1998 law relates to online music. The panel on March 12 notified interested parties that it would gauge "whether consensus exists on meaningful solutions to address identifiable harms."

Though the panel traditionally has been sympathetic to content creators, Chairman F. James Sensenbrenner Jr., R-Wis., has backed expanded consumer rights before. He included language in the 1998 copyright extension law that exempted taverns and other small businesses from paying music licensing fees to play radio or television sets in their establishments.

The hearings are expected to provide a forum for an ongoing feud between Boucher and the Recording Industry Association of America, which represents major record labels.

The industry association contends that file-swapping services facilitate billions of illegal downloads a month, and it is pursuing several court cases to shut them down. The industry took a similar tack last year when it persuaded a California court to shut down Napster's free file-sharing network.

Boucher and Cannon's bill would create a new system ensuring that online music services that are not owned by major labels would get access to copyrighted music at a fair price.

The lawmakers also may address the music industry's practice of placing copy protection on CDs so they cannot be played and copied on computer hard drives. The recent country release "Charley Pride — A Tribute to Jim Reeves" and a soundtrack album called "More Fast and Furious" each used types of this technology. Boucher and Cannon may press for a new labeling system that would require the recording industry to explicitly state on CD packages what equipment the discs can be played on.

The recording industry is asking Congress to be patient while it pursues the court cases. "The many millions of music fans around the world ... will continue to have access to the broad and diverse array of musical offerings that only a healthy music industry can provide," association President and CEO Hilary Rosen wrote Boucher in February.

Consumer electronics-makers also would like any legislation that emerges to include some affirmation of consumer rights in the digital world — something they say could counter Congress' tendency to back content creators. However, people on both sides of the debate say it would be difficult for the Judiciary panel or the broader Congress to agree on wording.

Another contentious issue is the provision in the 1998 act that prevents the circumvention of technological protection of digital works. Academic researchers and librarians worry that the law allows content creators to restrict access to material beyond what Congress envisioned. This could lead to a re-evaluation of the fair use doctrine and debate over what material researchers and others should reasonably expect access to.

Even if Congress does not pass major copyright legislation, many on both sides of the debate say it will at least encourage negotiations among the industries, something that has happened before.

Policymakers, for example, have been gridlocked for three years over whether databases, or compilations of unoriginal facts, deserve special protection, or whether copyright and trespass laws already offer enough protection. (Box, p. 108)

Also, the debate could spur passage of some narrowly tailored, noncontroversial measures concentrating on copyright.

One such bill (S 487) by Leahy and Orrin G. Hatch, R-Utah, would amend copyright law to allow educators to send excerpts of books, music and movies to students over the Internet without first obtaining a license. The House has yet to act on the bill, but is expected to address it before the end of the year.

"It's a critical time in that we're rapidly developing new uses for technology," said the University of Minnesota's Burk, "and Congress has to decide between protecting business models or hoping the market sorts things out." ◆

Industry

Bush Breaks With Position, Moves to Protect Steel Industry

President's action could affect midterm elections, fast-track legislation

The telephones in Ed O'Brien's office were ringing nonstop. President Bush had just announced his decision to put a temporary 30 percent tariff on most steel imports, and the Democratic House candidate in Pennsylvania's Lehigh Valley, the heart of steel country, was telling yet another reporter that Bush's remedy for the ailing industry was not enough.

O'Brien, a United Steelworkers Union official who once worked at the nearby Bethlehem Steel plant, was not just disagreeing with Bush. He also was trying to drive a wedge between district voters and the House member he wants to unseat: Patrick J. Toomey, a Republican free-trader who voted last December for Bush's fast-track trade negotiating authority, which would reduce congressional oversight on trade deals.

"He votes his mind," O'Brien said of Toomey. "But is his mind the right thinking for his constituents? I think not."

It is candidates such as O'Brien in political battleground states across the industrial Rust Belt who helped move Bush, a strident free-trader, to take a protectionist stand in favor of the steel industry.

By imposing tariffs ranging from 8 percent to 30 percent in 10 different categories of steel over three years, the president also stepped onto a politically perilous tightrope.

Bush reached out to the domestic steel industry at the risk of alienating global trading partners who also are allies in the war on terrorism.

He sought to show Congress that he can be trusted with fast-track trade authority by standing up for a domestic industry, but at the same time he upset businesses that use a lot of steel, such as automakers and appliance makers, as well as the shippers and seaports that make money from imports.

He tried to help one industry fend off foreign competition, but has all but invited other groups from textiles to timber to seek help with their trade problems. And he has disappointed free-trade purists in his own party who see any tariffs as evil.

"This is the triumph of politics over principle and policy," said Brink Lindsey, director of the Cato Institute's trade policy center. "This surrender to special interests could mark the end of the president's trade agenda for some time to come."

However, such steel states as Pennsylvania, Ohio, Michgan, Illinois and West Virginia also will be crucial to Bush if he runs for re-election in 2004. He carried traditionally Democratic West Virginia in 2000 partly on his promise to help steel battle low-priced imports — something the Clinton administration had avoided — and on March 5 imposed a 30 percent tariff on imported tin mill steel, which is produced by Weirton Steel, one of the largest employers in West Virginia.

"The president helped steel because they have got lots of political power in important states in the union," said Sen. Phil Gramm, R-Texas, a free-trader who expressed disappointment with Bush's decision. "If Enron had been a steel company, they never would have gone broke. I can assure you of that."

Back-Seat Debate

Sen. Arlen Specter, R-Pa., contends it was economics, not politics, that moved Bush.

"You cannot separate anything that's done in Washington from political consequences," Specter said. "But I believe that the president did not have that in mind when he made his decision."

Part of Bush's education on the dying steel industry occurred about a year ago, during a

Quick Contents

Most of the nation's top steel-producing states also are political battlegrounds in this year's congressional elections and in the 2004 presidential campaign. That is a key reason President Bush decided to raise tariffs on steel imports even though he preaches free trade. His decision could upset industries that use a lot of steel and some overseas allies.

Santorum, here addressing a steelworkers' rally near the White House Feb. 28, wanted higher steel tariffs but said it would not affect his upport for fast track.

CQ Weekly March 9, 2002

Politics and Public Policy

Steel States Pack Political Clout

The nation's top steel-producing states, shown here in black, are concentrated in the Midwest, and most have been political battlegrounds in recent presidential and congressional elections. President Bush and former Vice President Al Gore ran close in all the top steel states except Alabama, Indiana and North Carolina.

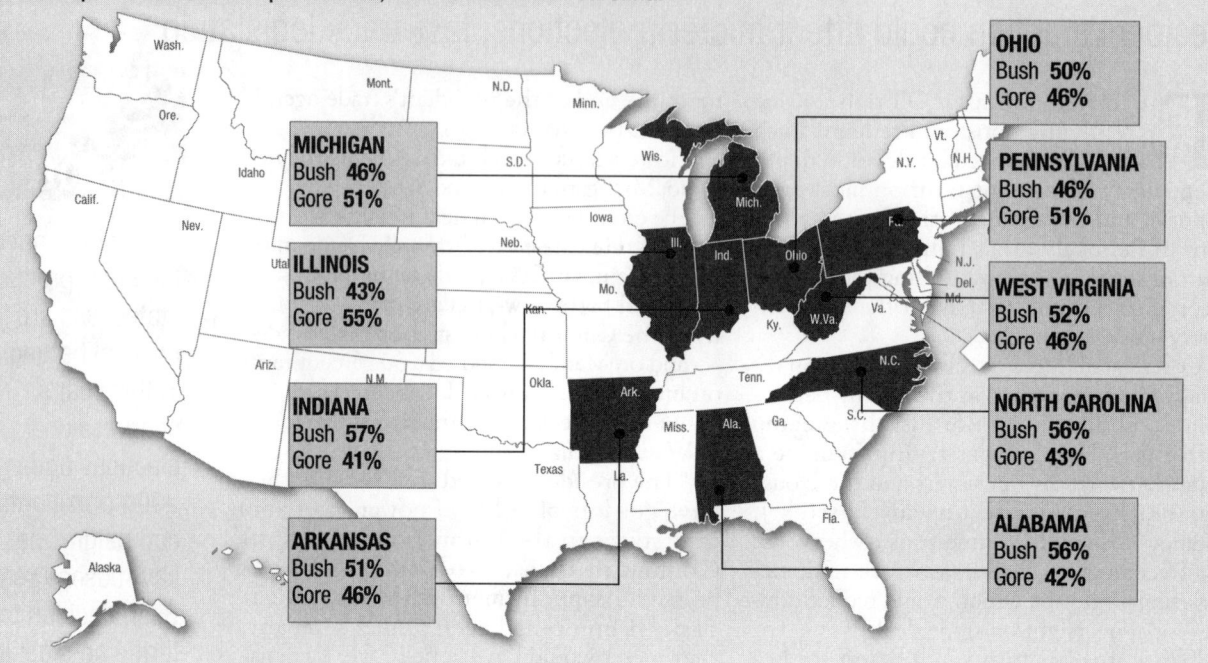

MICHIGAN Bush 46% Gore 51%
ILLINOIS Bush 43% Gore 55%
INDIANA Bush 57% Gore 41%
ARKANSAS Bush 51% Gore 46%
OHIO Bush 50% Gore 46%
PENNSYLVANIA Bush 46% Gore 51%
WEST VIRGINIA Bush 52% Gore 46%
NORTH CAROLINA Bush 56% Gore 43%
ALABAMA Bush 56% Gore 42%

CQ GRAPHIC / MARILYN GATES-DAVIS

40-minute limousine ride in Pennsylvania. Pennsylvania's two GOP senators, Specter and Rick Santorum, used the opportunity to talk steel with the president. They were joined by fellow Republicans Rep. Melissa A. Hart and then-Gov. Tom Ridge, now Bush's director of Homeland Security.

Industrywide, 46,000 jobs have been lost through 31 bankruptcies since 1997 because of cheaper steel imports, according to the pro-steel coalition. Another 326,000 jobs are on the verge of being lost.

Bush's initiation of an investigation last year by the U.S. International Trade Commission that found that higher tariffs were warranted persuaded Specter and other Republican steel-state lawmakers that the president would move to enforce anti-dumping laws.

The unknown factor until the week of March 4 was how far Bush was willing to go. The steel industry and unions wanted a 40 percent tariff over four years in order to have time to restructure and regain some momentum. Bush did not go that far, but he still surprised many with his decision to go as high as 30 percent over three years. (2002 CQ Weekly, p. 598)

Republicans said the decision would help Bush win congressional support for the fast-track bill (HR 3005), which the administration calls trade promotion authority. The bill would give the president more freedom to negotiate trade deals that Congress would have to approve or disapprove quickly and with no amendments. The measure passed the House by one vote last December and faces a contentious debate in the Senate this spring. Further, it will have to go back to the House because it already has been changed in committee. (2001 CQ Weekly, p. 2917)

Bush's ruling also gave political cover to Republicans in tough races, such as Toomey, and to others who backed fast track with reservations.

Rep. Bob Ney, R-Ohio, voted for fast track even though he has been backed by labor unions that oppose the bill. "The steel industry has been on life support with the plug half pulled out of the wall," Ney said. "This does the job for us at this point in time."

Toomey said he never doubted he would vote for fast track. One of the largest employers in his district, Air Products and Chemicals Inc., has about one-third of its sales overseas, for example. Fast track "is not tough in terms of me making my decision, but it's tough in terms of the political ramifications," he said. "I constantly feel the need to make the case." The president's [steel] decision will help, he said.

Other steel-state Republicans contend that Bush has purchased good will with his decision. "This will help Republicans in a lot of marginal races," said Rep. Phil English, R-Pa., chairman of the congressional steel caucus. "A lot of blue-collar voters . . . are going to feel more comfortable supporting Republican candidates," he added. "There is a clear political benefit."

Democrats also think they might benefit from the steel debate. The party picked O'Brien, Toomey's opponent, to deliver the Democratic response to Bush's March 9 radio address.

Leaving Legacies

Bush was not willing to commit the government to one steel industry priority: a $10 billion plan to cover health insurance and pensions for retirees who lost their benefits because of steel plant shutdowns. The industry says such federal support is vital to companies seeking to consolidate and cut costs.

Sen. John D. Rockefeller IV, D-W.Va., who specifically voted against fast track during the Senate Finance Committee markup because of inaction by the executive branch on steel, said he wanted to see how Bush would handle the retiree benefits issue now that he has shown sympathy for the steel industry.

"I will not play around with this issue. This is life or death for West Virginia," Rockefeller said.

A discharge petition that would release from committee a bill (HR 808) to pay for legacy costs has been signed by 123 House members, 95 short of the 218 signatures required.

Senate Finance Committee Chairman Max Baucus, D-Mont., also has warned that passage of fast track may depend on whether Republicans support a strong Trade Adjustment Assistance Act bill (S 1209). The $12.4 billion, 10-year legislation would authorize federal subsidies for wages and health care costs for workers displaced by trade pacts.

Even among some Republicans, support for fast track was not guaranteed by the steel decision. Although Specter praised Bush, for instance, he said he objects to the diminished congressional oversight of trade negotiations that comes with fast track.

"I don't want to give up my right to offer an amendment for the 12 million people I represent," Specter said.

Ohio Republican Sen. George V. Voinovich said he would not commit to Bush's trade promotion bill unless the Commerce Department can prove that it has the necessary manpower to police trade law violations.

"I'm getting complaints back from people in Ohio about China right now," Voinovich said. "I'm not kidding. It's very important."

Pro and Con

Free-traders such as Federal Reserve Board Chairman Alan Greenspan disapproved of the steel tariff decision, though Greenspan said he understood Bush's difficulties balancing trade and a troubled domestic industry. "I recognize that it is a very, very tough judgment," he said.

Rep. David Vitter, R-La., predicted that thousands of jobs could be lost in his district because of a drop in imports through the Port of New Orleans. He repeated an earlier threat to reconsider his vote for fast track.

"You can bend over backwards for people who are fundamentally against you on the issue and they will still be against you on the issue, and meanwhile you have turned your back on your base and alienated them," Vitter said.

House Rules Committee Chairman David Dreier, R-Calif., said the administration's protectionist move had "done a disservice to its long-term trade policy."

Numerous U.S. allies, including the European Union, Japan, Australia and New Zealand, launched formal complaints with the World Trade Organization. Korea, Taiwan, Brazil and China also are expected to protest.

Administration officials generally presented the ruling as a fair compromise: a necessary fix for the steel industry without setting tariffs so high they might impede economic recovery.

"We're a free-trading nation, and in order to remain a free-trading nation, we must enforce the law. And that's exactly what I did," Bush said.

At a White House briefing, U.S. Trade Representative Robert B. Zoellick was pressed to reconcile the administration's earlier statements against tariffs because they effectively function as tax increases.

"The nature of the relief — and I think this is a key distinction — is focused on foreigners, not Americans," Zoellick said. ◆

Politics and Public Policy

Welfare Overhaul Points Up Intra-Party Differences

Federal aid proposals focus on details of work hours, child care funds

Quick Contents

Republican leaders have managed to push President Bush's welfare plan through the House. Now all eyes are on a bipartisan coalition in the Senate.

With the House having passed a welfare bill along party lines, hope for a compromise rests now on the Senate.

A bipartisan group of senators are working on plans for reauthorizing the landmark 1996 welfare law (PL 104-193), and there are areas of broad agreement among them. Republican moderates agree with Democrats, for example, that low-income families need more help paying for child care than House Republicans and President Bush propose.

But the welfare debate this time around is largely in the details. In the Senate, any coalition could fracture along a number of lines, complicating the search for a deal.

Centrist Democrats support the president's call for longer work hours for welfare recipients, putting them at odds with many in their own party. But they balk at Republican initiatives aimed at promoting marriage.

Moderate Republicans, while they have crossed party lines to call generally for a boost in child care funding, could split with their Democratic allies over how much extra spending to propose.

Both parties are divided internally over how far to go in extending federal aid to legal immigrants, most of whom were denied cash welfare benefits in the 1996 overhaul.

With a midterm election looming and a summer calendar crowded with appropriations bills and other items, some observers speculate that the usually slow-moving Senate might run down the clock this year wrangling over the fine points of welfare policy, then simply opt for a one-year extension of the law with no major changes.

Senators close to the discussions, however, say they are determined to pass a meaningful reauthorization bill, hammer out a deal with the House and get it to the president before adjourning for the year.

"We ought to be able to work these issues out," said Sen. Thomas R. Carper, D-Del. "I always say if something's not perfect, make it better. And the law wasn't perfect."

Carper has proposed a bill with fellow Democrat Evan Bayh of Indiana that would embrace the tighter work requirements proposed by Bush and House Republicans but tie them to larger child care subsidies for states.

Meanwhile, Democrats and Republicans on the Senate Finance Committee promise legislation that would put more dollars into day care but keep the required workweek for welfare recipients at the current 30 hours.

With senators from both parties involved, it is the effort in Senate Finance that holds the most promise for producing legislation that could lead to consensus on renewing the welfare law.

Lawmakers are already warning against distracting side fights that would hinder progress on getting the rewrite done this year.

"This is important; we have got to do it," said Sen. Orrin G. Hatch, R-Utah, a panel conservative who is backing the committee's bipartisan effort.

Along Party Lines

On May 16, after hours of debate and some behind-the-scenes nipping and tucking by GOP leaders, the House passed a welfare bill (HR 4737) that closely follows the Bush proposals. The vote was 229-197, with 14 Democrats voting for the measure. (*2002 CQ Weekly, p. 1344*)

The House bill would require that welfare clients work a 40-hour week. It also would require states to have 70 percent of their welfare recipients employed by 2007, up from 50 percent now.

It would maintain current funding for federal welfare block grants to states at $16.5

CQ Weekly May 18, 2002

President Bush, who stumped for his welfare proposals May 13 in Chicago, claimed victory after the House vote. The Senate, however, is making other plans.

billion a year, but add $2 billion over the next five years to the current $4.8 billion in child care grants.

It would authorize up to $300 million a year in federal and matching state grants for marriage-promotion programs and continue $50 million a year for initiatives aimed at encouraging teenagers to abstain from sex.

It also would give states new authority to retool other federal anti-poverty programs, such as housing and food stamps, and to direct more aid to families on welfare. (2002 CQ Weekly, p. 1229)

Republican leaders hailed the legislation as the next logical step in the overhaul of the nation's welfare system, which replaced guaranteed welfare checks with work rules and time limits. (1996 Almanac, p. 6-3)

"House Republicans made a good plan better," said Majority Leader Dick Armey of Texas.

Since President Bill Clinton signed the 1996 law, nearly 2.3 million families have left welfare nationwide. But an estimated 58 percent of adults on welfare still do not have jobs, and House Republicans said their bill will help move them into jobs and toward financial independence.

"History tells us we were right, absolutely right in what we did in taking people out of a life of dependence," said Rep. E. Clay Shaw Jr., R-Fla., the main author of the 1996 measure.

Bush, who has made rewriting the welfare law a centerpiece of his social agenda this year, praised the House for passing the legislation and urged quick action in the Senate.

"This compassionate approach builds upon our past successes by moving more Americans from welfare to work, encouraging strong families and healthy marriages, and freeing states to innovate as they help people find the independence of a job," he said in a statement.

Looking to the Senate

The welfare debate this year lacks the stark ideological divides of six years ago, when the choice was whether to end welfare as an open-ended entitlement. Today, few question the new philosophy of welfare of temporary assistance only. (2002 CQ Weekly, p. 301)

But the House bill still was passed over Democrats' objections that the measure would demand more of low-income parents without helping them get adequate education and training, or pay for care for their children while they work.

House Democrats took the opportunity to point out the similarities between their proposed substitute and the plans being circulated by Senate Democrats and moderate Republicans.

The substitute (HR 3526) was defeated 198-222. (2002 CQ Weekly, p. 1344)

"Thank God, there's a Senate, and thank God they are working in a much more bipartisan way," said Rep. Benjamin L. Cardin, the top Democrat on the House Ways and Means Human Resources Subcommittee, which oversaw the bulk of the rewrite.

Cardin was referring to members of the Senate Finance Committee, including Hatch, John B. Breaux, D-La.; James M. Jeffords, I-Vt;, Olympia J. Snowe, R-Maine; and John D. Rockefeller IV, D-W.Va.

Like the House GOP bill, the plan those senators are writing would require states to have at least 70 percent of their welfare recipients working by 2007, but would allow states a credit against that requirement for every

A Marriage Tax Mishap

House Republicans thought a marriage tax bill deserved to be in the spotlight. It is an idea they now may be filing under the category, "Be careful of what you ask for."

The bill (HR 4626), the tax component of the GOP welfare package, is popular and non-controversial. At a cost of about $860 million, it would shave about $22 off tax bills of typical families — but only in 2003 and 2004 — by increasing the standard deduction for married couples. It also would combine two tax credits for employers who hire welfare recipients, at-risk youth, veterans and ex-felons.

House leaders slated the bill for just 40 minutes of debate on the May 14 "suspension of the rules" calendar, under which amendments are barred and a two-thirds majority is required for passage.

Then the leadership decided it should call the bill up under the regular ground rules for debate, which allow at least an hour of discussion and generally bring a bill more media exposure. "This is a big bill . . . an enormous increase to the take-home pay for about 21 million Americans," said Majority Leader Dick Armey, R-Texas.

Seeing their own chance to score some public relations points, Democrats prepared to offer an amendment that would have eliminated the tax advantage U.S. corporations obtain when they relocate headquarters to avoid paying U.S. taxes. Such an amendment would not have been in order had Republicans stuck to the original plan. (Background CQ Weekly, p. 1079)

Some Republicans, including Ways and Means Committee Chairman Bill Thomas of California, argue there is nothing wrong or illegal about so-called corporate inversions, but Scott McInnis of Colorado and other GOP members have criticized companies that relocated.

"I smell a skunk in the crowd," McInnis said after Stanley Works Ltd. stockholders on May 9 ratified the company's move to Bermuda. "Maybe they should move their whole operation to Bermuda, because they've already turned their back on the American worker."

To avoid having to vote against the amendment, GOP leaders pulled the bill from the agenda.

Democrats on Ways and Means quickly fired off a news release with a boldfaced headline in all-capital letters: "Republicans Cancel Vote on Marriage Penalty Relief in Order to Protect Corporate Traitors."

Republicans countered that the tax code is to blame, not businesses that need to stay competitive in the world market. "To suggest that it is not patriotic is a political ploy, simple election-year politics," said Christin Tinsworth, spokeswoman for Ways and Means.

GOP leaders now are taking no chances. They marriage bill is on the May 21 suspension calendar and presumably will stay there this time.

Politics and Public Policy

client who finds a job.

It would allow states to provide cash assistance to legal immigrants.

The coalition backs increased funding for child care grants to states, but so far has not settled on a dollar figure. The senators are waiting for a report from congressional budget analysts.

They are all but sure to propose a bigger increase than the $2 billion included in the House bill, but the $11 billion proposed by House Democrats could be a stretch for fiscal conservatives among the group, worried about covering those costs while also paying for the war on terrorism and other priorities in a year when money is tight.

"We are considering more," said Arlen Specter of Pennsylvania, the top Republican on the Labor, Health and Human Services, and Education Appropriations Subcommittee. "It is a question of balancing our priorities."

Finance Committee Chairman Max Baucus, D-Mont., has expressed interest in the coalition's plans, especially the proposal for more child care funding, but has yet to introduce a bill for panel markup.

Workweek Struggle

The Senate could see considerable debate over how many hours welfare recipients should have to work each week as a condition for receiving their benefits.

Bayh and Carper side with House Republicans and Bush in calling for a 40-hour workweek. The two centrists are members of the Democratic Leadership Council, founded by Clinton, who signed the 1996 welfare law over the objections of liberals in his party.

Requiring more work from welfare recipients is the only way to keep faith with typical working Americans, who themselves must put in at least 40 hours a week, Bayh and Carper say.

"I know this is controversial in some quarters," said Bayh, a former governor. "People on the system should put in the same 40 hours to become independent."

He and Carper would add $8 billion to child care through 2007, four times the amount voted for in the House bill, and make the longer workweek contingent upon Congress appropriating that extra money.

But other Democrats and some GOP moderates remain skeptical.

> "Many senators in both parties want to restore welfare cash benefits to immigrants, but making them eligible for health insurance is more controversial."

Charles E. Grassley of Iowa, the ranking Republican on the Senate Finance Committee, noted the House's 40-hour proposal would allow for 16 hours a week to be spent in classrooms or training programs.

"I like the 40-hour thing if it was really a hard-and-fast rule," Grassley said. "But there's so much subterfuge involved in how you qualify for the 40 hours that I think it might be more intellectually honest to stick with something less than 40 to make sure that it's legitimate work."

He added he would support a substantial increase in child care funding, but that any extra funds would be accompanied by some higher work requirements.

Marriage Problems

There also will be fights over whether to restore federal health benefits to immigrants. Many senators in both parties want to restore welfare cash benefits to immigrants, but making them eligible for health insurance is more controversial.

Bayh and Carper want to spend $585 million over five years to extend Medicaid to immigrants. But while spending on welfare block grants is fixed and easy for Congress to control, Medicaid, as an entitlement, grows with the need, which potentially makes it a much more costly item.

And there could be skirmishes over deciding how much federal money to put into programs that encourage single parents to get married.

Republicans say research has proven that children with married parents are healthier and do better in school than those with single parents.

"Why are we neutral on this issue if we are about children?" said Sen. Rick Santorum, R-Pa.

But lawmakers such as Breaux and Blanche Lincoln, D-Ark., say they fear such programs would instead encourage mothers to stay with abusive men for fear of losing welfare benefits.

Wade Horn, assistant secretary of Health and Human Services and the Bush administration's point man on welfare, appeared before the Finance Committee on May 16 to press the administration's case on that issue and welfare overall.

"It's time to step back and focus on what still needs to be done," he told the panel.

Marriage-promotion provisions in the current welfare law have not worked, Horn and others said. The goal of encouraging stable, two-parent families is important enough to try a new approach, they said.

Horn said the White House is not concerned about the apparent gap between the House-passed bill and plans now in the works in the Senate.

"We're encouraged by areas of overlap," he said.

Waivers for States

The House bill passed after a last-minute debate within the GOP caucus over the waiver program that would let states win special permission to combine anti-poverty block grants from welfare, housing, nutrition and other programs. Appropriators and authorizers both complained that the measure would allow states to flout the conditions Congress often places on grant programs.

It was a tricky balance to strike: States complain that the new rules in the House bill would undermine the state control that was central to the 1996 overhaul. The waiver proposal is an effort to allay those concerns.

In the end, the provision was changed to clarify that states could not get waivers for conditions that Congress puts on funding, especially against moving funds from one account to another.

Supporters of the waivers main-

Social Policy

House, Senate Welfare Plans: A Comparison

ISSUE	HOUSE BILL (HR 4735)	BREAUX-SNOWE PLAN	BAYH-CARPER PLAN
Work requirements	State would have to raise the percentage of welfare recipients working from 50 percent in 2003 to 70 percent in 2007.	Same.	Same.
Work hours	The number of hours welfare recipients would have to work each week would increase to 40, with at least 24 hours spent at a work site. Recipients could spend up to 16 hours in training.	The required workweek would remain at 30 hours. Recipients would have to spend at least 24 hours at a work site and could use the remaining six hours for training.	The required workweek would increase to 40 hours, as long as child care subsides for families also increase.
Child care	Federal child care subsidies, now $4.8 billion a year, would increase by $2 billion over five years.	Child care subsidies would increase by an amount yet to be determined, pending a cost estimate from the Congressional Budget Office.	Child care block grants to states would increase by $8 billion over five years.
Legal immigrants	The bill would continue the ban on welfare benefits to most legal immigrants.	States would have the option of restoring cash welfare benefits to legal immigrants.	States could restore cash welfare benefits for all legal immigrants and Medicaid for some children and pregnant women.
State waivers	States would get waivers from Cabinet secretaries to combine housing, nutrition and education programs to direct more help to welfare recipients.	No provision.	No provision.
Marriage and abstinence education	The bill would provide up to $300 million per year in federal and matching state grants for programs aimed at promoting marriage, and $50 million a year for programs that encourage sexual abstinence among teens.	States would get $200 million in annual block grants for marriage promotion and teen pregnancy prevention.	The plan would provide $300 million annually for teen pregnancy prevention and other initiatives.

tained that the language would take away the flexibility they had hoped to give to states. House Ways and Means Chairman Bill Thomas, R-Calif., argued that changing the proposal would effectively hinder its mission: allowing states to provide creative services for welfare families, such as putting food stamp coupons and welfare payments on the same debit cards or designing a single application for housing and job-training aid.

Despite the final partisan vote in the House, Republicans have shown they are willing to deal.

Before putting their bill on the floor, House leaders added child care money to win over GOP moderates, agreed to allow parents a few months out of the year for full-time education or drug rehabilitation to appease Democrats, and agreed on the waiver program to help Bush sell the plan to governors.

The two Senate proposals do not include the House waiver provision or their plan to let a handful of states experiment with a food stamps block grant.

Bush says such policies would cut down on bureaucracy and provide better services. Democrats contend that states could shortchange clients by shifting money from one program to another.

A General Accounting Office report issued May 16 said states are increasingly trying to blend social programs, such as coordinating cash assistance services with employment training. But the congressional accountants said such attempts have caused trouble.

In one case, a local welfare office was screening out recipients for job training funds who had little work history in order to ensure they would meet federally required job-retention quotas.

Some waiver opponents complain that such practices will keep welfare families in poverty.

Senate panel debate is expected to start next month. ◆

Appendix

The Legislative Process in Brief   119

The Budget Process in Brief   124

Glossary of Congressional Terms   126

Congressional Information on the Internet   150

The Legislative Process in Brief

Note: Parliamentary terms used below are defined in the glossary.

Introduction of Bills

A House member (including the resident commissioner of Puerto Rico and nonvoting delegates of the District of Columbia, Guam, the Virgin Islands and American Samoa) may introduce any one of several types of bills and resolutions by handing it to the clerk of the House or placing it in a box called the hopper. A senator first gains recognition of the presiding officer to announce the introduction of a bill.

As the usual next step in either the House or Senate, the bill is numbered, referred to the appropriate committee, labeled with the sponsor's name and sent to the Government Printing Office so that copies can be made for subsequent study and action. House and Senate bills may be jointly sponsored and carry several senators' names. A bill written in the executive branch and proposed as an administration measure usually is introduced by the chairman of the congressional committee that has jurisdiction, as a courtesy to the White House.

Bills—Prefixed with HR in the House, S in the Senate, followed by a number. Used as the form for most legislation, whether general or special, public or private.

Joint Resolutions—Designated H J Res or S J Res. Subject to the same procedure as bills, with the exception of a joint resolution proposing an amendment to the Constitution. The latter must be approved by two-thirds of both houses and is then sent directly to the administrator of general services for submission to the states for ratification instead of being presented to the president for his approval.

Concurrent Resolutions—Designated H Con Res or S Con Res. Used for matters affecting the operations of both houses. These resolutions do not become law.

Resolutions—Designated H Res or S Res. Used for a matter concerning the operation of either house alone and adopted only by the chamber in which it originates.

Committee Action

With few exceptions, bills are referred to the appropriate standing committees. The job of referral formally is the responsibility of the Speaker of the House and the presiding officer of the Senate, but this task usually is carried out on their behalf by the parliamentarians of the House and Senate. Precedent, statute and the jurisdictional mandates of the committees as set forth in the rules of the House and Senate determine which committees receive what kinds of bills. Bills are technically considered "read for the first time" when referred to House committees.

When a bill reaches a committee it is placed on the committee's calendar. Failure of a committee to act on a bill is equivalent to killing it and most fall by the legislative roadside. The measure can be withdrawn from the committee's purview only by a discharge petition signed by a majority of the House membership on House bills, or by adoption of a special resolution in the Senate. Discharge attempts rarely succeed and the Senate procedure has not been used for decades.

The first committee action taken on a bill usually is a request for comment on it by interested agencies of the government. The committee chairman may assign the bill to a subcommittee for study and hearings, or it may be considered by the full committee. Hearings may be public, closed (executive session) or both. A subcommittee, after considering a bill, reports to the full committee its recommendations for action and any proposed amendments.

The full committee then votes on its recommendation to the House or Senate. This procedure is called "ordering a bill reported." Occasionally a committee may order a bill reported unfavorably; most of the time a report, submitted by the chairman of the committee to the House or Senate, calls for favorable action on the measure since the committee can effectively "kill" a bill by simply failing to take any action.

After the bill is reported, the committee chairman instructs the staff to prepare a written report. The report describes the purposes and scope of the bill, explains the committee revisions, notes proposed changes in existing law and, usually, includes the views of the executive branch agencies consulted. Often committee members opposing a measure issue dissenting minority statements that are included in the report.

Usually, the committee "marks up" or proposes amendments to the bill. If the amendments are substantial and the measure is complicated, the committee may order a "clean bill" introduced, which will embody the proposed amendments. The original bill then is put aside and the clean bill, with a new number, is reported to the floor.

The chamber must approve, alter or reject the committee amendments before the bill itself can be put to a vote.

Floor Action

After a bill is reported back to the house where it originated, it is placed on the calendar.

There are five legislative calendars in the House, issued in one cumulative calendar titled *Calendars of the United States House of Representatives and History of Legislation*. The House calendars are:

The Union Calendar to which are referred bills raising revenues, general appropriations bills and any measures directly or indirectly appropriating money or property. It is the Calendar of the Committee of the Whole House on the State of the Union.

Appendix

The House Calendar to which are referred bills of public character not raising revenue or appropriating money.

The Corrections Calendar to which are referred bills to repeal rules and regulations deemed excessive or unnecessary when the Corrections Calendar is called the second and fourth Tuesday of each month. (Instituted in the 104th Congress to replace the seldom-used Consent Calendar.) A three-fifths majority is required for passage.

The Private Calendar to which are referred bills for relief in the nature of claims against the United States or private immigration bills that are passed without debate when the Private Calendar is called the first and third Tuesdays of each month.

The Discharge Calendar to which are referred motions to discharge committees when the necessary signatures are signed to a discharge petition.

There is only one legislative calendar in the Senate and one "executive calendar" for treaties and nominations submitted to the Senate.

Debate. A bill is brought to debate by varying procedures. In the Senate the majority leader, in consultation with the minority leader and others, schedules the bills that will be taken up for debate. If it is urgent or important it can be taken up in the Senate either by unanimous consent or by a majority vote.

In the House, precedence is granted if a special rule is obtained from the Rules Committee. A request for a special rule usually is made by the chairman of the committee that favorably reported the bill. The request is considered by the Rules Committee in the same fashion that other committees consider legislative measures. The committee proposes a resolution providing for immediate consideration of the bill. The Rules Committee reports the resolution to the House where it is debated and voted on in the same fashion as regular bills.

The resolutions providing special rules are important because they specify how long the bill may be debated and whether it may be amended from the floor. If floor amendments are banned, the bill is considered under a "closed rule."

When a bill is debated under an "open rule," amendments may be offered from the floor. Committee amendments always are taken up first but may be changed, as may all amendments up to the second degree; that is, an amendment to an amendment to an amendment is not in order.

Duration of debate in the House depends on whether the bill is under discussion by the House proper or before the House when it is sitting as the Committee of the Whole House on the State of the Union. In the former, the amount of time for debate is allocated with an hour for each member if the measure is under consideration without a rule. In the Committee of the Whole the amount of time agreed on for general debate is equally divided between proponents and opponents. At the end of general discussion, the bill is often read section by section for amendment. Debate on an amendment is limited to five minutes for each side; this is called the "five-minute rule." In practice, amendments regularly are debated more than ten minutes, with members gaining the floor by offering pro forma amendments or obtaining unanimous consent to speak longer than five minutes.

Senate debate usually is unlimited. It can be halted only by unanimous consent or by "cloture," which requires a three-fifths majority of the entire Senate except for proposed changes in the Senate rules. The latter requires a two-thirds vote.

The House considers almost all important bills within a parliamentary framework known as the Committee of the Whole. It is not a committee as the word usually is understood; it is the full House meeting under another name for the purpose of speeding action on legislation. Technically, the House sits as the Committee of the Whole when it considers any tax measure or bill dealing with public appropriations. Upon adoption of a special rule, the Speaker declares the House resolved into the Committee of the Whole and appoints a member of the majority party to serve as the chairman. The rules of the House permit the Committee of the Whole to meet when a quorum of 100 members is present on the floor and to amend and act on bills. When the Committee of the Whole has acted, it "rises," the Speaker returns as the presiding officer of the House and the member appointed chairman of the Committee of the Whole reports the action of the committee and its recommendations. The Committee of the Whole cannot pass a bill; instead it reports the measure to the full House with whatever changes it has approved. The full House then may pass or reject the bill — or, on occasion, recommit the bill to committee. Amendments adopted in the Committee of the Whole may be put to a second vote in the full House.

Votes. Voting on bills may occur repeatedly before they are finally approved or rejected. The House votes on the rule for the bill and on various amendments to the bill. Voting on amendments often is a more illuminating test of a bill's support than is the final tally. Sometimes members approve final passage of bills after vigorously supporting amendments that, if adopted, would have scuttled the legislation.

The Senate has three different methods of voting: an untabulated voice vote, a standing vote (called a division) and a recorded roll call to which members answer "yea" or "nay" when their names are called. The House also employs voice and standing votes, but since January 1973 yeas and nays have been recorded by an electronic voting device, eliminating the need for time-consuming roll calls.

After amendments to a bill have been voted upon, a vote may be taken on a motion to recommit the bill to committee. If carried, this vote is usually a death blow to the bill. If the motion is unsuccessful, the bill then is "read for the third time." After the third reading a vote on passage is taken. The final vote may be followed by a motion to reconsider, and this motion may be followed by a move to lay the motion on the table. Usually, those voting for the bill's passage vote for the tabling motion, thus safeguarding the final passage action. With that, the bill has been formally passed by the chamber.

Action in Second Chamber

After a bill is passed it is sent to the other chamber. This body may then take one of several steps. It may pass the bill as is — accepting the other chamber's language. It may send the bill to committee for scrutiny or alteration, or reject the entire bill, advising the other chamber of its actions. Or it simply may ignore the bill submitted while it continues work on its own version of the proposed legislation. Frequently, one chamber may approve a version of a bill that is greatly at variance with the version already passed by the other chamber, and then substitute its contents for the language of the other, retaining only the latter's bill number.

Often the second chamber makes only minor changes. If these are readily agreed to by the other chamber, the bill then is routed to the president. However, if the opposite chamber significantly alters the bill submitted to it, the measure usually is "sent to conference." The chamber that has possession of the "papers" (engrossed bill, engrossed amendments, messages of transmittal) requests a conference and the other chamber may agree to it. If the second chamber does not agree, the bill dies.

How a Bill Becomes a Law

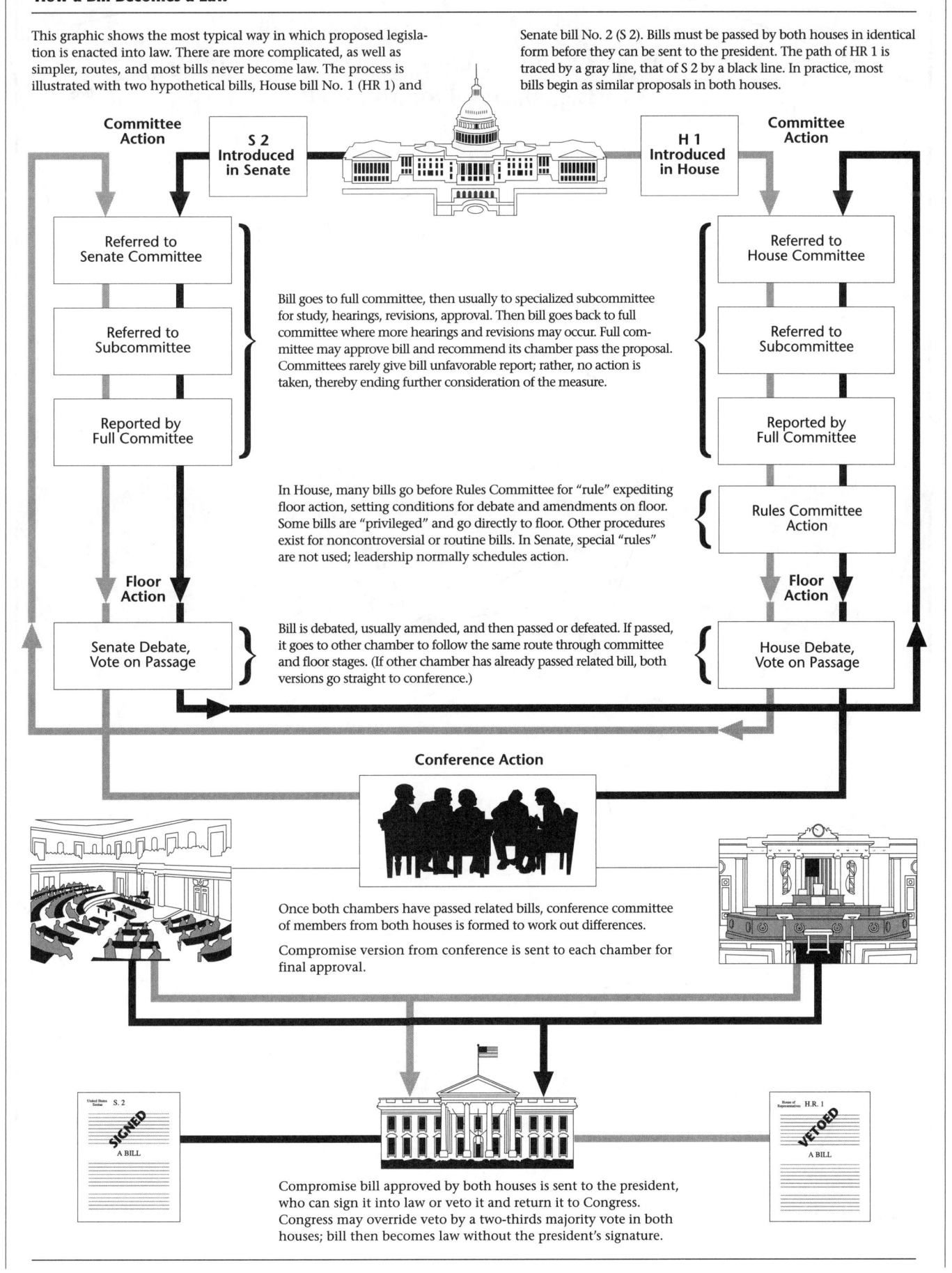

This graphic shows the most typical way in which proposed legislation is enacted into law. There are more complicated, as well as simpler, routes, and most bills never become law. The process is illustrated with two hypothetical bills, House bill No. 1 (HR 1) and Senate bill No. 2 (S 2). Bills must be passed by both houses in identical form before they can be sent to the president. The path of HR 1 is traced by a gray line, that of S 2 by a black line. In practice, most bills begin as similar proposals in both houses.

Committee Action

S 2 Introduced in Senate

H 1 Introduced in House

Committee Action

Referred to Senate Committee

Referred to Subcommittee

Reported by Full Committee

Referred to House Committee

Referred to Subcommittee

Reported by Full Committee

Bill goes to full committee, then usually to specialized subcommittee for study, hearings, revisions, approval. Then bill goes back to full committee where more hearings and revisions may occur. Full committee may approve bill and recommend its chamber pass the proposal. Committees rarely give bill unfavorable report; rather, no action is taken, thereby ending further consideration of the measure.

In House, many bills go before Rules Committee for "rule" expediting floor action, setting conditions for debate and amendments on floor. Some bills are "privileged" and go directly to floor. Other procedures exist for noncontroversial or routine bills. In Senate, special "rules" are not used; leadership normally schedules action.

Rules Committee Action

Floor Action

Senate Debate, Vote on Passage

House Debate, Vote on Passage

Floor Action

Bill is debated, usually amended, and then passed or defeated. If passed, it goes to other chamber to follow the same route through committee and floor stages. (If other chamber has already passed related bill, both versions go straight to conference.)

Conference Action

Once both chambers have passed related bills, conference committee of members from both houses is formed to work out differences.

Compromise version from conference is sent to each chamber for final approval.

S. 2 SIGNED A BILL

H.R. 1 VETOED A BILL

Compromise bill approved by both houses is sent to the president, who can sign it into law or veto it and return it to Congress. Congress may override veto by a two-thirds majority vote in both houses; bill then becomes law without the president's signature.

121

Examples of Legislative Documents

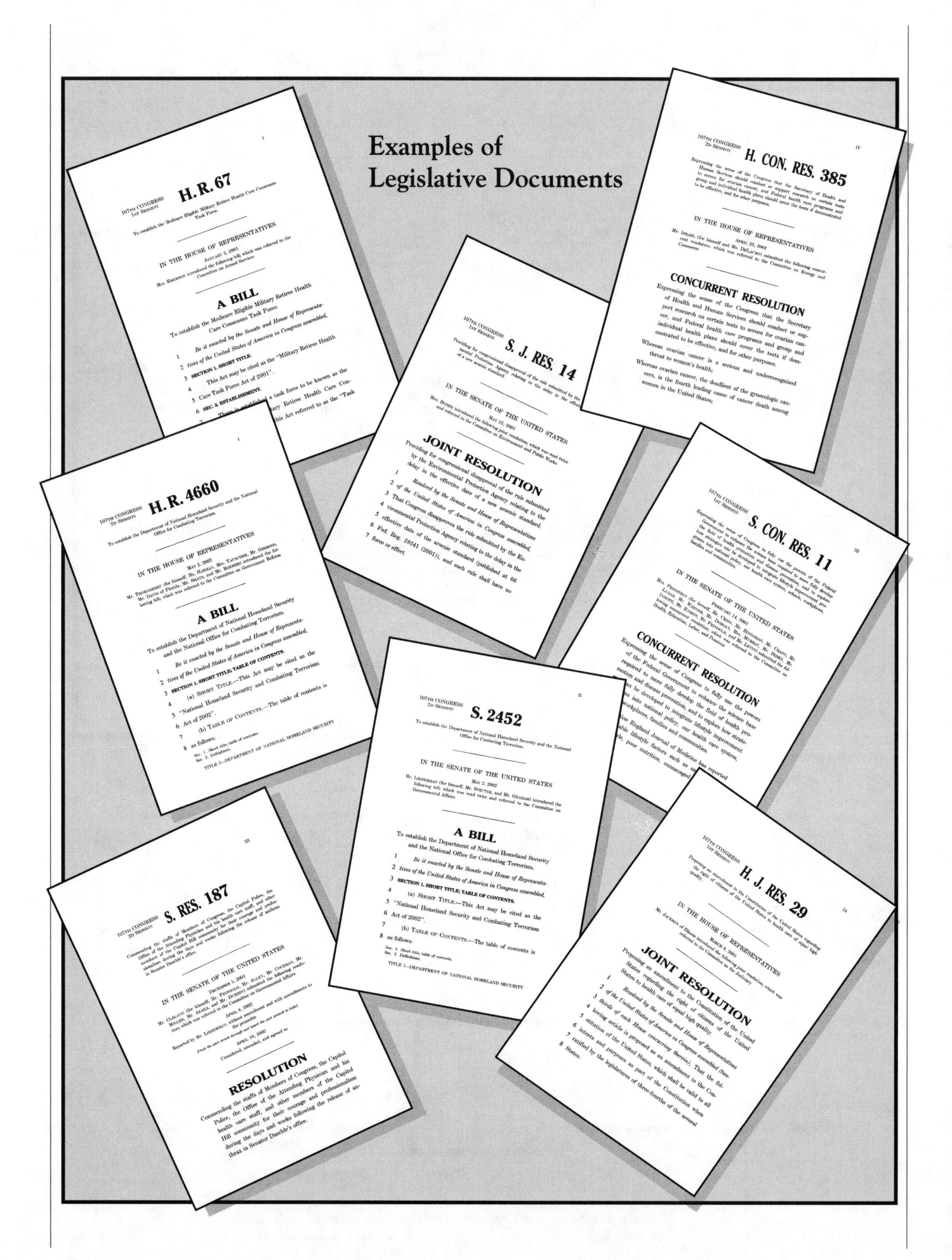

Conference Action

A conference works out conflicting House and Senate versions of a legislative bill. The conferees usually are senior members from the committees that managed the legislation who are appointed by the presiding officers of the two houses. Under this arrangement the conferees of one house have the duty of trying to maintain their chamber's position in the face of amending actions by the conferees (also referred to as "managers") of the other house.

The number of conferees from each chamber may vary, the range usually being from seven to nine members in each group, depending on the length or complexity of the bill involved. But a majority vote controls the action of each group so that a large representation does not give one chamber a voting advantage over the other chamber's conferees.

Theoretically, conferees are not allowed to write new legislation in reconciling the two versions before them, but this curb sometimes is bypassed. Many bills have been put into acceptable compromise form only after new language was provided by the conferees. Frequently the ironing out of difficulties takes days or even weeks. Conferences on involved, complex and controversial bills sometimes are particularly drawn out.

As a conference proceeds, conferees reconcile differences between the versions, but generally they grant concessions only insofar as they remain sure that the chamber they represent will accept the compromises. Occasionally, uncertainty over how either house will react, or the positive refusal of a chamber to back down on a disputed amendment, results in an impasse, and the bills die in conference even though each was approved by its sponsoring chamber.

When the conferees have reached agreement, they prepare a conference report embodying their recommendations (compromises) and a joint explanatory statement. The report, in document form, must be submitted to each house. The conference report must be approved by each house. Consequently, approval of the report is approval of the compromise bill. In the order of voting on conference reports, the chamber that asked for a conference yields to the other chamber the opportunity to vote first.

Final Action

After a bill has been passed by both the House and Senate in identical form, all of the original papers are sent to the enrolling clerk of the chamber in which the bill originated. The clerk then prepares an enrolled bill, which is printed on parchment paper.

When this bill has been certified as correct by the secretary of the Senate or the clerk of the House, depending on which chamber originated the bill, it is signed first (no matter whether it originated in the Senate or House) by the Speaker of the House and then by the president of the Senate. It is next sent to the White House to await action.

If the president approves the bill, he signs it, dates it and usually writes the word "approved" on the document. If the president does not sign it within 10 days (Sundays excepted) and Congress is in session, the bill becomes law without his signature.

If Congress adjourns *sine die* at the end of the second session the president can pocket veto a bill and it dies without Congress having the opportunity to override.

A president vetoes a bill by refusing to sign it and, before the ten-day period expires, returning it to Congress with a message stating his reasons. The message is sent to the chamber that originated the bill. If no action is taken on the message, the bill dies. Congress, however, can attempt to override the president's veto and enact the bill, "the objections of the president to the contrary notwithstanding." Overriding a veto requires a two-thirds vote of those present in each chamber, who must number a quorum and vote by roll call.

If the president's veto is overridden by a two-thirds vote in both houses, the bill becomes law. Otherwise it is dead.

When bills are passed finally and signed, or passed over a veto, they are given law numbers in numerical order as they become law. There are two series of numbers, one for public and one for private laws, starting at the number "1" for each two-year term of Congress. They are then identified by law number and by Congress — for example, Private Law 10, 105th Congress; Public Law 33, 106th Congress (or PL 106-33).

The Budget Process in Brief

Through the budget process, the president and Congress decide how much to spend and tax during the upcoming fiscal year. More specifically, they decide how much to spend on each activity, ensure that the government spends no more than that and spends it only for that activity and report on that spending at the end of each budget cycle.

The President's Budget

The law requires that, by the first Monday in February, the president submit to Congress his proposed federal budget for the next fiscal year, which begins on October 1. To accomplish this the president establishes general budget and fiscal policy guidelines. Based on these guidelines, executive branch agencies make requests for funds and submit them to the White House's Office of Management and Budget (OMB) nearly a year before the start of a new fiscal year. The OMB, receiving direction from the president and administration officials, reviews the agencies' requests and develops a detailed budget by December. From December to January the OMB prepares the budget documents, so that the president can deliver it to Congress in February.

The president's budget is the executive branch's plan for the next year — but it is just a proposal. After receiving it, Congress has its own budget process to follow from February to October. Only after Congress passes the required spending bills — and the president signs them — has the government created its actual budget.

Action in Congress

Congress first must pass a "budget resolution" — a framework within which the members of Congress will make their decisions about spending and taxes. It includes targets for total spending, total revenues and the deficit, and allocations within the spending target for the two types of spending — discretionary and mandatory.

Discretionary spending, which currently accounts for about 33 percent of all federal spending, is what the president and Congress must decide to spend for the next year through the thirteen annual appropriations bills. It includes money for such activities as the FBI and the Coast Guard, for housing and education, for NASA and highway and bridge construction and for defense and foreign aid.

Mandatory spending, which currently accounts for 67 percent of all spending, is authorized by laws that have already been passed. It includes entitlement spending — such as for Social Security, Medicare, veterans' benefits and food stamps — through which individuals receive benefits because they are eligible based on their age, income or other criteria. It also includes interest on the national debt, which the government pays to individuals and institutions that hold Treasury bonds and other government securities. The only way the president and Congress can change the spending on entitlement and other mandatory programs is if they change the laws that authorized the programs.

Currently, the law requires that legislation that would raise mandatory spending or lower revenues — compared to existing law — be offset by spending cuts or revenue increases. This requirement, called "pay-as-you-go" is designed to prevent new legislation from increasing the deficit.

Once Congress passes the budget resolution, legislators turn their attention to passing the 13 annual appropriations bills and, if they choose, "authorizing" bills to change the laws governing mandatory spending and revenues.

Congress begins by examining the president's budget in detail. Scores of committees and subcommittees hold hearings on proposals under their jurisdiction. The House and Senate Armed Services Authorizing Committees, and the Defense and Military Construction Subcommittees of the Appropriations Committees, for instance, hold hearings on the president's defense budget. The White House budget director, cabinet officers and other administration officials work with Congress as it accepts some of the president's proposals, rejects others and changes still others. Congress can change funding levels, eliminate programs or add programs not requested by the president. It can add or eliminate taxes and other sources of revenue, or make other changes that affect the amount of revenue collected. Congressional rules require that these committees and subcommittees take actions that reflect the congressional budget resolution.

The president's budget, the budget resolution and the appropriations or authorizing bills measure spending in two ways — "budget authority" and "outlays." Budget authority is what the law authorizes the federal government to spend for certain programs, projects or activities. What the government actually spends in a particular year, however, is an outlay. For example, when the government decides to build a space exploration system, the president and Congress may agree to appropriate $1 billion in budget authority. But the space system may take ten years to build. Thus, the government may spend $100 million in outlays in the first year to begin construction and the remaining $900 million during the next nine years as the construction continues.

Congress must provide budget authority before the federal agencies can obligate the government to make outlays. When Congress fails to complete action on one or more of the regular annual appropriations bills before the fiscal year begins on October 1, budget authority may be made on a temporary basis through continuing resolutions. Continuing resolutions make budget authority available for limited periods of time, generally at rates related through some formula to the rate provided in the previous year's appropriation.

Monitoring the Budget

Once Congress passes and the president signs the federal appropriations bills or authorizing laws for the fiscal year, the government monitors the budget through (1) agency program managers and budget officials, including the Inspectors General, who report only to the agency head; (2) the Office of Management and Budget; (3) congressional committees; and (4) the General Accounting Office, an auditing arm of Congress.

This oversight is designed to (1) ensure that agencies comply with legal limits on spending and that agencies use budget authority only for the purposes intended; (2) see that programs are operating consistently with legal requirements and existing policy; and (3) ensure that programs are well managed and achieving the intended results.

The president may withhold appropriated amounts from obligation only under certain limited circumstances — to provide for contingencies, to achieve savings made possible through changes in requirements or greater efficiency of operations or as otherwise provided by law. The Impoundment Control Act of 1974 specifies the procedures that must be followed if funds are withheld. Congress can also cancel previous authorized budget authority by passing a rescissions bill — but it also must be signed by the president.

Glossary of Congressional Terms

AA—(See Administrative Assistant.)

Absence of a Quorum—Absence of the required number of members to conduct business in a house or a committee. When a quorum call or roll-call vote in a house establishes that a quorum is not present, no debate or other business is permitted except a motion to adjourn or motions to request or compel the attendance of absent members, if necessary by arresting them.

Absolute Majority—A vote requiring approval by a majority of all members of a house rather than a majority of members present and voting. Also referred to as constitutional majority.

Account—Organizational units used in the federal budget primarily for recording spending and revenue transactions.

Act—(1) A bill passed in identical form by both houses of Congress and signed into law by the president or enacted over the president's veto. A bill also becomes an act without the president's signature if he does not return it to Congress within ten days (Sundays excepted) and if Congress has not adjourned within that period. (2) Also, the technical term for a bill passed by at least one house and engrossed.

Ad Hoc Select Committee—A temporary committee formed for a special purpose or to deal with a specific subject. Conference committees are ad hoc joint committees. A House rule adopted in 1975 authorizes the Speaker to refer measures to special ad hoc committees, appointed by the Speaker with the approval of the House.

Adjourn—A motion to adjourn is a formal motion to end a day's session or meeting of a house or a committee. A motion to adjourn usually has no conditions attached to it, but it sometimes may specify the day or time for reconvening or make reconvening subject to the call of the chamber's presiding officer or the committee's chairman. In both houses, a motion to adjourn is of the highest privilege, takes precedence over all other motions, is not debatable and must be put to an immediate vote. Adjournment of a house ends its legislative day. For this reason, the House or Senate sometimes adjourns for only one minute, or some other very brief period of time, during the course of a day's session. The House does not permit a motion to adjourn after it has resolved into Committee of the Whole or when the previous question has been ordered on a measure to final passage without an intervening motion.

Adjourn for More Than Three Days—Under Article I, Section 5 of the Constitution, neither house may adjourn for more than three days without the approval of the other. The necessary approval is given in a concurrent resolution to which both houses have agreed.

Adjournment *Sine Die*—Final adjournment of an annual or two-year session of Congress; literally, adjournment without a day. The two houses must agree to a privileged concurrent resolution for such an adjournment. A sine die adjournment precludes Congress from meeting again until the next constitutionally fixed date of a session (Jan. 3 of the following year) unless Congress determines otherwise by law or the president calls it into special session. Article II, Section 3 of the Constitution authorizes the president to adjourn both houses until such time as the president thinks proper when the two houses cannot agree to a time of adjournment. No president, however, has ever exercised this authority.

Adjournment to a Day (and Time) Certain—An adjournment that fixes the next date and time of meeting for one or both houses. It does not end an annual session of Congress.

Administration Bill—A bill drafted in the executive office of the president or in an executive department or agency to implement part of the president's program. An administration bill is introduced in Congress by a member who supports it or as a courtesy to the administration.

Administrative Assistant (AA)—The title usually given to a member's chief aide, political advisor and head of office staff. The administrative assistant often represents the member at meetings with visitors or officials when the member is unable (or unwilling) to attend.

Adoption—The usual parliamentary term for approval of a conference report. It is also commonly applied to amendments.

Advance Appropriation—In an appropriation act for a particular fiscal year, an appropriation that does not become available for spending or obligation until a subsequent fiscal year. The amount of the advance appropriation is counted as part of the budget for the fiscal year in which it becomes available for obligation.

Advance Funding—A mechanism whereby statutory language may allow budget authority for a fiscal year to be increased, and obligations to be incurred, with an offsetting decrease in the budget authority available in the succeeding fiscal year. If not used, the budget authority remains available for obligation in the succeeding fiscal year. Advance funding is sometimes used to provide contingency funding of a few benefit programs.

Adverse Report—A committee report recommending against approval of a measure or some other matter. Committees usually pigeonhole measures they oppose instead of reporting them adversely, but they may be required to report them by a statutory rule or an instruction from their parent body.

Advice and Consent—The Senate's constitutional role in consenting to or rejecting the president's nominations to executive branch and judicial offices and treaties with other nations. Confirmation of nominees requires a simple majority vote of senators present and voting. Treaties must be approved by a two-thirds majority of those present and voting.

Aisle—The center aisle of each chamber. When facing the presiding officer, Republicans usually sit to the right of the aisle, Democrats to the left. When members speak of "my side of the aisle" or "this side," they are referring to their party.

Glossary

Amendment—A formal proposal to alter the text of a bill, resolution, amendment, motion, treaty or some other text. Technically, it is a motion. An amendment may strike out (eliminate) part of a text, insert new text or strike out and insert — that is, replace all or part of the text with new text. The texts of amendments considered on the floor are printed in full in the Congressional Record.

Amendment in the Nature of a Substitute—Usually, an amendment to replace the entire text of a measure. It strikes out everything after the enacting clause and inserts a version that may be somewhat, substantially or entirely different. When a committee adopts extensive amendments to a measure, it often incorporates them into such an amendment. Occasionally, the term is applied to an amendment that replaces a major portion of a measure's text.

Amendment Tree—A diagram showing the number and types of amendments that the rules and practices of a house permit to be offered to a measure before any of the amendments is voted on. It shows the relationship of one amendment to the others, and it may also indicate the degree of each amendment, whether it is a perfecting or substitute amendment, the order in which amendments may be offered and the order in which they are put to a vote. The same type of diagram can be used to display an actual amendment situation.

Annual Authorization—Legislation that authorizes appropriations for a single fiscal year and usually for a specific amount. Under the rules of the authorization-appropriation process, an annually authorized agency or program must be reauthorized each year if it is to receive appropriations for that year. Sometimes Congress fails to enact the reauthorization but nevertheless provides appropriations to continue the program, circumventing the rules by one means or another.

Appeal—A member's formal challenge of a ruling or decision by the presiding officer. On appeal, a house or a committee may overturn the ruling by majority vote. The right of appeal ensures the body against arbitrary control by the chair. Appeals are rarely made in the House and are even more rarely successful. Rulings are more frequently appealed in the Senate and occasionally overturned, in part because its presiding officer is not the majority party's leader, as in the House.

Apportionment—The action, after each decennial census, of allocating the number of members in the House of Representatives to each state. By law, the total number of House members (not counting delegates and a resident commissioner) is fixed at 435. The number allotted to each state is based approximately on its proportion of the nation's total population. Because the Constitution guarantees each state one representative no matter how small its population, exact proportional distribution is virtually impossible. The mathematical formula currently used to determine the apportionment is called the Method of Equal Proportions. (See Method of Equal Proportions.)

Appropriated Entitlement—An entitlement program, such as veterans' pensions, that is funded through annual appropriations rather than by a permanent appropriation. Because such an entitlement law requires the government to provide eligible recipients the benefits to which they are entitled, whatever the cost, Congress must appropriate the necessary funds.

Appropriation—(1) Legislative language that permits a federal agency to incur obligations and make payments from the Treasury for specified purposes, usually during a specified period of time. (2) The specific amount of money made available by such language. The Constitution prohibits payments from the Treasury except "in Consequence of Appropriations made by Law." With some exceptions, the rules of both houses forbid consideration of appropriations for purposes that are unauthorized in law or of appropriation amounts larger than those authorized in law. The House of Representatives claims the exclusive right to originate appropriation bills — a claim the Senate denies in theory but accepts in practice.

At-Large—Elected by and representing an entire state instead of a district within a state. The term usually refers to a representative rather than to a senator. (See Apportionment; Congressional District; Redistricting.)

August Adjournment—A congressional adjournment during the month of August in odd-numbered years, required by the Legislative Reorganization Act of 1970. The law instructs the two houses to adjourn for a period of at least thirty days before the second day after Labor Day, unless Congress provides otherwise or if, on July 31, a state of war exists by congressional declaration.

Authorization—(1) A statutory provision that establishes or continues a federal agency, activity or program for a fixed or indefinite period of time. It may also establish policies and restrictions and deal with organizational and administrative matters. (2) A statutory provision, as described in (1), may also, explicitly or implicitly, authorize congressional action to provide appropriations for an agency, activity or program. The appropriations may be authorized for one year, several years or an indefinite period of time, and the authorization may be for a specific amount of money or an indefinite amount ("such sums as may be necessary"). Authorizations of specific amounts are construed as ceilings on the amounts that subsequently may be appropriated in an appropriation bill, but not as minimums; either house may appropriate lesser amounts or nothing at all.

Authorization-Appropriation Process—The two-stage procedural system that the rules of each house require for establishing and funding federal agencies and programs: first, enactment of authorizing legislation that creates or continues an agency or program; second, enactment of appropriations legislation that provides funds for the authorized agency or program.

Automatic Roll Call—Under a House rule, the automatic ordering of the yeas and nays when a quorum is not present on a voice or division vote and a member objects to the vote on that ground. It is not permitted in the Committee of the Whole.

Backdoor Spending Authority—Authority to incur obligations that evades the normal congressional appropriations process because it is provided in legislation other than appropriation acts. The most common forms are borrowing authority, contract authority and entitlement authority.

Baseline—A projection of the levels of federal spending, revenues and the resulting budgetary surpluses or deficits for the upcoming and subsequent fiscal years, taking into account laws enacted to date and assuming no new policy decisions. It provides a benchmark for measuring the budgetary effects of proposed changes in federal revenues or spending, assuming certain economic conditions.

Bells—A system of electric signals and lights that informs members of activities in each chamber. The type of activity taking place is indicated by the number of signals and the interval between them. When the signals are sounded, a corresponding number of lights are lit around the perimeter of many clocks in House or Senate offices.

Bicameral—Consisting of two houses or chambers. Congress is a bicameral legislature whose two houses have an equal role in enacting legislation. In most other national bicameral legislatures, one house is significantly more powerful than the other.

Appendix

Bigger Bite Amendment—An amendment that substantively changes a portion of a text including language that had previously been amended. Normally, language that has been amended may not be amended again. However, a part of a sentence that has been changed by amendment, for example, may be changed again by an amendment that amends a "bigger bite" of the text — that is, by an amendment that also substantively changes the unamended parts of the sentence or the entire section or title in which the previously amended language appears. The biggest possible bite is an amendment in the nature of a substitute that amends the entire text of a measure. Once adopted, therefore, such an amendment ends the amending process.

Bill—The term for the chief vehicle Congress uses for enacting laws. Bills that originate in the House of Representatives are designated as HR, those in the Senate as S, followed by a number assigned in the order in which they are introduced during a two-year Congress. A bill becomes a law if passed in identical language by both houses and signed by the president, or passed over the president's veto, or if the president fails to sign it within ten days after receiving it while Congress is in session.

Bill of Attainder—An act of a legislature finding a person guilty of treason or a felony. The Constitution prohibits the passage of such a bill by the U.S. Congress or any state legislature.

Bills and Resolutions Introduced—Members formally present measures to their respective houses by delivering them to a clerk in the chamber when their house is in session. Both houses permit any number of members to join in introducing a bill or resolution. The first member listed on the measure is the sponsor; the other members listed are its cosponsors.

Bills and Resolutions Referred—After a bill or resolution is introduced, it is normally sent to one or more committees that have jurisdiction over its subject, as defined by House and Senate rules and precedents. A Senate measure is usually referred to the committee with jurisdiction over the predominant subject of its text, but it may be sent to two or more committees by unanimous consent or on a motion offered jointly by the majority and minority leaders. In the House, a rule requires the Speaker to refer a measure to the committee that has primary jurisdiction. The Speaker is also authorized to refer measures sequentially to additional committees and to impose time limits on such referrals.

Bipartisan Committee—A committee with an equal number of members from each political party. The House Committee on Standards of Official Conduct and the Senate Select Committee on Ethics are the only bipartisan, permanent full committees.

Borrowing Authority—Statutory authority permitting a federal agency, such as the Export-Import Bank, to borrow money from the public or the Treasury to finance its operations. It is a form of backdoor spending. To bring such spending under the control of the congressional appropriation process, the Congressional Budget Act requires that new borrowing authority shall be effective only to the extent and in such amounts as are provided in appropriations acts.

Budget—A detailed statement of actual or anticipated revenues and expenditures during an accounting period. For the national government, the period is the federal fiscal year (Oct. 1 to Sept. 30). The budget usually refers to the president's budget submission to Congress early each calendar year. The president's budget estimates federal government income and spending for the upcoming fiscal year and contains detailed recommendations for appropriation, revenue and other legislation. Congress is not required to accept or even vote directly on the president's proposals, and it often revises the president's budget extensively. (See Fiscal Year.)

Budget Act—Common name for the Congressional Budget and Impoundment Control Act of 1974, which established the basic procedures of the current congressional budget process; created the House and Senate Budget Committees; and enacted procedures for reconciliation, deferrals and rescissions. (See Budget Process; Deferral; Impoundment; Reconciliation; Rescission. See also Gramm-Rudman-Hollings Act of 1985.)

Budget and Accounting Act of 1921—The law that, for the first time, authorized the president to submit to Congress an annual budget for the entire federal government. Before passage of the act, most federal agencies sent their budget requests to the appropriate congressional committees without review by the president.

Budget Authority—Generally, the amount of money that may be spent or obligated by a government agency or for a government program or activity. Technically, it is statutory authority to enter into obligations that normally result in outlays. The main forms of budget authority are appropriations, borrowing authority and contract authority. It also includes authority to obligate and expend the proceeds of offsetting receipts and collections. Congress may make budget authority available for only one year, several years or an indefinite period, and it may specify definite or indefinite amounts.

Budget Enforcement Act of 1990—An act that revised the sequestration process established by the Gramm-Rudman-Hollings Act of 1985, replaced the earlier act's fixed deficit targets with adjustable ones, established discretionary spending limits for fiscal years 1991 through 1995, instituted pay-as-you-go rules to enforce deficit neutrality on revenue and mandatory spending legislation and reformed the budget and accounting rules for federal credit activities. Unlike the Gramm-Rudman-Hollings Act, the 1990 act emphasized restraints on legislated changes in taxes and spending instead of fixed deficit limits.

Budget Enforcement Act of 1997—An act that revised and updated the provisions of the Budget Enforcement Act of 1990, including by extending the discretionary spending caps and pay-as-you-go rules through 2002.

Budget Process—(1) In Congress, the procedural system it uses (a) to approve an annual concurrent resolution on the budget that sets goals for aggregate and functional categories of federal expenditures, revenues and the surplus or deficit for an upcoming fiscal year; and (b) to implement those goals in spending, revenue and, if necessary, reconciliation and debt-limit legislation. (2) In the executive branch, the process of formulating the president's annual budget, submitting it to Congress, defending it before congressional committees, implementing subsequent budget-related legislation, impounding or sequestering expenditures as permitted by law, auditing and evaluating programs and compiling final budget data. The Budget and Accounting Act of 1921 and the Congressional Budget and Impoundment Control Act of 1974 established the basic elements of the current budget process. Major revisions were enacted in the Gramm-Rudman-Hollings Act of 1985 and the Budget Enforcement Act of 1990.

Budget Resolution—A concurrent resolution in which Congress establishes or revises its version of the federal budget's broad financial features for the upcoming fiscal year and several additional fiscal years. Like other concurrent resolutions, it does not have the force of law, but it provides the framework within which Congress subsequently considers revenue, spending and other budget-implementing legislation. The framework consists of two basic elements: (1) aggregate budget amounts (total revenues, new budget authority, outlays, loan obligations and loan guarantee commitments, deficit or surplus and debt limit); and (2) subdivisions of the relevant aggregate amounts among the functional categories of the budget. Although it does not allocate funds to specific programs or accounts, the budget committees' reports accompanying the resolution often discuss the major program assumptions underlying its functional amounts. Unlike those amounts, however, the assumptions are not binding on Congress.

By Request—A designation indicating that a member has introduced a measure on behalf of the president, an executive agency or a private individual or organization. Members often introduce such measures as a courtesy because neither the president nor any person other than a member of Congress can do so. The term, which appears next to the sponsor's name, implies that the member who introduced the measure does not necessarily endorse it. A House rule dealing with by-request introductions dates from 1888, but the practice goes back to the earliest history of Congress.

Byrd Rule—The popular name of an amendment to the Congressional Budget Act that bars the inclusion of extraneous matter in any reconciliation legislation considered in the Senate. The ban is enforced by points of order that the presiding officer sustains. The provision defines different categories of extraneous matter, but it also permits certain exceptions. Its chief sponsor was Sen. Robert C. Byrd, D-W.Va.

Calendar—A list of measures or other matters (most of them favorably reported by committees) that are eligible for floor consideration. The House has five calendars; the Senate has two. A place on a calendar does not guarantee consideration. Each house decides which measures and matters it will take up, when and in what order, in accordance with its rules and practices.

Calendar Wednesday—A House procedure that on Wednesdays permits its committees to bring up for floor consideration nonprivileged measures they have reported. The procedure is so cumbersome and susceptible to dilatory tactics, however, that it is rarely used.

Call Up—To bring a measure or report to the floor for immediate consideration.

Casework—Assistance to constituents who seek assistance in dealing with federal and local government agencies. Constituent service is a high priority in most members' offices.

Caucus—(1) A common term for the official organization of each party in each house. (2) The official title of the organization of House Democrats. House and Senate Republicans and Senate Democrats call their organizations "conferences." (3) A term for an informal group of members who share legislative interests, such as the Black Caucus, Hispanic Caucus and Children's Caucus.

Censure—The strongest formal condemnation of a member for misconduct short of expulsion. A house usually adopts a resolution of censure to express its condemnation, after which the presiding officer reads its rebuke aloud to the member in the presence of his or her colleagues.

Chairman—The presiding officer of a committee, a subcommittee or a task force. At meetings, the chairman preserves order, enforces the rules, recognizes members to speak or offer motions and puts questions to a vote. The chairman of a committee or subcommittee usually appoints its staff and sets its agenda, subject to the panel's veto.

Chamber—The Capitol room in which a house of Congress normally holds its sessions. The chamber of the House of Representatives, officially called the Hall of the House, is considerably larger than that of the Senate because it must accommodate 435 representatives, four delegates and one resident commissioner. Unlike the Senate chamber, members have no desks or assigned seats. In both chambers, the floor slopes downward to the well in front of the presiding officer's raised desk. A chamber is often referred to as "the floor," as when members are said to be on or going to the floor. Those expressions usually imply that the member's house is in session.

Christmas Tree Bill—Jargon for a bill adorned with amendments, many of them unrelated to the bill's subject, that provide benefits for interest groups, specific states, congressional districts, companies and individuals.

Classes of Senators—A class consists of the thirty-three or thirty-four senators elected to a six-year term in the same general election. Because the terms of approximately one-third of the senators expire every two years, there are three classes.

Clean Bill—After a House committee extensively amends a bill, it often assembles its amendments and what is left of the bill into a new measure that one or more of its members introduces as a "clean bill." The revised measure is assigned a new number.

Clerk of the House—An officer of the House of Representatives responsible principally for administrative support of the legislative process in the House. The clerk is invariably the candidate of the majority party.

Cloakrooms—Two rooms with access to the rear of each chamber's floor, one for each party's members, where members may confer privately, sit quietly or have a snack. The presiding officer sometimes urges members who are conversing too loudly on the floor to retire to their cloakrooms.

Closed Hearing—A hearing closed to the public and the media. A House committee may close a hearing only if it determines that disclosure of the testimony to be taken would endanger national security, violate any law or tend to defame, degrade or incriminate any person. The Senate has a similar rule. Both houses require roll-call votes in open session to close a hearing.

Closed Rule—A special rule reported from the House Rules Committee that prohibits amendments to a measure or that only permits amendments offered by the reporting committee.

Cloture—A Senate procedure that limits further consideration of a pending proposal to thirty hours in order to end a filibuster. Sixteen senators must first sign and submit a cloture motion to the presiding officer. One hour after the Senate meets on the second calendar day thereafter, the chair puts the motion to a yea-and-nay vote following a live quorum call. If three-fifths of all senators (sixty if there are no vacancies) vote for the motion, the Senate must take final action on the cloture proposal by the end of the thirty hours of consideration and may consider no other business until it takes that action. Cloture on a proposal to amend the Senate's standing rules requires approval by two-thirds of the senators present and voting.

Code of Official Conduct—A House rule that bans certain actions by House members, officers and employees; requires them to conduct themselves in ways that "reflect creditably" on the House; and orders them to adhere to the spirit and the letter of House rules and those of its committees. The code's provisions govern the receipt of outside compensation, gifts and honoraria and the use of campaign funds; prohibit members from using their clerk-hire allowance to pay anyone who does not perform duties commensurate with that pay; forbids discrimination in members' hiring or treatment of employees on the grounds of race, color, religion, sex, handicap, age or national

Appendix

origin; orders members convicted of a crime who might be punished by imprisonment of two or more years not to participate in committee business or vote on the floor until exonerated or reelected; and restricts employees' contact with federal agencies on matters in which they have a significant financial interest. The Senate's rules contain some similar prohibitions.

College of Cardinals—A popular term for the subcommittee chairmen of the appropriations committees, reflecting their influence over appropriation measures. The chairmen of the full appropriations committees are sometimes referred to as popes.

Comity—The practice of maintaining mutual courtesy and civility between the two houses in their dealings with each other and in members' speeches on the floor. Although the practice is largely governed by long-established customs, a House rule explicitly cautions its members not to characterize any Senate action or inaction, refer to individual senators except under certain circumstances, or quote from Senate proceedings except to make legislative history on a measure. The Senate has no rule on the subject but references to the House have been held out of order on several occasions. Generally the houses do not interfere with each other's appropriations although minor conflicts sometimes occur. A refusal to receive a message from the other house has also been held to violate the practice of comity.

Committee—A panel of members elected or appointed to perform some service or function for its parent body. Congress has four types of committees: standing, special or select, joint, and, in the House, a Committee of the Whole. Committees conduct investigations, make studies, issue reports and recommendations and, in the case of standing committees, review and prepare measures on their assigned subjects for action by their respective houses. Most committees divide their work among several subcommittees. With rare exceptions, the majority party in a house holds a majority of the seats on its committees, and their chairmen are also from that party.

Committee Jurisdiction—The legislative subjects and other functions assigned to a committee by rule, precedent, resolution or statute. A committee's title usually indicates the general scope of its jurisdiction but often fails to mention other significant subjects assigned to it.

Committee of the Whole—Common name of the Committee of the Whole House on the State of the Union, a committee consisting of all members of the House of Representatives. Measures from the union calendar must be considered in the Committee of the Whole before the House officially completes action on them; the committee often considers other major bills as well. A quorum of the committee is 100, and it meets in the House chamber under a chairman appointed by the Speaker. Procedures in the Committee of the Whole expedite consideration of legislation because of its smaller quorum requirement, its ban on certain motions and its five-minute rule for debate on amendments. Those procedures usually permit more members to offer amendments and participate in the debate on a measure than is normally possible. The Senate no longer uses a Committee of the Whole.

Committee Ratios—The ratios of majority to minority party members on committees. By custom, the ratios of most committees reflect party strength in their respective houses as closely as possible.

Committee Report on a Measure—A document submitted by a committee to report a measure to its parent chamber. Customarily, the report explains the measure's purpose, describes provisions and any amendments recommended by the committee and presents arguments for its approval.

Committee Veto—A procedure that requires an executive department or agency to submit certain proposed policies, programs or action to designated committees for review before implementing them. Before 1983, when the Supreme Court declared that a legislative veto was unconstitutional, these provisions permitted committees to veto the proposals. Committees no longer conduct this type of policy review, and the term is now something of a misnomer. Nevertheless, agencies usually take the pragmatic approach of trying to reach a consensus with the committees before carrying out their proposals, especially when an appropriations committee is involved.

Concur—To agree to an amendment of the other house, either by adopting a motion to concur in that amendment or a motion to concur with an amendment to that amendment. After both houses have agreed to the same version of an amendment, neither house may amend it further, nor may any subsequent conference change it or delete it from the measure. Concurrence by one house in all amendments of the other house completes action on the measure; no vote is then necessary on the measure as a whole because both houses previously passed it.

Concurrent Resolution—A resolution that requires approval by both houses but does not need the president's signature and therefore cannot have the force of law. Concurrent resolutions deal with the prerogatives or internal affairs of Congress as a whole. Designated H. Con. Res. in the House and S. Con. Res. in the Senate, they are numbered consecutively in each house in their order of introduction during a two-year Congress.

Conferees—A common title for managers, the members from each house appointed to a conference committee. The Senate usually authorizes its presiding officer to appoint its conferees. The Speaker appoints House conferees, and under a rule adopted in 1993, can remove conferees "at any time after an original appointment" and also appoint additional conferees at any time. Conferees are expected to support the positions of their houses despite their personal views, but in practice this is not always the case. The party ratios of conferees generally reflect the ratios in their houses. Each house may appoint as many conferees as it pleases. House conferees often outnumber their Senate colleagues; however, each house has only one vote in a conference, so the size of its delegation is immaterial.

Conference—(1) A formal meeting or series of meetings between members representing each house to reconcile House and Senate differences on a measure (occasionally several measures). Because one house cannot require the other to agree to its proposals, the conference usually reaches agreement by compromise. When a conference completes action on a measure, or as much action as appears possible, it sends its recommendations to both houses in the form of a conference report, accompanied by an explanatory statement. (2) The official title of the organization of all Democrats or Republicans in the Senate and of all Republicans in the House of Representatives. (See Party Caucus.)

Conference Committee—A temporary joint committee formed for the purpose of resolving differences between the houses on a measure. Major and controversial legislation usually requires conference committee action. Voting in a conference committee is not by individuals but within the House and Senate delegations. Consequently, a conference committee report requires the support of a majority of the conferees from each house. Both houses require that conference committees open their meetings to the public. The Senate's rule permits the committee to close its meetings if a majority of conferees in each delegation agree by a roll-call vote. The House rule permits closed meetings only if the House authorizes them to do so on a roll-call vote. Otherwise, there are no congressional rules governing the organization of, or procedure in, a conference committee. The committee chooses its chairman, but on measures that go to conference annually, such as general appropriation bills, the chairmanship traditionally rotates between the houses.

Conference Report—A document submitted to both houses that contains a conference committee's agreements for resolving their differences on a measure. It must be signed by a majority of the conferees from each house separately and must be accompanied by an explanatory statement. Both houses prohibit amendments to a conference report and require it to be accepted or rejected in its entirety.

Congress—(1) The national legislature of the United States, consisting of the House of Representatives and the Senate. (2) The national legislature in office during a two-year period. Congresses are numbered sequentially; thus, the 1st Congress of 1789–1791 and the 106th Congress of 1999–2001. Before 1935, the two-year period began on the first Monday in December of odd-numbered years. Since then it has extended from January of an odd-numbered year through noon on Jan. 3 of the next odd-numbered year. A Congress usually holds two annual sessions, but some have had three sessions and the 67th Congress had four. When a Congress expires, measures die if they have not yet been enacted.

Congressional Accountability Act of 1995 (CAA)—An act applying eleven labor, workplace and civil rights laws to the legislative branch and establishing procedures and remedies for legislative branch employees with grievances in violation of these laws. The following laws are covered by the CAA: the Fair Labor Standards Act of 1938; Title VII of the Civil Rights Act of 1964; Americans with Disabilities Act of 1990; Age Discrimination in Employment Act of 1967; Family and Medical Leave Act of 1993; Occupational Safety and Health Act of 1970; Chapter 71 of Title 5, U.S. Code (relating to federal service labor-management relations); Employee Polygraph Protection Act of 1988; Worker Adjustment and Retraining Notification Act; Rehabilitation Act of 1973; and Chapter 43 of Title 38, U.S. Code (relating to veterans' employment and reemployment).

Congressional Budget and Impoundment Control Act of 1974—The law that established the basic elements of the congressional budget process, the House and Senate Budget Committees, the Congressional Budget Office and the procedures for congressional review of impoundments in the form of rescissions and deferrals proposed by the president. The budget process consists of procedures for coordinating congressional revenue and spending decisions made in separate tax, appropriations and legislative measures. The impoundment provisions were intended to give Congress greater control over executive branch actions that delay or prevent the spending of funds provided by Congress.

Congressional Budget Office (CBO)—A congressional support agency created by the Congressional Budget and Impoundment Control Act of 1974 to provide nonpartisan budgetary information and analysis to Congress and its committees. CBO acts as a scorekeeper when Congress is voting on the federal budget, tracking bills to ensure they comply with overall budget goals. The agency also estimates what proposed legislation would cost over a five-year period. CBO works most closely with the House and Senate Budget Committees.

Congressional Directory—The official who's who of Congress, usually published during the first session of a two-year Congress.

Congressional District—The geographical area represented by a single member of the House of Representatives. For states with only one representative, the entire state is a congressional district. As of 2001 seven states had only one representative each: Alaska, Delaware, Montana, North Dakota, South Dakota, Vermont and Wyoming.

Congressional Record—The daily, printed and substantially verbatim account of proceedings in both the House and Senate chambers. Extraneous materials submitted by members appear in a section titled "Extensions of Remarks." A "Daily Digest" appendix contains highlights of the day's floor and committee action plus a list of committee meetings and floor agendas for the next day's session.

Although the official reporters of each house take down every word spoken during the proceedings, members are permitted to edit and "revise and extend" their remarks before they are printed. In the Senate section, all speeches, articles and other material submitted by senators but not actually spoken or read on the floor are set off by large black dots, called bullets. However, bullets do not appear when a senator reads part of a speech and inserts the rest. In the House section, undelivered speeches and materials are printed in a distinctive typeface. The term "permanent Record" refers to the bound volumes of the daily Records of an entire session of Congress.

Congressional Research Service (CRS)—Established in 1917, a department of the Library of Congress whose staff provide nonpartisan, objective analysis and information on virtually any subject to committees, members and staff of Congress. Originally the Legislative Reference Service, it is the oldest congressional support agency.

Congressional Support Agencies—A term often applied to three agencies in the legislative branch that provide nonpartisan information and analysis to committees and members of Congress: the Congressional Budget Office, the Congressional Research Service of the Library of Congress and the General Accounting Office. A fourth support agency, the Office of Technology Assessment, formerly provided such support but was abolished in the 104th Congress.

Congressional Terms of Office—A term normally begins on Jan. 3 of the year following a general election and runs two years for representatives and six years for senators. A representative chosen in a special election to fill a vacancy is sworn in for the remainder of the predecessor's term. An individual appointed to fill a Senate vacancy usually serves until the next general election or until the end of the predecessor's term, whichever comes first. Some states, however, require their governors to call a special election to fill a Senate vacancy shortly after an appointment has been made.

Constitutional Rules—Constitutional provisions that prescribe procedures for Congress. In addition to certain types of votes required in particular situations, these provisions include the following: (1) the House chooses its Speaker, the Senate its president pro tempore and both houses their officers; (2) each house requires a majority quorum to conduct business; (3) less than a majority may adjourn from day to day and compel the attendance of absent members; (4) neither house may adjourn for more than three days without the consent of the other; (5) each house must keep a journal; (6) the yeas and nays are ordered when supported by one-fifth of the members present; (7) all revenue-raising bills must originate in the House, but the Senate may propose amendments to them. The Constitution also sets out the procedure in the House for electing a president, the procedure in the Senate for electing a vice president, the

Appendix

procedure for filling a vacancy in the office of vice president and the procedure for overriding a presidential veto.

Constitutional Votes—Constitutional provisions that require certain votes or voting methods in specific situations. They include (1) the yeas and nays at the desire of one-fifth of the members present; (2) a two-thirds vote by the yeas and nays to override a veto; (3) a two-thirds vote by one house to expel one of its members and by both houses to propose a constitutional amendment; (4) a two-thirds vote of senators present to convict someone whom the House has impeached and to consent to ratification of treaties; (5) a two-thirds vote in each house to remove political disabilities from persons who have engaged in insurrection or rebellion or given aid or comfort to the enemies of the United States; (6) a majority vote in each house to fill a vacancy in the office of vice president; (7) a majority vote of all states to elect a president in the House of Representatives when no candidate receives a majority of the electoral votes; (8) a majority vote of all senators when the Senate elects a vice president under the same circumstances; and (9) the casting vote of the vice president in case of tie votes in the Senate.

Contempt of Congress—Willful obstruction of the proper functions of Congress. Most frequently, it is a refusal to obey a subpoena to appear and testify before a committee or to produce documents demanded by it. Such obstruction is a misdemeanor and persons cited for contempt are subject to prosecution in federal courts. A house cites an individual for contempt by agreeing to a privileged resolution to that effect reported by a committee. The presiding officer then refers the matter to a U.S. attorney for prosecution.

Continuing Body—A characterization of the Senate on the theory that it continues from Congress to Congress and has existed continuously since it first convened in 1789. The rationale for the theory is that under the system of staggered six-year terms for senators, the terms of only about one-third of them expire after each Congress and, therefore, a quorum of the Senate is always in office. Consequently, under this theory, the Senate, unlike the House, does not have to adopt its rules at the beginning of each Congress because those rules continue from one Congress to the next. This makes it extremely difficult for the Senate to change its rules against the opposition of a determined minority because those rules require a two-thirds vote of the senators present and voting to invoke cloture on a proposed rules change.

Continuing Resolution (CR)—A joint resolution that provides funds to continue the operation of federal agencies and programs at the beginning of a new fiscal year if their annual appropriation bills have not yet been enacted; also called continuing appropriations. Continuing resolutions are enacted shortly before or after the new fiscal year begins and usually make funds available for a specified period. Additional resolutions are often needed after the first expires. Some continuing resolutions have provided appropriations for an entire fiscal year. Continuing resolutions for specific periods customarily fix a rate at which agencies may incur obligations based either on the previous year's appropriations, the president's budget request, or the amount as specified in the agency's regular annual appropriation bill if that bill has already been passed by one or both houses. In the House, continuing resolutions are privileged after Sept. 15.

Contract Authority—Statutory authority permitting an agency to enter into contracts or incur other obligations even though it has not received an appropriation to pay for them. Congress must eventually fund them because the government is legally liable for such payments. The Congressional Budget Act of 1974 requires that new contract authority may not be used unless provided for in advance by an appropriation act, but it permits a few exceptions.

Correcting Recorded Votes—The rules of both houses prohibit members from changing their votes after a vote result has been announced. Nevertheless, the Senate permits its members to withdraw or change their votes, by unanimous consent, immediately after the announcement. In rare instances, senators have been granted unanimous consent to change their votes several days or weeks after the announcement. Votes tallied by the electronic voting system in the House may not be changed. But when a vote actually given is not recorded during an oral call of the roll, a member may demand a correction as a matter of right. On all other alleged errors in a recorded vote, the Speaker determines whether the circumstances justify a change. Occasionally, members merely announce that they were incorrectly recorded; announcements can occur hours, days or even months after the vote and appear in the Congressional Record.

Cosponsor—A member who has joined one or more other members to sponsor a measure.

Credit Authority—Authority granted to an agency to incur direct loan obligations or to make loan guarantee commitments. The Congressional Budget Act of 1974 bans congressional consideration of credit authority legislation unless the extent of that authority is made subject to provisions in appropriation acts.

C-SPAN—Cable-Satellite Public Affairs Network, which provides live, gavel-to-gavel coverage of Senate floor proceedings on one cable television channel and coverage of House floor proceedings on another channel. C-SPAN also televises important committee hearings in both houses. Each house also transmits its televised proceedings directly to congressional offices.

Current Services Estimates—Executive branch estimates of the anticipated costs of federal programs and operations for the next and future fiscal years at existing levels of service and assuming no new initiatives or changes in existing law. The president submits these estimates to Congress with the annual budget and includes an explanation of the underlying economic and policy assumptions on which they are based, such as anticipated rates of inflation, real economic growth and unemployment, plus program caseloads and pay increases.

Custody of the Papers—Possession of an engrossed measure and certain related basic documents that the two houses produce as they try to resolve their differences over the measure.

Dance of the Swans and the Ducks—A whimsical description of the gestures some members use in connection with a request for a recorded vote, especially in the House. When members want their colleagues to stand in support of the request, they move their hands and arms in a gentle upward motion resembling the beginning flight of a graceful swan. When they want their colleagues to remain seated to avoid such a vote, they move their hands and arms in a vigorous downward motion resembling a diving duck.

Dean—Within a state's delegation in the House of Representatives, the member with the longest continuous service.

Debate—In congressional parlance, speeches delivered during consideration of a measure, motion or other matter, as distinguished from speeches in other parliamentary situations, such as one-minute and special order speeches when no business is pending. Virtually all debate in the House of Representatives is under some kind of time limitation. Most debate in the Senate is unlimited; that is, a senator, once recognized, may speak for as long as he or she chooses, unless the Senate invokes cloture.

Debt Limit—The maximum amount of outstanding federal public debt permitted by law. The limit (or ceiling) covers virtually all debt incurred by the government except agency debt. Each congressional budget resolution sets forth the new debt limit that may be required under its provisions.

Deferral—An impoundment of funds for a specific period of time that may not extend beyond the fiscal year in which it is proposed. Under the Impoundment Control Act of 1974, the president must notify Congress that he is deferring the spending or obligation of funds provided by law for a project or activity. Congress can disapprove the deferral by legislation.

Deficit—The amount by which the government's outlays exceed its budget receipts for a given fiscal year. Both the president's budget and the annual congressional budget resolution provide estimates of the deficit or surplus for the upcoming and several future fiscal years.

Degrees of Amendment—Designations that indicate the relationships of amendments to the text of a measure and to each other. In general, an amendment offered directly to the text of a measure is an amendment in the first degree, and an amendment to that amendment is an amendment in the second degree. Both houses normally prohibit amendments in the third degree — that is, an amendment to an amendment to an amendment.

Delegate—A nonvoting member of the House of Representatives elected to a two-year term from the District of Columbia, the territory of Guam, the territory of the Virgin Islands or the territory of American Samoa. By law, delegates may not vote in the full House but they may participate in debate, offer motions (except to reconsider) and serve and vote on standing and select committees. On their committees, delegates possess the same powers and privileges as other members and the Speaker may appoint them to appropriate conference committees and select committees.

Denounce—A formal action that condemns a member for misbehavior; considered by some experts to be equivalent to censure. (See Censure.)

Dilatory Tactics—Procedural actions intended to delay or prevent action by a house or a committee. They include, among others, offering numerous motions, demanding quorum calls and recorded votes at every opportunity, making numerous points of order and parliamentary inquiries and speaking as long as the applicable rules permit. The Senate rules permit a battery of dilatory tactics, especially lengthy speeches, except under cloture. In the House, possible dilatory tactics are more limited. Speeches are always subject to time limits and debate-ending motions. Moreover, a House rule instructs the Speaker not to entertain dilatory motions and lets the Speaker decide whether a motion is dilatory. However, the Speaker may not override the constitutional right of a member to demand the yeas and nays, and in practice usually waits for a point of order before exercising that authority. (See Cloture.)

Discharge a Committee—Remove a measure from a committee to which it has been referred in order to make it available for floor consideration. Noncontroversial measures are often discharged by unanimous consent. However, because congressional committees have no obligation to report measures referred to them, each house has procedures to extract controversial measures from recalcitrant committees. Six discharge procedures are available in the House of Representatives. The Senate uses a motion to discharge, which is usually converted into a discharge resolution.

District Office—Representatives maintain one or more offices in their districts for the purpose of assisting and communicating with constituents. The costs of maintaining these offices are paid from members' official allowances. Senators can use the official expense allowance to rent offices in their home state, subject to a funding formula based on their state's population and other factors.

District Work Period—The House term for a scheduled congressional recess during which members may visit their districts and conduct constituency business.

Division Vote—A vote in which the chair first counts those in favor of a proposition and then those opposed to it, with no record made of how each member votes. In the Senate, the chair may count raised hands or ask senators to stand, whereas the House requires members to stand; hence, often called a standing vote. Committees in both houses ordinarily use a show of hands. A division usually occurs after a voice vote and may be demanded by any member or ordered by the chair if there is any doubt about the outcome of the voice vote. The demand for a division can also come before a voice vote. In the Senate, the demand must come before the result of a voice vote is announced. It may be made after a voice vote announcement in the House, but only if no intervening business has transpired and only if the member was standing and seeking recognition at the time of the announcement. A demand for the yeas and nays or, in the House, for a recorded vote, takes precedence over a division vote.

Doorkeeper of the House—A former officer of the House of Representatives who was responsible for enforcing the rules prohibiting unauthorized persons from entering the chamber when the House is in session. The doorkeeper was usually the candidate of the majority party. In 1995 the office was abolished and its functions transferred to the sergeant at arms.

Effective Dates—Provisions of an act that specify when the entire act or individual provisions in it become effective as law. Most acts become effective on the date of enactment, but it is sometimes necessary or prudent to delay the effective dates of some provisions.

Electronic Voting—Since 1973 the House has used an electronic voting system to record the yeas and nays and to conduct recorded votes. Members vote by inserting their voting cards in one of the boxes at several locations in the chamber. They are given at least fifteen minutes to vote. When several votes occur immediately after each other, the Speaker may reduce the voting time to five minutes on the second and subsequent votes. The Speaker may allow additional time on each vote but may also close a vote at any time after the minimum time has expired. Members can change their votes at any time before the Speaker announces the result. The House also uses the electronic system for quorum calls. While a vote is in progress, a large panel above the Speaker's desk displays how each member has voted. Smaller panels on either side of the chamber display running totals of the votes and the time remaining. The Senate does not have electronic voting.

Enacting Clause—The opening language of each bill, beginning "Be it enacted by the Senate and House of Representatives of the United States of America in Congress assembled..." This language gives legal force to measures approved by Congress and signed by the president or enacted over the president's veto. A successful motion to strike it from a bill kills the entire measure.

Engrossed Bill—The official copy of a bill or joint resolution as passed by one chamber, including the text as amended by floor action and certified by the clerk of the House or the secretary of the Senate (as appropriate). Amendments by one house to a measure or amendments of the other also are engrossed. House engrossed documents are printed on blue paper; the Senate's are printed on white paper.

Enrolled Bill—The final official copy of a bill or joint resolution passed in identical form by both houses. An enrolled bill is printed on parchment. After it is certified by the chief officer of the house in which it originated and signed by the House Speaker and the Senate president pro tempore, the measure is sent to the White House for the president's signature.

Entitlement Program—A federal program under which individuals, businesses or units of government that meet the requirements or qualifications established by law are entitled to receive certain payments if they seek such payments. Major examples include Social Security, Medicare, Medicaid, unemployment insurance and military and federal civilian pensions. Congress cannot control their expenditures by refusing to appropriate the sums necessary to fund them because the government is legally obligated to pay eligible recipients the amounts to which the law entitles them.

Equality of the Houses—A component of the Constitution's emphasis on checks and balances under which each house is given essentially equal status in the enactment of legislation and in the relations and negotiations between the two houses. Although the House of Representatives initiates revenue and appropriation measures, the Senate has the right to amend them. Either house may initiate any other type of legislation, and neither can force the other to agree to, or even act on, its measures. Moreover, each house has a potential veto over the other because legislation requires agreement by both. Similarly, in a conference to resolve their differences on a measure, each house casts one vote, as determined by a majority of its conferees. In most other national bicameral legislatures, the powers of one house are markedly greater than those of the other.

Ethics Rules—Several rules or standing orders in each house that mandate certain standards of conduct for members and congressional employees in finance, employment, franking and other areas. The Senate Permanent Select Committee on Ethics and the House Committee on Standards of Official Conduct investigate alleged violations of conduct and recommend appropriate actions to their respective houses.

Exclusive Committee—(1) Under the rules of the Republican Conference and House Democratic Caucus, a standing committee whose members usually cannot serve on any other standing committee. As of 2000 the Appropriations, Energy and Commerce (beginning in the 105th Congress), Ways and Means and Rules Committees were designated as exclusive committees. (2) Under the rules of the two party conferences in the Senate, a standing committee whose members may not simultaneously serve on any other exclusive committee.

Executive Calendar—The Senate's calendar for committee reports on its executive business, namely treaties and nominations. The calendar numbers indicate the order in which items were referred to the calendar but have no bearing on when or if the Senate will consider them. The Senate, by motion or unanimous consent, resolves itself into executive session to consider them.

Executive Document—A document, usually a treaty, sent by the president to the Senate for approval. It is referred to a committee in the same manner as other measures. Resolutions to ratify treaties have their own "treaty document" numbers. For example, the first treaty submitted in the 106th Congress would be "Treaty Doc 106-1."

Executive Order—A unilateral proclamation by the president that has a policy-making or legislative impact. Members of Congress have challenged some executive orders on the grounds that they usurped the authority of the legislative branch. Although the Supreme Court has ruled that a particular order exceeded the president's authority, it has upheld others as falling within the president's general constitutional powers.

Executive Privilege—The assertion that presidents have the right to withhold certain information from Congress. Presidents have based their claim on (1) the constitutional separation of powers; (2) the need for secrecy in military and diplomatic affairs; (3) the need to protect individuals from unfavorable publicity; (4) the need to safeguard the confidential exchange of ideas in the executive branch; and (5) the need to protect individuals who provide confidential advice to the president.

Executive Session—(1) A Senate meeting devoted to the consideration of treaties or nominations. Normally, the Senate meets in legislative session; it resolves itself into executive session, by motion or by unanimous consent, to deal with its executive business. It also keeps a separate Journal for executive sessions. Executive sessions are usually open to the public, but the Senate may choose to close them.

Expulsion—A member's removal from office by a two-thirds vote of his or her house; the supermajority is required by the Constitution. It is the most severe and most rarely used sanction a house can invoke against a member. Although the Constitution provides no explicit grounds for expulsion, the courts have ruled that it may be applied only for misconduct during a member's term of office, not for conduct before the member's election. Generally, neither house will consider expulsion of a member convicted of a crime until the judicial processes have been exhausted. At that stage, members sometimes resign rather than face expulsion. In 1977 the House adopted a rule urging members convicted of certain crimes to voluntarily abstain from voting or participating in other legislative business.

Extensions of Remarks—An appendix to the daily Congressional Record that consists primarily of miscellaneous extraneous material submitted by members. It often includes members' statements not delivered on the floor, newspaper articles and editorials, praise for a member's constituents and noteworthy letters received by a member, among other material. Representatives supply the bulk of this material; senators submit very little. "Extensions of Remarks" pages are separately numbered, and each number is preceded by the letter "E." Materials may be placed in the Extensions of Remarks section only by unanimous consent. Usually, one member of each party makes the request each day on behalf of his or her party colleagues after the House has completed its legislative business of the day.

Federal Debt—The total amount of monies borrowed and not yet repaid by the federal government. Federal debt consists of public debt and agency debt. Public debt is the portion of the federal debt borrowed by the Treasury or the Federal Financing Bank directly from the public or from another federal fund or account. For example, the Treasury regularly borrows money from the Social Security trust fund. Public debt accounts for about 99 percent of the federal debt. Agency debt refers to the debt incurred by federal agencies such as the Export-Import Bank but excluding the Treasury and the Federal Financing Bank, which are authorized by law to borrow funds from the public or from another government fund or account.

Filibuster—The use of obstructive and time-consuming parliamentary tactics by one member or a minority of members to delay, modify or defeat proposed legislation or rules changes. Filibusters are also sometimes used to delay urgently needed measures to force the body to accept other legislation. The Senate's rules permitting unlimited debate and the extraordinary majority it requires to impose cloture make filibustering particularly effective in that chamber. Under the stricter rules of the House, filibusters in that body are short-lived and therefore ineffective and rarely attempted.

Fiscal Year—The federal government's annual accounting period. It begins Oct. 1 and ends on the following Sept. 30. A fiscal year is designated by the calendar year in which it ends and is often referred to as FY. Thus, fiscal year 1998 began Oct. 1, 1997, ended Sept. 30, 1998, and is called FY98. In theory, Congress is supposed to complete action on all budgetary measures applying to a fiscal year before that year begins. It rarely does so.

Five-Minute Rule—A House rule that limits debate on an amendment offered in Committee of the Whole to five minutes for its sponsor and five minutes for an opponent. In practice, the committee routinely permits longer debate by two devices: the offering of pro forma amendments, each debatable for five minutes, and unanimous consent for a member to speak longer than five minutes. Consequently, debate on an amendment sometimes continues for hours. At any time after the first ten minutes, however, the committee may shut off debate immediately or by a specified time, either by unanimous consent or by majority vote on a nondebatable motion. The motion, which dates from 1847, is also used in the House as in Committee of the Whole, where debate also may be shut off by a motion for the previous question.

Floor—The ground level of the House or Senate chamber where members sit and the houses conduct their business. When members are attending a meeting of their house they are said to be on the floor. Floor action refers to the procedural actions taken during floor consideration such as deciding on motions, taking up measures, amending them and voting.

Floor Manager—A majority party member responsible for guiding a measure through its floor consideration in a house and for devising the political and procedural strategies that might be required to get it passed. The presiding officer gives the floor manager priority recognition to debate, offer amendments, oppose amendments and make crucial procedural motions.

Frank—Informally, members' legal right to send official mail postage free under their signatures; often called the franking privilege. Technically, it is the autographic or facsimile signature used on envelopes instead of stamps that permits members and certain congressional officers to send their official mail free of charge. The franking privilege has been authorized by law since the first Congress, except for a few months in 1873. Congress reimburses the U.S. Postal Service for the franked mail it handles.

Function or Functional Category—A broad category of national need and spending of budgetary significance. A category provides an accounting method for allocating and keeping track of budgetary resources and expenditures for that function because it includes all budget accounts related to the function's subject or purpose such as agriculture, administration of justice, commerce and housing and energy. Functions do not necessarily correspond with appropriations acts or with the budgets of individual agencies. As of 2000 there were twenty functional categories, each divided into a number of subfunctions.

Gag Rule—A pejorative term for any type of special rule reported by the House Rules Committee that proposes to prohibit amendments to a measure or only permits amendments offered by the reporting committee.

Glossary

Galleries—The balconies overlooking each chamber from which the public, news media, staff and others may observe floor proceedings.

General Accounting Office (GAO)—A congressional support agency, often referred to as the investigative arm of Congress. It evaluates and audits federal agencies and programs in the United States and abroad on its initiative or at the request of congressional committees or members.

General Appropriation Bill—A term applied to each of the thirteen annual bills that provide funds for most federal agencies and programs and also to the supplemental appropriation bills that contain appropriations for more than one agency or program.

Germaneness—The requirement that an amendment be closely related — in terms of subject or purpose, for example — to the text it proposes to amend. A House rule requires that all amendments be germane. In the Senate, only amendments offered to general appropriation bills and budget measures or proposed under cloture must be germane. Germaneness rules can be waived by suspension of the rules in both houses, by unanimous consent agreements in the Senate and by special rules from the Rules Committee in the House. Moreover, presiding officers usually do not enforce germaneness rules on their own initiative; therefore, a nongermane amendment can be adopted if no member raises a point of order against it. Under cloture in the Senate, however, the chair may take the initiative to rule amendments out of order as not being germane, without a point of order being made. All House debate must be germane except during general debate in the Committee of the Whole, but special rules invariably require that such debate be "confined to the bill." The Senate requires germane debate only during the first three hours of each daily session. Under the precedents of both houses, an amendment can be relevant but not necessarily germane. A crucial factor in determining germaneness in the House is how the subject of a measure or matter is defined. For example, the subject of a measure authorizing construction of a naval vessel is defined as being the construction of a single vessel; therefore, an amendment to authorize an additional vessel is not germane.

Gerrymandering—The manipulation of legislative district boundaries to benefit a particular party, politician or minority group. The term originated in 1812 when the Massachusetts legislature redrew the lines of state legislative districts to favor the party of Gov. Elbridge Gerry, and some critics said one district looked like a salamander. (See also Congressional District; Redistricting.)

Gramm-Rudman-Hollings Act of 1985—Common name for the Balanced Budget and Emergency Deficit Control Act of 1985, which established new budget procedures intended to balance the federal budget by fiscal year 1991. (The timetable subsequently was extended and then deleted.) The act's chief sponsors were senators Phil Gramm (R-Texas), Warren Rudman (R-N.H.) Ernest Hollings (D-S.C.).

Grandfather Clause—A provision in a measure, law or rule that exempts an individual, entity or a defined category of individuals or entities from complying with a new policy or restriction. For example, a bill that would raise taxes on persons who reach the age of sixty-five after a certain date inherently grandfathers out those who are sixty-five before that date. Similarly, a Senate rule limiting senators to two major committee assignments also grandfathers some senators who were sitting on a third major committee before a specified date.

Grants-in-Aid—Payments by the federal government to state and local governments to help provide for assistance programs or public services.

Appendix

Hearing—Committee or subcommittee meetings to receive testimony on proposed legislation during investigations or for oversight purposes. Relatively few bills are important enough to justify formal hearings. Witnesses often include experts, government officials, spokespersons for interested groups, officials of the General Accounting Office and members of Congress.

Hold—A senator's request that his or her party leaders delay floor consideration of certain legislation or presidential nominations. The majority leader usually honors a hold for a reasonable period of time, especially if its purpose is to assure the senator that the matter will not be called up during his or her absence or to give the senator time to gather necessary information.

Hold (or Have) the Floor—A member's right to speak without interruption, unless he or she violates a rule, after recognition by the presiding officer. At the member's discretion, he or she may yield to another member for a question in the Senate or for a question or statement in the House, but may reclaim the floor at any time.

Hold-Harmless Clause—In legislation providing a new formula for allocating federal funds, a clause to ensure that recipients of those funds do not receive less in a future year than they did in the current year if the new formula would result in a reduction for them. Similar to a grandfather clause, it has been used most frequently to soften the impact of sudden reductions in federal grants. (See Grandfather Clause.)

Hopper—A box on the clerk's desk in the House chamber into which members deposit bills and resolutions to introduce them. In House jargon, to drop a bill in the hopper is to introduce it.

Hour Rule—A House rule that permits members, when recognized, to hold the floor in debate for no more than one hour each. The majority party member customarily yields one-half the time to a minority member. Although the hour rule applies to general debate in Committee of the Whole as well as in the House, special rules routinely vary the length of time for such debate and its control to fit the circumstances of particular measures.

House As In Committee of the Whole—A hybrid combination of procedures from the general rules of the House and from the rules of the Committee of the Whole, sometimes used to expedite consideration of a measure on the floor.

House Calendar—The calendar reserved for all public bills and resolutions that do not raise revenue or directly or indirectly appropriate money or property when they are favorably reported by House committees.

House Manual—A commonly used title for the handbook of the rules of the House of Representatives, published in each Congress. Its official title is Constitution, Jefferson's Manual and Rules of the House of Representatives.

House of Representatives—The house of Congress in which states are represented roughly in proportion to their populations, but every state is guaranteed at least one representative. By law, the number of voting representatives is fixed at 435. Four delegates and one resident commissioner also serve in the House; they may vote in their committees but not on the House floor. Although the House and Senate have equal legislative power, the Constitution gives the House sole authority to originate revenue measures. The House also claims the right to originate appropriation measures, a claim the Senate disputes in theory but concedes in practice. The House has the sole power to impeach, and it elects the president when no candidate has received a majority of the electoral votes. It is sometimes referred to as the lower body.

Immunity—(1) Members' constitutional protection from lawsuits and arrest in connection with their legislative duties. They may not be tried for libel or slander for anything they say on the floor of a house or in committee. Nor may they be arrested while attending sessions of their houses or when traveling to or from sessions of Congress, except when charged with treason, a felony or a breach of the peace. (2) In the case of a witness before a committee, a grant of protection from prosecution based on that person's testimony to the committee. It is used to compel witnesses to testify who would otherwise refuse to do so on the constitutional ground of possible selfincrimination. Under such a grant, none of a witness's testimony may be used against him or her in a court proceeding except in a prosecution for perjury or for giving a false statement to Congress. (See also Contempt of Congress.)

Impeachment—The first step to remove the president, vice president or other federal civil officers from office and to disqualify them from any future federal office "of honor, Trust or Profit." An impeachment is a formal charge of treason, bribery or "other high Crimes and Misdemeanors." The House has the sole power of impeachment and the Senate the sole power of trying the charges and convicting. The House impeaches by a simple majority vote; conviction requires a two-thirds vote of all senators present.

Impeachment Trial, Removal and Disqualification—The Senate conducts an impeachment trial under a separate set of twenty-six rules that appears in the Senate Manual. Under the Constitution, the chief justice of the United States presides over trials of the president, but the vice president, the president pro tempore or any other senator may preside over the impeachment trial of another official.

The Constitution requires senators to take an oath for an impeachment trial. During the trial, senators may not engage in colloquies or participate in arguments, but they may submit questions in writing to House managers or defense counsel. After the trial concludes, the Senate votes separately on each article of impeachment without debate unless the Senate orders the doors closed for private discussions. During deliberations senators may speak no more than once on a question, not for more than ten minutes on an interlocutory question and not more than fifteen minutes on the final question. These rules may be set aside by unanimous consent or suspended on motion by a two-thirds vote.

The Senate's impeachment trial of President Clinton in 1999 was only the second such trial involving a president. It continued for five weeks, with the Senate voting not to convict on the two impeachment articles.

Senate impeachment rules allow the Senate, at its own discretion, to name a committee to hear evidence and conduct the trial, with all senators thereafter voting on the charges. The impeachment trials of three federal judges were conducted this way, and the Supreme Court upheld the validity of these rules in Nixon v. United States, 506 U.S. 224, 1993.

An official convicted on impeachment charges is removed from office immediately. However, the convicted official is not barred from holding a federal office in the future unless the Senate, after its conviction vote, also approves a resolution disqualifying the convicted official from future office. For example, federal judge Alcee L. Hastings was impeached and convicted in 1989, but the Senate did not vote to bar him from office in the future. In 1992 Hastings was elected to the House of Representatives, and no challenge was raised against seating him when he took the oath of office in 1993.

Impoundment—An executive branch action or inaction that delays or withholds the expenditure or obligation of budget authority provided by law. The Impoundment Control Act of 1974 classifies impoundments as either deferrals or rescissions, requires the president to notify Congress about all such actions and gives Congress authority to approve or reject them.

Inspector General (IG) In the House of Representatives—A position established with the passage of the House Administrative Reform Resolution of 1992. The duties of the office have been revised several times and are now contained in House Rule II. The inspector general (IG), who is subject to the policy direction and oversight of the Committee on House Administration, is appointed for a Congress jointly by the Speaker and the majority and minority leaders of the House. The IG communicates the results of audits to the House officers or officials who were the subjects of the audits and suggests appropriate corrective measures. The IG submits a report of each audit to the Speaker, the majority and minority leaders and the chairman and ranking minority member of the House Administration Committee; notifies these five members in the case of any financial irregularity discovered; and reports to the Committee on Standards of Official Conduct on possible violations of House rules or any applicable law by any House member, officer or employee. The IG's office also has certain duties to audit various financial operations of the House that had previously been performed by the General Accounting Office.

Instruct Conferees—A formal action by a house urging its conferees to uphold a particular position on a measure in conference. The instruction may be to insist on certain provisions in the measure as passed by that house or to accept a provision in the version passed by the other house. Instructions to conferees are not binding because the primary responsibility of conferees is to reach agreement on a measure and neither House can compel the other to accept particular provisions or positions.

Investigative Power—The authority of Congress and its committees to pursue investigations, upheld by the Supreme Court but limited to matters related to, and in furtherance of, a legitimate task of the Congress. Standing committees in both houses are permanently authorized to investigate matters within their jurisdictions. Major investigations are sometimes conducted by temporary select, special or joint committees established by resolutions for that purpose.

Some rules of the House provide certain safeguards for witnesses and others during investigative hearings. These permit counsel to accompany witnesses, require that each witness receive a copy of the committee's rules and order the committee to go into closed session if it believes the testimony to be heard might defame, degrade or incriminate any person. The committee may subsequently decide to hear such testimony in open session. The Senate has no rules of this kind.

Item Veto—Item veto authority, which is available to most state governors, allows governors to eliminate or reduce items in legislative measures presented for their signature without vetoing the entire measure and sign the rest into law. A similar authority was briefly granted to the U.S. president under the Line Item Veto Act of 1996. According to the majority opinion of the Supreme Court in its 1998 decision overturning that law, a constitutional amendment would be necessary to give the president such item veto authority.

Jefferson's Manual—Short title of Jefferson's Manual of Parliamentary Practice, prepared by Thomas Jefferson for his guidance when he was president of the Senate from 1797 to 1801. Although it reflects English parliamentary practice in his day, many procedures in both houses of Congress are still rooted in its basic precepts. Under a House rule adopted in 1837, the manual's provisions govern House procedures when applicable and when they are not inconsistent with its standing rules and orders. The Senate, however, has never officially acknowledged it as a direct authority for its legislative procedure.

Johnson Rule—A policy instituted in 1953 under which all Democratic senators are assigned to one major committee before any Democrat is assigned to two. The Johnson Rule is named after its author, Sen. Lyndon B. Johnson, D-Texas, then the Senate's Democratic leader. Senate Republicans adopted a similar policy soon thereafter.

Joint Committee—A committee composed of members selected from each house. The functions of most joint committees involve investigation, research or oversight of agencies closely related to Congress. Permanent joint committees, created by statute, are sometimes called standing joint committees. Once quite numerous, only four joint committees remained as of 2002: Joint Economic, Joint Taxation, Joint Library and Joint Printing. None has authority to report legislation.

Joint Resolution—A legislative measure that Congress uses for purposes other than general legislation. Similar to a bill, it has the force of law when passed by both houses and either approved by the president or passed over the president's veto. Unlike a bill, a joint resolution enacted into law is not called an act; it retains its original title. Most often, joint resolutions deal with such relatively limited matters as the correction of errors in existing law, continuing appropriations, a single appropriation or the establishment of permanent joint committees. Unlike bills, however, joint resolutions also are used to propose constitutional amendments; these do not require the president's signature and become effective only when ratified by three-fourths of the states. The House designates joint resolutions as H.J. Res., the Senate as S.J. Res. Each house numbers its joint resolutions consecutively in the order of introduction during a two-year Congress.

Joint Session—Informally, any combined meeting of the Senate and the House. Technically, a joint session is a combined meeting to count the electoral votes for president and vice president or to hear a presidential address, such as the State of the Union message; any other formal combined gathering of both houses is a joint meeting. Joint sessions are authorized by concurrent resolutions and are held in the House chamber, because of its larger seating capacity. Although the president of the Senate and the Speaker sit side by side at the Speaker's desk during combined meetings, the former presides over the electoral count and the latter presides on all other occasions and introduces the president or other guest speaker. The president and other guests may address a joint session or meeting only by invitation.

Joint Sponsorship—Two or more members sponsoring the same measure.

Journal—The official record of House or Senate actions, including every motion offered, every vote cast, amendments agreed to, quorum calls and so forth. Unlike the Congressional Record, it does not provide reports of speeches, debates, statements and the like. The Constitution requires each house to maintain a Journal and to publish it periodically.

Junket—A member's trip at government expense, especially abroad, ostensibly on official business but, it is often alleged, for pleasure.

Killer Amendment—An amendment that, if agreed to, might lead to the defeat of the measure it amends, either in the house in which the amendment is offered or at some later stage of the legislative process. Members sometimes deliberately offer or vote for such an amendment in the expectation that it will

Appendix

undermine support for the measure in Congress or increase the likelihood that the president will veto it.

King of the Mountain (or Hill) Rule—(See Queen of the Hill Rule.)

LA—(See Legislative Assistant.)

Lame Duck—Jargon for a member who has not been reelected, or did not seek reelection, and is serving the balance of his or her term.

Lame Duck Session—A session of a Congress held after the election for the succeeding Congress, so-called after the lame duck members still serving.

Last Train Out—Colloquial name for last must-pass bill of a session of Congress.

Law—An act of Congress that has been signed by the president, passed over the president's veto or allowed to become law without the president's signature.

Lay on the Table—A motion to dispose of a pending proposition immediately, finally and adversely; that is, to kill it without a direct vote on its substance. Often simply called a motion to table, it is not debatable and is adopted by majority vote or without objection. It is a highly privileged motion, taking precedence over all others except the motion to adjourn in the House and all but three additional motions in the Senate. It can kill a bill or resolution, an amendment, another motion, an appeal or virtually any other matter.

Tabling an amendment also tables the measure to which the amendment is pending in the House, but not in the Senate. The House does not allow the motion against the motion to recommit, in Committee of the Whole, and in some other situations. In the Senate it is the only permissible motion that immediately ends debate on a proposition, but only to kill it.

(The) Leadership—Usually, a reference to the majority and minority leaders of the Senate or to the Speaker and minority leader of the House. The term sometimes includes the majority leader in the House and the majority and minority whips in each house and, at other times, other party officials as well.

Legislation—(1) A synonym for legislative measures: bills and joint resolutions. (2) Provisions in such measures or in substantive amendments offered to them. (3) In some contexts, provisions that change existing substantive or authorizing law, rather than provisions that make appropriations.

Legislation on an Appropriation Bill—A common reference to provisions changing existing law that appear in, or are offered as amendments to, a general appropriation bill. A House rule prohibits the inclusion of such provisions in general appropriation bills unless they retrench expenditures. An analogous Senate rule permits points of order against amendments to a general appropriation bill that propose general legislation.

Legislative Assistant (LA)—A member's staff person responsible for monitoring and preparing legislation on particular subjects and for advising the member on them; commonly referred to as an LA.

Legislative Day—The day that begins when a house meets after an adjournment and ends when it next adjourns. Because the House of Representatives normally adjourns at the end of a daily session, its legislative and calendar days usually coincide. The Senate, however, frequently recesses at the end of a daily session, and its legislative day may extend over several calendar days, weeks or months. Among other uses, this technicality permits the Senate to save time by circumventing its morning hour, a procedure required at the beginning of every legislative day.

Legislative History—(1) A chronological list of actions taken on a measure during its progress through the legislative process. (2) The official documents relating to a measure, the entries in the Journals of the two houses on that measure and the Congressional Record text of its consideration in both houses. The documents include all committee reports and the conference report and joint explanatory statement, if any. Courts and affected federal agencies study a measure's legislative history for congressional intent about its purpose and interpretation.

Legislative Process—(1) Narrowly, the stages in the enactment of a law from introduction to final disposition. An introduced measure that becomes law typically travels through reference to committee; committee and subcommittee consideration; report to the chamber; floor consideration; amendment; passage; engrossment; messaging to the other house; similar steps in that house, including floor amendment of the measure; return of the measure to the first house; consideration of amendments between the houses or a conference to resolve their differences; approval of the conference report by both houses; enrollment; approval by the president or override of the president's veto; and deposit with the Archivist of the United States. (2) Broadly, the political, lobbying and other factors that affect or influence the process of enacting laws.

Legislative Veto—A procedure, declared unconstitutional in 1983, that allowed Congress or one of its houses to nullify certain actions of the president, executive branch agencies or independent agencies. Sometimes called congressional vetoes or congressional disapprovals. Following the Supreme Court's 1983 decision, Congress amended several legislative veto statutes to require enactment of joint resolutions, which are subject to presidential veto, for nullifying executive branch actions.

Limitation on a General Appropriation Bill—Language that prohibits expenditures for part of an authorized purpose from funds provided in a general appropriation bill. Precedents require that the language be phrased in the negative: that none of the funds provided in a pending appropriation bill shall be used for a specified authorized activity. Limitations in general appropriation bills are permitted on the grounds that Congress can refuse to fund authorized programs and, therefore, can refuse to fund any part of them as long as the prohibition does not change existing law. House precedents have established that a limitation does not change existing law if it does not impose additional duties or burdens on executive branch officials, interfere with their discretionary authority or require them to make judgments or determinations not required by existing law. The proliferation of limitation amendments in the 1970s and early 1980s prompted the House to adopt a rule in 1983 making it more difficult for members to offer them. The rule bans such amendments during the reading of an appropriation bill for amendments, unless they are specifically authorized in existing law. Other limitations may be offered after the reading, but the Committee of the Whole can foreclose them by adopting a motion to rise and report the bill back to the House. In 1995 the rule was amended to allow the motion to rise and report to be made only by the majority leader or his or her designee. The House Appropriations Committee, however, can include limitation provisions in the bills it reports.

Line Item—An amount in an appropriation measure. It can refer to a single appropriation account or to separate amounts within the account. In the congressional budget process, the term usually refers to assumptions about the funding of particular programs or accounts that underlie the broad functional amounts in a budget resolution. These assumptions are

Glossary

discussed in the reports accompanying each resolution and are not binding.

Line-Item Veto—(See Item Veto.)

Line Item Veto Act of 1996—A law, in effect only from January 1997 until June 1998, that granted the president authority intended to be functionally equivalent to an item veto, by amending the Impoundment Control Act of 1974 to incorporate an approach known as enhanced rescission. Key provisions established a new procedure that permitted the president to cancel amounts of new discretionary appropriations (budget authority), new items of direct spending (entitlements) or certain limited tax benefits. It also required the president to notify Congress of the cancellation in a special message within five calendar days after signing the measure. The cancellation would become permanent unless legislation disapproving it was enacted within thirty days. On June 25, 1998, in Clinton v. City of New York the Supreme Court held the Line Item Veto Act unconstitutional, on the grounds that its cancellation provisions violated the presentment clause in Article I, clause 7, of the Constitution.

Live Pair—A voluntary and informal agreement between two members on opposite sides of an issue, one of whom is absent for a recorded vote, under which the member who is present withholds or withdraws his or her vote to offset the failure to vote by the member who is absent. Usually the member in attendance announces that he or she has a live pair, states how each would have voted and votes "present." In the House, under a rules change enacted in the 106th Congress, a live pair is only permitted on the rare occasions when electronic voting is not used.

Live Quorum—In the Senate, a quorum call to which senators are expected to respond. Senators usually suggest the absence of a quorum, not to force a quorum to appear, but to provide a pause in the proceedings during which senators can engage in private discussions or wait for a senator to come to the floor. A senator desiring a live quorum usually announces his or her intention, giving fair warning that there will be an objection to any unanimous consent request that the quorum call be dispensed with before it is completed.

Loan Guarantee—A statutory commitment by the federal government to pay part or all of a loan's principal and interest to a lender or the holder of a security in case the borrower defaults.

Lobby—To try to persuade members of Congress to propose, pass, modify or defeat proposed legislation or to change or repeal existing laws. Lobbyists attempt to promote their preferences or those of a group, organization or industry. Originally the term referred to persons frequenting the lobbies or corridors of legislative chambers in order to speak to lawmakers. In a general sense, lobbying includes not only direct contact with members but also indirect attempts to influence them, such as writing to them or persuading others to write or visit them, attempting to mold public opinion toward a desired legislative goal by various means and contributing or arranging for contributions to members' election campaigns. The right to lobby stems from the First Amendment to the Constitution, which bans laws that abridge the right of the people to petition the government for a redress of grievances.

Lobbying Disclosure Act of 1995—The principal statute requiring disclosure of — and also, to a degree, circumscribing — the activities of lobbyists. In general, it requires lobbyists who spend more than 20 percent of their time on lobbying activities to register and make semiannual reports of their activities to the clerk of the House and the secretary of the Senate, although the law provides for a number of exemptions. Among the statute's prohibitions, lobbyists are not allowed to make contributions to the legal defense fund of a member or high government official or to reimburse for official travel. Civil penalties for failure to comply may include fines of up to $50,000. The act does not include grassroots lobbying in its definition of lobbying activities.

The act amends several other lobby laws, notably the Foreign Agents Registration Act (FARA), so that lobbyists can submit a single filing. Since the measure was enacted, the number of lobby registrations has risen from about 12,000 to more than 20,000. In 1998 expenditures on federal lobbying, as disclosed under the Lobbying Disclosure Act, totaled $1.42 billion. The 1995 act supersedes the 1946 Federal Regulation of Lobbying Act, which was repealed in Section 11 of the 1995 Act.

Logrolling—Jargon for a legislative tactic or bargaining strategy in which members try to build support for their legislation by promising to support legislation desired by other members or by accepting amendments they hope will induce their colleagues to vote for their bill.

Lower Body—A way to refer to the House of Representatives, which is considered pejorative by House members.

Mace—The symbol of the office of the House sergeant at arms. Under the direction of the Speaker, the sergeant at arms is responsible for preserving order on the House floor by holding up the mace in front of an unruly member, or by carrying the mace up and down the aisles to quell boisterous behavior. When the House is in session, the mace sits on a pedestal at the Speaker's right; when the House is in Committee of the Whole, it is moved to a lower pedestal. The mace is forty-six inches high and consists of thirteen ebony rods bound in silver and topped by a silver globe with a silver eagle, wings outstretched, perched on it.

Majority Leader—The majority party's chief floor spokesperson, elected by that party's caucus — sometimes called floor leader. In the Senate, the majority leader also develops the party's political and procedural strategy, usually in collaboration with other party officials and committee chairmen. The majority leader negotiates the Senate's agenda and committee ratios with the minority leader and usually calls up measures for floor action. The chamber traditionally concedes to the majority leader the right to determine the days on which it will meet and the hours at which it will convene and adjourn. In the House, the majority leader is the Speaker's deputy and heir apparent and helps plan the floor agenda and the party's legislative strategy and often speaks for the party leadership in debate.

Managers—(1) The official title of members appointed to a conference committee, commonly called conferees. The ranking majority and minority managers for each house also manage floor consideration of the committee's conference report. (2) The members who manage the initial floor consideration of a measure. (3) The official title of House members appointed to present impeachment articles to the Senate and to act as prosecutors on behalf of the House during the Senate trial of the impeached person.

Mandatory Appropriations—Amounts that Congress must appropriate annually because it has no discretion over them unless it first amends existing substantive law. Certain entitlement programs, for example, require annual appropriations.

Markup—A meeting or series of meetings by a committee or subcommittee during which members mark up a measure by offering, debating and voting on amendments to it.

Appendix

Means-Tested Programs—Programs that provide benefits or services to low-income individuals who meet a test of need. Most are entitlement programs, such as Medicaid, food stamps and Supplementary Security Income. A few—for example, subsidized housing and various social services—are funded through discretionary appropriations.

Members' Allowances—Official expenses that are paid for or for which members are reimbursed by their houses. Among these are the costs of office space in congressional buildings and in their home states or districts; office equipment and supplies; postage-free mailings (the franking privilege); a set number of trips to and from home states or districts, as well as travel elsewhere on official business; telephone and other telecommunications services; and staff salaries.

Member's Staff—The personal staff to which a member is entitled. The House sets a maximum number of staff and a monetary allowance for each member. The Senate does not set a maximum staff level, but it does set a monetary allowance for each member. In each house, the staff allowance is included with office expenses allowances and official mail allowances in a consolidated allowance. Representatives and senators can spend as much money in their consolidated allowances for staff, office expenses or official mail, as long as they do not exceed the monetary value of the three allowances combined. This provides members with flexibility in operating their offices.

Method of Equal Proportions—The mathematical formula used since 1950 to determine how the 435 seats in the House of Representatives should be distributed among the fifty states in the apportionment following each decennial census. It minimizes as much as possible the proportional difference between the average district population in any two states. Because the Constitution guarantees each state at least one representative, fifty seats are automatically apportioned. The formula calculates priority numbers for each state, assigns the first of the 385 remaining seats to the state with the highest priority number, the second to the state with the next highest number and so on until all seats are distributed. (See Apportionment.)

Midterm Election—The general election for members of Congress that occurs in November of the second year in a presidential term.

Minority Leader—The minority party's leader and chief floor spokesman, elected by the party caucus; sometimes called minority floor leader. With the assistance of other party officials and the ranking minority members of committees, the minority leader devises the party's political and procedural strategy.

Minority Staff—Employees who assist the minority party members of a committee. Most committees hire separate majority and minority party staffs but they also may hire nonpartisan staff. Senate rules state that a committee's staff must reflect the relative number of its majority and minority party committee members, and the rules guarantee the minority at least one-third of the funds available for hiring partisan staff. In the House, each committee is authorized thirty professional staff, and the minority members of most committees may select up to ten of these staff (subject to full committee approval). Under House rules, the minority party is to be "treated fairly" in the apportionment of additional staff resources. Each House committee determines the portion of its additional staff it allocates to the minority; some committees allocate one-third; and others allot less.

Modified Rule—A special rule from the House Rules Committee that permits only certain amendments to be offered to a measure during its floor consideration or that bans certain specified amendments or amendments on certain subjects.

Morning Business—In the Senate, routine business that is to be transacted at the beginning of the morning hour. The business consists, first, of laying before the Senate, and referring to committees, matters such as messages from the president and the House, federal agency reports and unreferred petitions, memorials, bills and joint resolutions. Next, senators may present additional petitions and memorials. Then committees may present their reports, after which senators may introduce bills and resolutions. Finally, resolutions coming over from a previous day are taken up for consideration. In practice, the Senate adopts standing orders that permit senators to introduce measures and file reports at any time, but only if there has been a morning business period on that day. Because the Senate often remains in the same legislative day for several days, weeks or months at a time, it orders a morning business period almost every calendar day for the convenience of senators who wish to introduce measures or make reports.

Morning Hour—A two-hour period at the beginning of a new legislative day during which the Senate is supposed to conduct routine business, call the calendar on Mondays and deal with other matters described in a Senate rule. In practice, the morning hour very rarely, if ever, occurs, in part because the Senate frequently recesses, rather than adjourns, at the end of a daily session. Therefore the rule does not apply when the senate next meets. The Senate's rules reserve the first hour of the morning for morning business. After the completion of morning business, or at the end of the first hour, the rules permit a motion to proceed to the consideration of a measure on the calendar out of its regular order (except on Mondays). Because that normally debatable motion is not debatable if offered during the morning hour, the majority leader may, but rarely does, use this procedure in anticipating a filibuster on the motion to proceed. If the Senate agrees to the motion, it can consider the measure until the end of the morning hour, and if there is no unfinished business from the previous day it can continue considering it after the morning hour. But if there is unfinished business, a motion to continue consideration is necessary, and that motion is debatable.

Motion—A formal proposal for a procedural action, such as to consider, to amend, to lay on the table, to reconsider, to recess or to adjourn. It has been estimated that at least eighty-five motions are possible under various circumstances in the House of Representatives, somewhat fewer in the Senate. Not all motions are created equal; some are privileged or preferential and enjoy priority over others. Some motions are debatable, amendable or divisible, while others are not.

Multiple and Sequential Referrals—The practice of referring a measure to two or more committees for concurrent consideration (multiple referral) or successively to several committees in sequence (sequential referral). A measure may also be divided into several parts, with each referred to a different committee or to several committees sequentially (split referral). In theory this gives all committees that have jurisdiction over parts of a measure the opportunity to consider and report on them.

Before 1975, House precedents banned such referrals. A 1975 rule required the Speaker to make concurrent and sequential referrals "to the maximum extent feasible." On sequential referrals, the Speaker could set deadlines for reporting the measure. The Speaker ruled that this provision authorized him to discharge a committee from further consideration of a measure and place it on the appropriate calendar of the House if the committee fails to meet the Speaker's deadline. The Speaker also used combinations of concurrent and sequential referrals. In 1995 joint referrals were prohibited. Now each measure is referred to a primary committee and also may be referred, either concurrently or sequentially, to one or more other committees, but usually only for consideration of portions of the measure that fall within the jurisdiction of each of those other committees.

In the Senate, before 1977 concurrent and sequential referrals were permitted only by unanimous consent. In that year, a rule authorized a privileged motion for such a referral if offered jointly by the majority and minority leaders. Debate on the motion and all amendments to it is limited to two hours. The motion may set deadlines for reporting and provide for discharging the committees involved if they fail to meet the deadlines. To date, this procedure has never been invoked; multiple referrals in the Senate continue to be made by unanimous consent.

Multiyear Appropriation—An appropriation that remains available for spending or obligation for more than one fiscal year; the exact period of time is specified in the act making the appropriation.

Multiyear Authorization—(1) Legislation that authorizes the existence or continuation of an agency, program or activity for more than one fiscal year. (2) Legislation that authorizes appropriations for an agency, program or activity for more than one fiscal year.

Nomination—A proposed presidential appointment to a federal office submitted to the Senate for confirmation. Approval is by majority vote. The Constitution explicitly requires confirmation for ambassadors, consuls, "public Ministers" (department heads) and Supreme Court justices. By law, other federal judges, all military promotions of officers and many high-level civilian officials must be confirmed.

Oath of Office—Upon taking office, members of Congress must swear or affirm that they will "support and defend the Constitution...against all enemies, foreign and domestic," that they will "bear true faith and allegiance" to the Constitution, that they take the obligation "freely, without any mental reservation or purpose of evasion," and that they will "well and faithfully discharge the duties" of their office. The oath is required by the Constitution, and the wording is prescribed by a statute. All House members must take the oath at the beginning of each new Congress. Usually, the member with the longest continuous service in the House swears in the Speaker, who then swears in the other members. The president of the Senate or a surrogate administers the oath to newly elected or reelected senators.

Obligation—A binding agreement by a government agency to pay for goods, products, services, studies and the like, either immediately or in the future. When an agency enters into such an agreement, it incurs an obligation. As the agency makes the required payments, it liquidates the obligation. Appropriation laws usually make funds available for obligation for one or more fiscal years but do not require agencies to spend their funds during those specific years. The actual outlays can occur years after the appropriation is obligated, as with a contract for construction of a submarine that may provide for payment to be made when it is delivered in the future. Such obligated funds are often said to be "in the pipeline." Under these circumstances, an agency's outlays in a particular year can come from appropriations obligated in previous years as well as from its current-year appropriation. Consequently, the money Congress appropriates for a fiscal year does not equal the total amount of appropriated money the government will actually spend in that year.

Off-Budget Entities—Specific federal entities whose budget authority, outlays and receipts are excluded by law from the calculation of budget totals, although they are part of government spending and income. As of early 2001, these included the Social Security trust funds (Federal Old-Age and Survivors Insurance Fund and the Federal Disability Insurance Trust Fund) and the Postal Service. Government-sponsored enterprises are also excluded from the budget because they are considered private rather than public organizations.

Office of Management and Budget (OMB)—A unit in the Executive Office of the President, reconstituted in 1970 from the former Bureau of the Budget. The Office of Management and Budget (OMB) assists the president in preparing the budget and in formulating the government's fiscal program. The OMB also plays a central role in supervising and controlling implementation of the budget, pursuant to provisions in appropriations laws, the Budget Enforcement Act and other statutes. In addition to these budgetary functions, the OMB has various management duties, including those performed through its three statutory offices: Federal Financial Management, Federal Procurement Policy and Information and Regulatory Affairs.

Officers of Congress—The Constitution refers to the Speaker of the House and the president of the Senate as officers and declares that each house "shall chuse" its "other Officers," but it does not name them or indicate how they should be selected. A House rule refers to its clerk, sergeant at arms and chaplain as officers. Officers are not named in the Senate's rules, but Riddick's Senate Procedure lists the president pro tempore, secretary of the Senate, sergeant at arms, chaplain and the secretaries for the majority and minority parties as officers. A few appointed officials are sometimes referred to as officers, including the parliamentarians and the legislative counsels. The House elects its officers by resolution at the beginning of each Congress. The Senate also elects its officers, but once elected Senate officers serve from Congress to Congress until their successors are chosen.

Omnibus Bill—A measure that combines the provisions of several disparate subjects into a single and often lengthy bill.

One-Minute Speeches—Addresses by House members that can be on any subject but are limited to one minute. They are usually permitted at the beginning of a daily session after the chaplain's prayer, the pledge of allegiance and approval of the Journal. They are a customary practice, not a right granted by rule. Consequently, recognition for one-minute speeches requires unanimous consent and is entirely within the Speaker's discretion. The Speaker sometimes refuses to permit them when the House has a heavy legislative schedule or limits or postpones them until a later time of the day.

Open Rule—A special rule from the House Rules Committee that permits members to offer as many floor amendments as they wish as long as the amendments are germane and do not violate other House rules.

Order of Business (House)—The sequence of events prescribed by a House rule during the meeting of the House on a new legislative day that is supposed to take place, also called the general order of business. The sequence consists of (1) the chaplain's prayer; (2) reading and approval of the Journal; (3) the pledge of allegiance; (4) correction of the reference of public bills to committee; (5) disposal of business on the Speaker's table; (6) unfinished business; (7) the morning hour call of committees and consideration of their bills; (8) motions to go into Committee of the Whole; and (9) orders of the day. In practice, the House never fully complies with this rule. Instead, the items of business that follow the pledge of allegiance are supplanted by any special orders of business that are in order on that day (for example, conference reports; the corrections, discharge or private calendars; or motions to suspend the rules) and by other privileged business (for example,

Appendix

general appropriation bills and special rules) or measures made in order by special rules or unanimous consent. The regular order of business is also modified by unanimous consent practices and orders that govern recognition for one-minute speeches (which date from 1937) and for morning-hour debates, begun in 1994. By this combination of an order of business with privileged interruptions, the House gives precedence to certain categories of important legislation, brings to the floor other major legislation from its calendars in any order it chooses and provides expeditious processing for minor and noncontroversial measures.

Order of Business (Senate)—The sequence of events at the beginning of a new legislative day, as prescribed by Senate rules and standing orders. The sequence consists of (1) the chaplain's prayer; (2) the pledge of allegiance; (3) the designation of a temporary presiding officer if any; (4) Journal reading and approval; (5) recognition of the majority and minority leaders or their designees under the standing order; (6) morning business in the morning hour; (7) call of the calendar during the morning hour (largely obsolete); and (8) unfinished business from the previous session day.

Organization of Congress—The actions each house takes at the beginning of a Congress that are necessary to its operations. These include swearing in newly elected members, notifying the president that a quorum of each house is present, making committee assignments and fixing the hour for daily meetings. Because the House of Representatives is not a continuing body, it must also elect its Speaker and other officers and adopt its rules.

Original Bill—(1) A measure drafted by a committee and introduced by its chairman or another designated member when the committee reports the measure to its house. Unlike a clean bill, it is not referred back to the committee after introduction. The Senate permits all its legislative committees to report original bills. In the House, this authority is referred to in the rules as the "right to report at any time," and five committees (Appropriations, Budget, House Administration, Rules and Standards of Official Conduct) have such authority under circumstances specified in House Rule XIII, clause 5.

(2) In the House, special rules reported by the Rules Committee often propose that an amendment in the nature of a substitute be considered as an original bill for purposes of amendment, meaning that the substitute, as with a bill, may be amended in two degrees. Without that requirement, the substitute may only be amended in one further degree. In the Senate, an amendment in the nature of a substitute automatically is open to two degrees of amendment, as is the original text of the bill, if the substitute is offered when no other amendment is pending.

Original Jurisdiction—The authority of certain committees to originate a measure and report it to the chamber. For example, general appropriation bills reported by the House Appropriations Committee are original bills, and special rules reported by the House Rules Committee are original resolutions.

Other Body—A commonly used reference to a house by a member of the other house. Congressional comity discourages members from directly naming the other house during debate.

Outlays—Amounts of government spending. They consist of payments, usually by check or in cash, to liquidate obligations incurred in prior fiscal years as well as in the current year, including the net lending of funds under budget authority. In federal budget accounting, net outlays are calculated by subtracting the amounts of refunds and various kinds of reimbursements to the government from actual spending.

Override a Veto—Congressional enactment of a measure over the president's veto. A veto override requires a recorded two-thirds vote of those voting in each house, a quorum being present. Because the president must return the vetoed measure to its house of origin, that house votes first, but neither house is required to attempt an override, whether immediately or at all. If an override attempt fails in the house of origin, the veto stands and the measure dies.

Oversight—Congressional review of the way in which federal agencies implement laws to ensure that they are carrying out the intent of Congress and to inquire into the efficiency of the implementation and the effectiveness of the law. The Legislative Reorganization Act of 1946 defined oversight as the function of exercising continuous watchfulness over the execution of the laws by the executive branch.

Oxford-Style Debate—The House held three Oxford-style debates in 1994, modeled after the famous debating format favored by the Oxford Union in Great Britain. Neither chamber has held Oxford-style debates since then. The Oxford-style debates aired nationally over C-SPAN television and National Public Radio. The organized event featured eight participants divided evenly into two teams, one team representing the Democrats (then holding the majority in the chamber) and the other the Republicans. Both teams argued a single question chosen well ahead of the event. A moderator regulated the debate, and began it by stating the resolution at issue. The order of the speakers alternated by team, with a debater for the affirmative speaking first and a debater for the opposing team offering a rebuttal. The rest of the speakers alternated in kind until all gained the chance to speak.

Parliamentarian—The official advisor to the presiding officer in each house on questions of procedure. The parliamentarian and his or her assistants also answer procedural questions from members and congressional staff, refer measures to committees on behalf of the presiding officer and maintain compilations of the precedents. The House parliamentarian revises the House Manual at the beginning of every Congress and usually reviews special rules before the Rules Committee reports them to the House. Either a parliamentarian or an assistant is always present and near the podium during sessions of each house.

Party Caucus—Generic term for each party's official organization in each house. Only House Democrats officially call their organization a caucus. House and Senate Republicans and Senate Democrats call their organizations conferences. The party caucuses elect their leaders, approve committee assignments and chairmanships (or ranking minority members, if the party is in the minority), establish party committees and study groups and discuss party and legislative policies. On rare occasions, they have stripped members of committee seniority or expelled them from the caucus for party disloyalty.

Pay-as-You-Go (PAYGO)—A provision first instituted under the Budget Enforcement Act of 1990 that applies to legislation enacted before Oct. 1, 2002. It requires that the cumulative effect of legislation concerning either revenues or direct spending should not result in a net negative impact on the budget. If legislation does provide for an increase in spending or decrease in revenues, that effect is supposed to be offset by legislated spending reductions or revenue increases. If Congress fails to enact the appropriate offsets, the act requires presidential sequestration of sufficient offsetting amounts in specific direct spending accounts. Congress and the president can circumvent this requirement if both agree that an emergency requires a particular action or if a law is enacted declaring that deteriorated economic circumstances make it necessary to suspend the requirement.

Glossary

Permanent Appropriation—An appropriation that remains continuously available, without current action or renewal by Congress, under the terms of a previously enacted authorization or appropriation law. One such appropriation provides for payment of interest on the public debt and another the salaries of members of Congress.

Permanent Authorization—An authorization without a time limit. It usually does not specify any limit on the funds that may be appropriated for the agency, program or activity that it authorizes, leaving such amounts to the discretion of the appropriations committees and the two houses.

Permanent Staff—Term used formerly for committee staff authorized by law, who were funded through a permanent authorization and also called statutory staff. Most committees were authorized thirty permanent staff members. Most committees also were permitted additional staff, often called investigative staff, who were authorized by annual or biennial funding resolutions. The Senate eliminated the primary distinction between statutory and investigative staff in 1981. The House eliminated the distinction in 1995 by requiring that funding resolutions authorize money to hire both types of staff.

Personally Obnoxious (or Objectionable)—A characterization a senator sometimes applies to a president's nominee for a federal office in that senator's state to justify his or her opposition to the nomination.

Pocket Veto—The indirect veto of a bill as a result of the president withholding approval of it until after Congress has adjourned sine die. A bill the president does not sign but does not formally veto while Congress is in session automatically becomes a law ten days (excluding Sundays) after it is received. But if Congress adjourns its annual session during that ten-day period the measure dies even if the president does not formally veto it.

Point of Order—A parliamentary term used in committee and on the floor to object to an alleged violation of a rule and to demand that the chair enforce the rule. The point of order immediately halts the proceedings until the chair decides whether the contention is valid.

Pork or Pork Barrel Legislation—Pejorative terms for federal appropriations, bills or policies that provide funds to benefit a legislator's district or state, with the implication that the legislator presses for enactment of such benefits to ingratiate himself or herself with constituents rather than on the basis of an impartial, objective assessment of need or merit. The terms are often applied to such benefits as new parks, post offices, dams, canals, bridges, roads, water projects, sewage treatment plants and public works of any kind, as well as demonstration projects, research grants and relocation of government facilities. Funds released by the president for various kinds of benefits or government contracts approved by him allegedly for political purposes are also sometimes referred to as pork.

Postcloture Filibuster—A filibuster conducted after the Senate invokes cloture. It employs an array of procedural tactics rather than lengthy speeches to delay final action. The Senate curtailed the postcloture filibuster's effectiveness by closing a variety of loopholes in the cloture rule in 1979 and 1986.

Power of the Purse—A reference to the constitutional power Congress has over legislation to raise revenue and appropriate monies from the Treasury. Article I, Section 8 states that Congress "shall have Power To lay and collect Taxes, Duties, Imposts and Excises, [and] to pay the Debts." Section 9 declares: "No Money shall be drawn from the Treasury, but in Consequence of Appropriations made by Law."

Preamble—Introductory language describing the reasons for and intent of a measure, sometimes called a whereas clause. It occasionally appears in joint, concurrent and simple resolutions but rarely in bills.

Precedent—A previous ruling on a parliamentary matter or a long-standing practice or custom of a house. Precedents serve to control arbitrary rulings and serve as the common law of a house.

President of the Senate—One constitutional role of the vice president is serving as the presiding officer of the Senate, or president of the Senate. The Constitution permits the vice president to cast a vote in the Senate only to break a tie, but the vice president is not required to do so.

President Pro Tempore—Under the Constitution, an officer elected by the Senate to preside over it during the absence of the vice president of the United States. Often referred to as the "pro tem," this senator is usually a member of the majority party with the longest continuous service in the chamber and also, by virtue of seniority, a committee chairman. When attending to committee and other duties the president pro tempore appoints other senators to preside.

Presiding Officer—In a formal meeting, the individual authorized to maintain order and decorum, recognize members to speak or offer motions and apply and interpret the chamber's rules, precedents and practices. The Speaker of the House and the president of the Senate are the chief presiding officers in their respective houses.

Previous Question—A nondebatable motion which, when agreed to by majority vote, usually cuts off further debate, prevents the offering of additional amendments and brings the pending matter to an immediate vote. It is a major debate-limiting device in the House; it is not permitted in Committee of the Whole in the House or in the Senate.

Private Bill—A bill that applies to one or more specified persons, corporations, institutions or other entities, usually to grant relief when no other legal remedy is available to them. Many private bills deal with claims against the federal government, immigration and naturalization cases and land titles.

Private Calendar—Commonly used title for a calendar in the House reserved for private bills and resolutions favorably reported by committees. The private calendar is officially called the Calendar of the Committee of the Whole House.

Private Law—A private bill enacted into law. Private laws are numbered in the same fashion as public laws.

Privilege—An attribute of a motion, measure, report, question or proposition that gives it priority status for consideration. Privileged motions and motions to bring up privileged questions are not debatable.

Privilege of the Floor—In addition to the members of a house, certain individuals are admitted to its floor while it is in session. The rules of the two houses differ somewhat but both extend the privilege to the president and vice president, Supreme Court justices, cabinet members, state governors, former members of that house, members of the other house, certain officers and officials of Congress, certain staff of that house in the discharge of official duties and the chamber's former parliamentarians. They also allow access to a limited number of committee and members' staff when their presence is necessary.

Pro Forma Amendment—In the House, an amendment that ostensibly proposes to change a measure or another amendment by moving "to strike the last word" or "to strike the requisite number of words." A member offers it not to make any actual change in the measure or amendment but only to obtain time for debate.

Appendix

Pro Tem—A common reference to the president pro tempore of the Senate or, occasionally, to a Speaker pro tempore. (See President Pro Tempore; Speaker Pro Tempore.)

Procedures—The methods of conducting business in a deliberative body. The procedures of each house are governed first by applicable provisions of the Constitution, and then by its standing rules and orders, precedents, traditional practices and any statutory rules that apply to it. The authority of the houses to adopt rules in addition to those specified in the Constitution is derived from Article I, Section 5, clause 2, of the Constitution, which states: "Each House may determine the Rules of its Proceedings...." By rule, the House of Representatives also follows the procedures in Jefferson's Manual that are not inconsistent with its standing rules and orders. Many Senate procedures also conform with Jefferson's provisions, but by practice rather than by rule. At the beginning of each Congress, the House uses procedures in general parliamentary law until it adopts its standing rules.

Proxy Voting—The practice of permitting a member to cast the vote of an absent colleague in addition to his or her own vote. Proxy voting is prohibited on the floors of the House and Senate, but the Senate permits its committees to authorize proxy voting, and most do. In 1995, House rules were changed to prohibit proxy voting in committee.

Public Bill—A bill dealing with general legislative matters having national applicability or applying to the federal government or to a class of persons, groups or organizations.

Public Debt—Federal government debt incurred by the Treasury or the Federal Financing Bank by the sale of securities to the public or borrowings from a federal fund or account.

Public Law—A public bill or joint resolution enacted into law. It is cited by the letters "PL" followed by a hyphenated number. The digits before the hyphen indicate the number of the Congress in which it was enacted; the digits after the hyphen indicate its position in the numerical sequence of public measures that became law during that Congress. For example, the Budget Enforcement Act of 1990 became PL 101-508 because it was the 508th measure in that sequence for the 101st Congress. (See also Private Law.)

Qualification (of Members)—The Constitution requires members of the House of Representatives to be twenty-five years of age at the time their terms begin. They must have been citizens of the United States for seven years before that date and, when elected, must be "Inhabitant[s]" of the state from which they were elected. There is no constitutional requirement that they reside in the districts they represent. Senators are required to be thirty years of age at the time their terms begin. They must have been citizens of the United States for nine years before that date and, when elected, must be "Inhabitant[s]" of the states in which they were elected. The "Inhabitant" qualification is broadly interpreted, and in modern times a candidate's declaration of state residence has generally been accepted as meeting the constitutional requirement.

Queen of the Hill Rule—A special rule from the House Rules Committee that permits votes on a series of amendments, especially complete substitutes for a measure, in a specified order, but directs that the amendment receiving the greatest number of votes shall be the winning one. This kind of rule permits the House to vote directly on a variety of alternatives to a measure. In doing so, it sets aside the precedent that once an amendment has been adopted, no further amendments may be offered to the text it has amended. Under an earlier practice, the Rules Committee reported "king of the hill" rules under which there also could be votes on a series of amendments, again in a specified order. If more than one of the amendments was adopted under this kind of rule, it was the last amendment to receive a majority vote that was considered as having been finally adopted, whether or not it had received the greatest number of votes.

Quorum—The minimum number of members required to be present for the transaction of business. Under the Constitution, a quorum in each house is a majority of its members: 218 in the House and 51 in the Senate when there are no vacancies. By House rule, a quorum in Committee of the Whole is 100. In practice, both houses usually assume a quorum is present even if it is not, unless a member makes a point of no quorum in the House or suggests the absence of a quorum in the Senate. Consequently, each house transacts much of its business, and even passes bills, when only a few members are present. For House and Senate committees, chamber rules allow a minimum quorum of one-third of a committee's members to conduct most types of business.

Quorum Call—A procedure for determining whether a quorum is present in a chamber. In the Senate, a clerk calls the roll (roster) of senators. The House usually employs its electronic voting system.

Ramseyer Rule—A House rule that requires a committee's report on a bill or joint resolution to show the changes the measure, and any committee amendments to it, would make in existing law. The rule requires the report to present the text of any statutory provision that would be repealed and a comparative print showing, through typographical devices such as stricken-through type or italics, other changes that would be made in existing law. The rule, adopted in 1929, is named after its sponsor, Rep. Christian W. Ramseyer, R-Iowa. The Senate's analogous rule is called the Cordon Rule.

Rank or Ranking—A member's position on the list of his or her party's members on a committee or subcommittee. When first assigned to a committee, a member is usually placed at the bottom of the list, then moves up as those above leave the committee. On subcommittees, however, a member's rank may not have anything to do with the length of his or her service on it.

Ranking Member—(1) Most often a reference to the minority member with the highest ranking on a committee or subcommittee. (2) A reference to the majority member next in rank to the chairman or to the highest ranking majority member present at a committee or subcommittee meeting.

Ratification—(1) The president's formal act of promulgating a treaty after the Senate has approved it. The resolution of ratification agreed to by the Senate is the procedural vehicle by which the Senate gives its consent to ratification. (2) A state legislature's act in approving a proposed constitutional amendment. Such an amendment becomes effective when ratified by three-fourths of the states.

Reapportionment—(See Apportionment.)

Recess—(1) A temporary interruption or suspension of a meeting of a chamber or committee. Unlike an adjournment, a recess does not end a legislative day. Because the Senate often recesses from one calendar day to another, its legislative day may extend over several calendar days, weeks or even months. (2) A period of adjournment for more than three days to a day certain, especially over a holiday or in August during odd-numbered years.

Recess Appointment—A presidential appointment to a vacant federal position made after the Senate has adjourned sine die or has adjourned or recessed for more than thirty days. If the president submits the recess appointee's nomination during the

Glossary

next session of the Senate, that individual can continue to serve until the end of the session even though the Senate might have rejected the nomination. When appointed to a vacancy that existed thirty days before the end of the last Senate session, a recess appointee is not paid until confirmed.

Recommit—To send a measure back to the committee that reported it; sometimes called a straight motion to recommit to distinguish it from a motion to recommit with instructions. A successful motion to recommit kills the measure unless it is accompanied by instructions.

Recommit a Conference Report—To return a conference report to the conference committee for renegotiation of some or all of its agreements. A motion to recommit may be offered with or without instructions.

Recommit with Instructions—To send a measure back to a committee with instructions to take some action on it. Invariably in the House and often in the Senate, when the motion recommits to a standing committee, the instructions require the committee to report the measure "forthwith" with specified amendments.

Reconciliation—A procedure for changing existing revenue and spending laws to bring total federal revenues and spending within the limits established in a budget resolution. Congress has applied reconciliation chiefly to revenues and mandatory spending programs, especially entitlements. Discretionary spending is controlled through annual appropriation bills.

Recorded Vote—(1) Generally, any vote in which members are recorded by name for or against a measure; also called a record vote or roll-call vote. The only recorded vote in the Senate is a vote by the yeas and nays and is commonly called a roll-call vote. (2) Technically, a recorded vote is one demanded in the House of Representatives and supported by at least one-fifth of a quorum (forty-four members) in the House sitting as the House or at least twenty-five members in Committee of the Whole.

Recorded Vote by Clerks—A voting procedure in the House where members pass through the appropriate "aye" or "no" aisle in the chamber and cast their votes by depositing a signed green (yea) or red (no) card in a ballot box. These votes are tabulated by clerks and reported to the chair. The electronic voting system is much more convenient and has largely supplanted this procedure. (See Committee of the Whole; Recorded Vote; Teller Vote.)

Redistricting—The redrawing of congressional district boundaries within a state after a decennial census. Redistricting may be required to equalize district populations or to accommodate an increase or decrease in the number of a state's House seats that might have resulted from the decennial apportionment. The state governments determine the district lines. (See Apportionment; Congressional District; Gerrymandering.)

Referral—The assignment of a measure to committee for consideration. Under a House rule, the Speaker can refuse to refer a measure if the Speaker believes it is "of an obscene or insulting character."

Report—(1) As a verb, a committee is said to report when it submits a measure or other document to its parent chamber. (2) A clerk is said to report when he or she reads a measure's title, text or the text of an amendment to the body at the direction of the chair. (3) As a noun, a committee document that accompanies a reported measure. It describes the measure, the committee's views on it, its costs and the changes it proposes to make in existing law; it also includes certain impact statements. (4) A committee document submitted to its parent chamber that describes the results of an investigation or other study or provides information it is required to provide by rule or law.

Representative—An elected and duly sworn member of the House of Representatives who is entitled to vote in the chamber. The Constitution requires that a representative be at least twenty-five years old, a citizen of the United States for at least seven years and an inhabitant of the state from which he or she is elected. Customarily, the member resides in the district he or she represents. Representatives are elected in even-numbered years to two-year terms that begin the following January.

Reprimand—A formal condemnation of a member for misbehavior, considered a milder reproof than censure. The House of Representatives first used it in 1976. The Senate first used it in 1991. (See also Censure; Code of Official Conduct; Denounce; Ethics Rules; Expulsion; Seniority Loss.)

Rescission—A provision of law that repeals previously enacted budget authority in whole or in part. Under the Impoundment Control Act of 1974, the president can impound such funds by sending a message to Congress requesting one or more rescissions and the reasons for doing so. If Congress does not pass a rescission bill for the programs requested by the president within forty-five days of continuous session after receiving the message, the president must make the funds available for obligation and expenditure. If the president does not, the comptroller general of the United States is authorized to bring suit to compel the release of those funds. A rescission bill may rescind all, part or none of an amount proposed by the president, and may rescind funds the president has not impounded.

Reserving the Right To Object—Members' declaration that at some indefinite future time they may object to a unanimous consent request. It is an attempt to circumvent the requirement that members may prevent such an action only by objecting immediately after it is proposed.

Resident Commissioner from Puerto Rico—A nonvoting member of the House of Representatives, elected to a four-year term. The resident commissioner has the same status and privileges as delegates. Like the delegates, the resident commissioner may not vote in the House or Committee of the Whole.

Resolution—(1) A simple resolution; that is, a nonlegislative measure effective only in the house in which it is proposed and not requiring concurrence by the other chamber or approval by the president. Simple resolutions are designated H. Res. in the House and S. Res. in the Senate. Simple resolutions express nonbinding opinions on policies or issues or deal with the internal affairs or prerogatives of a house. (2) Any type of resolution: simple, concurrent or joint. (See Concurrent Resolution; Joint Resolution.)

Resolution of Inquiry—A resolution usually simple rather than concurrent calling on the president or the head of an executive agency to provide specific information or papers to one or both houses.

Resolution of Ratification—The Senate vehicle for agreeing to a treaty. The constitutionally mandated vote of two-thirds of the senators present and voting applies to the adoption of this resolution. However, it may also contain amendments, reservations, declarations or understandings that the Senate had previously added to it by majority vote.

Revenue Legislation—Measures that levy new taxes or tariffs or change existing ones. Under Article I, Section 7, clause 1 of the Constitution, the House of Representatives originates federal revenue measures, but the Senate can propose amendments to them. The House Ways and Means Committee and

Appendix

the Senate Finance Committee have jurisdiction over such measures, with a few minor exceptions.

Revise and Extend One's Remarks—A unanimous consent request to publish in the Congressional Record a statement a member did not deliver on the floor, a longer statement than the one made on the floor or miscellaneous extraneous material.

Revolving Fund—A trust fund or account whose income remains available to finance its continuing operations without any fiscal year limitation.

Rider—Congressional slang for an amendment unrelated or extraneous to the subject matter of the measure to which it is attached. Riders often contain proposals that are less likely to become law on their own merits as separate bills, either because of opposition in the committee of jurisdiction, resistance in the other house or the probability of a presidential veto. Riders are more common in the Senate.

Roll Call—A call of the roll to determine whether a quorum is present, to establish a quorum or to vote on a question. Usually, the House uses its electronic voting system for a roll call. The Senate does not have an electronic voting system; its roll is always called by a clerk.

Rule—(1) A permanent regulation that a house adopts to govern its conduct of business, its procedures, its internal organization, behavior of its members, regulation of its facilities, duties of an officer or some other subject it chooses to govern in that form. (2) In the House, a privileged simple resolution reported by the Rules Committee that provides methods and conditions for floor consideration of a measure or, rarely, several measures.

Rule Twenty-Two—A common reference to the Senate's cloture rule. (See Cloture)

Second-Degree Amendment—An amendment to an amendment in the first degree. It is usually a perfecting amendment.

Secretary of the Senate—The chief financial, administrative and legislative officer of the Senate. Elected by resolution or order of the Senate, the secretary is invariably the candidate of the majority party and usually chosen by the majority leader. In the absence of the vice president and pending the election of a president pro tempore, the secretary presides over the Senate. The secretary is subject to policy direction and oversight by the Senate Committee on Rules and Administration. The secretary manages a wide range of functions that support the administrative operations of the Senate as an organization as well as those functions necessary to its legislative process, including record keeping, document management, certifications, housekeeping services, administration of oaths and lobbyist registrations. The secretary is responsible for accounting for all funds appropriated to the Senate and conducts audits of Senate financial activities. On a semiannual basis the secretary issues the Report of the Secretary of the Senate, a compilation of Senate expenditures.

Section—A subdivision of a bill or statute. By law, a section must be numbered and, as nearly as possible, contain "a single proposition of enactment."

Select or Special Committee—A committee established by a resolution in either house for a special purpose and, usually, for a limited time. Most select and special committees are assigned specific investigations or studies but are not authorized to report measures to their chambers. However, both houses have created several permanent select and special committees and have given legislative reporting authority to a few of them: the Ethics Committee in the Senate and the Intelligence Committees in both houses. There is no substantive difference between a select and a special committee; they are so called depending simply on whether the resolution creating the committee calls it one or the other.

Senate—The house of Congress in which each state is represented by two senators; each senator has one vote. Article V of the Constitution declares that "No State, without its Consent, shall be deprived of its equal Suffrage in the Senate." The Constitution also gives the Senate equal legislative power with the House of Representatives. Although the Senate is prohibited from originating revenue measures, and as a matter of practice it does not originate appropriation measures, it can amend both. Only the Senate can give or withhold consent to treaties and nominations from the president. It also acts as a court to try impeachments by the House and elects the vice president when no candidate receives a majority of the electoral votes. It is often referred to as "the upper body," but not by members of the House.

Senate Manual—The handbook of the Senate's standing rules and orders and the laws and other regulations that apply to the Senate, usually published once each Congress.

Senator—A duly sworn elected or appointed member of the Senate. The Constitution requires that a senator be at least thirty years old, a citizen of the United States for at least nine years and an inhabitant of the state from which he or she is elected. Senators are usually elected in even-numbered years to six-year terms that begin the following January. When a vacancy occurs before the end of a term, the state governor can appoint a replacement to fill the position until a successor is chosen at the state's next general election or, if specified under state law, the next feasible date for such an election, to serve the remainder of the term. Until the Seventeenth Amendment was ratified in 1913, senators were chosen by their state legislatures.

Senatorial Courtesy—The Senate's practice of declining to confirm a presidential nominee for an office in the state of a senator of the president's party unless that senator approves.

Seniority—The priority, precedence or status accorded members according to the length of their continuous service in a house or on a committee.

Seniority Loss—A type of punishment that reduces a member's seniority on his or her committees, including the loss of chairmanships. Party caucuses in both houses have occasionally imposed such punishment on their members, for example, for publicly supporting candidates of the other party.

Seniority Rule—The customary practice, rather than a rule, of assigning the chairmanship of a committee to the majority party member who has served on the committee for the longest continuous period of time.

Seniority System—A collection of long-standing customary practices under which members with longer continuous service than their colleagues in their house or on their committees receive various kinds of preferential treatment. Although some of the practices are no longer as rigidly observed as in the past, they still pervade the organization and procedures of Congress.

Sequestration—A procedure for canceling budgetary resources — that is, money available for obligation or spending — to enforce budget limitations established in law. Sequestered funds are no longer available for obligation or expenditure.

Sergeant at Arms—The officer in each house responsible for maintaining order, security and decorum in its wing of the Capitol, including the chamber and its galleries. Although elected by their respective houses, both sergeants at arms are invariably the candidates of the majority party.

Session—(1) The annual series of meetings of a Congress. Under the Constitution, Congress must assemble at least once a year at noon on Jan. 3 unless it appoints a different day by law. (2) The special meetings of Congress or of one house convened by the president, called a special session. (3) A house is said to be in session during the period of a day when it is meeting.

Severability (or Separability) Clause—Language stating that if any particular provisions of a measure are declared invalid by the courts the remaining provisions shall remain in effect.

Sine Die—Without fixing a day for a future meeting. An adjournment sine die signifies the end of an annual or special session of Congress.

Slip Law—The first official publication of a measure that has become law. It is published separately in unbound, single-sheet form or pamphlet form. A slip law usually is available two or three days after the date of the law's enactment.

Speaker—The presiding officer of the House of Representatives and the leader of its majority party. The Speaker is selected by the majority party and formally elected by the House at the beginning of each Congress. Although the Constitution does not require the Speaker to be a member of the House, in fact, all Speakers have been members.

Speaker Pro Tempore—A member of the House who is designated as the temporary presiding officer by the Speaker or elected by the House to that position during the Speaker's absence.

Speaker's Vote—The Speaker is not required to vote, and the Speaker's name is not called on a roll-call vote unless so requested. Usually, the Speaker votes either to create a tie vote, and thereby defeat a proposal or to break a tie in favor of a proposal. Occasionally, the Speaker also votes to emphasize the importance of a matter.

Special Session—A session of Congress convened by the president, under his constitutional authority, after Congress has adjourned sine die at the end of a regular session. (See Adjournment Sine Die; Session.)

Spending Authority—The technical term for backdoor spending. The Congressional Budget Act of 1974 defines it as borrowing authority, contract authority and entitlement authority for which appropriation acts do not provide budget authority in advance. Under the Budget Act, legislation that provides new spending authority may not be considered unless it provides that the authority shall be effective only to the extent or in such amounts as provided in an appropriation act.

Spending Cap—The statutory limit for a fiscal year on the amount of new budget authority and outlays allowed for discretionary spending. The Budget Enforcement Act of 1997 requires a sequester if the cap is exceeded.

Split Referral—A measure divided into two or more parts, with each part referred to a different committee.

Sponsor—The principal proponent and introducer of a measure or an amendment.

Staff Director—The most frequently used title for the head of staff of a committee or subcommittee. On some committees, that person is called chief of staff, clerk, chief clerk, chief counsel, general counsel or executive director. The head of a committee's minority staff is usually called minority staff director.

Standing Committee—A permanent committee established by a House or Senate standing rule or standing order. The rule also describes the subject areas on which the committee may report bills and resolutions and conduct oversight. Most introduced measures must be referred to one or more standing committees according to their jurisdictions.

Standing Order—A continuing regulation or directive that has the force and effect of a rule, but is not incorporated into the standing rules. The Senate's numerous standing orders, like its standing rules, continue from Congress to Congress unless changed or the order states otherwise. The House uses relatively few standing orders, and those it adopts expire at the end of a session of Congress.

Standing Rules—The rules of the Senate that continue from one Congress to the next and the rules of the House of Representatives that it adopts at the beginning of each new Congress.

Standing Vote—An alternative and informal term for a division vote, during which members in favor of a proposal and then members opposed stand and are counted by the chair.

Star Print—A reprint of a bill, resolution, amendment or committee report correcting technical or substantive errors in a previous printing; so called because of the small black star that appears on the front page or cover.

State of the Union Message—A presidential message to Congress under the constitutional directive that the president shall "from time to time give to the Congress Information of the State of the Union, and recommend to their Consideration such Measures as he shall judge necessary and expedient." Customarily, the president sends an annual State of the Union message to Congress, usually late in January.

Statutes at Large—A chronological arrangement of the laws enacted in each session of Congress. Though indexed, the laws are not arranged by subject matter nor is there an indication of how they affect or change previously enacted laws. The volumes are numbered by Congress, and the laws are cited by their volume and page number. The Gramm-Rudman-Hollings Act, for example, appears as 99 Stat. 1037.

Straw Vote Prohibition—Under a House precedent, a member who has the floor during debate may not conduct a straw vote or otherwise ask for a show of support for a proposition. Only the chair may put a question to a vote.

Strike From the Record—Expunge objectionable remarks from the Congressional Record, after a member's words have been taken down on a point of order.

Subcommittee—A panel of committee members assigned a portion of the committee's jurisdiction or other functions. On legislative committees, subcommittees hold hearings, mark up legislation and report measures to their full committee for further action; they cannot report directly to the chamber. A subcommittee's party composition usually reflects the ratio on its parent committee.

Subpoena Power—The authority granted to committees by the rules of their respective houses to issue legal orders requiring individuals to appear and testify, or to produce documents pertinent to the committee's functions, or both. Persons who do not comply with subpoenas can be cited for contempt of Congress and prosecuted.

Subsidy—Generally, a payment or benefit made by the federal government for which no current repayment is required. Subsidy payments may be designed to support the conduct of an economic enterprise or activity, such as ship operations, or to support certain market prices, as in the case of farm subsidies.

Sunset Legislation—A term sometimes applied to laws authorizing the existence of agencies or programs that expire annually or at the end of some other specified period of time. One of the purposes of setting specific expiration dates for agencies

Appendix

and programs is to encourage the committees with jurisdiction over them to determine whether they should be continued or terminated.

Sunshine Rules—Rules requiring open committee hearings and business meetings, including markup sessions, in both houses, and also open conference committee meetings. However, all may be closed under certain circumstances and using certain procedures required by the rules.

Supermajority—A term sometimes used for a vote on a matter that requires approval by more than a simple majority of those members present and voting; also referred to as extraordinary majority.

Supplemental Appropriation Bill—A measure providing appropriations for use in the current fiscal year, in addition to those already provided in annual general appropriation bills. Supplemental appropriations are often for unforeseen emergencies.

Suspension of the Rules (House)—An expeditious procedure for passing relatively noncontroversial or emergency measures by a two-thirds vote of those members voting, a quorum being present.

Suspension of the Rules (Senate)—A procedure to set aside one or more of the Senate's rules; it is used infrequently, and then most often to suspend the rule banning legislative amendments to appropriation bills.

Task Force—A title sometimes given to a panel of members assigned to a special project, study or investigation. Ordinarily, these groups do not have authority to report measures to their respective houses.

Tax Expenditure—Loosely, a tax exemption or advantage, sometimes called an incentive or loophole; technically, a loss of governmental tax revenue attributable to some provision of federal tax laws that allows a special exclusion, exemption or deduction from gross income or that provides a special credit, preferential tax rate or deferral of tax liability.

Televised Proceedings—Television and radio coverage of the floor proceedings of the House of Representatives has been available since 1979 and of the Senate since 1986. They are broadcast over a coaxial cable system to all congressional offices and to some congressional agencies on channels reserved for that purpose. Coverage is also available free of charge to commercial and public television and radio broadcasters. The Cable-Satellite Public Affairs Network (C-SPAN) carries gavel-to-gavel coverage of both houses.

Teller Vote—A voting procedure, formerly used in the House, in which members cast their votes by passing through the center aisle to be counted, but not recorded by name, by a member from each party appointed by the chair. The House deleted the procedure from its rules in 1993, but during floor discussion of the deletion a leading member stated that a teller vote would still be available in the event of a breakdown of the electronic voting system.

Third-Degree Amendment—An amendment to a second-degree amendment. Both houses prohibit such amendments.

Third Reading—A required reading to a chamber of a bill or joint resolution by title only before the vote on passage. In modern practice, it has merely become a pro forma step.

Three-Day Rule—(1) In the House, a measure cannot be considered until the third calendar day on which the committee report has been available. (2) In the House, a conference report cannot be considered until the third calendar day on which its text has been available in the Congressional Record. (3) In the House, a general appropriation bill cannot be considered until the third calendar day on which printed hearings on the bill have been available. (4) In the Senate, when a committee votes to report a measure, a committee member is entitled to three calendar days within which to submit separate views for inclusion in the committee report. (In House committees, a member is entitled to two calendar days for this purpose, after the day on which the committee votes to report.) (5) In both houses, a majority of a committee's members may call a special meeting of the committee if its chairman fails to do so within three calendar days after three or more of the members, acting jointly, formally request such a meeting.

In calculating such periods, the House omits holiday and weekend days on which it does not meet. The Senate makes no such exclusion.

Tie Vote—When the votes for and against a proposition are equal, it loses. The president of the Senate may cast a vote only to break a tie. Because the Speaker is invariably a member of the House, the Speaker is entitled to vote but usually does not. The Speaker may choose to do so to break, or create, a tie vote.

Title—(1) A major subdivision of a bill or act, designated by a roman numeral and usually containing legislative provisions on the same general subject. Titles are sometimes divided into subtitles as well as sections. (2) The official name of a bill or act, also called a caption or long title. (3) Some bills also have short titles that appear in the sentence immediately following the enacting clause. (4) Popular titles are the unofficial names given to some bills or acts by common usage. For example, the Balanced Budget and Emergency Deficit Control Act of 1985 (short title) is almost invariably referred to as Gramm-Rudman (popular title). In other cases, significant legislation is popularly referred to by its title number (see definition (1) above). For example, the federal legislation that requires equality of funding for women's and men's sports in educational institutions that receive federal funds is popularly called Title IX.

Track System—An occasional Senate practice that expedites legislation by dividing a day's session into two or more specific time periods, commonly called tracks, each reserved for consideration of a different measure.

Transfer Payment—A federal government payment to which individuals or organizations are entitled under law and for which no goods or services are required in return. Payments include welfare and Social Security benefits, unemployment insurance, government pensions and veterans benefits.

Treaty—A formal document containing an agreement between two or more sovereign nations. The Constitution authorizes the president to make treaties, but the president must submit them to the Senate for its approval by a two-thirds vote of the senators present. Under the Senate's rules, that vote actually occurs on a resolution of ratification. Although the Constitution does not give the House a direct role in approving treaties, that body has sometimes insisted that a revenue treaty is an invasion of its prerogatives. In any case, the House may significantly affect the application of a treaty by its equal role in enacting legislation to implement the treaty.

Trust Funds—Special accounts in the Treasury that receive earmarked taxes or other kinds of revenue collections, such as user fees, and from which payments are made for special purposes or to recipients who meet the requirements of the trust funds as established by law. Of the more than 150 federal government trust funds, several finance major entitlement programs, such as Social Security, Medicare and retired federal employees' pensions. Others fund infrastructure construction and improvements, such as highways and airports.

Unanimous Consent—Without an objection by any member. A unanimous consent request asks permission, explicitly or implicitly, to set aside one or more rules. Both houses and their committees frequently use such requests to expedite their proceedings.

Uncontrollable Expenditures—A frequently used term for federal expenditures that are mandatory under existing law and therefore cannot be controlled by the president or Congress without a change in the existing law. Uncontrollable expenditures include spending required under entitlement programs and also fixed costs, such as interest on the public debt and outlays to pay for prior-year obligations. In recent years, uncontrollables have accounted for approximately three-quarters of federal spending in each fiscal year.

Unfunded Mandate—Generally, any provision in federal law or regulation that imposes a duty or obligation on a state or local government or private sector entity without providing the necessary funds to comply. The Unfunded Mandates Reform Act of 1995 amended the Congressional Budget Act of 1974 to provide a mechanism for the control of new unfunded mandates.

Union Calendar—A calendar of the House of Representatives for bills and resolutions favorably reported by committees that raise revenue or directly or indirectly appropriate money or property. In addition to appropriation bills, measures that authorize expenditures are also placed on this calendar. The calendar's full title is the Calendar of the Committee of the Whole House on the State of the Union.

Upper Body—A common reference to the Senate, but not used by members of the House.

U.S. Code—Popular title for the United States Code: Containing the General and Permanent Laws of the United States in Force on.... It is a consolidation and partial codification of the general and permanent laws of the United States arranged by subject under 50 titles. The first six titles deal with general or political subjects, the other forty-four with subjects ranging from agriculture to war, alphabetically arranged. A supplement is published after each session of Congress, and the entire Code is revised every six years.

User Fee—A fee charged to users of goods or services provided by the federal government. When Congress levies or authorizes such fees, it determines whether the revenues should go into the general collections of the Treasury or be available for expenditure by the agency that provides the goods or services.

Veto—The president's disapproval of a legislative measure passed by Congress. The president returns the measure to the house in which it originated without his signature but with a veto message stating his objections to it. When Congress is in session, the president must veto a bill within ten days, excluding Sundays, after the president has received it; otherwise it becomes law without his signature. The ten-day clock begins to run at midnight following his receipt of the bill. (See also Committee Veto; Item Veto; Line Item Veto Act of 1996; Override a Veto; Pocket Veto.)

Voice Vote—A method of voting in which members who favor a question answer aye in chorus, after which those opposed answer no in chorus, and the chair decides which position prevails.

Voting—Members vote in three ways on the floor: (1) by shouting "aye" or "no" on voice votes; (2) by standing for or against on division votes; and (3) on recorded votes (including the yeas and nays), by answering "aye" or "no" when their names are called or, in the House, by recording their votes through the electronic voting system.

War Powers Resolution of 1973—An act that requires the president "in every possible instance" to consult Congress before committing U.S. forces to ongoing or imminent hostilities. If the president commits them to a combat situation without congressional consultation, the president must notify Congress within forty-eight hours. Unless Congress declares war or otherwise authorizes the operation to continue, the forces must be withdrawn within sixty or ninety days, depending on certain conditions. No president has ever acknowledged the constitutionality of the resolution.

Well—The sunken, level, open space between members' seats and the podium at the front of each chamber. House members usually address their chamber from their party's lectern in the well on its side of the aisle. Senators usually speak at their assigned desks.

Whip—The majority or minority party member in each house who acts as assistant leader, helps plan and marshal support for party strategies, encourages party discipline and advises his or her leader on how colleagues intend to vote on the floor. In the Senate, the Republican whip's official title is assistant leader.

Yeas and Nays—A vote in which members usually respond "aye" or "no" (despite the official title of the vote) on a question when their names are called in alphabetical order. The Constitution requires the yeas and nays when a demand for it is supported by one-fifth of the members present, and it also requires an automatic yea-and-nay vote on overriding a veto. Senate precedents require the support of at least one-fifth of a quorum, a minimum of eleven members with the present membership of 100.

Congressional Information on the Internet

A huge array of congressional information is available for free at Internet sites operated by the federal government, colleges and universities and commercial firms. The sites offer the full text of bills introduced in the House and Senate, voting records, campaign finance information, transcripts of selected congressional hearings, investigative reports and much more.

THOMAS

The most important site for congressional information is THOMAS (http://thomas.loc.gov), which is named for Thomas Jefferson and operated by the Library of Congress. THOMAS' highlight is its databases containing the full text of all bills introduced in Congress since 1989, the full text of the *Congressional Record* since 1989 and the status and summary information for all bills introduced since 1973.

THOMAS also offers special links to bills that have received or are expected to receive floor action during the current week and newsworthy bills that are pending or that have recently been approved. Finally, THOMAS has selected committee reports, answers to frequently asked questions about accessing congressional information, publications titled *How Our Laws Are Made* and *Enactment of a Law* and links to lots of other congressional Web sites.

House of Representatives

The U.S. House of Representatives site (http://www.house.gov) offers the schedule of bills, resolutions and other legislative issues the House will consider in the current week. It also has updates about current proceedings on the House floor and a list of the next day's meeting of House committees. Other highlights include a database that helps users identify their representative, a directory of House members and committees, the House ethics manual, links to Web pages maintained by House members and committees, a calendar of congressional primary dates and candidate-filing deadlines for ballot access, the full text of all amendments to the Constitution that have been ratified and those that have been proposed but not ratified and lots of information about Washington, D.C., for visitors.

Another key House site is The Office of the Clerk On-line Information Center (http://clerkweb.house.gov), which has records of all roll-call votes taken since 1990. The votes are recorded by bill, so it is a lengthy process to compile a particular representative's voting record. The site also has lists of committee assignments, a telephone directory for members and committees, mailing label templates for members and committees, rules of the current Congress, election statistics from 1920 to the present, biographies of Speakers of the House, biographies of women who have served since 1917 and a virtual tour of the House Chamber.

One of the more interesting House sites is operated by the Subcommittee on Rules and Organization of the House Committee on Rules (http://www.house.gov/rules/crs_reports.htm). Its highlight is dozens of Congressional Research Service reports about the legislative process. Some of the available titles include *Legislative Research in Congressional Offices: A Primer, How to Follow Current Federal Legislation and Regulations; Investigative Oversight: An Introduction to the Law, Practice and Procedure of Congressional Inquiry;* and *Presidential Vetoes 1789 – Present: A Summary Overview.*

Senate

At least in the Internet world, the Senate is not as active as the House. Its main Web site (http://www.senate.gov) has records of all roll-call votes taken since 1989 (arranged by bill), brief descriptions of all bills and joint resolutions introduced in the Senate during the past week and a calendar of upcoming committee hearings. The site also provides the standing rules of the Senate, a directory of senators and their committee assignments, lists of nominations that the president has submitted to the Senate for approval, links to Web pages operated by senators and committees and a virtual tour of the Senate.

Information about the membership, jurisdiction and rules of each congressional committee is available at the U.S. Government Printing Office site (http://www.access.gpo.gov/congress/index.html). It also has transcripts of selected congressional hearings, the full text of selected House and Senate reports and the House and Senate rules manuals.

General Reference

The U.S. General Accounting Office, the investigative arm of Congress, operates a site (http://www.gao.gov) that provides the full text of its reports from 1975 to the present. The reports cover a wide range of topics: aviation safety, combating terrorism, counternarcotics efforts in Mexico, defense contracting, electronic warfare, food assistance programs, Gulf War illness, health insurance, illegal aliens, information technology, long-term care, mass transit, Medicare, military readiness, money laundering, national parks, nuclear waste, organ donation and student loan defaults, among others.

The GAO Daybook is an excellent current awareness tool. This electronic mailing list distributes a daily list of reports and testimony released by the GAO. Subscriptions are available by sending an e-mail message to majordomo@www.gao.gov, and in the message area typing "subscribe daybook" (without the quotation marks).

Current budget and economic projections are provided at the Congressional Budget Office Web site (http://www.cbo.gov). The site also has reports about the economic and budget outlook for the next decade, the president's budget proposals, federal civilian employment, Social Security privatization, tax reform, water use conflicts in the West, marriage and the federal income tax and the role of foreign aid in development, among other topics. Other highlights include monthly budget updates, historical budget data, cost estimates for bills reported by congressional committees and transcripts of congressional testimony by CBO officials.

Campaign Finance

Several Internet sites provide detailed campaign finance data for congressional elections. The official site is operated by the Federal Election Commission *(http://www.fec.gov)*, which regulates political spending. The site's highlight is its database of campaign reports filed from May 1996 to the present by House and presidential candidates, political action committees and political party committees. Senate reports are not included because they are filed with the Secretary of the Senate. The reports in the FEC's database are scanned images of paper reports filed with the commission.

The FEC site also has summary financial data for House and Senate candidates in the current election cycle, abstracts of court decisions pertaining to federal election law from 1976 to 1997, a graph showing the number of political action committees in existence each year from 1974 to the present and a directory of national and state agencies that are responsible for releasing information about campaign financing, candidates on the ballot, election results, lobbying and other issues. Another useful feature is a collection of brochures about federal election law, public funding of presidential elections, the ban on contributions by foreign nationals, independent expenditures supporting or opposing a candidate for federal office, contribution limits, filing a complaint, researching public records at the FEC and other topics. Finally, the site provides the FEC's legislative recommendations, its annual report, a report about its first twenty years in existence, the FEC's monthly newsletter, several reports about voter registration, election results for the most recent presidential and congressional elections and campaign guides for corporations and labor organizations, congressional candidates and committees, political party committees and nonconnected committees.

The best online source for campaign finance data is Political Money Line *(http://www.tray.com)*. The site's searchable databases provide extensive itemized information about receipts and expenditures by federal candidates and political action committees from 1980 to the present. The data, which are obtained from the FEC, are quite detailed. For example, for candidates contributions can be searched by Zip Code. The site also has lists of the top political action committees in various categories, lists of the top contributors from each state and much more.

Another interesting site is the American University Campaign Finance Website *(http://www1.soc.american.edu/campfin)*, which is operated by the American University School of Communication. It provides electronic files from the FEC that have been reformatted in .dbf format so they can be used in database programs such as Paradox, Access and FoxPro. The files contain data on PAC, committee and individual contributions to individual congressional candidates.

More campaign finance data is available from the Center for Responsive Politics *(http://www.opensecrets.org)*, a public interest organization. The center provides a list of all "soft money" donations to political parties of $100,000 or more in the current election cycle and data about "leadership" political action committees associated with individual politicians. Other databases at the site provide information about travel expenses that House members received from private sources for attending meetings and other events, activities of registered federal lobbyists and activities of foreign agents who are registered in the United States.

Index

accounting industry reform, 93–96
Afghanistan, 52–55
airport security screeners, 7
Appropriations committees, 10–11, 84. *See also* budget and expenditures
Arafat, Yasser, 60–61
Armitage, Richard L., 69, 72
Army modernization plan, 74–78
Arthur Andersen LLP, 93–96
ASCAP (American Society of Composers, Authors and Publishers), 106
Ashcroft, John, 86
Audio Home Recording Act, 106
auditing industry, 93–96
aviation security law, 58

Baird, Brian (D-Wash.), 13–15
Balanced Budget Act, 102, 103
Bates, John D., 20, 21
Bayh, Evan (D-Ind.), 71, 114, 116
Bennett, Robert F. (R-Utah), 7
Biden, Joseph R., Jr. (D-Del.), 68
bio-terrorism, defending against, 82
Bishop, Sanford D. (D-Ga.), 36
Blue Dog coalition, 64
border security, 4, 83
Boren, David L. (D-Okla.), 46
Boucher, Rick (D-Va.), 25, 105, 110
Brinkley, Alan, 51
budget and expenditures
  contingency fund, 89
  cuts, 63–64, 65, 84
  defense, 63–64, 88–92
  deficit spending, 63–67
  emergency supplemental bill, 84
  foreign aid and peacekeeping, 52–53
  Homeland Security, 10–11, 57, 80–84
  Medicare, 99–100
bunker busters, 88, 89
Burton, Dan (R-Ind.), 17, 18
Bush, George, 57, 59
Bush, George W.
  Afghanistan, 52–53, 54
  campaign finance, 42, 44
  Congress, communication with, 69–71, 72, 73
  Daschle, policy struggle with, 56–59
  defense budget, 63–64, 88–92
  deficit spending, 63–67

document disclosure, 16–21, 51
fast-track trade authority, 112–113
foreign policy, Congress and, 68–69
Homeland Security proposal, 2–12, 80–84
Medicare and Social Security reform, 64–65
Mideast policy, 60–62, 68–69
Netanyahu criticism of, 68
nuclear program expansion, 88–89, 90
patients' rights, 100, 101
prescription drug plan, 65
secrecy, pattern of, 8, 18
steel tariffs, 111–113
welfare, 114–117
Byrd, Robert C. (D-W.Va.), 64

California redistricting plan, 26–27
campaign finance
  bill, passage of, 41–46
  court challenge, 43
  incumbents, advantage of, 33, 34–35, 36
  soft money and hard money, 41–42
Campbell, Ben Nighthorse (R-Colo.), 84
Cannon, Christopher B. (R-Utah), 105, 110
Capps, Lois (D-Calif.), 29
Carper, Thomas R. (D-Del.), 114, 116
Carter, Jimmy, 18
Chabot, Steve (R-Ohio), 30
Chambliss, Saxby (R-Ga.), 55
Cheney, Dick, 16–21, 67
Cleveland, Grover, 16
Clinton, Bill, 19, 32, 59
Clyburn, James E. (D-S.C.), 39, 40
Coast Guard, 4, 7
Cochran, Thad (R-Miss.), 44
committee assignments, congressional, 35–36
computer security, 83
Condit, Gary A. (D-Calif.), 28
confidentiality, in executive branch, 19, 21
Congress
  Afghanistan, 52–55
  Appropriations committees, 10–11
  Armed Service committees, 77, 78
  Army modernization plan, 74–78
  budget deficits, 63–64, 67

Bush administration, communication with, 69–71, 72, 73
copyright, 104–110
defense budget, 88–92
Democratic leadership races, 37–40
Enron/Andersen scandal, 93–96
fast-track bill, 112–113
FBI reorganization, 85–87
foreign policy, 60–62, 70–71
health care policy, 32, 97–101, 102–103
Homeland Security, 3–5, 7–8, 9–12, 81–84
House vacancies, in case of disaster, 13–15
incumbents, re-election of, 24–36
nuclear program, 88–89, 90
party balance in House, 24
polarization, political, 32–33
"safe seats" projection, 34–35
seniority issues, 31, 32–33, 34
Sept. 11, 2001, intelligence investigations, 48–51, 85, 87
State Department, relationship with, 68–69, 71–73
steel tariffs, 111–113
welfare, 114–117
Copy Protection Technical Working Group, 109
copyright, 104–110
Corzine, Jon (D-N.J.), 96
counterterrorism. *See* Homeland Security Department, proposed; terrorism
Cox, Christopher (R-Calif.), 14
Crusader cannon, 89, 92
Cs3, Inc., 83
Culberson, John (R-Texas), 25, 31

Daniels, Mitchell E., Jr., 66, 67
Darman, Richard G., 66
Daschle, Tom (D-S.D.)
  Bush, policy struggle with, 56–59
  campaign finance, 45–46
  Homeland Security proposal, 9
  Mideast policy, 61
  Pakistan, 54–55
  Sept. 11, 2001, investigations, 48–50
defense. *See also* Homeland Security Department, proposed
  Army modernization plan, 74–78

152

Index

budget, 63–64, 88–92
counterterrorism budget, 83
environmental law exemptions, 78
pensions vs. disability, military, 92
Saudi Arabia, U.S. forces in, 55
deficit spending, 63–67
DeLauro, Rosa (D-Conn.), 38–39
DeLay, Tom (R-Texas), 61
Democrats
health care policy, 98–99
House leadership races, 37–40
Sept. 11, 2001, investigation, 48–51
welfare, 114–117
derivatives regulation, 94
Digital Millennium Copyright Act, 105, 106, 110
digital technology, copyright and, 104–110
Dingell, John D. (D-Mich.), 16, 95
districting, 24, 25, 26–29, 30–31
document disclosure issues, 16–21, 51
Dole, Bob, 59
Durch, William, 54
Dyer, James W., 67

economic stimulus package, 58, 59
Eisenhower, Dwight D., 17
Eisner, Michael, 107
emergency response units, 80, 82
Energy and Commerce Committee, House, 93, 95, 96
energy policy, 94
Engel, Eliot L. (D-N.Y.), 62
English, Phil (R-Pa.), 27
Enron Corporation, 17–18, 44, 93–96
environmental policy, military exemptions to, 78
Evans, Lane (D-Ill.), 27
Everett, Terry (R-Ala.), 36
executive branch, document disclosure, 16–21
executive privilege, 21

farm bill, 57–58
FBI (Federal Bureau of Investigation), 48, 49, 51, 85–87
FEC (Federal Election Commission), 46
Feingold, Russell (D-Wis.), 42, 46
Feinstein, Dianne (D-Calif.), 61, 62
FEMA (Federal Emergency Management Agency), 4
file-sharing services, 107, 110
finance, campaign. *See* campaign finance
Fitzgerald, Peter G. (R-Ill.), 44–45
Focal Communications Corp., 83
Foley, Thomas S., 14, 15
Ford, Gerald R., 18
foreign policy
Afghanistan, 52–55
congressional panels, 70–71
Iraq, 62

Israeli-Palestinian conflict, 60–62
National Security Agency, Congress and, 69–70, 73
Saudi Arabia, U.S. forces in, 55
State Department, Congress and, 68–69, 71–73
Syria, 62
Fowler, Tillie, 84
free trade, 111–113
Frost, Martin (D-Texas), 37–38
fundraising. *See* campaign finance

General Accounting Office (GAO), 16–21
General Dynamics, 91
Gephardt, Richard A. (D-Mo.), 37–38
gerrymandered districts, 25, 36
Gingrich, Newt, 14, 15
Goss, Porter J. (R-Fla.), 70, 71, 86
Grassley, Charles E. (R-Iowa), 86, 116
Greenberger, I. Michael, 81
Gregg, Judd (R-N.H.), 10–11, 84
gridlock, entrenched incumbents and, 32

Hagel, Chuck (R-Neb.), 71, 80
Hastert, J. Dennis (R-Ill.), 9, 26–27
Hayes, Robin (R-N.C.), 113
health care policy
costs, rising, 97–101
Medicare, 64–65, 99–101, 102–103
patients' bill of rights, 32, 97, 100, 101
Hill, Eleanor, 87
Hollings, Ernest F. (D-S.C.), 105, 107, 109
Homeland Security Department, proposed
budget, 3, 11, 80–84
Congress, committee organization and, 4, 9–12
Congress response to, 3–5, 7–8
historical pattern of agency expansion, 6
organization and scope, 2–5, 7
secretive planning process, 8
homeland security office, 57
Hoover, Herbert, 17
Horn, Wade, 116
House of Representatives
filling vacancies, in case of disaster, 13–15
incumbents, re-election of, 24–36
party balance in House, 24
polarization, 32–33
"safe seats" projection, 34–35
Hoyer, Steny H. (D-Md.), 10–11, 38, 39, 40
Hussein, Saddam, 62
HydroGeoLogic Inc., 83–84

Illinois redistricting plan, 26–27
immigrants, welfare and, 116
immigration services, 4
incumbents
committee assignments and, 35–36

fundraising advantage, 33, 34–35, 36
ideological rigidity and, 32–33
minority districts and, 28, 30–31
redistricting and, 24, 25, 26–29
reelection of, 24–26
"safe seats" projection, 34–35
seniority, 31, 32–33, 34
India, 53
information analysis and infrastructure protection, 5, 83
insurance, health, 32, 97–101
intellectual property rights, 104–110
Internet, copyright issues, 104–110
Iraq, 62
Islamic countries, 55
Islamic militants, 55
Israeli-Palestinian conflict, 60–62

Jackson, Andrew, 16
Jackson, Jesse L., Jr. (D-Ill.), 28
Johnson, Lyndon B., 17
Johnson, Nancy L. (R-Conn.), 102, 103

Kashmir, 53
Kelly, Paul V., 72–73
Kennedy, Edward M. (D-Mass.), 100, 101
Kennedy, John F., 17
Kirk, Mark Steven (R-Ill.), 27
Kmiec, Douglas, 20
Kolbe, Jim (R-Ariz.), 54
Kraus, Joe, 107

Lantos, Tom (D-Calif.), 54
Leahy, Patrick J. (D-Vt.), 61, 109
Levin, Carl (D-Mich.), 55
liability, health care policy and, 65, 100, 101
Lieberman, Joseph I. (D-Conn.)
on Afghanistan and Islamic countries, 55
on Army modernization, 74–75, 76
homeland security bill, 3, 5, 7
Lipinski, William O. (D-Ill.), 26–27, 36
Lofgren, Zoe (D-Calif.), 39–40
Lowey, Nita M. (D-N.Y.), 61
Lugar, Richard G. (R-Ind.), 53

managed care, 97–98
marriage tax, 115
Mason, David, 46
McCain, John (R-Ariz.), 42, 44
McConnell, Mitch (R-Ky.), 43, 45, 61–62
Medicaid, 99, 116
Medicare, 64–65, 99–101, 102–103
Meeks, Gregory W. (D-N.Y.), 39, 40
Menendez, Robert (D-N.J.), 38, 39
Middle East crisis, 60–62
military. *See* defense
minorities, district lines and, 28, 30–31
Mitchell, George J., 51

Index

moderates, and redistricting, 32–33
Mueller, Robert S., 85–87
Murtha, John P. (D-Pa.), 34–35
music, online, 110

Napster, 107, 110
Narayanaswamy, K., 83
National Security Council (NSC), 69–70, 73
National Treasury Employees Union, 7
Netanyahu, Benjamin, 68
Nixon, Richard M., 18
nuclear arsenals, in India and Pakistan, 53
nuclear program, U.S., 88–89, 90
Nunn-Lugar nuclear safeguard program, 53
Nussle, Jim (R-Iowa), 84

Oberstar, James L. (D-Minn.), 7
O'Brien, Ed, 111, 112
Office of Management and Budget (OMB), 66, 67
Ornstein, Norman J., 14–15
Osborne, Tom (R-Neb.), 25

Pakistan, 53, 54–55
Palestinian-Israeli conflict, 60–62
Palestinian Liberation Organization (PLO), 73
Panetta, Leon E., 66
partisanship, redistricting and, 32
patients' bill of rights, 32, 97, 100, 101
pay-as-you-go requirements (PAYGO), 67
peacekeeping forces, in Afghanistan, 53–54
Pelosi, Nancy (D-Calif.), 37–38
Pentagon. *See* defense
Phoenix memo, 49, 51
Pitt, Harvey, 93–94, 96
PLO (Palestinian Liberation Organization), 73
Powell, Colin L.
  Afghanistan, 52
  Congress, relationship with, 68–69, 71–73
  Middle East, 60, 61
prescription drug coverage, 65, 99, 100
Private Securities Litigation Reform Act of 1995, 96

Reagan, Ronald, 19, 64
redistricting, 24, 25, 26–29, 36

Reischauer, Robert D., 64, 65
Reorganization Act (1949), 6
Republicans
  health care policy, 99
  homeland security spending dilemma, 81–82
  Mideast policy divisions, 60
  Sept. 11, 2001, investigations, 48
  welfare, 114–117
retirement plans, 94
Rice, Condoleeza, 69–71, 73
Ridge, Tom, 5
Riggs, Lt. Gen. John M., 75
Rockefeller, John D. IV (D-W.Va.), 112–113
Rogers, Mike (R-Mich.), 36
Rohrabacher, Dana (R-Calif.), 54
Rowley, Coleen, 85
Rumsfeld, Donald H., 89, 92
Ryan, Paul D. (R-Wisc.), 36

Sanders, Bernard (I-Vt.), 26
Satellite Home Viewer Act, 106
Saudi Arabia, 55
Scardaville, Michael, 81
Schroeder, Pat, 107
Securities and Exchange Commission (SEC), 93–96
Seiffert, Grant E., 83
Senate. *See also* Congress
  Armed Services Committee, 77
  Foreign Relations Committee, 70–71
  welfare, 114–117
seniority, in the House, 31, 32–33, 34
Sensatex, Inc., 83
Sensenbrenner, F. James, Jr. (R-Wis.), 108, 110
Sept. 11, 2001, attacks, intelligence failures, 48–51, 85, 87
Serrano, Jose E. (D-N.Y.), 25
Shane, Peter M., 20
Shays, Christopher (R-Conn.), 8
Shinseki, Gen. Eric K., 74, 75
Social Security reform, 64–65
Specter, Arlen (R-Pa.), 15, 61, 111–112
State Department, 68–69, 71–73
steel tariffs, 111–113
Stockman, David, 66
Supreme Court copyright case, 105
swing districts, 32

Syria, 62

tariffs, steel, 111–113
Tauzin, Billy (R-La.), 93, 95, 96, 108
tax, marriage, 115
technology, digital, 106–110
term limits, incumbents and, 33
terrorism. *See also* Homeland Security Department, proposed
  bio-terrorism defense, 82
  budget deficits and, 63
  computer security, 83
  Congress recovery plan, 13–15
  Sept. 11, 2001, investigations, 48–51, 85, 87
terrorism insurance bill, 32
textile industry, 113
Thompson, Fred (R-Tenn.), 70, 71
Thornberry, William M. "Mac" (R-Texas), 3, 5
Thurber, James, 2
Toomey, Patrick J. (R-Penn.), 111, 112
Transportation and Security Administration (TSA), 3, 7
transportation security, 4, 83
Truman, Harry S, 17
Turkey, 55
Tyler, John, 16

unions of federal workers, 7
US PIRG, 45

Vitter, David (R-La.), 113

Walker, David M., 16–17
Walker v. Cheney, 16–21
war on terrorism. *See* Homeland Security Department, proposed; terrorism
Washington, George, 16
watermarking technology, 110
water projects, spending on, 84
Waxman, Henry A. (D-Calif.), 7, 16
weapons of mass destruction, 5
welfare, 114–117
Wellstone, Paul (D-Minn.), 54

Young, C.W. Bill (R-Fla.), 25, 84
Young, Don (D-Alaska), 7, 12